GM SUBCOMPACT 1971-80

Chevrolet Vega 1971-77 • Chevrolet Monza 1975-80 • Pontiac Astre 1975-77 • Pontiac Sunbird 1975-80 • Oldsmobile Starfire 1975-80 • Buick Skyhawk 1975-80

President LAWRENCE A. FORNASIERI
Vice President and General Manager JOHN P. KUSHNERICK
Executive Editor KERRY A. FREEMAN, S.A.E
Senior Editor RICHARD J. RIVELE, S.A.E.
Editor MARTIN J. GUNTHER

CHILTON BOOK COMPANY
Radnor, Pennsylvania
19089

SAFETY NOTICE

Proper service and repair procedures are vital to the safe, reliable operation of all motor vehicles, as well as the personal safety of those performing repairs. This book outlines procedures for servicing and repairing vehicles using safe, effective methods. The procedures contain many NOTES, CAUTIONS and WARNINGS which should be followed along with standard safety procedures to eliminate the possibility of personal injury or improper service which could damage the vehicle or compromise its safety.

It is important to note that repair procedures and techniques, tools and parts for servicing motor vehicles, as well as the skill and experience of the individual performing the work vary widely. It is not possible to anticipate all of the conceivable ways or conditions under which vehicles may be serviced, or to provide cautions as to all of the possible hazards that may result. Standard and accepted safety precautions and equipment should be used when handling toxic or flammable fluids, and safety goggles or other protection should be used during cutting, grinding, chiseling, prying, or any other process that can cause material removal or projectiles.

Some procedures require the use of tools specially designed for a specific purpose. Before substituting another tool or procedure, you must be completely satisfied that neither your personal safety, nor the performance of the vehicle will be endangered.

Although the information in this guide is based on industry sources and is as complete as possible at the time of publication, the possibility exists that the manufacturer made later changes which could not be included here. While striving for total accuracy, Chilton Book Company cannot assume responsibility for any errors, changes, or omissions that may occur in the compilation of this data.

PART NUMBERS

Part numbers listed in this reference are not recommendations by Chilton for any product by brand name. They are references that can be used with interchange manuals and aftermarket supplier catalogs to locate each brand supplier's discrete part number.

ACKNOWLEDGMENTS

The Chilton Book Company expresses its appreciation to the General Motors Corporation, Detroit, Michigan for their generous assistance.

Information has been selected from shop manuals, owners manuals, service bulletins and technical training manuals.

Manufactured in the United States of America
Twelfth Printing, January 1986

Chilton's Repair & Tune-Up Guide: GM Subcompact 1971–80
ISBN 0-8019-6935-2 pbk.
Library of Congress Catalog Card No. 79-8303

CONTENTS

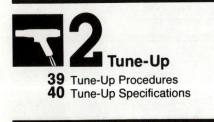

Quick Reference Specifications For Your Vehicle

Fill in this chart with the most commonly used specifications for your vehicle. Specifications can be found in Chapters 1 through 3 or on the tune-up decal under the hood of the vehicle.

Tune-Up

Firing Order_____

Spark Plugs:

    Type_____

    Gap (in.)_____

Point Gap (in.)_____

Dwell Angle (°)_____

Ignition Timing (°)_____

    Vacuum (Connected/Disconnected)_____

Valve Clearance (in.)

    Intake_____ Exhaust_____

Capacities

Engine Oil (qts)

    With Filter Change_____

    Without Filter Change_____

Cooling System (qts)_____

Manual Transmission (pts)_____

    Type_____

Automatic Transmission (pts)_____

    Type_____

Front Differential (pts)_____

    Type_____

Rear Differential (pts)_____

    Type_____

Transfer Case (pts)_____

    Type_____

FREQUENTLY REPLACED PARTS

Use these spaces to record the part numbers of frequently replaced parts.

PCV VALVE	OIL FILTER	AIR FILTER
Manufacturer_____	Manufacturer_____	Manufacturer_____
Part No._____	Part No._____	Part No._____

General Information and Maintenance

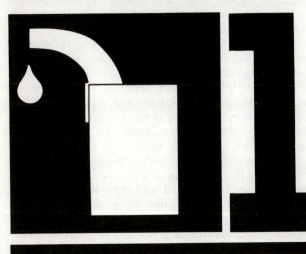

HOW TO USE THIS BOOK

Chilton's Repair & Tune-Up Guide for the GM Sub-Compact is intended to help you learn more about the inner workings of your vehicle and save you money on its upkeep and operation.

The first two chapters will be the most used, since they contain maintenance and tune-up information and procedures. Studies have shown that a properly tuned and maintained car can get at least 10% better gas mileage than an out-of-tune car. Chapters Three thru Nine deal with the more complex systems of your car. Operating systems from engine through brakes are covered to the extent that the average do-it-yourselfer becomes mechanically involved. This book will not explain such things as rebuilding the differential for the simple reason that the expertise required and the investment in special tools make this task uneconomical. It will give you detailed instructions to help you change your own brake pads and shoes, replace points and plugs, and do many more jobs that will save you money, give you personal satisfaction, and help you avoid expensive problems. Chapter Ten is devoted to body repair and refinishing and Chapter Eleven to troubleshooting.

A secondary purpose of this book is a reference for owners who want to understand their car and/or their mechanics better. In this case, no tools at all are required.

Before removing any bolts, read through the entire procedure. This will give you the overall view of what tools and supplies will be required. There is nothing more frustrating than having to walk to the bus stop on Monday morning because you were short one bolt on Sunday afternoon. So read ahead and plan ahead. Each operation should be approached logically and all procedures thoroughly understood before attempting any work.

All chapters contain adjustments, maintenance, removal and installation procedures, and repair or overhaul procedures. When repair is not considered practical, we tell you how to remove the part and then how to install the new or rebuilt replacement. In this way, you at least save the labor costs. Backyard repair of such components as the alternator is just not practical.

Two basic mechanic's rules should be mentioned here. One, whenever the left side of the car or engine is referred to, it is meant to specify the driver's side of the car. Conversely, the right side of the car means the passenger's side. Secondly, most screws and bolts are removed' by turning counterclockwise, and tightened by turning clockwise.

Safety is always the most important rule. Constantly be aware of the dangers involved in working on an automobile and take the proper precautions. (See the section in this chapter "Servicing Your Vehicle Safely" and the SAFETY NOTICE on the acknowledgement page.)

Pay attention to the instructions provided. There are 3 common mistakes in mechanical work:

1. Incorrect order of assembly, disassembly or adjustment. When taking something apart or putting it together, doing things in the wrong order usually justs costs you extra time; however, it CAN break something. Read the entire procedure before beginning disassembly. Do everything in the order in which the instructions say you should do it, even if you can't immediately see a reason for it. When you're taking apart something that is very intricate (for example, a carburetor), you might want to draw a picture of how it looks when assembled at one point in order to make sure you get everything back in its proper position. (We will supply an exploded view whenever possible). When making adjustments, especially tune-up adjustments, do them in order; often, one adjustment affects another, and you cannot expect even satisfactory results unless each adjustment is made only when it cannot be changed by any other.

2. Overtorquing (or undertorquing). While it is more common for overtorquing to cause damage, undertorquing can cause a fastener to vibrate loose causing serious damage. Especially when dealing with aluminum parts, pay attention to torque specifications and utilize a torque wrench in assembly. If a torque figure is not available, remember that if you are using the right tool to do the job, you will probably not have to strain yourself to get a fastener tight enough. The pitch of most threads is so slight that the tension you put on the wrench will be multiplied many, many times in actual force on what you are tightening. A good example of how critical torque is can be seen in the case of spark plug installation, especially where you are putting the plug into an aluminum cylinder head. Too little torque can fail to crush the gasket, causing leakage of combustion gases and consequent overheating of the plug and engine parts. Too much torque can damage the threads, or distort the plug, which changes the spark gap.

There are many commercial products available for ensuring that fasteners won't come loose, even if they are not torqued just right (a very common brand is "Loctite®"). If you're worried about getting something together tight enough to hold, but loose enough to avoid mechanical damage during assembly, one of these products might offer substantial insurance. Read the label on the package and make sure the product is compatible with the materials, fluids, etc. involved before choosing one.

3. Crossthreading. This occurs when a part such as a bolt is screwed into a nut or casting at the wrong angle and forced. Cross threading is more likely to occur if access is difficult. It helps to clean and lubricate fasteners, and to start threading with the part to be installed going straight in. Then, start the bolt, spark plug, etc. with your fingers. If you encounter resistance, unscrew the part and start over again at a different angle until it can be inserted and turned several turns without much effort. Keep in mind that many parts, especially spark plugs, use tapered threads so that gentle turning will automatically bring the part you're threading to the proper angle if you don't force it or resist a change in angle. Don't put a wrench on the part until it's been turned a couple of turns by hand. If you suddenly encounter resistance, and the part has not seated fully, don't force it. Pull it back out and make sure it's clean and threading properly.

Always take your time and be patient; once you have some experience, working on your car will become an enjoyable hobby.

TOOLS AND EQUIPMENT

Naturally, without the proper tools and equipment it is impossible to properly service your vehicle. It would be impossible to catalog each tool that you would need to perform each or any operation in this book. It would also be unwise for the amateur to rush out and buy an expensive set of tools on the theory that he may need one or more of them at sometime.

The best approach is to proceed slowly, gathering together a good quality set of those tools that are used most frequently. Don't be misled by the low cost of bargain tools. It is far better to spend a little more for better quality. Forged wrenches, 10 or 12 point sockets and fine tooth ratchets are by far preferable to their less expensive counterparts. As any good mechanic can tell you, there are few worse experiences than trying to work on a car or truck with bad tools. Your monetary

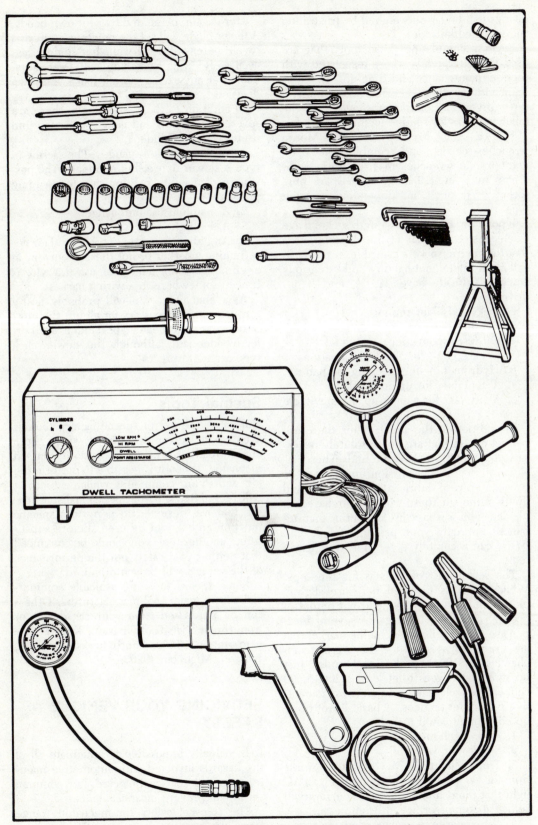

The tools and equipment shown here will handle the majority of the maintenance on a car

savings will be far outweighed by frustration and mangled knuckles.

Begin accumulating those tools that are used most frequently; those associated with routine maintenance and tune-up.

In addition to the normal assortment of screwdrivers and pliers you should have the following tools for routine maintenance jobs:

1. SAE (or Metric) or SAE/Metric wrenches-sockets and combination open end/box end wrenches in sizes from ⅛ in. (3mm) to ¾ in. (19 mm) and a spark plug socket (¹³/₁₆ or ⅝ in. depending on plug type).

If possible, buy various length socket drive extensions. One break in this department is that the metric sockets available in the U.S. will fit all the ratchet handles and extensions you may already have (¼, ⅜, and ½ in. drive.)

2. Jackstands—for support
3. Oil filter wrench
4. Oil filter spout—for pouring oil
5. Grease gun—for chassis lubrication
6. Hydrometer—for checking the battery
7. A container for draining oil
8. Many rags for wiping up the inevitable mess.

In addition to the above items there are several others that are not absolutely necessary, but handy to have around. These include oil dry, a transmission funnel and the usual supply of lubricants, antifreeze and fluids, although these can be purchased as needed. This is a basic list for routine maintenance, but only your personal needs and desire can accurately determine your list of tools.

The second list of tools is for tune-ups. While the tools involved here are slightly more sophisticated, they need not be outrageously expensive. There are several inexpensive tach/dwell meters on the market that are every bit as good for the average mechanic as a $100.00 professional model. Just be sure that it goes to at least 1,200–1,500 rpm on the tach scale and that it works on 4, 6 or 8 cylinder engines. A basic list of tune-up equipment could include:

1. Tach-dwell meter;
2. Spark plug wrench;
3. Timing light (a DC light that works from the car's battery is best, although an AC light that plugs into 110V house current will suffice at some sacrifice in brightness);
4. Wire spark plug gauge/adjusting tools
5. Set of feeler blades

Here again, be guided by your own needs. A feeler blade will set the points as easily as a dwell meter will read well, but slightly less accurately. And since you will need a tachometer anyway . . . well, make your own decision.

In addition to these basic tools, there are several other tools and gauges you may find useful. These include:

1. A compression gauge. The screw-in type is slower to use, but eliminates the possibility of a faulty reading due to escaping pressure.
2. A manifold vacuum gauge.
3. A test light.
4. An induction meter. This is used for determining whether or not there is current in a wire. These are handy for use if a wire is broken somewhere in a wiring harness.

As a final note, you will probably find a torque wrench necessary for all but the most basic work. The beam type models are perfectly adequate, although the newer click type are more precise.

Special Tools

Normally, the use of special factory tools is avoided for repair procedures, since these are not readily available for the do-it-yourself mechanic. When it is possible to perform the job with more commonly available tools, it will be pointed out, but occasionally, a special tool was designed to perform a specific function and should be used. Before substituting another tool, you should be convinced that neither your safety nor the performance of the vehicle will be compromised.

Some special tools are available commercially from major tool manufacturers. Others can be purchased from your car dealer or from the Service Tool Division, Kent-Moore Corporation, 1501 South Jackson Street, Jackson, Michigan 49203.

SERVICING YOUR VEHICLE SAFELY

It is virtually impossible to anticipate all of the hazards involved with automotive maintenance and service but care and common sense will prevent most accidents.

The rules of safety for mechanics range from "don't smoke around gasoline," to "use the proper tool for the job." The trick to avoiding injuries is to develop safe work habits and take every possible precaution.

Do's

• Do keep a fire extinguisher and first aid kit within easy reach.

• Do wear safety glasses or goggles when cutting, drilling, grinding or prying, even if you have 20–20 vision. If you wear glasses for the sake of vision, then they should be made of hardened glass that can serve also as safety glasses, or wear safety goggles over your regular glasses.

• Do shield your eyes whenever you work around the battery. Batteries contain sulphuric acid; in case of contact with the eyes or skin, flush the area with water or a mixture of water and baking soda and get medical attention immediately.

• Do use safety stands for any undercar service. Jacks are for raising vehicles; safety stands are for making sure the vehicle stays raised until you want it to come down. Whenever the vehicle is raised, block the wheels remaining on the ground and set the parking brake.

• Do use adequate ventilation when working with any chemicals. Like carbon monoxide, the asbestos dust resulting from brake lining wear can be poisonous in sufficient quantities.

• Do disconnect the negative battery cable when working on the electrical system. The primary ignition system can contain up to 40,000 volts.

• Do follow manufacturer's directions whenever working with potentially hazardous materials. Both brake fluid and antifreeze are poisonous if taken internally.

• Do properly maintain your tools. Loose hammerheads, mushroomed punches and chisels, frayed or poorly grounded electrical cords, excessively worn screwdrivers, spread wrenches (open end), cracked sockets, slipping ratchets, or faulty droplight sockets can cause accidents.

• Do use the proper size and type of tool for the job being done.

• Do when possible, pull on a wrench handle rather than push on it, and adjust your stance to prevent a fall.

• Do be sure that adjustable wrenches are tightly adjusted on the nut or bolt and pulled so that the face is on the side of the fixed jaw.

• Do select a wrench or socket that fits the nut or bolt. The wrench or socket should sit straight, not cocked.

• Do strike squarely with a hammer—avoid glancing blows.

• Do set the parking brake and block the drive wheels if the work requires that the engine be running.

Dont's

• Don't run an engine in a garage or anywhere else without proper ventilation—EVER! Carbon monoxide is poisonous; it takes a long time to leave the human body and you can build up a deadly supply of it in your system by simply breathing in a little every day. You may not realize you are slowly poisoning yourself. Always use power vents, windows, fans or open the garage doors.

• Don't work around moving parts while wearing a necktie or other loose clothing. Short sleeves are much safer than long, loose sleeves and hard-tored shoes with neoprene soles protect your toes and give a better grip on slippery surfaces. Jewelry such as watches, fancy belt buckles, beads or body adornment of any kind is not safe working around a car. Long hair should be hidden under a hat or cap.

• Don't use pockets for toolboxes. A fall or bump can drive a screwdriver deep into your body. Even a wiping cloth hanging from the back pocket can wrap around a spinning shaft or fan.

• Don't smoke when working around gasoline, cleaning solvent or other flammable material.

• Don't smoke when working around the battery. When the battery is being charged, it gives off explosive hydrogen gas.

• Don't use gasoline to wash your hands; there are excellent soaps available. Gasoline may contain lead, and lead can enter the body through a cut, accumulating in the body until you are very ill. Gasoline also removes all the natural oils from the skin so that bone dry hands will suck up oil and grease.

• Don't service the air conditioning system unless you are equipped with the necessary tools and training. The refrigerant, R-12, is extremely cold and when exposed to the air, will instantly freeze any surface it comes in contact with, including your eyes. Although the refrigerant is normally non-toxic, R-12 becomes a deadly poisonous gas in the presence of an open flame. One good whiff of the vapors from burning refrigerant can be fatal.

HISTORY

The models covered in this book are the Chevrolet Vega, Monza; Pontiac Astre, Sunbird; Oldsmobile Starfire and the Buick Skyhawk. All these models are classified as subcompacts and are also designated by General Motors as their "H" body series. The first model of the "H" body series was the Vega introduced in 1971 by Chevrolet. In 1975, Chevrolet added the Monza and produced both models through 1977. In 1978 the Vega name was discontinued and only the Monza remained. Pontiac introduced their version of the "H" body in 1975 and called it the Astre. In 1976 the Sunbird model was added and Pontiac produced both models through 1977. In 1978 the Astre name was discontinued and only the name Sunbird was used. The Buick Skyhawk and the Oldsmobile Starfire were both introduced in 1975 and each produced only one model through 1980.

NOTE: *This book does not contain any specifications or service procedures for the Cosworth Vega.*

MODEL IDENTIFICATION

Body Identification Plate

The body identification plate is located on the upper horizontal surface of the shroud. The body identification plate identifies: model year, car division, body type, series, body style, assembly plant, body number, trim combination, modular seat code, paint code and date built code.

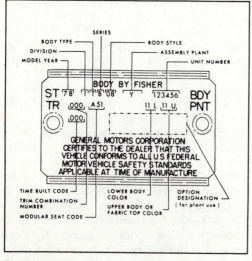

Body number plate

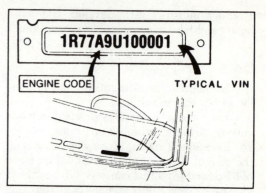

Vehicle identification number location

Vehicle Identification Number (VIN)

This is the legal identification of the vehicle. It appears on a plate which is attached to the left top of the instrument panel, and can easily be seen through the windshield from the outside of the car. The VIN also appears on the Vehicle Certificates of Title of Registration.

Vehicle Identification Number (VIN)

Manufacturer's Identity ①	Series Code Letter ②	Body Code Letter ③	Engine Model ④	Model Year ⑤	Assembly Plant ⑥	Unit Number ⑦
1	V	77	B	5	U	200025

NOTE: *Vega VIN shown above as example*

1. Manufacturer's idenity number assigned to all vehicles. Chevrolet-1, Pontiac-2, Oldsmobile-3, Buick-4

2. Series (Model identification)

3. Body style

4. Engine size

5. Last number of the model year (1975 shown)

6. Assembly plant (example U—Lordstown)

7. Unit numbering (example unit number will start at 200001.

Engine Identification

The engine can be identified by the letter code in the Vehicle Identification Number (VIN) plate located on the top left side of the dash panel or by code letters stamped on a pad at the right side of the cylinder block above the starter. The following chart identifies the engine code letter found in the VIN plate on the dash panel.

Engine Code Letter in the VIN Plate

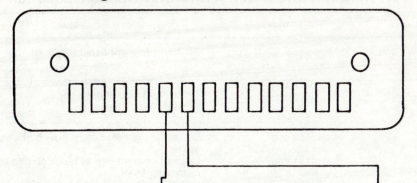

	Engine Code				Model Year Code	
Code	Eng. Disp. (cu in.)	Eng. Config.	Carb	Eng. Mfgr.	Code	Year
B	140	L4	1V	Chev	1, 2	1971–72
B	140	L4	2V	Chev		
A	140	L4	1V	Chev	3	1973
B	140	L4	2V	Chev		
A	140	L4	1V	Chev	4	1974
B	140	L4	2V	Chev		
A	140	L4	1V	Chev	5	1975
B	140	L4	2V	Chev		
C	231	V6	2V	Buick		
F	260	V8	2V	Olds		
G	262	V8	2V	Chev		
O	122	L4	FI	Chev	6	1976
A	140	L4	1V	Chev		
B	140	L4	2V	Chev		
C	231	V6	2V	Buick		
F	260	V8	2V	Olds		
G	262	V8	2V	Chev		
Q	305	V8	2V	Chev		
B	140	L4	2V	Chev	7	1977
V	151	L4	2V	Pont		
C	231	V6	2V	Buick		
U	305	V8	2V	Chev		
V	151	L4	2V	Pont	8	1978
C	196	V6	2V	Buick		
A	231	V6	2V	Buick		
U	305	V8	2V	Chev		
V	151	L4	2V	Pont	9	1979
I	151	L4	2V	Pont		
C	196	V6	2V	Buick		
A	231	V6	2V	Buick		
G	305	V8	2V	Chev		

Vehicle Component Serial and Unit Number Location

Component	Model	Location
Vehicle Identification Number Plate	All	Top of instrument panel left, front.
Body Number, Trim and Point Plate	All	Upper right side of dash panel.
Engine	4 cyl. 140 eng.	On pad at right side of cylinder block above starter.
	4 cyl. 151 eng.	Located on right side of block on pad at rear of distributor shaft.
	V6 & V8 eng.	Located on pad at front right hand side of cylinder block.
Transmission	3-spd.	Centered on lower rear face of case.
	4-spd.	On metal tag bolted to right side of case.
	5-spd.	On right vertical surface of oil pan.
	Powerglide, Torque Drive	On the left upper flange of the converter opening of the transmission housing.
	Turbo Hydra-Matic	On right vertical surface of oil pan.
Rear Axle Number	All	On right or left axle tube adjacent to carrier.
Delcotron	All	On top drive end frame.
Starter	All	Stamped on outer case, toward rear.
Battery	All	On cell cover segment, top of battery.

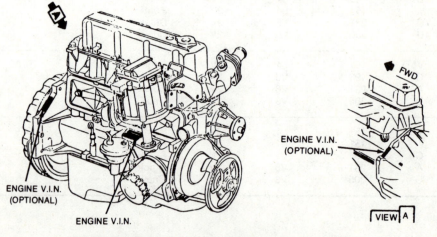

Engine identification number location—4 cyl. 151 engine

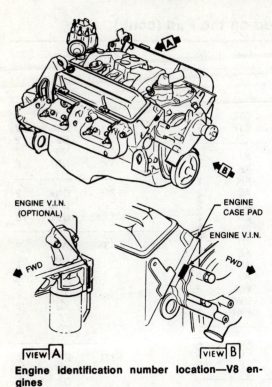

ENGINE V.I.N.
(OPTIONAL)

ENGINE
CASE PAD

ENGINE V.I.N.

FWD

FWD

VIEW A

VIEW B

Engine identification number location—V8 engines

Engine identification number location—V6 engines

The following charts identify the engine codes located on the pad on the cylinder block.

Engine Codes Located on the Pad

VEGA, MONZA

Year	Engine	Code	Bbl	Year	Engine	Code	Bbl	Year	Engine	Code	Bbl
1971	4-140	CHA	1			CAC	2			CBX	NA
		CHC	1			CAL	2			CBY	NA
		CHB	2			CAK	2			CBZ	2
		CHD	2	1975	4-140	CAA	1		8-262	CZT	2
1972	4-140	CHA	1			CAB	1			CZU	2
		CHC	1			CAH	1			CGA	2
		CHB	2			CAJ	1			CGB	2
		CHD	2			CAC	2				
						CAD	2	1977	4-140	CAY	2
1973	4-140	CAA	1			CAK	2			CAZ	2
		CAB	1			CAF	2			CBK	2
		CAH	1							CBL	2
		CAJ	1	8-262.5		CZF	2			CBS	2
		CAC	2			CZH	2			CBT	2
		CAD	2			CZT	2			CAB	2
		CAK	2			CZU	2			CAB	2
		CAL	2							CAA	2
				1976	4-140	CBK	2			CAC	2
1974	4-140	CAA	1			CBL	2			CBY	2
		CAS	1			CBS	2			CBZ	2
		CAB	1			CBT	2				
		CAH	1			CBU	NA	8-305		CPK	2
		CAD	2			CBW	NA			CPL	2

Engine Codes Located on the Pad (cont.)

VEGA, MONZA

Year	Engine	Code	Bbl	Year	Engine	Code	Bbl	Year	Engine	Code	Bbl
1977	4-140	CPU	2			CTD	2			NC	2
		CPX	2			CTF	2			SM	2
		CRC	2							SS	2
		CRD	2	1979	4-151	XJ	2			NS	2
						XK	2			NR	2
1978	4-151V	WH	2			AB	2				
		WD	2			AD	2		8-305	DNK	2
		WB	2			ZA	2			DND	2
		XL	2			ZB	2			DTL	2
		ZFZA	2			ZP	2				
		ZBZH	2			ZR	2	1980	4-151	WD	2
		XN	2			AF	2			WJ	2
						AH	2			A9	2
	6-196	PC	2			AJ	2			A7	2
		PD	2			WN	2			XC	2
						PWN	2			XD	2
	6-231A	OD	2			PWP	2			ZA	2
		OF	2							ZB	2
		OC	2		6-196	FD	2				
		OE	2			FC	2		6-231	EX	2
						FF	2			EZ	2
	8-305U	CTA	2							OA	2
		CTB	2		6-231	NA	2			OB	2
		CTC	2			NE	2			OC	2
						NH	2			EA	2

ASTRE, SUNBIRD

Year	Engine	Code	Bbl	Year	Engine	Code	Bbl	Year	Engine	Code	Bbl
1975	4-140	CBB	1			CBX	2		4-151-V	WB	2
		CBC	1			CBY	2			WD	2
		CAM	2			CBZ	2			WH	2
		CAS	2							XN	2
		CAR	2		4-151	WD	2			XL	2
		CAT	2			WC	2			ZA	2
						YL	2			ZH	2
1976	4-140	CBH	1			YM	2			ZF	2
		CBJ	1			ZH	2			ZB	2
		CBS	2			ZJ	2				
		CBT	2			ZN	2		6-231	OA	2
		CBK	2			ZP	2			OD	2
		CBL	2			ZD	2			OF	2
						ZF	2			OB	2
	V6-231	FM	2							OE	2
		FH	2		6-231	SA	2			OC	2
		FK	2			SB	2				
		FI	2			SD	2	1979	4-151-1	AC	2
		FO	2			SO	2			AD	2
		FJ	2			SX	2			ZJ	2
						SY	2			ZK	2
1977	4-140	CAY	2								
		CAZ	2	1978	4-151-1	AC	2		4-151-9	AB	2
		CAK	2			AD	2			ZA	2
		CBL	2			ZC	2			ZB	2
		CBS	2			ZD	2				
		CBT	2			ZJ	2		6-231	NA	2
		CBU	2			ZL	2			NB	2
		CBW	2			ZN	2			NC	2

Engine Codes Located on the Pad (cont.)

ASTRE, SUNBIRD

Year	Engine	Code	Bbl	Year	Engine	Code	Bbl	Year	Engine	Code	Bbl
1979	4-140	NE	2			DNZ	2			WJ	2
		NG	2	1980	4-151	ZA	2		6-231	EX	2
		NH	2			ZB	2			EY	2
		NM	2			XC	2			OA	2
	8-305	DNF	2			XD	2			OB	2
		DNK	2			A7	2			EZ	2
		DNJ	2			A9	2			OC	2

STARFIRE

Year	Engine	Code	Bbl	Year	Engine	Code	Bbl	Year	Engine	Code	Bbl
1975	V6-231	FP	2			CRT	2		4-151-9	AB	2
		FR	2			CRM	2			ZA	2
		FS	2	1978	4-151-1	AC	2			ZB	2
1976	4-140	CBS	2			AD	2		4-151-V	WB	2
		CBZ	2			ZC	2			WD	2
		CAZ	2			ZD	2			WH	2
		CBT	2			ZJ	2			WJ	2
		CBK	2			ZK	2			XL	2
		CBY	2			ZL	2			XN	2
		CAY	2			ZN	2			XJ	2
		CBL	2	4-151-V		WD	2			XK	2
	V6-231	FH	2			WH	2				
		FI	2			ZA	2		6-231	NA	2
		FO	2			ZB	2			NB	2
		FJ	2			WB	2			NC	2
1977	4-140	CBS	2			XL	2			NE	2
		CAZ	2			XN	2			NH	2
		CBT	2	6-231		OA	2			NG	2
		CBK	2			OB	2			NM	2
		CAY	2			OC	2				
		CBL	2			OD	2		8-305	DNF	2
	6-231	SA	2			OE	2				
		SB	2			OF	2	1980	4-151	DNJ	2
		SD	2			OH	2			WD	2
		SE	2	8-305		CTA	2			WJ	2
		SF	2			CTB	2			A9	2
		SQ	2			CTC	2			A7	2
		SR	2			CTD	2			ZA	2
		SW	2			CTC	2			ZB	2
		SY	2	1979	4-151-1	AC	2		6-231	EX	2
	8-305	CPX	2			AD	2			EZ	2
		CRL	2			ZK	2			EY	2
						ZJ	2			OC	2

SKYHAWK

Year	Engine	Code	Bbl	Year	Engine	Code	Bbl	Year	Engine	Code	Bbl
1975	6-231	AD	2			FO	2			SD	2
						FJ	2			SO	2
1976	6-231	FH	2	1977	6-231	SA	2			SX	2
		FI	2			SB	2			SY	2

Engine Codes Located on the Pad (cont.)

Year	Engine	Code	Bbl	Year	Engine	Code	Bbl	Year	Engine	Code	Bbl
SKYHAWK											
1978	6-231	OA	2	1979	6-231	NA	2	1980	6-231	EX	2
		OB	2			NB	2			EY	2
		OC	2			NC	2			EZ	2
		OD	2			NE	2			DA	2
		OE	2			NG	2			OB	2
		OF	2			NH	2			OC	2
		OG	2			NM	2				

Transmission

Identification of your transmission can be made by referring to the Vehicle Component Serial and Unit Number Location Chart, finding out the transmission code letters and applying them to the following chart:

Transmission Identification Chart

Year	Code	Transmission
ASTRE, SUNBIRD		
1975	HJ	Saginaw 3-sp
	HK	Saginaw 4-sp
	DJ	Turbo Hydra-Matic 350
1976	UY	Saginaw 3-sp
	SF,SH,SR	Saginaw 4-sp
	DX,SM,SN	Warner 5-sp
	BH	Turbo Hydra-Matic 200
1977	DJ,KD	Turbo Hydra-Matic 350
	JY,UY	Saginaw 3-sp
	SF,SH,SR	Saginaw 4-sp
	SM,SN,DX	Warner 5-sp
	BH,BU,BY	Turbo Hydra-Matic 200
	DJ	Turbo Hydra-Matic 350
1978		Saginaw 4-sp
	RJ,U6	Warner 5-sp
	PY	Turbo Hydra-Matic 200
	KA,KL	Turbo Hydra-Matic 350
1979	ZR	Saginaw 4-sp
	UM,US	Warner 5-sp
	PB,PY	Turbo Hydra-Matic 200
	KC,KL,JC,JD	Turbo Hydra-Matic 350
1980	KA,WD	Turbo Hydra-Matic 350, 375
	SH	Saginaw 4-sp

Transmission Identification Chart (cont.)

Year	Code	Transmission
	PY,PB	Turbo Hydra-Matic 200
	KA	Turbo Hydra-Matic 350, 375
STARFIRE		
1975	BX	Saginaw 4-sp
	KD,KX	Turbo Hydra-Matic 350
1976	SF,SH	Saginaw 4-sp
	UC,SJ	Warner 5-sp
	BH	Turbo Hydra-Matic 200
	KD	Turbo Hydra-Matic 350
1977	ZS,ZN,RY,RH	Saginaw 4-sp
	RM,RN,RK,RJ	Warner 5-sp
	BH,CK,BU	Turbo Hydra-Matic 200
	AP,AO,KL,KP	Turbo Hydra-Matic 250
1978	ZR,RH	Saginaw 4-sp
	RJ,U6	Warner 5-sp
	KL	Turbo Hydra-Matic 250
	PY	Turbo Hydra-Matic 200
	WC	Turbo Hydra-Matic 350
1979	SH,RH,SJ	Saginaw 4-sp
	UM,US	Warner 5-sp
	PB,PY	Turbo Hydra-Matic 200
	KL,JC,JD	Turbo Hydra-Matic 250
	KA,WD	Turbo Hydra-Matic 350
1980		Saginaw 4-sp
		Warner 5-sp
	KA	Turbo Hydra-Matic 350
SKYHAWK		
1975		Saginaw 4-sp
		Turbo Hydra-Matic 350

Transmission Identification
Chart (cont.)

Year	Code	Transmission
1976	SF,SH	Saginaw 4-sp
	SJ,UC	Warner 5-sp
	BH	Turbo Hydra-Matic 200
	KD	Turbo Hydra-Matic 350
1977	ZS,RY	Saginaw 4-sp
	RM,RN	Warner 5-sp
	BH,BU	Turbo Hydra-Matic 200
	KL,KP	Turbo Hydra-Matic 350
1978	ZR	Saginaw 4-sp
	UZ,U6	Warner 5-sp
	KA,KL	Turbo Hydra-Matic 250
1979		Saginaw 4-sp
	US	Warner 5-sp
	KL,JC,JD	Turbo Hydra-Matic 250
	KA	Turbo Hydra-Matic 350
1980	SH	Saginaw 4-sp
		Warner 5-sp
	KA	Turbo Hydra-Matic 350

VEGA, MONZA

Year	Code	Transmission
1971–75	S	Saginaw 3-sp
	R	Saginaw 4-sp
	C	Powerglide
	B,Y	Turbo Hydra-Matic
	A	Torque Drive
1976		Saginaw 3-sp
		Saginaw 4-sp
		Warner 5-sp
		Turbo Hydra-Matic 200
		Turbo Hydra-Matic 250
1977		Saginaw 4-sp
		Warner 5-sp
		Turbo Hydra-Matic 200
		Turbo Hydra-Matic 250
1978	U2,U3	Saginaw 4-sp
	RK,RJ,U6,U7	Warner 5-sp
	CA	Turbo Hydra-Matic 200
	KK,KL,WC	Turbo Hydra-Matic 350
1979	SH,SJ,SK	Saginaw 4-sp
	UM,US,UT	Warner 5-sp
	PA,PB,PC,PY	Turbo Hydra-Matic 200
	KA,KL,KK,WD	Turbo Hydra-Matic 350
1980	SH	Saginaw 4-sp
	PA,PY,PB	Turbo Hydra-Matic 200
	KA	Turbo Hydra-Matic 350

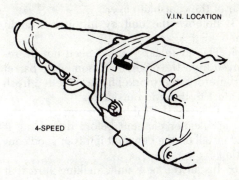

5-SPEED

4-SPEED

MANUAL

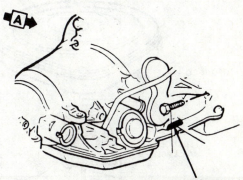

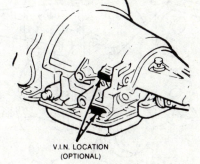

AUTOMATIC

Transmission identification number location

ROUTINE MAINTENANCE

Air Cleaner

4 cyl. 140, 151 engine

The air cleaner is a welded non–serviceable unit designed to be discarded every 50,000 miles under normal driving conditions. To replace the unit:

1. Some air cleaners are secured by a single bolt or wing nut, others by four nuts on studs.

2. Lift the front of the unit up and turn it to release the crankcase vent pipe from the rear of the camshaft cover.

3. Remove the unit by lifting it straight up.

4. The air intake snorkel need not be removed from the engine. On some two barrel carburetors, the snorkel has a screened fresh air duct to bring in outside air.

5. Remove the rubber grommet from the old air cleaner element before discarding it and install on the new unit if it is in good condition.

6. Install the new unit, making sure that the crankshaft vent pipe is in place. Replace the wing nut.

V6 & V8 engines

The air cleaner on these models consist of a metal housing for a replaceable paper filter and the necessary hoses connecting it to the crankcase ventilation system.

The air cleaner cover is held in place by a wing nut on all models. The condition of the air filter should be checked every 6,000 miles and replaced at least every 30,000 miles.

Positive Crankcase Ventilation Valve (PCV)

The crankcase ventilation system (PCV) must be operating properly in order to allow evaporation of fuel vapors and water from the crankcase. This system should be checked at every oil change and serviced after one year or 12,000 miles. The PCV valve is replaced after 2 years or 24,000 miles. For 1975 and later cars, the service interval has been upgraded to one year or 15,000 miles, with PCV valve replacement scheduled for two years or

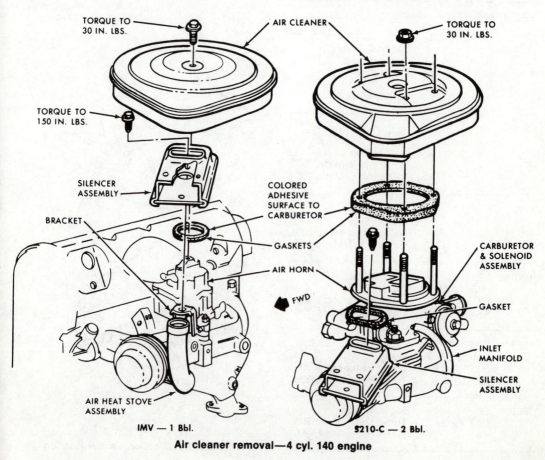

Air cleaner removal—4 cyl. 140 engine

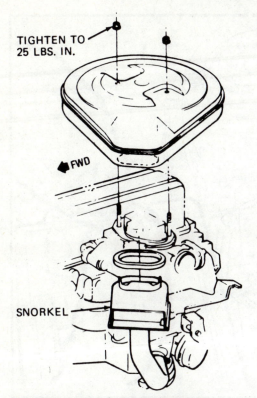

TIGHTEN TO
25 LBS. IN.

◄ FWD

SNORKEL

Air cleaner removal—4 cyl. 151 engine

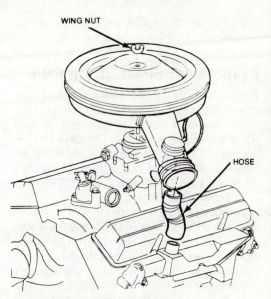

WING NUT

HOSE

Air cleaner removal—V8 engine

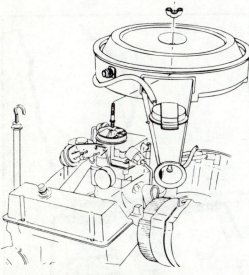

Air cleaner removal—V6 engine

30,000 miles. Normal service entails cleaning the passages of the system hoses with solvent, inspecting them for cracks and breaks, and replacing them as necessary. The PCV valve contains a check valve and, when working properly, this valve will make a rattling sound when the outside case is tapped. If it fails to rattle, then it is probably stuck in a closed position and needs to be replaced.

The PCV system is designed to prevent the emission of gases from the crankcase. It does this by connecting a crankcase outlet (valve cover, oil filler tube, back of engine) to the intake manifold with a hose. The crankcase gases travel through the hose to the intake manifold where they are returned to the combustion chamber to be burned. If maintained properly, this system reduces condensation in the crankcase and the resultant formation of harmful acids and oil dilution. A clogged PCV valve will often cause a slow or rough idle due to a richer fuel mixture. A car equipped with a PCV system has air going through a hose to the intake manifold from an outlet at the valve cover, oil filler tube, or rear of the engine. To compensate for this extra air going to the manifold, carburetor specifications require a richer (more gas) mixture at the carburetor. If the PCV valve or hose is clogged, this air doesn't go to the intake manifold and the fuel mixture is too rich. A rough, slow idle results. The valve should be checked before making any carburetor adjustments. Disconnect the valve from the engine or merely clamp the hose shut. If the engine speed decreases less than 50 rpm, the valve is clogged and should be replaced. If the engine speed decreases much more than 50 rpm, then the valve is good. The PCV valve is an inexpensive item and it is suggested that it be replaced. If the new valve doesn't noticeably improve engine idle, the problem might be a restriction in the PCV hose. For details on PCV valve operation see the chapter covering emission controls.

Evaporation Emission Canister

The canister stores carburetor and fuel tank vapors while the engine is off, holding them to be drawn into the engine and burned when the engine is started. The form filter in the base of the canister is designed to be replaced at 12,000 mile or 12-month intervals (24 months or 30,000 miles after 1974).

To replace the filter:

1. Remove all the hoses from the top of the canister, which is in the left front of the engine compartment. The clamps can be removed by squeezing them with pliers.

2. Loosen the screw holding the canister restraining strap.

3. Pull the canister straight up and out.

4. Invert the canister and pull out the foam filter.

5. Insert the new filter under the retaining wire.

6. Replace the canister and tighten the strap.

7. Connect the hoses to the top of the canister. All the fittings are labeled.

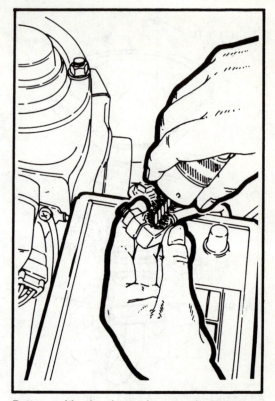

Battery cable cleaning tool-top terminal type

Battery

Loose, dirty, or corroded battery terminals are a major cause of "no-start." Every 3 months or so, remove the battery terminals and clean them, giving them a light coating of petroleum jelly when you are finished. This will help to retard corrosion.

Check the battery cables for signs of wear or chafing and replace any cable or terminal that looks marginal. Battery terminals can be easily cleaned and inexpensive terminal cleaning tools are an excellent investment that will pay for themselves many times over. They can usually be purchased from any well-equipped auto store or parts department. Side terminal batteries require a different tool to clean the threads in the battery case. The accumulated white powder and corrosion can be cleaned from the top of the battery with an old toothbrush and a solution of baking soda and water.

Unless you have a "maintenance-free" battery, check the electrolyte level (see Battery under Fluid Level Checks in this chapter) and check the specific gravity of each cell. Be sure that the vent holes in each cell cap are not blocked by grease or dirt. The vent holes

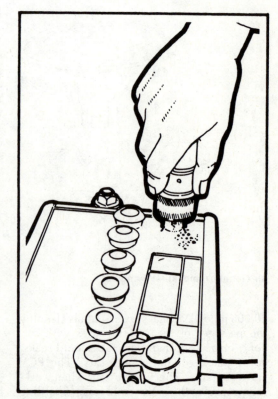

Battery terminal cleaning tool-top terminal type

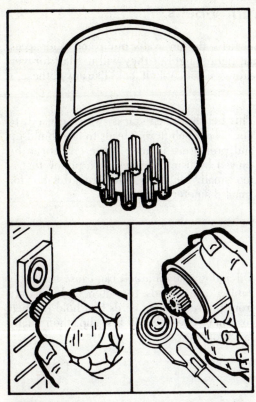

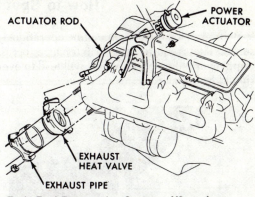

Early Fuel Evaporation System—V8 engines

Battery cleaning tool—side mounted terminal battery

allow hydrogen gas, formed by the chemical reaction in the battery, to escape safely.

REPLACEMENT BATTERIES

The cold power rating of a battery measures battery starting performance and provides an approximate relationship between battery size and engine size. The cold power rating of a replacement battery should match or exceed your engine size in cubic inches.

Early Fuel Evaporation (EFE) System

This is a more effective form of heat riser which is vacuum actuated. It is used on V-8 engines in 1975 and later years. It heats incoming mixture during the engine warm-up process, utilizing a ribbed heat exhanger of thin metal that is located in the intake manifold. This pre-heating allows the choke to open more rapidly, thus reducing emissions. Problems in this system might be indicated by poor engine operation during warmup.

This valve should be checked initially at 6 months/7500 miles, and, thereafter, at 18 month/22,500 mile intervals.

To check, move the valve through its full stroke by hand, making sure that linkage does not bind and is properly connected. If the valve sticks, free it up with a solvent. Also check that all vacuum hoses are properly connected and free of cracks or breaks. Replace hoses or broken or bent linkage parts as necessary.

Belts

TENSION CHECKING AND ADJUSTMENT

Check the drive belts every 6,000 miles or four months for evidence of wear such as cracking, fraying, and incorrect tension. Determine belt tension at a point halfway between the pulleys by pressing on the belt with moderate thumb pressure. If the distance between the pulleys (measured at the center of the pulley) is 13–16 in., the belt should deflect ½ in. at the halfway point or ¼ in. if the distance is 7–10 in. If the deflection is found to be too much or too little, loosen the mounting bolts and make the adjustments.

Before you attempt to adjust any of your

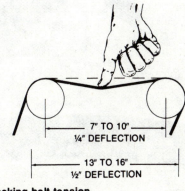

7" TO 10"
¼" DEFLECTION

13" TO 16"
½" DEFLECTION

Checking belt tension

How to Spot Worn V-Belts

V-Belts are vital to efficient engine operation—they drive the fan, water pump and other accessories. They require little maintenance (occasional tightening) but they will not last forever. Slipping or failure of the V-belt will lead to overheating. If your V-belt looks like any of these, it should be replaced.

Cracking or weathering

This belt has deep cracks, which cause it to flex. Too much flexing leads to heat build-up and premature failure. These cracks can be caused by using the belt on a pulley that is too small. Notched belts are available for small diameter pulleys.

Softening (grease and oil)

Oil and grease on a belt can cause the belt's rubber compounds to soften and separate from the reinforcing cords that hold the belt together. The belt will first slip, then finally fail altogether.

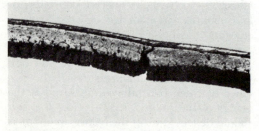

Glazing

Glazing is caused by a belt that is slipping. A slipping belt can cause a run-down battery, erratic power steering, overheating or poor accessory performance. The more the belt slips, the more glazing will be built up on the surface of the belt. The more the belt is glazed, the more it will slip. If the glazing is light, tighten the belt.

Worn cover

The cover of this belt is worn off and is peeling away. The reinforcing cords will begin to wear and the belt will shortly break. When the belt cover wears in spots or has a rough jagged appearance, check the pulley grooves for roughness.

Separation

This belt is on the verge of breaking and leaving you stranded. The layers of the belt are separating and the reinforcing cords are exposed. It's just a matter of time before it breaks completely.

engine's belts, you should take an old rag soaked in solvent and clean the mounting bolts of any road grime which has accumulated there. On some of the harder-to-reach bolts, an application of penetrating oil will make them easier to loosen. When you're adjusting belts, especially on late model V8's with air conditioning and power steering, it would be especially helpful to have a variety of socket extensions and universals to get to those hard-to-reach bolts.

NOTE: *When adjusting the air pump belt, if you are using a pry bar, make sure that you pry against the cast iron end cover and not against the aluminum housing. Excessive force on the housing itself will damage it.*

Hoses

HOSE REPLACEMENT

1. Remove the radiator cap.
2. Open the radiator petcock to drain the coolant. To replace the bottom hose drain all the radiator coolant. If only the top hose is to be replaced drain just enough fluid to bring the level down below the level of the top hose. If the coolant is over a year old discard it.
3. Remove the hose clamps and remove the hose.
4. Use new hose clamps if the old ones are badly rusted or damaged. Slide the hose clamps over each end of the new hose then slide the hose over the hose connections.
5. Position each clamp about ¼″ from the end of the hose and tighten.
6. Close the petcock and refill with the old fluid if it is less than a year old or with a new mixture of 50/50, coolant/water.
7. Start the engine and idle it for 15 minutes with the radiator cap off and check for leaks. Add coolant if necessary and install the radiator cap.

Cooling System

At least once every 2 years, the engine cooling system should be inspected, flushed, and refilled with fresh coolant. If the coolant is left in the system too long, it loses its ability to prevent rust and corrosion. If the coolant has too much water, it won't protect against freezing.

The pressure cap should be looked at for signs of age or deterioration. Fan belt and other drive belts should be inspected and ad-

justed to the proper tension. (See checking belt tension).

Hose clamps should be tightened, and soft or cracked hoses replaced. Damp spots, or accumulations of rust or dye near hoses, water pump or other areas, indicate possible leakage, which must be corrected before filling the system with fresh coolant.

CHECK THE RADIATOR CAP

While you are checking the coolant level, check the radiator cap for a worn or cracked gasket. If the cap doesn't seal properly, fluid will be lost and the engine will overheat.

Worn caps should be replaced with a new one.

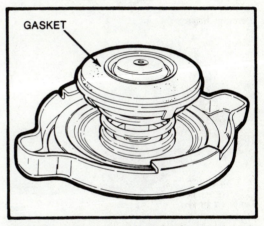

Check the radiator cap and gasket for proper seal

CLEAN RADIATOR OF DEBRIS

Periodically clean any debris—leaves, paper, insects, etc.—from the radiator fins. Pick the larges pieces off by hand. The smaller pieces can be washed away with water pressure from a hose.

Carefully straighten any bent radiator fins with a pair of needle nose pliers. Be careful—the fins are very soft. Don't wiggle the fins back and forth too much. Straighten them once and try not to move them again.

DRAIN AND REFILL THE COOLING SYSTEM

Completely draining and refilling the cooling system every two years at least will remove accumulated rust, scale and other deposits. Coolant in late model cars is a 50–50 mixture of ethylene glycol and water for year round use. Use a good quality antifreeze with water pump lubricants, rust inhibitors and other corrosion inhibitors along with acid neutralizers.

How To Spot Bad Hoses

Both the upper and lower radiator hoses are called upon to perform difficult jobs in an inhospitable environment. They are subject to nearly 18 psi at under hood temperatures often over 280°F., and must circulate nearly 7500 gallons of coolant an hour—3 good reasons to have good hoses.

Swollen hose

A good test for any hose is to feel it for soft or spongy spots. Frequently these will appear as swollen areas of the hose. The most likely cause is oil soaking. This hose could burst at any time, when hot or under pressure.

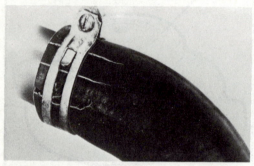

Cracked hose

Cracked hoses can usually be seen but feel the hoses to be sure they have not hardened; a prime cause of cracking. This hose has cracked down to the reinforcing cords and could split at any of the cracks.

Frayed hose end (due to weak clamp)

Weakened clamps frequently are the cause of hose and cooling system failure. The connection between the pipe and hose has deteriorated enough to allow coolant to escape when the engine is hot.

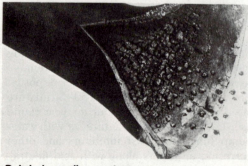

Debris in cooling system

Debris, rust and scale in the cooling system can cause the inside of a hose to weaken. This can usually be felt on the outside of the hose as soft or thinner areas.

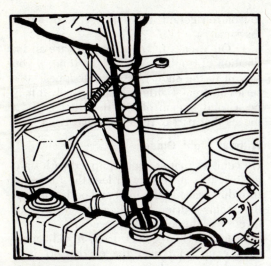

Antifreeze tester

1. Drain the existing antifreeze and coolant. Open the radiator and engine drain petcocks, or disconnect the bottom radiator hose, at the radiator outlet.

NOTE: *Before opening the radiator petcock, spray it with some penetrating lubricant.*

2. Close the petcock or re-connect the lower hose and fill the system with water.

3. Add a can of quality radiator flush.

4. Idle the engine until the upper radiator hose gets hot.

5. Drain the system again.

6. Repeat this process until the drained water is clear and free of scale.

7. Close all petcocks and connect all the hoses.

8. If equipped with a coolant recovery system, flush the reservoir with water and leave empty.

9. Determine the capacity of your cooling system (see capacities specifications). Add a 50/50 mix of quality antifreeze (ethylene glycol) and water to provide the desired protection.

10. Run the engine to operating temperature.

11. Stop the engine and check the coolant level.

12. Check the level of protection with an anti-freeze tester, replace the cap and check for leaks.

Air-Conditioning Safety Precautions

There are two particular hazards associated with air conditioning systems and they both relate to the refrigerant gas.

First, the refrigerant gas is an extremely cold substance. When exposed to air, it will instantly freeze any surface it comes in contact with, including your eyes. The other hazard relates to fire. Although normally non-toxic, refrigerant gas becomes highly poisonous in the presence of an open flame. One good whiff of the vapor formed by burning refrigerant can be fatal. Keep all forms of fire (including cigarettes) well clear of the air-conditioning system.

Any repair work to an air conditioning system should be left to a professional. Do not, under any circumstances, attempt to loosen or tighten any fittings or perform any work other than that outlined here.

CHECKING FOR OIL LEAKS

Refrigerant leaks show up as oily areas on the various components because the compressor oil is transported around the entire system along with the refrigerant. Look for oily spots on all the hoses and lines, and especially on the hose and tubing connections. If there are oily deposits, the system may have a leak, and you should have it checked by a qualified repairman.

NOTE: *A small area of oil on the front of the compressor is normal and no cause for alarm.*

CHECK THE COMPRESSOR BELT

Refer to the section in this chapter on "Drive Belts."

KEEP THE CONDENSER CLEAR

Periodically inspect the front of the condenser for bent fins or foreign material (dirt, bugs, leaves, etc.) If any cooling fins are bent, straighten them carefully with needle-nosed pliers. You can remove any debris with a stiff bristle brush or hose.

OPERATE THE A/C SYSTEM PERIODICALLY

A lot of A/C problems can be avoided by simply running the air conditioner at least once a week, regardless of the season. Simply let the system run for at least 5 minutes a week (even in the winter, and you'll keep the internal parts lubricated as well as preventing the hoses from hardening.

REFRIGERANT LEVEL CHECK

There are two ways to check refrigerant level, depending on how your model is equipped.

With Sight Glass

The first order of business when checking the sight glass is to find the sight glass. It will either be in the head of the receiver/drier, or in one of the metal lines leading from the top of the receiver/drier. Once you've found it, wipe it clean and proceed as follows:

1. With the engine and the air conditioning system running, look for the flow of refrigerant through the sight glass. If the air conditioner is working properly, you'll be able to see a continuous flow of clear refrigerant through the sight glass, with perhaps an occasional bubble at very high temperatures.

2. Cycle the air conditioner on and off to make sure what you are seeing is clear refrigerant. Since the refrigerant is clear, it is possible to mistake a completely discharged system for one that is fully charged. Turn the system off and watch the sight glass. If there is refrigerant in the system, you'll see bubbles during the off cycle. If you observe no bubbles when the system is running, and the air flow from the unit in the car is delivering cold air, everything is OK.

3. If you observe bubbles in the sight glass while the system is operating, the system is

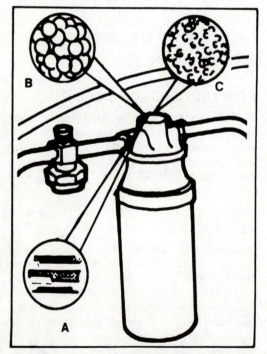

Oil streaks (A), constant bubbles (B) or foam (C) indicate there is not enough refrigerant in the system. Occasional bubbles during initial operation is normal. A clear sight glass indicates a proper charge or no refrigerant at all

low on refrigerant. Have it checked by a professional.

4. Oil streaks in the sight glass are an indication of trouble. Most of the time, if you see oil in the sight glass, it will appear as a series of streaks, although occasionally it may be a solid stream of oil. In either case, it means that part of the charge has been lost.

Without Sight Glass

On vehicles that are not equipped with sight glasses, it is necessary to feel the temperature difference in the inlet and outlet lines at the receiver/drier to gauge the refrigerant level. Use the following procedure:

1. Locate the receiver/drier. It will generally be up front near the condenser. It is shaped like a small fire extinguisher and will always have two lines connected to it. One line goes to the expansion valve and the other goes to the condenser.

2. With the engine and the air conditioner running, hold a line in each hand and gauge their relative temperatures. If they are both the same approximate temperature, the system is correctly charged.

3. If the line from the expansion valve to the receiver/drier is a lot colder than the line from the receiver/drier to the condenser, then the system is overcharged. It should be noted that this is an extremely rare condition.

4. If the line that leads from the receiver/drier to the condenser is a lot colder than the other line, the system is undercharged.

5. If the system is undercharged or overcharged, have it checked by a professional air conditioning mechanic.

Windshield Wipers

Intense heat from the sun, snow and ice, road oils and the chemicals used in windshield washer solvents combine to deteriorate the rubber wiper refills. The refills should be replaced about twice a year or whenever the blades begin to streak or chatter.

WIPER REFILL REPLACEMENT

Normally, if the wipers are not cleaning the windshield properly, only the refill has to be replaced. The blade and arm usually require replacement only in the event of damage. It is not necessary (except on new Tridon refills) to remove the arm or the balde to replace the refill (rubber part), though you may have to

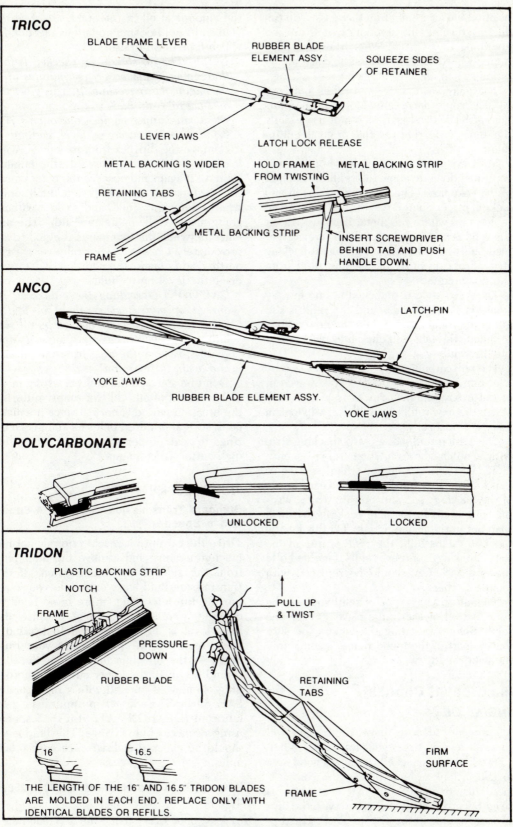

Wiper insert replacement

position the arm higher on the glass. You can do this turning the ignition switch on and operating the wipers. When they are positioned where they are accessible, turn the ignition switch off.

There are several types of refills and your vehicle could have any kind, since aftermarket blades and arms may not use exactly the same type refill as the original equipment.

Most Trico styles uses a release button that is pushed down to allow the refill to slide out of the yoke jaws. The new refill slides in and locks in place. Some Trico refills are removed by locating where the metal backing strip or the refill is wider. Insert a small screwdriver blade between the frame and metal backing strip. Press down to release the refill from the retaining tab.

The Anco style is unlocked at one end by squeezing 2 metal tabs, and the refill is slid out of the frame jaws. When the new refill is installed, the tabs will click into place, locking the refill.

The polycarbonate type is held in place by a locking lever that is pushed downward out of the groove in the arm to free the refill. When the new refill is installed, it will lock in place automatically.

The Tridon refill has a plastic backing strip with a notch about an inch from the end. Hold the blade (frame) on a hard surface so that the frame is tightly bowed. Grip the tip of the backing strip and pull up while twisting counterclockwise. The backing strip will snap out of the retaining tab. Do this for the remaining tabs until the refill is free of the arm. The length of these refills is molded into the end and they should be replaced with identical types.

No matter which type of refill you use, be sure that all of the frame claws engage the refill. Before operating the wipers, be sure that no part of the metal frame is contacting the windshield.

Fluid Level Checks
ENGINE OIL

It's a good idea to have the engine oil checked every time you buy gas. When you're having it checked, it's also a good idea to take a look around the engine compartment just to make sure that everything is alright. The oil level is checked with the dipstick at the side of the engine block. The dipstick protrudes into the oil pan and measures the amount of oil in the crankcase. See the "Oil and Fuel Recommendations" section for which type of oil to use.

NOTE: *The oil should be checked before the engine is started or five minutes after the engine has been shut off. This gives the oil time to drain back to the pan from the valves and upper engine components preventing an inaccurate oil level reading.*

Remove the dipstick from its holder, wipe it clean, and insert it back into the engine. Remove it again and observe the point where the oil stops on the stick. It should fall somewhere between "full" and "add" without going above "full" or below "add." The distance between the two marks is equal to approximately 1 qt, so, if your oil level is right on the "add" mark, the addition of 1 qt will bring the level up to "full."

CAUTION: *Overfilling the crankcase by one qt or more may result in oil-fouled spark plugs or oil leaks caused by oil seal failure. To avoid weakening oil seals and gaskets, remove the plug from the oil pan and drain the extra oil.*

Don't be alarmed if a new car uses a moderate amount of oil. Oil consumption during the break-in period is normal since it usually takes several hundred miles for the piston oil rings to seat properly and often longer for high-performance engines.

TRANSMISSION FLUID
Standard Transmission (3 Speed, 4 Speed and 5 Speed)

Drive the car until it reaches normal operating temperature and remove the filler plug from the side of the transmission. If the transmission fluid leaks out while you're removing the filler plug, there is no need to completely remove the plug because the fluid level is alright. If no fluid leaks out when removing the plug, insert your little finger in the opening and feel for fluid. It should be up to the lower edge of the filler plug opening; if not, fill with a high-quality SAE 80 or SAE 80–90 multipurpose gear lubricant (DEXRON® ATF if it's a 5 speed) using a squeeze bulb syringe. This fluid level should be checked at least once each 6,000 miles.

Powerglide, Turbo Hydra-Matic 200, 250, and 350

At least once every 6,000 miles (7,500 miles in 1975 and later cars), check the fluid level

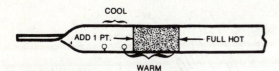

Automatic transmission dipstick

with the dipstick. The dipstick is located on the right-side of the engine, near the firewall. When checking the transmission fluid, make sure that the cap of the dipstick seats properly on the filler tube. Failure to do so may result in an inaccurate reading.

Drive the car until the transmission is hot (at least 15 miles) and then stop it on a level surface. With the transmission in Park (parking brake on) and the engine idling, the fluid level on the dipstick should be between the "full" mark and ¼ in. below "full."

If the car hasn't been driven enough to heat the transmission, the fluid level should be checked in the following manner. Set the parking brake, put the transmission lever in Park and start the engine. With the engine at idle, move the selector lever through each position. Return the lever to Park and, with the engine at a slow idle, check the fluid level on the transmission dipstick. The level should be between the "add" mark and ¼ in. below "add" or, on 1976 and later cars, between the two dimples. If additional fluid is required, add just enough to bring the level to ¼ in. below the "add" mark, or above the lower dimple. As the transmission temperature rises from room temperature (80° F), to operating temperature (180° F), the fluid will expand and rise on the dipstick. Drive the car until the transmission is hot and recheck the fluid level. It should now appear at the "full" mark or ¼ in. below it. Replace the dipstick making sure that it is pushed fully into the filler tube.

CAUTION: *Do not overfill an automatic transmission; internal damage may result. Overfilling will bring the fluid level up to the planetary gear causing the gear to pass through the oil with every revolution. This aerates and foams the oil before it goes to the rest of the transmission. This condition can cause overheating. If the transmission dipstick indicates a level above "full," the additional fluid should be drained immediately.*

Use only General Motors DEXRON® Automatic Transmission Fluid or any other fluid with DEXRON® marked on the can in 1975 and earlier cars. Use DEXRON II® in 1976

and later cars. One pint raises the level from "add" to "full."

The automatic transmission fluid must be drained periodically. See Chapter 6, "Clutch and Transmission" for the procedure and intervals.

BRAKE MASTER CYLINDER

At least once every 6,000 miles (7,500 miles on 1975 and later cars), check the brake fluid level in the master cylinder. The master cylinder, which is mounted on the left-side of the engine compartment firewall, is divided into two sections (reservoirs), and the fluid level must be maintained about ¼ in. below the top edge of both reservoirs. Use only a top grade SAE approved brake fluid with the words "DOT 3" on the can. This will assure you that the brake fluid meets the specifications for your car.

CAUTION: *Be careful when using brake fluid around painted surfaces; it will quickly dissolve paint if not immediately diluted with water. Never operate the brake pedal with the master cylinder cover*

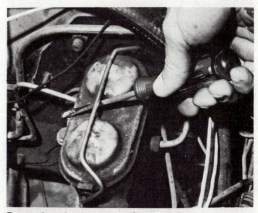

Removing the master cylinder cover

Proper brake fluid level

removed. Fluid pressure created by pushing the pedal will force fuild from the reservoirs.

COOLANT

Check the coolant level when the engine is cold by opening the radiator cap. Turn the cap to its first stop. If you hear steam or water escaping, close the cap and let the engine cool further before you try again. *Never get your face near a radiator cap when you're opening it.* If you wish to check the coolant with the engine hot, you can do so without opening the radiator cap by squeezing the top radiator hose. This will tell you if there is coolant in the system. This method is permissible for occasionally checking the coolant, but should not be substituted for removing the cap on a permanent basis. With the radiator cap removed, the level of coolant should be maintained 2 in. below the bottom of the filler neck, or if equipped with an expansion tank, at the proper level line on the side of the tank.

CAUTION: *Allow the engine to cool considerably and then add water while the engine is running.*

REAR AXLE

Whether the axle is standard or positraction, the same procedure for checking fluid level is the same. About once every 6,000 miles or four months (or 7,500 miles and six months on 1975 and later models), remove the filler plug and see that fluid is to the level of the filler plug hold at operating temperatures or ½ in. below the hole when cold. Fill standard axles with SAE 80 or SAE 80-90 multipurpose gear lubricant. On positraction units, use only the special positraction fluid available from your Chevrolet parts department. Also available from Chevrolet is a positraction fluid additive helpful in silencing noisy units and reducing clutch slippage.

POWER STEERING RESERVOIR

Power steering fluid level should be checked at least once every 6,000 miles or four months (7,500 miles and six months for 1975 and later models). To prevent possible overfilling, check the fluid level only when fluid has warmed to operating temperatures and the wheels are turned straight ahead. If the level is low, fill the pump reservoir with DEXRON® Automatic Transmission Fluid

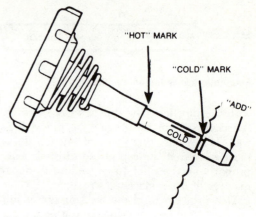

Power steering dipstick

required by the transmission on 1976 and earlier cars. 1977–79 cars require GM power steering fluid, until the fluid level measures "full" on the reservoir dipstick. Low fluid level usually produces a moaning sound as the wheels are turned (especially when standing still or parking) and increases steering wheel effort.

BATTERY

The electrolyte level in the battery should be checked about once every month and more often during hot weather or long trips. If the level is below the bottom of the split ring, distilled water should be added until the level reaches the ring. 1976 and later models are offered with an optional Freedom® battery which is sealed at the factory and never needs water added to it.

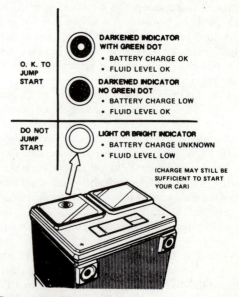

Battery condition indicator

Capacities

Year	Model	Engine Displacement Cu In. (cc)	Engine Crankcase (qts)		Transmission (pts)			Drive Axle (pts)	Gasoline Tank (gals)	Cooling System (qts)	
			With Filter	Without Filter	Manual 3-spd	4–5 spd	Automatic			W/ AC	W/O AC
1971	All	4-140	4	3	2.4	3	6	2.3	11	6.5	6.5
1972	All	4-140	4	3	2.4	3	6	2.8	11	9.0	8.6
1973	All	4-140	4	3	3	3	6	2.8	11	9.0	8.6
1974	All	4-140	4	3	3	3	8	2.8	16	9.0	8.6
1975	Vega/Monza	4-140	4.5	3.5	3	3	8	2.8	16	8.0	8.0
	Astre	4-140	4	3	2.4	2.4①	5	2.8	16	7.0	7.5
	Sunbird	4-140	4	3	2.4	2.4①	5	2.8	18.5	7.0	7.5
	All	6-231	5	4	—	3.5②	6	2.8	18.5	14	13
	Monza	8-262	4	3	—	3②	8	2.8	18.5	18	18
	Monza	8-350③	4	3	—	3②	8	2.8	18.5	18	18
1976	Vega/Monza	4-140	4	3	—	3②	8	2.8	18.5	18	18
	Astre	4-140	4	3	—	2.4①	5	2.8	16.0	7.0	7.5
	Sunbird	4-140	4	3	—	2.4①	5	2.8	18.5	7.0	7.5
	Starfire	6-231	5	4	—	2.5①	6	4.25	18.5	14	13
	Sunbird	6-231	5	4	2.4	2.4①	5	2.8	18.5	7.0	7.5
	Skyhawk	6-231	5	4	—	3.5②	6	2.8	18.5	14	13
	Astre	6-231	5	4	2.4	2.4①	5	2.8	16.0	7.0	7.5
	Monza	8-262, 305	5	4	—	3②	8	2.8	18.5	18	18
1977	Vega	4-140	4.5	3.5	3	3②	8	2.8	16	8.0	8.0
	Monza	4-140	4.5	3.5	3	3②	8	2.8	18.5	8.0	8.0
	Astre	4-140	4.5	3.5	—	3	8	2.8④	16	7.0	8.0
	Sunbird	4-140	4.5	3.5	—	3	8	2.8④	18.5	7.0	8.0
	Starfire	4-140	4.5	3.5	—	3	6	4.25	18.5	9.3	8.1
	Astre	4-151	4	3	—	3	6	2.8④	16	10.7	10.7

Capacities (cont.)

Year	Model	Engine Displacement Cu In. (cc)	Engine Crankcase (qts) With Filter	Engine Crankcase (qts) Without Filter	Transmission (pts) Manual 3-spd	Transmission (pts) Manual 4–5 spd	Transmission (pts) Automatic	Drive Axle (pts)	Gasoline Tank (gals)	Cooling System (qts) W/ AC	Cooling System (qts) W/O AC
1977	Sunbird	4-151	4	3	—	3	6	2.8④	18.5	10.7	10.7
	Astre	6-231	5	4	2.4	3	6	2.8④	16	12.0	12.0
	Sunbird	6-231	5	4	2.4	3	6	2.8④	18.5	12.0	12.0
	Starfire	6-231	5	4	—	3	6	4.25	18.5	12.2	11.8
	Skyhawk	6-231	5	4	—	3.1①	6	2.8	18.5	12.0	12.0
	Monza	8-305	5	4	—	3②	8	2.8	18.5	18.0	18.0
1978–79	Monza	4-151	4	3	—	3②	6	2.8	18.5⑤	10.8	10.8
	Sunbird	4-151	4	3	—	3.5	6	3.5	18.5⑥	⑦	⑧
	Starfire	4-151	4	3	—	3.5	6	3.5	18.5	11.5	11.0
	Monza	6-196	5	4	—	3②	6	2.8	18.5⑤	11.6	11.6
	Monza	6-231	5	4	—	3②	6	2.8	18.5⑤	11.6	11.6
	Sunbird	6-231	5	4	—	3.5	7.5	3.5	18.5⑥	12.8	12.7
	Starfire	6-231	5	4	—	3.5	6	3.5	18.5	12.25	11.75
	Skyhawk	6-231	5	4	—	3.5②	6	3.75	18.5	1.21	11.8
	All	8-305	5	4	—	3②	8	2.8	18.5	18.0	18.0
1980	Monza	4-151	4	3	3.4	—	7.5	3.5	18.5	11.5	11.6
		6-231	5	4	3.4	—	7.0	3.5	18.5	11.9	11.9
	Sunbird	4-151	4	3	3.0	3.5	8.0	3.5	18.5⑨	11.5	11.0
		6-231	5	4	3.4	—	7.0	3.5	18.5⑨	11.9	11.9
	Starfire	4-151	4	3	3.0	—	6.0	3.5	18.5	11.5	11.0
		6-231	5	4	3.0	—	6.0	3.5	18.5	12.4	11.9
	Skyhawk	6-231	5	4	3.0	—	6.0	3.5	18.5	12.2	12.3

① 3.5–5-speed
② 5-speed uses Dexron® II Auto. Trans. Fluid
③ California only
④ 3.5 with 7½" ring gear axle
⑤ Sta. wag. and Monza "S" hatchback—15.0
⑥ Sta. wag: early production—15.9 late production—15.0
⑦ Man. trans.—10.9
⑧ Man. trans.—10.9 Auto. trans.—11.4
Auto. trans.—11.6
⑨ Sta. wag.—15.0

RECOMMENDED TIRE PRESSURES

GM

VEHICLE LOAD	(PSI COLD)	
	FRONT	REAR
UP TO VEHICLE CAPACITY	XX	XX

RECOMMENDED TIRE SIZE(S)

(USE ONLY IN SETS)	LOAD RANGE
XXX(X)XX XXX(X)XX XX(X)XXX	

BECAUSE OF POSSIBLE ADVERSE EFFECTS ON VEHICLE HANDLING, DO NOT MIX RADIAL PLY TIRES WITH OTHER TYPE TIRES ON THE SAME VEHICLE.

VEHICLE CAPACITY

BUCKET SEAT

4 OCCUPANTS
2 FRONT—2 REAR
125 LBS. CARGO LOAD

TOTAL 725 LBS.

SEE OWNERS MANUAL FOR ADDITIONAL INFORMATION

XX XXXXXXX   PRINTED IN U.S.A.

The tire pressure placard found on the left door gives the proper pressures for the tires originally installed on your car

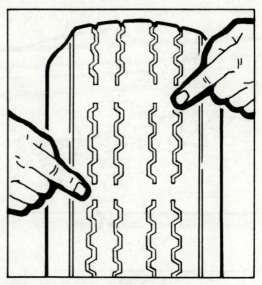

Built-in tread wear indicator bars

Tires

INFLATION PRESSURE

Tire inflation is the most ignored item of auto maintenance. Gasoline mileage can drop as much as .8% for every 1 pound per square inch (psi) of under inflation.

Two items should be a permanent fixture in every glove compartment; a tire pressure gauge and a tread depth gauge. Check the tire air pressure (including the spare) regularly with a pocket type gauge. Kicking the tires won't tell you a thing, and the gauge on the service station air hose is notoriously inaccurate.

The tire pressures recommended for your car are usually found on the left door or in the owner's manual. Ideally, inflation pressure should be checked when the tires are cool. When the air becomes heated it expands and the pressure increases. Every 10° rise (or drop) in temperature means a difference of 1 psi, which also explains why the tire appears to lose air on a very cold night. When it is impossible to check the tires "cold," allow for pressure build-up due to heat. If the "hot" pressure exceeds the "cold" pressure by more than 15 psi, reduce your speed, load or both. Otherwise internal heat is created in the tire. When the heat approaches the temperature at which the tire was cured, during manufacture, the tread can separate from the body.

CAUTION: *Never counteract excessive pressure build-up by bleeding off air pressure (letting some air out). This will only further raise the tire operating temperature.*

Before starting a long trip with lots of luggage, you can add about 2–4 psi to the tires to make them run cooler, but never exceed the maximum inflation pressure on the side of the tire.

TREAD DEPTH

All tires made since 1968, have 8 built-in tread wear indicator bars that show up as ½" wide smooth bands across the tire when 1/16" of tread remains. The appearance of tread wear indicators means that the tires should be replaced. In fact, many states have laws prohibiting the use of tires with less than 1/16" tread.

You can check your own tread depth with an inexpensive gauge or by using a Lincoln head penny. Slip the Lincoln penny into several tread grooves. If you can see the top of Lincoln's head in 2 adjacent gooves, the tires have less than 1/16" tread left and should be replaced. You can measure snow tires in the same manner by using the "tails" side of the Lincoln penny. If you can see the top of the Lincoln memorial, it's time to replace the snow tires.

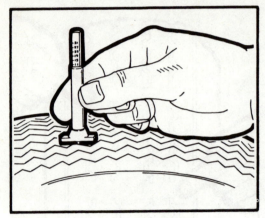

Checking tread depth using a gauge

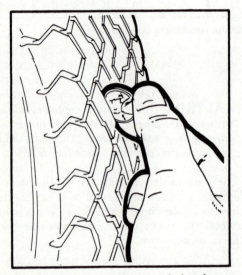

Checking tread depth with a Lincoln head penny

TIRE ROTATION

Tire wear can be equalized by switching the position of the tires about every 6000 miles. Including a conventional spare in the rotation pattern can give up to 20% more tire life.

CAUTION: *Do not include the new "Space Saver®" or temporary spare tires in the rotation pattern.*

There are certain exceptions to tire rotation, however. Studded snow tires should not be rotated, and radials should be kept on the same side of the car (maintain the same direction of rotation). The belts on radial tires get set in a pattern. If the direction of rotation is reversed, it can cause rough ride and vibration.

NOTE: *When radials or studded snows are*

taken off the car, mark them, so you can maintain the same direction of rotation.

TIRE STORAGE

Store the tires at proper inflation pressures if they are mounted on wheels. All tires should be kept in a cool, dry place. If they are stored in the garage or basement, do not let them stand on a concrete floor; set them on strips of wood.

Fuel Filter

The carburetor inlet fuel filter should be replaced every twelve months or 12,000 miles (15,000 miles on 1975 and later models).

Filters may become clogged before replacement time causing hard starting, hesitation when accelerating, and poor performance and sputtering at higher speeds. This occurs because the dirty filter restricts the flow of gasoline. The filter should be inspected and replaced if found to be excessively dirty. To replace the inlet filter:

1. Using an open-end wrench (preferably a flare nut wrench), disconnect the fuel line connection from the larger fuel filter nut.

2. Remove the larger nut from the carburetor with a box-end wrench or socket.

3. Remove the filter element and spring from the carburetor.

4. Check the bronze element for dirt blockage by blowing on the cone end. If the element is good, air should pass through easily.

5. If the car has a paper element instead of

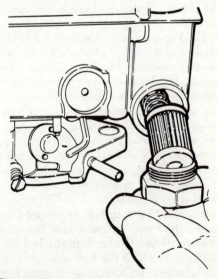

Fuel filter replacement

a bronze element, check by blowing into the inlet end. If air does not pass through easily, replace the element. Do not attempt to clean elements.

6. Install the spring and then the element into the carburetor, making sure that the small side of the bronze cone is facing outward.

7. Install a new gasket on the large nut and tighten the nut securely.

8. Insert the fuel line and tighten the nut.

LUBRICATION

Oil and Fuel Recommendations

GM recommends the use of high quality heavy-duty detergent oil having the proper viscosity and an SE service rating.

Engine oil must be selected according to its viscosity and to its service rating. The selection is determined by two major factors: the climate in which the car will be operated and the work the engine will be doing. Engine oils are sold in a variety of viscosities. Each oil can top is stamped with a viscosity number (SEA 20, 30, 10W-30, etc.,) and a service rating (SA, SB, SC, SD, or SE). Oil viscosity refers to the body and thickness of the oil. The Society of Automotive Engineers (SAE) devised an oil viscosity rating system in which the thicker oils receive a higher viscosity number than the thinner oils. SAE 30 oil is a straight-weight, single-viscosity oil having a fairly high viscosity.

As mentioned earlier, engine oil must be selected by viscosity and service rating. An engine oil is refined and then rated according to its ability to lubricate, control deposits, retard oil oxidation, and protect the engine from rust and corrosion. Today there are five categories of oil ratings. Now it is possible for the comsumer to merely look at the two letter classification on the can and determine more accurately which oil is best for his particular engine. The five ratings are:

1. SA—This oil is for those engines operated under mild conditions. It contains no protective qualities.

2. SB—For those engines undergoing light duty. It has antiscuff properties and will slow down oil oxidation and bearing corrosion.

3. SC—This oil meets the minimum requirement for all 1964–67 passenger cars and light trucks. It will control high and low-temperature deposits and retard rust and corrosion.

4. SD—This oil meets the requirements for 1968 gasoline engine warranty service and controls deposits better than the SC oil in addition to resisting rust and corrosion.

5. SE—This oil has increased detergency and can withstand higher temperatures and produce more pressure. It is equivalent to the old MS rating.

Your 1971–74 car is designed to run well on regular gasoline. All 1975 and later models are equipped with catalytic converters. These cars *must* use unleaded fuel. The use of a leaded fuel in a car equipped with a catalytic converter will render the converter useless. A nonfunctioning converter will not reduce emissions and as a result the car will not pass an emissions inspection.

An engine using the improper grade of gasoline will produce a "spark knock" or pinging sound when accelerating because the octane (antiknock ingredient) is too low for the high compression of the engine. Gasoline octane rating determines the speed at which the gas will burn. The lower the octane, the faster it burns. A low octane gas will complete its burning too rapidly before downward motion of the piston can prevent the production of very high pressure. If this occurs, try a higher grade of gasoline and, if the knocking persists, consult your authorized Chevrolet dealer since excessive spark knocking can

Oil Viscosity Selection Chart

	Anticipated Temperature Range	SAE Viscosity
Multi-grade	Above 20° F.	20W–40 20W–50
	Above 0° F.	10W–30 10W–40
	Below 60° F.	5W–30
	Below 20° F.	5W–20[1]
Single grade	Above 40° F.	30
	Above 20° F.	20W–20
	0° F.–60° F.	10W

[1] GM does not recommend the use of 5W–20 oil for high speed driving.

Maintenance Schedule

Maintenance Operation	1971–74	1975–80
Air conditioning system—Check condition of hoses and refrigerant charge	Every 4 months or 6,000 miles	Every 12 months or 7,500 miles
Air cleaner element—replace	Every 50,000 miles③	Every 30,000 miles③
Automatic transmission filter and change	Every 24,000 miles②	Every 100,000 miles②
Carburetor mounting—Torque carburetor attaching bolts and/or nuts	At 1st 4 months or 6,000 miles	At 1st 6 months or 7,500 miles then every 24,000 miles
Chassis lubrication—Lubricate all grease fittings	Every 4 months or 6,000 miles	Every 12 months or 7,500 miles
Cooling system—Flushing and fluid change	Every 12 months or 12,000 miles	Every 24 months or 30,000 miles
Disc brakes—Check brake pads and condition of rotor	Every 6,000 miles	Every 12 months or 7,500 miles
Drive belts—Check for tension and wear and adjust or replace as required	Every 4 months or 6,000 miles	Every 12 months or 15,000 miles
Drum brakes and parking brake—Check drum and lining condition and adjust parking brake	Every 12 months or 12,000 miles	Every 12 months or 15,000 miles
ECS system—Replace canister filter	Every 24 months or 24,000 miles	Every 24 months or 30,000 miles
EGR system—Inspect and clean as necessary	Every 12 months or 12,000 miles	Every 12 months or 15,000 miles
Engine timing—Check and adjust	Every 12 months or 12,000 miles	Every 30,000 miles
Engine oil filter	Every oil change	Every oil change
Engine oil change	Every 4 months or 6,000 miles	Every 12 months or 7,500 miles
Fluid levels—Check battery, engine, axle, transmission, steering pump, engine coolant and windshield washer	Every 4 months or 6,000 miles	Every 12 months or 7,500 miles
Fuel filter—Replace	Every 12 months or 12,000 miles	Every 12 months or 15,000 miles
Manifold heat valve (EFE)—Inspect and lubricate as necessary		Every 18 months or 22,500 miles
Mechanical valve lifters—Adjust intake and exhaust valves	Every 24,000 miles	—
Oxygen sensor—replace	—	Every 15,000 miles

Maintenance Schedule (cont.)

Maintenance Operation	1971–74	1975–80
PCV filter—Check and replace	Every 12 months or 12,000 miles	Every 12 months or 15,000 miles
PCV valve—Check and replace	Every 12 months or 15,000 miles	Every 12 months or 15,000 miles
Rear axle fluid:① Positraction axle (change fluid) Standard axle (check level)	After 1st 12,000 miles Every 4 months or 6,000 miles	After 1st 7,500 miles Every 12 months or 7,500 miles
Spark plugs (leaded fuels)—Replace	Every 6,000 miles	—
Spark plugs (unleaded fuels)—Replace	Every 12,000 miles	Every 22,500 miles
Spark plug wires—Clean and inspect for damage and replace as necessary	Every 12 months or 12,000 miles	Every 15,000 miles
Tire pressures	At least once a month	At least once a month
Tire rotation—Rotate to equalize wear	Every 6,000 miles	1st 7,500 miles then every 15,000 miles
Wheel bearings—Clean and repack	Every 24,000 miles	Every 30,000 miles

① Change the lubricant every 12,000 miles on all type rear axles when using the vehicle to pull a trailer.
② Change the lubricant every 12,000 miles after constantly pulling a trailer or driving in heavy city traffic.
③ Change more often under dusty driving conditions.

cause engine damage. The proper fuel for your car is available throughout the United States and Canada but may be difficult to find in other countries where fuel is much lower in octane. This lower grade of gasoline may cause excessive spark knock and serious engine damage. After arriving in the foreign country, it is advisable to contact the nearest General Motors dealer for advice on usage and availability of proper fuels.

Oil Changes

Engine oil and filter should be changed every four months or 6,000 miles on all 1971–1974 models. On 1975 and later models, the interval is six months and 7,500 miles. Make *sure* you change oil based on the time interval if it arrives before you've accumulated enough mileage. Chevrolet bases these recommendations on the assumption that your car is being used for average driving. Certain types of driving requires that this interval not exceed three months or 3,000 miles. These include:
1. Operating the car under dusty conditions or during a dust storm. A dust storm may necessitate an immediate oil change.
2. Long periods of idling.
3. Trailer hauling.
4. Short trips at freezing temperatures when the engine hasn't had time to warm up sufficiently.
5. Commercial driving such as that performed by patrol cars, taxicabs, or limousines.

These recommended oil change intervals are based upon the assumption that a high-quality SE oil is used; otherwise the intervals would have to be made shorter for the lower quality oil. Long engine life, low maintenance, and good performance cannot be ensured if these oil changes are not performed at the proper intervals.

Always drain the oil after the engine has been running long enough to bring it to operating temperature. Hot oil will flow easier and more contaminants will be removed along with the oil than if it were drained cold. You will need a large capacity drain pan, which you can purchase at any store which sells automotive parts. Another necessity is containers for the used oil. You will find that plastic bottles, such as those used for bleach or fabric softener, make excellent storage jugs.

After draining your oil you should find some way of disposing of the old oil without damaging the environment. One way to do this would be to ask at your local gas station if you could dump your old oil into his holding tank. Some quantity of the old oil could be kept around for miscellaneous lubrication of things which are exposed to the elements all the time.

CHANGING YOUR OIL

1. Run the engine until it reaches normal operating temperature.
2. Jack up the front of the car and support it on safety stands.
3. Slide a drain pan of at least 6 quarts capacity under the oil pan.
4. Loosen the drain plug. Turn the plug out by hand. By keeping an inward pressure on the plug as you unscrew it, oil won't escape past the threads and you can remove it without being burned by hot oil.
5. Allow the oil to drain completely, then wipe clean and install the drain plug. Don't overtighten the plug, or force it in and strip the threads or you'll end up with a headache and a repair bill. If you do happen to damage the plug, there are other types of replacement plugs available from auto supply stores which will do the job.
6. Using a strap wrench, remove the oil filter. Keep in mind that it's holding about one quart of dirty, hot oil.
7. Empty the old filter into the drain pan and dispose of the filter.
8. Using a clean rag, wipe off the filter adapter on the engine block. Be sure that the rag doesn't leave any lint which could clog an oil passage.
9. Coat the rubber gasket on the filter

Removing the oil filter with a strap wrench

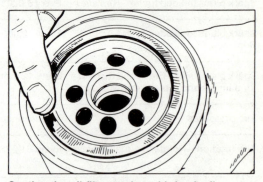
Coating the oil filter gasket with fresh oil

with fresh oil. Spin it onto the engine *by hand;* when the gasket touches the adapter surface give it another ½–¾ turn. No more, or you'll squash the gasket and it will leak.
10. Refill the engine with the correct amount of fresh oil. See the "Capacities" chart.
11. Crank the engine over several times and then start it without touching the accelerator. If the oil pressure "idiot light" doesn't go out or the pressure gauge shows zero, after 10 seconds or so, shut the engine down and find out what's wrong.
12. If the oil pressure is OK and there are no leaks, shut the engine off and lower the car.
13. Wait a few minutes and check the oil level. Add oil, as necessary, to bring the level up to Full.

Chassis Lubrication

Chassis lubrication can be performed by a shop or gas station using a pressurized grease gun or it can be performed at home using a hand-operated grease gun. Before applying grease, wipe the grease fittings clean to prevent the possibility of forcing any dirt into the component. Upon completion of lubrica-

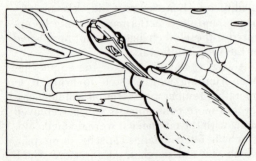
Removing the oil pan drain plug

tion, wipe each fitting clean to keep dirt build-up to a minimum. Installing plastic fitting caps or aluminum foil around each fitting is an even better idea. Periodic lubrication is necessary for the components listed in the paragraphs below. Unless otherwise indicated, maintenance intervals are: 1971–74 cars: 6,000 miles or four months. 1975–76 cars: 7,500 miles or six months. 1977 and later cars: 7,500 miles or 1 year.

FRONT SUSPENSION BALL JOINTS

Lubricate the four fittings with a water resistant EP chassis lubricant. Do not grease the ball joints unless they are warmer than 10° F.

STEERING LINKAGE

Lubricate the seven fittings with a water-resistant EP chassis lubricant. Locations for these fittings are: one at each end of each tie rod, one at each end of the relay rod, and one at the idler shaft.

FRONT WHEEL BEARINGS

Clean and repack the wheel bearings with a high-melting-point wheel bearing lubricant. On those cars with disc brakes, use a more durable lubricant—GM part no. 1051195 available at your Chevrolet parts department.

CAUTION: *Do not use a "long fiber" or "viscous" type lubricant in wheel bearings. Never mix wheel bearing lubricants. To prevent mixing, completely clean any old lubricant from the bearings and hubs before repacking them with new grease.*

It is important that the wheel bearings be properly adjusted after installation. Improperly adjusted wheel bearings can cause steering instability, front end shimmy and wander, and increased tire wear. For complete adjustment procedures, see "Wheel Bearings" in the "Brakes" chapter.

Lubrication Chart—1971–74

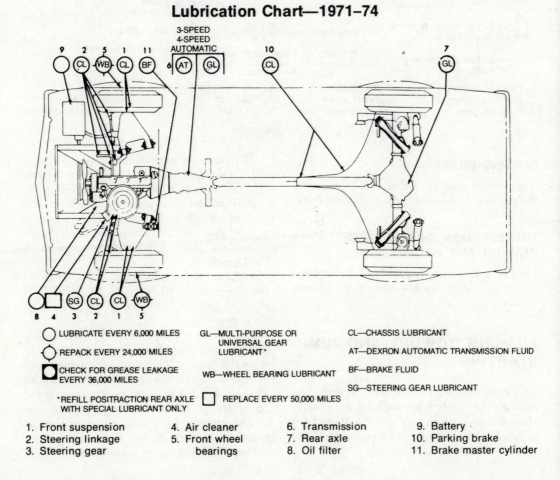

LUBRICATE EVERY 6,000 MILES

REPACK EVERY 24,000 MILES

CHECK FOR GREASE LEAKAGE EVERY 36,000 MILES

*REFILL POSITRACTION REAR AXLE WITH SPECIAL LUBRICANT ONLY

REPLACE EVERY 50,000 MILES

GL—MULTI-PURPOSE OR UNIVERSAL GEAR LUBRICANT*

WB—WHEEL BEARING LUBRICANT

CL—CHASSIS LUBRICANT

AT—DEXRON AUTOMATIC TRANSMISSION FLUID

BF—BRAKE FLUID

SG—STEERING GEAR LUBRICANT

1. Front suspension
2. Steering linkage
3. Steering gear
4. Air cleaner
5. Front wheel bearings
6. Transmission
7. Rear axle
8. Oil filter
9. Battery
10. Parking brake
11. Brake master cylinder

Lubrication Chart—1975–80

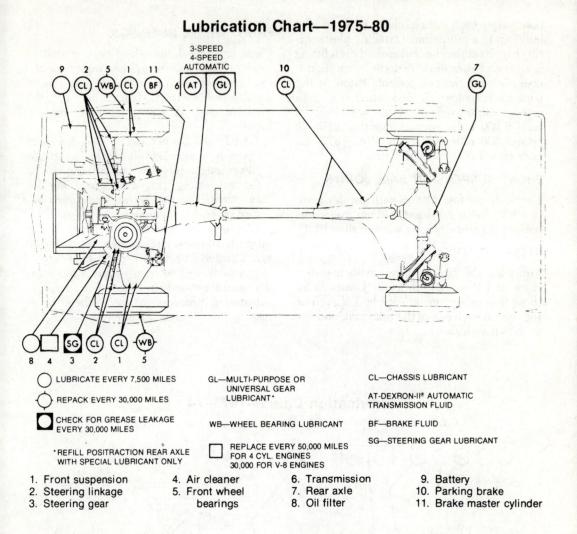

⭘ LUBRICATE EVERY 7,500 MILES	GL—MULTI-PURPOSE OR UNIVERSAL GEAR LUBRICANT*	CL—CHASSIS LUBRICANT
⭘ REPACK EVERY 30,000 MILES		AT-DEXRON-II® AUTOMATIC TRANSMISSION FLUID
◻ CHECK FOR GREASE LEAKAGE EVERY 30,000 MILES	WB—WHEEL BEARING LUBRICANT	BF—BRAKE FLUID
		SG—STEERING GEAR LUBRICANT
*REFILL POSITRACTION REAR AXLE WITH SPECIAL LUBRICANT ONLY	◻ REPLACE EVERY 50,000 MILES FOR 4 CYL. ENGINES 30,000 FOR V-8 ENGINES	

1. Front suspension	4. Air cleaner	6. Transmission
2. Steering linkage	5. Front wheel	7. Rear axle
3. Steering gear	bearings	8. Oil filter

9. Battery	
10. Parking brake	
11. Brake master cylinder	

PARKING BRAKE

Apply water-resistant EP chassis lubricant to the parking brake cable, cable guides, links, and levers.

TRANSMISSION SHIFT LINKAGE (MANUAL AND AUTOMATIC)

Lubricate all contacting surfaces throughout the linkage with water-resistant EP chassis lubricant.

PUSHING, TOWING, AND JUMP STARTING

Cars equipped with automatic transmissions may not be started by pushing or towing. Manual transmission cars may be started by pushing. The car need not be pushed to high speed to start.

To push a car with manual transmission:

1. Make sure that the bumpers of the two vehicles align so as not to damage either.

2. Turn on the ignition switch in the pushed car. Place the transmission in second or third gear and hold down the clutch pedal.

3. Have the car pushed to a speed of 10–15 mph.

4. Ease up the clutch and press down on the accelerator slightly. If the clutch is engaged abruptly, damage to the push vehicle may result.

The car should not be towed to start, since there is a chance of the towed vehicle ramming the tow car. The car may be towed with its rear wheels on the ground at speeds under 35 mph, for distances up to 50 miles. If the car must be towed further or faster, the driveshaft must be disconnected or the car must be towed on its front wheels.

Three and four speed manual transmission

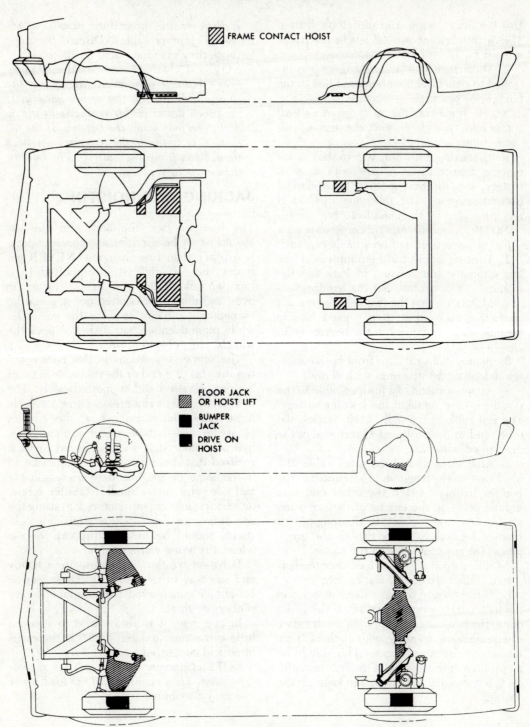

FRAME CONTACT HOIST

FLOOR JACK
OR HOIST LIFT

BUMPER
JACK

DRIVE ON
HOIST

Lifting and jacking points

vehicles can be towed on all four wheels at freeway speeds for extensive distances, provided that the following precautions are observed:

1. On 1971–72 models remove the TCS switch from the right side of the transmission and fill with lubricant to this level. On 1973 and later models remove the transmission filler plug and install a 90° ½″ pipe street elbow and add one quart (2 lbs) of lubricant.

Use the filler plug to cap the elbow fitting. The extra lubricant may be left in the transmission for normal operation.

2. Make sure that a sturdy towbar is attached to structural members, not just to the bumper or brackets.

NOTE: *Whenever the car is towed with all four wheels on the ground, the steering column must not be locked.*

Jump starting is the only way to start an automatic transmission vehicle with a weak battery, and the best method for a manual transmission car. The following method is recommended by the manufacturer:

NOTE: *Do not attempt this procedure on a frozen battery. It will very likely explode.*

1. Turn off all electrical equipment. Place the automatic transmission in Park and the manual unit in neutral. Set the handbrake.

2. Make sure that the two vehicles are not contacting each other. It is a good idea to keep the engine running in the booster vehicle.

3. Remove all vent caps from both batteries and cover the openings with cloths.

4. Attach one end of a jumper cable to the positive (+) terminal of the booster battery. The red cable is normally used. Attach the other end to the positive (+) terminal of the discharged battery.

5. Attach one end of the other cable (the black one) to the negative (−) terminal of the booster battery. Attach the other end to a ground point on the engine of the car being started. An ideal point is the engine lift bracket located between two of the spark plugs. Do not connect it to the battery.

NOTE: *Be careful not to lean over the battery while making this last connection.*

6. If the engine will not start, disconnect the batteries as soon as possible. If this is not done, the two batteries will soon reach a state of equilibrium, possibly with both of them too weak to start an engine. This should be no problem if the engine of the booster vehicle is left running fast enough to keep up the charge.

7. Reverse the procedure exactly to remove the jumper cables. Discard the rags, because they may have acid on them.

NOTE: *To jump start a Maintenance Free® battery, you must first check the charge indicator on top of the battery. If the green dot is visible or the indicator is dark, you may jump the battery. If the indicator is light, under no circumstances should you jump the battery. The battery then must be replaced.*

JACKING AND HOISTING

The bumper jack supplied with the car should never be used for any service operation other than tire changing. NEVER get under the car while it is supported by a bumper jack. If the jack should slip or tip over, as bumper jacks often do, it would be exceedingly difficult to raise the car again while pinned underneath. Always block the wheels when changing tires.

The service operations in this book often require that one end or the other, or both, of the car be raised and supported safely. The best arrangement is a grease pit or a vehicle hoist. The illustrations show the contact points for various types of lift equipment. A hydraulic floor jack is also referred to. It is realized that these items are not often found in the home garage, but there are reasonable and safe substitutes. Small hydraulic, screw, or scissors jacks are satisfactory for raising the car. Heavy wooden blocks or adjustable jackstands should be used to support the car while it is being worked on.

Drive-on trestles, or ramps, are a handy and safe way to raise the car. These can be bought or constructed from suitable heavy timbers or steel.

In any case, it is always best to spend a little extra time to make sure that the car is lifted and supported safely.

NOTE: *Concrete blocks are not recommended. They may break if the load is not evenly distributed.*

Tune-Up

TUNE-UP PROCEDURES

Breaker Type Systems—1971–74

The manufacturer recommends that you perform a tune-up every 12,000 miles. However, don't forget that parts are constantly wearing and their performance is becoming less efficient with each passing mile. The 12,000 mile limit is a safe limit for satisfactory performance. If the car is subjected to severe usage or if you experience unsatisfactory performance, it is advisable to perform a tune-up at more frequent intervals. A good idea would be to check plugs, points, rotor and distributor cap for signs of wear or impending failure at 6,000 mile intervals. This will ensure good performance, gas mileage, and prevent breakdowns. If, probably due to running production changes, the specifications following do not agree with the specifications on the underhood sticker, follow the sticker.

Breakerless Ignition System (HEI)

Starting in 1975, all GM cars are equipped with an electronic ignition system called HEI (High Energy Ignition). This system replaces the points and condenser of a conventional ignition system with an electronic module and pick-up assembly. The ignition coil has also been changed—the conventional coil has the iron core inside the windings, while the HEI system has the core outside the windings for more voltage. The coil on V8s and V6s with HEI has been placed inside the distributor cap, while on four-cylinder applications it retains conventional positioning. Although some of the parts are different, the system accomplishes the same effect, i.e., firing the plugs. This is accomplished as follows: When the teeth of the timer core rotating inside the pole piece, line up with the teeth of the pole piece, a pulse in the pick-up coil signals the module to open the coil primary circuit. This would be when the points open on a conventional ignition system. The primary current then decreases which induces a high voltage in the secondary winding, which then proceeds through the rotor to the spark plug lead to fire the plugs.

Spark Plugs

A typical spark plug consists of a metal shell surrounding a ceramic insulator. A metal electrode extends downward through the center of the insulator and protrudes a small

Tune-Up Specifications

Year	Model	Engine No. Cyl Displacement (cu in.)	(hp)	Spark Plugs Orig Type	Gap (in.)	Distributor Point Dwell (deg)	Point Gap (in.)	Ignition Timing (deg) Man	Auto	Intake Valve Opens (deg)	Fuel Pump Pressure (psi)	Idle Speed (rpm) ▲ Man	Auto
1971	Vega	4-140	90	R42TS	0.035	31–34	0.019	6B	6B	22	3-4½	850/700	650/550
	Vega	4-140	110	R42TS	0.035	31–34	0.019	6B	10B	25	3-4½	1200/700	650/550
1972	Vega	4-140	80	R42TS	0.035	31–34	0.019	6B	6B(4B)	22(28)	3-4½	700	700/550①
	Vega	4-140	90	R42TS	0.035	31–34	0.019	8B	8B	28	3-4½	700	700/550①
1973	Vega	4-140	75	R42TS	0.035	31–34	0.019	8B	8B	22	3-4½	1000/450	750/450
	Vega	4-140	85	R42TS	0.035	31–34	0.019	10B	12B	28	3-4½	1200/450	750/450①
1974	Vega	4-140	75	R42TS	0.035	31–34	0.019	10B(8B)	12B(8B)	22	3-4½	1000/700	750/550
	Vega	4-140	85	R42TS	0.035	31–34	0.019	10B(8B)	12B(8B)	28	3-4½	1200/700	750/500①
1975	All	4-140	75	R43TSX	0.060	Electronic		8B	10B	22	3-4½	1200/700	700/550
	All	4-140	85	R43TSX	0.060	Electronic		10B	12B	28	3-4½	1200/700	750/600
	All	6-231	110	R46TX	0.060	Electronic		12B	12B	17	3-4½②	800/600	700
	Monza	8-262	110	R44TX	0.060	Electronic		8B	8B	26	7-8½	800	600
	Monza	8-350		R44TX	0.060	Electronic		—	6B	28	7-8½	—	600
1976	All	4-140	75	R43TS	0.035	Electronic		8B	10B	22	3-4½	1200	750

Year	Model	Engine		Spark Plug	Gap	Distributor						
	All	4-140	85	R43TS	0.035	Electronic	10B	12B	28	3–4½	700	750
	Skyhawk/Starfire	6-231	105	R44SX	0.060	Electronic	12B	12B	17	3–4½②	800/600	600
	Sunbird	6-231	110	R44SX	0.060	Electronic	12B	12B	17	3–4½	800	600
	Monza	8-262		R45TS	0.045	Electronic	6B	8B③	26	3–4½	800	600
	Monza	8-305		R45TS	0.045	Electronic	8B	8B④	28	3–4½	600	500⑤
1977	Astre/Sunbird	4-140	87	R43TS	0.035	Electronic	10B	12B	34	3–4½	700	750
	Starfire	4-140	84	R43TS	0.035	Electronic	10B	12B	34	3–4½	1250/700⑩	850/650⑩
	Vega/Monza	4-140	84	R43TS	0.035	Electronic	TDC⑥	2B③	34	3–4½	700⑦	650⑧
	Sunbird	4-151	87	R44TSX	0.060	Electronic	14B	14B⑨	33	4–5½	1000	650
	Astre/Sunbird	6-231	105	R46TSX	0.060	Electronic	12B	12B	17	3–4½	800	600
	Skyhawk	6-231	105	R46TSX	0.060	Electronic	12B	12B	17	4¼–5¾	800/500	600
	Starfire	6-231	105	R46TSX	0.060	Electronic	12B	12B	17	3–4½	800/600	800/600
	Monza	8-305	145	R45TS	0.045	Electronic	8B	8B④	28	3–4½	600	500⑤
1978	Monza	4-151	85	R43TSX	0.060	Electronic	14B	14B⑮	33	4–5½	1000/500	⑫
	Starfire	4-151	90	R43TSX	0.060	Electronic	14B	14B	33	4–5	⑪	⑫
	Sunbird	4-151	87	R43TSX	0.060	Electronic	14B	12B⑬	33	4–5½	⑪	⑭

Tune-Up Specifications (cont.)

Year	Model	Engine No. Cyl Displacement (cu in.)	(hp)	Spark Plugs Orig Type	Gap (in.)	Distributor Point Dwell (deg)	Point Gap (in.)	Ignition Timing (deg) Man	Auto	Intake Valve Opens (deg)	Fuel Pump Pressure (psi)	Idle Speed (rpm) ▲ Man	Auto
	Monza	6-196	90	R46TSX	0.060	Electronic		15B	15B	17	5-6	800	600
	All	6-231	105	R46TSX	0.060	Electronic		15B	15B	17	3-4½	800⑯	600
	Monza	8-305	145	R45TS	0.045	Electronic		4B	6B⑰	28	4-5	600	500⑱
1979	Starfire	4-151	85	R44TSX	0.060	Electronic		14B	14B⑨	33	4-5½	1000	650
	Sunbird	4-151	85	R44TSX	0.060	Electronic		12B⑬	12B⑬	33	5-6½	1000	650
	Monza	4-151	85	R43TSX	0.060	Electronic		12B⑬	12B⑬	33	4-5.5	1000	650
	Monza	6-196	90	R46TSX	0.060	Electronic		15B	15B	16	4.5-7.5		
	All	6-231	115	R46TSX	0.060	Electronic		15B	15B	16	4-6.5	800	600
	Monza	8-305		R45TS	0.045	Electronic		4B	4B	28	7.5-9		
1980					See underhood specifications sticker								

① For air conditioned vehicles, adjust the idle speed to 800 rpm with the a/c on
② 4¼-5¾ on mechanical pumps
③ Calif.—TDC
④ Calif.—6B
⑤ High Altitude—800
⑥ Calif.—2B
⑦ Calif.—800
⑧ High Altitude—700
⑨ Calif.—12B
⑩ High Altitude: Man trans—1250/800, Auto trans—850/700
⑪ Without a/c—1000/500, With a/c—1200/1000
⑫ Without a/c—650/500, With a/c—850/650
⑬ Calif.—14B
⑭ With a/c—650, Without a/c—500
⑮ Calif. without EGR valve—12B
⑯ 600—Skyhawk, Starfire exc. Calif.
⑰ 8B—Calif.
⑱ 600—High Altitude
▲Lines separated by a slash show solenoid on/off
NOTE: The underhood specifications sticker often reflects tune-up specification changes made in production. Sticker figures must be used if they disagree with those in this chart.
NOTE: Where two figures are separated by a slash, the first figure is for idle speed with the solenoid connected, while the second is for the idle speed with the solenoid disconnected.

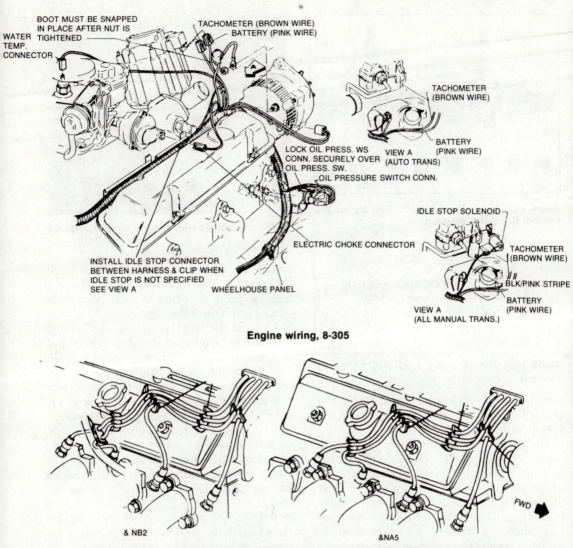

WATER TEMP. CONNECTOR

BOOT MUST BE SNAPPED IN PLACE AFTER NUT IS TIGHTENED

TACHOMETER (BROWN WIRE)
BATTERY (PINK WIRE)

TACHOMETER (BROWN WIRE)

BATTERY (PINK WIRE)

VIEW A (AUTO TRANS)

LOCK OIL PRESS. WS CONN. SECURELY OVER OIL PRESS. SW.

OIL PRESSURE SWITCH CONN.

IDLE STOP SOLENOID

ELECTRIC CHOKE CONNECTOR

TACHOMETER (BROWN WIRE)

BLK/PINK STRIPE

INSTALL IDLE STOP CONNECTOR BETWEEN HARNESS & CLIP WHEN IDLE STOP IS NOT SPECIFIED SEE VIEW A

WHEELHOUSE PANEL

VIEW A (ALL MANUAL TRANS.)

BATTERY (PINK WIRE)

Engine wiring, 8-305

& NB2

&NA5

FWD

Spark plug wire routing, 4-151, California engines on the left; all others on the right

distance. Located at the end of the plug and attached to the side of the outer metal shell is the side electrode. The side electrode bends in at a 90° angle so that its tip is even with, and parallel to, the tip of the center electrode. The distance between these two electrodes (measured in thousandths of an inch) is called the spark plug gap. The spark plug in no way produces a spark but merely provides a gap across which the current can arc. The coil produces anywhere from 20,000 to 40,000 volts which travels to the distributor where it is distributed through the spark plug wires to the spark plugs. The current passes along the center electrode and jumps the gap to the side electrode, and, in so doing, ignites the air/fuel mixture in the combustion chamber.

SPARK PLUG HEAT RANGE

Spark plug heat range is the ability of the plug to dissipate heat. The longer the insulator (or the farther it extends into the engine), the hotter the plug will operate; the shorter the insulator the cooler it will operate. A plug that absorbs little heat and remains too cool will quickly accumulate deposits of oil and carbon since it is not hot enough to burn them off. This leads to plug fouling and consequently to misfiring. A plug that absorbs too much heat will have no deposits, but, due to the excessive heat, the electrodes will burn away quickly and in some instances, preignition may result. Preignition takes place when plug tips get so hot that they glow sufficiently to ignite the fuel/air mixture be-

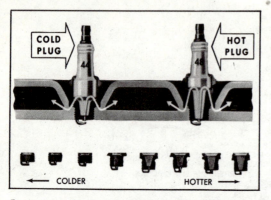

Spark plug heat range system. The higher the number the hotter the plug

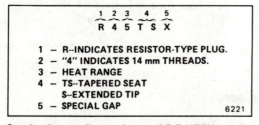

Spark plug coding using a AC-R45TSX as an example

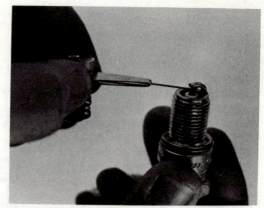

Checking plug gap with a round wire feeler gauge

fore the actual spark occurs. This early ignition will usually cause a pinging during low speeds and heavy loads.

The general rule of thumb for choosing the correct heat range when picking a spark plug is: if most of your driving is long distance, high speed travel, use a colder plug; if most of your driving is stop and go, use a hotter plug. Original equipment plugs are compromise plugs, but most people never have occasion to change their plugs from the factory-recommended heat range.

REPLACING SPARK PLUGS

A set of spark plugs usually requires replacement after about 10,000 miles on cars with conventional ignition systems and after about 20,000 to 30,000 miles on cars with electronic ignition, depending on your style of driving. In normal operation, plug gap increases about 0.001 in. for every 1,000–2,500 miles. As the gap increases, the plug's voltage requirement also increases. It requires a greater voltage to jump the wider gap and about two to three times as much voltage to fire a plug at high speeds than at idle.

When you're removing spark plugs, you should work on one at a time. Don't start by removing the plug wires all at once, because unless you number them, they may become mixed up. Take a minute before you begin and number the wires with tape. The best location for numbering is near where the wires come out of the cap.

1. Twist the spark plug boot and remove the boot and wire from the plug. Do not pull on the wire itself as this will ruin the wire.

2. If possible, use a brush or rag to clean the area around the spark plug. Make sure that all the dirt is removed so that none will enter the cylinder after the plug is removed.

3. Remove the spark plug using a ⅝ in. socket. Turn the socket counterclockwise to remove the plug. Be sure to hold the socket straight on the plug to avoid breaking the plug, or rounding off the hex on the plug.

4. Once the plug is out, check it against the plugs shown in this section to determine engine condition. This is crucial since plug readings are vital signs of engine condition.

5. Use a round wire feeler gauge to check

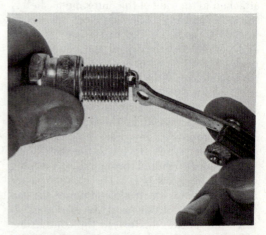

Adjusting the gap with an electrode bending tool

the plug gap. The correct size gauge should pass through the electrode gap with a slight drag. If you're in doubt, try one size smaller and one larger. The smaller gauge should go through easily while the larger one shouldn't go through at all. If the gap is incorrect, use the electrode bending tool on the end of the gauge to adjust the gap. When adjusting the gap, always bend the side electrode. The center electrode is non-adjustable.

6. Squirt a drop of penetrating oil on the threads of the new plug and install it. Don't oil the threats too heavily. Turn the plug in clockwise by hand until it is snug.

7. When the plug is finger tight, tighten it with a wrench. If you don't have a torque wrench, tighten the plug as shown.

8. Install the plug boot firmly over the plug. Proceed to the next plug.

CHECKING AND REPLACING SPARK PLUG CABLES

Visually inspect the spark plug cables for burns, cuts, or breaks in the insulation. Check the spark plug boots and the nipples on the distributor cap and coil. Replace any damaged wiring. If no physical damage is obvious, the wires can be checked with an ohmmeter for excessive resistance. (See the tune-up and troubleshooting section).

When installing a new set of spark plug cables, replace the cables one at a time so there will be no mixup. Start by replacing the longest cable first. Install the boot firmly over the spark plug. Route the wire exactly the same as the original. Insert the nipple firmly into the tower on the distributor cap. Repeat the process for each cable. If needed, refer to the firing order illustration in Chapter 3.

> NOTE: *To correct the problem of 1975 Vegas equipped with 2 bbl. carburetors failing to start in cold weather due to carbon fouling of spark plugs, it is recommended that the plug gap be changed from .060 to .035 in. When replacing the plugs use R43TS or equivalent.*
> NOTE: *Due to assembly variations some early model 1975 V-8 Monzas with power steering could have been built with insufficient clearance to provide access to the no. 3 spark plug. To gain permanent access to the no. 3 spark plug Chevrolet recommends the following procedure:*
> 1. Loosen the engine mount to frame

bracket bolts at both front mounts. These should be loose enough to permit sliding, but not removed.

2. In the same manner, loosen the two transmission support to transmission mount bolts.

3. Using a jack, with suitable protection to prevent engine oil pan damage, lift the engine until the weight on the mounts is negligible.

4. Pry the engine to the right to the limit of travel. Then tighten the right front mount to frame bolts to 35–40 pound feet.

5. With a combination of engine lifting and mount prying, locate the left front mount to frame bolts inboard of the center of the frame bracket slots. Tighten these bolts to 35–40 pound feet.

6. Tighten the transmission mount bolts to 21–31 pound feet.

Breaker Points and Condenser—1971–74

It is common practice to replace the condenser every time the point set is replaced. Although this is not always necessary, it is easy to do at this time and costs very little. After every breaker point adjustment or replacement, the ignition timing must be checked and, if necessary, adjusted. No special equipment other than a feeler gauge is required for point replacement or adjustment, although a dwell meter can be used to ensure the accuracy of the adjustment.

REPLACEMENT

1. Remove the two screws securing the distributor cap. Remove the cap.

2. Clean the cap inside and out. Check for cracks and carbon paths. A carbon path shows up as a dark line, usually from one of the cap sockets or inside terminals to a ground. Check the condition of the carbon button inside the center of the cap and the four inside terminals. Replace the cap if necessary.

3. Pull the rotor up and off the shaft. Clean off the metal end if it is burned or corroded. Replace the rotor if necessary.

4. The manufacturer states that the points need not be replaced if metal transfer from one contact to the other does not exceed 0.020 in. However, experience shows that it is more economical and reliable in the long run to replace the point set while the distrib-

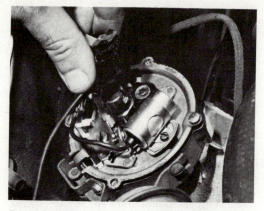

Removing the rotor on conventional ignition

utor is open, than to have to do this at a later (and possibly more inconvenient) time.

5. Pull off the two wire terminals connected to the points. Remove the point set hold-down screw, being very careful not to drop it into the inside of the distributor. If this happens, the distributor will probably have to be removed to get at the screw. If the screw is lost elsewhere, it must be replaced with one that is no longer than the original to avoid interference with distributor workings. Remove the point set, even if it is to be reused.

6. If the points are to be reused, clean them with a few strokes of a special point file. This is done with the points removed to prevent tiny metal filings getting into the distributor.

7. Remove the condenser, being careful not to drop the screw.

8. Install the new condenser. This must be done if the contact point metal transfer exceeded 0.020 in.

9. Attend to the cam lubricator as described under Routine Maintenance, Distributor in Chapter 1.

10. Replace the point set and tighten the screw lightly. Replace the two wire terminals.

11. Check that the contacts meet squarely. If they do not, bend the tab supporting the fixed contact.

12. Place a ¾ in. socket on the crankshaft pulley nut and turn the engine until a high point on the cam that opens the points contacts the rubbing block on the point arm. This is easier if the spark plugs have been removed. You could also have a friend turn the key to start for a second to turn the engine over or purchase a remove starter button so that you could do it yourself.

13. There is a screwdriver slot near the contacts. Insert a screwdriver and lever the points open or closed until they appear to be open about 0.016–0.019 in.

14. Point gap is 0.019 in. for new points and 0.016 for used ones. Insert the correct size feeler gauge and adjust the gap with the screwdriver until you can push the gauge in and out between the contacts with a slight drag but without moving the point arm. This operation takes a bit of experience to obtain the proper feel. If there is any doubt, have an experienced mechanic check the setting. Another check is to try the gauges 0.001–0.002 larger and smaller than the setting size. The larger one should disturb the point arm, whereas the smaller one should not drag at all. Tighten the point set hold-down screw snugly. Recheck the gap, because it often changes when the screw is tightened.

15. After all the point adjustments are complete, pull a white business card through

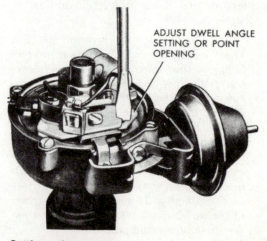

Adjusting the point gap

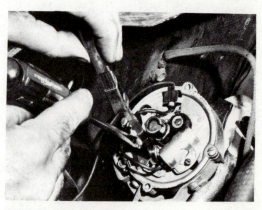

ADJUST DWELL ANGLE SETTING OR POINT OPENING

Setting point opening

(between) the contacts to remove any traces of oil. Oil will cause rapid point burning.

16. Push the rotor firmly down into place. It will only go on one way. If it is not installed properly, it will probably break when the starter is operated.

17. Replace the distributor cap and install the screws.

18. If a dwell meter is available, check the dwell. The dwell meter hookup is shown in the Troubleshooting Section. Dwell can be checked with the engine running or cranking. Dwell should be 31–34 degrees. Decrease dwell by increasing the point gap; increase by decreasing the gap. Dwell angle is simply the number of degrees of distributor shaft rotation during which the points stay closed. Theoretically, if the point gap is correct, the dwell should also be correct or nearly so. If dwell varies more than 3 degrees from idle speed to 1750 engine rpm, the distributor is worn.

19. Start the engine. If it won't start, check:

 a. That all the spark plug wires are in place.

 b. That the rotor has been installed.

 c. That the two wires inside the distributor are connected.

 d. That the points open and close when the engine turns.

 e. That the gap is correct and the hold-down screw is tight.

20. After the first 200 miles on a new set of points, the point gap often closes up due to initial rubbing block wear. For best performance, recheck the gap at this time.

21. Since changing the point gap affects the ignition timing setting, the timing should be checked and adjusted if necessary after each point replacement or adjustment.

Ignition Timing—1971–74

Timing should be checked at each tune-up and any time the points are adjusted or replaced. The timing marks are located on the crankshaft pulley and the front of the engine. A stroboscopic flash (dynamic) timing light must be used, as a static light is too inaccurate for emission controlled engines.

To check and adjust the timing:

1. Warm up the engine to normal operating temperature. Stop the engine and connect the timing light to the No. 1 (front) spark plug wire. Clean off the timing marks and mark the pulley notch with chalk.

Timing mark location

Checking ignition timing using a strobe light

2. Disconnect and plug the vacuum line at the distributor.

3. Disconnect the Fuel Tank line from the top of the evaporative emission canister.

4. Disconnect the electrical connector at the idle stop solenoid on the carburetor. Make sure that the connector does not short circuit to any engine parts.

5. Start the engine and set the idle to 700 rpm or less by adjusting the carburetor idle speed screw. This is done to prevent the distributor advance mechanism from being actuated.

6. Aim the timing light at the pointer marks. Be careful not to touch the fan, because it may appear to be standing still. If the pulley notch does not appear to be aligned with the proper timing mark (refer to the Tune-Up Specifications Chart), the timing will have to be adjusted.

NOTE: *The 0° mark is also referred to as TDC or Top Dead Center.*

7. Loosen the distributor clamp locknut and turn the distributor slowly to adjust. Turn counterclockwise to advance timing (toward before), and clockwise to retard (toward 0° or after).

8. Tighten the distributor clamp locknut but be careful not to overtighten it.

9. Adjust the carburetor idle speed screw to obtain the idle speed specified with the solenoid disconnected.

10. Reconnect the electrical connector to the idle stop solenoid. Speed up the engine to allow the solenoid plunger to extend and then adjust the solenoid plunger screw to obtain the idle speed specified with the solenoid connected.

11. Stop the engine and reconnect the vacuum line and the evaporative emission canister line. Disconnect the timing light.

Timing Light and Tachometer Hook-Up for HEI—1975 and Later

1. Use an adapter between the No. 1 spark plug and No. 1 spark plug lead, when con-

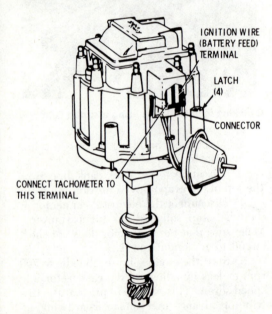

IGNITION WIRE (BATTERY FEED) TERMINAL

LATCH (4)

CONNECTOR

CONNECT TACHOMETER TO THIS TERMINAL

V8 HEI distributor, V6 and 4 cyl. 151 engine similar

necting a timing light. Connect the timing light to the adapter; DO NOT pierce the spark plug lead. Because of the higher voltage used in the HEI system, any break in the insulation will cause electricity to jump to the nearest ground, making the No. 1 plug misfire.

NOTE: *The No. 1 plug is the left-front on the V-6 and V-8 and on the RF on the 4 cyl.*

2. The tachometer terminal is next to the ignition switch connector on the cap of 151 cu. in. four cylinder, V6 and V8 distributors or next to the ignition switch connector on

the external mounted coil on the 140 cu. in. four cylinder engine.

3. Most new tachometers can be used. Tachometers without a relay can't be used. Check the tach's instructions if you aren't sure. If you don't have the instructions, hook up the tach and check the readings on both the high and low rpm scales. If they agree, the tach is OK; if they don't use another tach.

4. There is no way of adjusting dwell, since this is controlled by the electronic module.

5. If you want to crank the engine without starting it, disconnect the ignition switch wire at the distributor cap or at the coil (140 cu. in. engines).

Ignition Timing—1975 and Later

The timing marks are on a plate mounted on the front of the block and the timing notch is on the crankshaft pulley.

Timing is set as follows:

1. Bring the engine to normal operating temperature, shut the engine off, and connect a timing light according to the manufacturer's instructions. Clean the timing plate and mark the notch in the pulley with chalk.

2. Disconnect and plug the vacuum line to the distributor.

3. See the underhood sticker for the latest certified information on preparing the engine for ignition timing.

4. Set the idle speed to specifications, following the procedure outlined later in this chapter.

5. Aim the timing light at the timing marks. If the notch does not align with the correct value on the scale, loosen the distributor clamp locknut and slowly turn the distributor to adjust.

6. Tighten the clamp locknut. Adjust the carburetor idle speed screw to give the specified idle speed with the solenoid disconnected.

7. Reconnect the idle stop solenoid lead. Increase the engine speed to allow the solenoid to extend and then adjust the solenoid plunger screw to obtain the idle speed specified with the solenoid connected.

8. Shut the engine off and connect the vacuum and evaporative emission line.

Valve Lash 1971–75

Late 1975 and later cars are equipped with hydraulic lifters which do not require the ser-

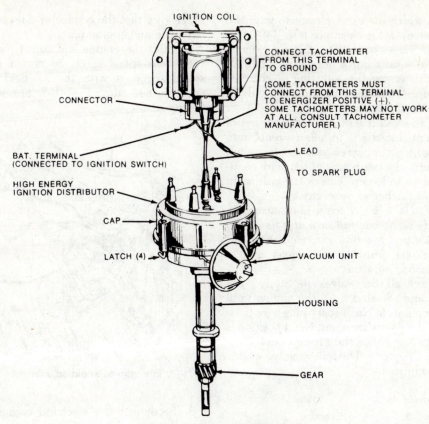

IGNITION COIL

CONNECT TACHOMETER
FROM THIS TERMINAL
TO GROUND

(SOME TACHOMETERS MUST
CONNECT FROM THIS TERMINAL
TO ENERGIZER POSITIVE (+).
SOME TACHOMETERS MAY NOT WORK
AT ALL. CONSULT TACHOMETER
MANUFACTURER.)

CONNECTOR

LEAD

BAT. TERMINAL
(CONNECTED TO IGNITION SWITCH)

TO SPARK PLUG

HIGH ENERGY
IGNITION DISTRIBUTOR

CAP

LATCH (4)

VACUUM UNIT

HOUSING

GEAR

4 cyl. 140 engine HEI distributor

vicing as listed below. As they seldom need attention, any adjustment procedures could not be considered part of a normal tune-up. For any procedures, see Chapter 3, "Engine and Engine Rebuilding."

Valve lash adjustment is required at 24,000-mile intervals. However, the adjustment could be checked at more frequent intervals for the very best performance. It should also be checked any time that there seems to be excessive noise from the valve mechanism.

NOTE: *Do not set the valve lash closer than specified in an attempt to quiet the valve mechanism. This will result in burned valves.*

1. Mark the location of No. 1 spark plug wire on the side of the distributor with chalk.

2. Remove the coil wire from the center of the distributor cap. Remove the two hold-down screws and the distributor cap.

3. Place a ¾ in. socket on the crankshaft pulley nut and turn the engine until the distributor rotor (the metal end) points to the chalk mark made in Step 1 and the points open. This is easier to do if the spark plugs

have been removed. The engine may also be turned with the starter, but it may be difficult to obtain the right position.

4. Remove the air cleaner and the camshaft cover.

5. With the rotor pointing to the chalk mark, the following valves can be adjusted:

Cylinder No.	Valve
1	Exhaust, Intake
2	Intake
3	Exhaust

The cylinders are numbered from front to rear. The intake and exhaust valves can be identified by the locations of the intake and exhaust manifolds on the engine. The intake valve is the front valve for each cylinder, and the exhaust valve is the rear one.

6. Intake valves are set at 0.015 in. and exhaust valves at 0.030 in. The lash is measured between the camshaft lobe and the valve tappet with a feeler gauge.

7. To check the lash, insert the correct size feeler gauge between the camshaft lobe and the valve tappet. If the gauge is loose or

tight, measure the exact clearance with the feeler gauges. If the clearance is 0.014–0.016 for intake valves or 0.029–0.031 for exhaust valves, no adjustment is necessary. The reason for this is that the adjusting mechanism allows adjustments in each direction only in increments of 0.003 in.

8. If the lash is 0.003 in. or more out of adjustment, insert a ⅛ in. allen wrench into the tappet adjusting screw and turn it one full turn. Turn clockwise to tighten and counterclockwise to loosen. Check the lash again and adjust further as necessary.

NOTE: *The adjuster screw must always be turned exactly one full turn at a time. The flat spot on the adjuster screw can be felt by pressing down on the tappet with a finger while adjusting.*

9. After all the valves in Step 5 are checked and adjusted, turn the engine until the rotor points to No. 4 spark plug wire position and the points are open. No. 4 position is 180° from No. 1. See the Firing Order Illustration in Chapter 3. The following valves can then be adjusted.

Cylinder No.	Valve
2	Exhaust
3	Intake
4	Intake, Exhaust

10. Replace the camshaft cover with a new gasket. Replace the air cleaner.

Idle Speed Adjustment

Idle speed specifications should always be checked against the tune-up decal located in the engine compartment. If a discrepancy exists between what we have listed and what is on your car, use the specification listed on the decal.

1971–72

1. The engine must be at normal operating temperature. The air cleaner must be in place. The air conditioner should be on in 1971 models and off in 1972 models. The manual transmission should be in neutral and the automatic in Drive, with the wheels blocked.

2. Detach the Fuel Tank line from the top of the evaporative emission canister.

3. Disconnect and plug the vacuum line at the distributor.

4. Disconnect the electrical connector at the idle stop solenoid on the carburetor.

Make sure that the connector does not short circuit to any engine parts.

5. Start the engine and adjust the carburetor idle speed screw to obtain the idle speed specified with the solenoid disconnected. See the Tune-Up Specifications Chart.

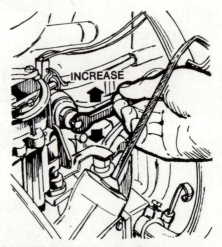

1971–72 idle stop solenoid adjustment

6. Reconnect the electrical connector to the idle stop solenoid. Speed up the engine to allow the solenoid plunger to extend and then adjust the solenoid plunger screw to obtain the idle speed specified with the solenoid connected.

7. Stop the engine and reconnect the vacuum line and the evaporative emission canister line.

1973–74

Prepare the vehicle as described in the next four steps, then proceed.

1. The engine must be at normal operating temperature and the air cleaner in place. Air conditioning should be off.

2. Detach the fuel tank line from the top of the evaporative emission canister.

3. Disconnect the distributor vacuum line and plug the carburetor hose.

4. Disconnect the electrical connector at the idle stop solenoid on the carburetor.

ROCHESTER MV 1 BBL

1. Start the engine and using a ⅛ in. allen wrench, adjust the idle speed to the figure given in the Tune-Up Specifications Chart (for speed with the solenoid disconnected).

2. Check the dwell and ignition timing. Check the idle speed again.

3. Reconnect the electrical wire to the solenoid.

4. Adjust the idle speed (for speed with solenoid connected) by turning the body of the solenoid itself.

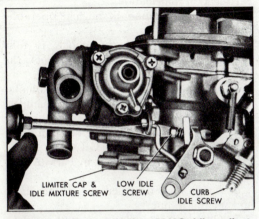

Rochester MV and Holley 5210C idle adjustments—1973-74

HOLLEY 5210-C2 BBL

1. Start the engine and adjust the idle speed screw for the speed listed in the Tune-Up Specifications Chart (speed with solenoid disconnected).

2. Check the dwell and ignition timing. Check the idle speed again.

3. Reconnect the electrical wire to the solenoid.

4. Adjust the screw on the throttle lever (not the same screw as Step 1). Set the idle speed to the figure given in the Tune-Up Specifications Chart (for speed with the solenoid connected).

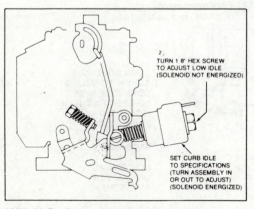

1975-76 Rochester MV idle adjustments

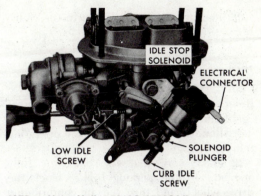

1975 and later Holley 5210C, 6510C idle adjustment

1975-77

1. The engine should be at normal operating temperature, air cleaner ON, choke open and the air conditioner OFF.

2. Set the parking brake.

3. Disconnect the fuel tank hose from the vapor canister.

4. Disconnect and plug the vacuum hose. Check and adjust the timing. Reconnect the vacuum hose on Rochester 1MV and 2GC carburetors.

5. Disconnect the electrical connector at the idle stop solenoid.

6. Place automatic transmissions in Drive

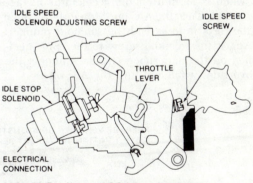

1975-78 Rochester 2GC idle adjustment

and manual transmissions in Neutral. On Rochester 1MV carburetors, turn the hex screw in the end of the solenoid body with a 1/8 in. allen wrench to set the low idle speed. On Holley 5210-C and Rochester 2GC models, set the low idle speed with the idle screw.

7. Reconnect the electrical connector and crack the throttle slightly.

8. Turn the solenoid in or out to set the curb idle speed.

9. Reconnect the vapor line to the canister.

1978
4-151

Refer to the underhood sticker for the latest certification information.

1. Run the engine to normal operating temperature.

2. Make sure that the choke is fully opened, set the parking brake, block the drive wheels and turn the air conditioning off.

3. Connect a timing light and tachometer to the engine according to their manufacturers instructions.

4. Disconnect and plug the PCV hose at the vapor canister. Disconnect and plug the vacuum advance hose at the distributor.

5. Place the transmission in Drive (AT) or Neutral (MT).

6. Check and adjust timing.

7. Connect the vacuum advance line.

8. On manual transmission cars without A/C: Turn the idle speed screw to achieve the specified rpm. On automatic transmission cars or manual transmission cars with A/C: Turn the idle speed screw to obtain the specified rpm. Disconnect the wire at the wide open throttle A/C override switch. The switch is located on the accelerator linkage bracket. Turn the A/C on. Momentarily open the throttle to extend the solenoid plunger. Adjust the solenoid screw to the rpm specified on the underhood sticker. Connect the override switch and turn the A/C off.

9. Connect all hoses and remove the timing light and tachometer.

6-196, 231, V8-305

Refer to the underhood sticker for the latest certification information.

1. Run the engine to normal operating temperature.

2. Make sure that the choke is fully opened, set the parking brake, block the drive wheels and turn the A/C off.

3. Connect a timing light and tachometer to the engine according to their manufacturers' instructions.

4. Disconnect and plug the vacuum hoses at the vapor canister and EGR valve.

5. Place the transmission in Park (AT) or Neutral (MT).

6. Disconnect the vacuum advance hose and set the timing.

7. On manual transmission without A/C: Adjust the idle speed screw to obtain the specified rpm. On automatic transmission cars without A/C: Open the throttle slightly to fully extend the solenoid plunger. Turn the idle speed screw to obtain the specified rpm. Disconnect the solenoid and turn the solenoid screw to obtain the rpm specified on the underhood sticker.

On cars with A/C: Turn the idle speed screw to obtain the specified rpm. Momentarily open the throttle to extend the solenoid plunger. Disconnect the A/C compressor clutch wire. Turn the A/C on. Place the AT in Drive, the MT in Neutral. Turn the solenoid screw to obtain the rpm specified on the underhood sticker.

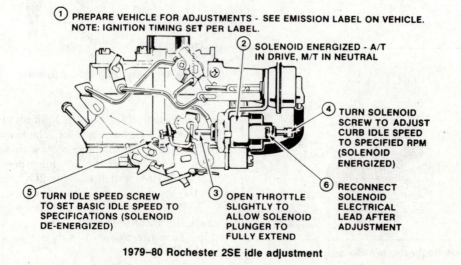

① PREPARE VEHICLE FOR ADJUSTMENTS - SEE EMISSION LABEL ON VEHICLE. NOTE: IGNITION TIMING SET PER LABEL.

② SOLENOID ENERGIZED - A/T IN DRIVE, M/T IN NEUTRAL

④ TURN SOLENOID SCREW TO ADJUST CURB IDLE SPEED TO SPECIFIED RPM (SOLENOID ENERGIZED)

⑤ TURN IDLE SPEED SCREW TO SET BASIC IDLE SPEED TO SPECIFICATIONS (SOLENOID DE-ENERGIZED)

③ OPEN THROTTLE SLIGHTLY TO ALLOW SOLENOID PLUNGER TO FULLY EXTEND

⑥ RECONNECT SOLENOID ELECTRICAL LEAD AFTER ADJUSTMENT

1979–80 Rochester 2SE idle adjustment

1979–80

4-151

Check the Vehicle Emission Control Information label for the latest certified information.

1. Run the engine to normal operating temperature with the choke fully open. The air conditioning should be off.

2. Connect a tachometer and a timing light according to the manufacturer's instructions.

3. Set the parking brake and block the drive wheels.

4. Disconnect and plug the PCV hose at the canister and the vacuum hose at the distributor.

5. Start the engine and place the transmission in drive (AT) or neutral (MT).

6. Check and, if necessary, adjust the timing.

7. Unplug and reconnect the vacuum hose at the distributor. Adjust the idle speed screw to obtain the specified rpm.

8. On cars with automatic transmission or manual transmission with A/C, turn the idle speed screw to obtain the specified rpm, then:

a. disconnect the electrical line at the wide open throttle A/C override switch located on the accelerator linkage bracket.

b. turn the A/C on.

c. momentarily open the throttle to allow the solenoid plunger to extend.

d. adjust the solenoid screw to the rpm specified in the Turn-Up table.

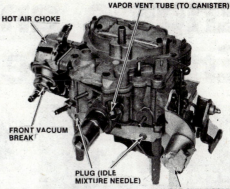

1979 and later Rochester 2MC/2ME idle adjustment

e. reconnect the electrical connector.

f. turn the A/C off.

g. reconnect the PCV hose at the canister.

V6 and V8

1. Prepare the vehicle according to the instructions found on the Emission label.

2. Turn the idle speed screw to obtain the rpm specified in the Tune-Up table.

3. Disconnect the A/C lead at the compressor clutch.

4. Turn the A/C on. Open the throttle slightly to extend the solenoid plunger.

5. Turn the solenoid screw to obtain the rpm specified in the Tune-Up table.

6. Reconnect the A/C lead.

Engine and Engine Rebuilding

3

ENGINE ELECTRICAL

Understanding a little bit about electricity will make electrical system troubleshooting much easier. For any electrical system to operate it must make a complete circuit. When an electrical component is operating, power flows from the battery to the component, passes through the component causing it to perform its function, and returns to the battery through the ground in the circuit. This ground is usually (but not always) the steel frame of the car. The ground terminal from the battery is attached to the chassis of the automobile, thus completing the circuit.

The flow of electricity can be measured. The unit of measurement is amperes, commonly refered to as "amps". A ammeter is used to measure the actual current flow in the circuit.

Just as water pressure is measured in units as pounds per square inch, electrical pressure is measured in volts. When a voltmeter's two probes are placed on two live parts of an electrical circuit with different electrical pressures, current will flow through the voltmeter and produce a reading which indicates the difference in electrical pressure between the two points. Increasing the voltage in a circuit will increase the amount of flow.

The actual flow of current depends not only on voltage but resistance. The standard unit for measuring resistance is the ohm, and is measured by an ohmmeter. The ohmmeter is similar to the ammeter but incorporates its own power source so that a standard voltage is always present.

Remember that in electrical testing, the voltmeter is connected in parallel with the circuit being tested (without disconnecting any wires); the ammeter is connected in series with the load (the circuit is separated at one point and the ammeter is inserted so it actually becomes part of the circuit); and the ohmmeter is self-powered, so that all the power in the circuit should be off and the portion of the circuit to be tested must be contacted at either end by one of the probes of the meter.

Electronic Ignition Systems

Electronic ignition systems are not as complicated as they may first appear. In actual fact, they differ only slightly from conventional ignition systems. Like conventional ignition systems, electronic systems have two circuits: a primary circuit, and a secondary circuit. *The entire secondary circuit is exactly the same as the secondary circuit in a conven-*

tional ignition system. Also, the section of the primary circuit from the battery to the BAT terminal at the coil is exactly the same as a conventional ignition system.

Electronic ignition systems differ from conventional ignition systems in the distributor component area. Instead of a distributor cam, breaker plate, points, and condenser, an electronic ignition system has an armature (called variously a trigger wheel, reluctor, etc.), a pickup coil (stator, sensor, etc), and an electronic control module. Essentially, all electronic ignition systems operate in the following manner:

With the ignition switch turned on, primary (battery) current flows from the battery through the ignition switch to the coil primary windings. Primary current is turned on and off by the action of the armature as it revolves. As the armature nears the pickup coil, it induces a voltage which signals the electronic module to turn off the coil primary current. A timing circuit in the module will turn the current on again after the coil field has collapsed. When the current is off, however, the magnetic field built up in the coil is allowed to collapse, inducing a high voltage in the secondary windings of the coil. It is now operating on the secondary ignition circuit, which, as noted, is exactly the same as a conventional ignition system.

Troubleshooting electronic ignition systems ordinarily requires the use of a voltmeter and/or an ohmmeter. Sometimes the use of an ammeter is required also. Because of differences is design and construction, troubleshooting is specific to each system.

The Charging System

The automobile charging system provides electrical power for operation of the vehicle's ignition and starting systems and all the electrical accessories. The battery serves as an electrical surge or storage tank, storing (in chemical form) the energy originally produced by the engine-driven generator. The system also provides a means of regulating generator output to protect the battery from being overcharged and to avoid excessive voltage to the accessories.

The storage battery is a chemical device incorporating parallel lead plates in a tank containing a sulfuric acid-water solution. Adjacent plates are slightly dissimilar, and the chemical reaction of the two dissimilar plates

produces electrial energy when the battery is connected to a load such as the starter motor. The chemical reaction is reversible, so that when the generator is producing a voltage (electrical pressure) greater than that produced by the battery, electricity is forced into the battery, and the battery is returned to its fully charged state.

The vehicle's generator is driven mechanically, through V belts, by the engine crankshaft. It consists of two coils of fine wire, one stationary (the "stator"), and one movable (the "rotor"). The rotor may also be known as the "armature," and consists of fine wire wrapped around an iron core which is mounted on a shaft. The electricity which flows through the two coils of wire (provided initially by the battery in some cases) creates an intense magnetic field around both rotor and stator, and the interaction between the two fields creates voltage, allowing the generator to power the accessories and charge the battery.

There are two types of generators; the earlier is the direct current (DC) type. The current produced by the DC generator is generated in the armature and carried off the spinning armature by stationary brushes contacting the commutator. The commutator is a series of smooth metal contact plates on the end of the armature. The commutator plates, which are separated from one another by a very short gap, are connected to the armature circuits so that current will flow in one direction only in the wires carrying the generator output. The generator stator consists of two stationary coils of wire which draw some of the output current of the generator to form a powerful magnetic field and create the interaction of fields which generates the voltage. The generator field is wired in series with the regulator.

Newer automobiles use alternating current generators or "alternators", because they are more efficient, can be rotated at higher speeds, and have fewer brush problems. In an alternator, the field rotates while all the current produced passes only through the stator windings. The brushes bear against continuous slip rings rather than a commutator. This causes the current produced to periodically reverse the direction of its flow. Diodes (electrical one-way switches) block the flow of current from traveling in the wrong direction. A series of diodes is wired together to permit the alternating flow of the stator to be converted to a pulsating, but unidirectional flow at the alternator output. The alternator's field is wired in series with the voltage regulator.

The regulator consists of several circuits. Each circuit has a core, or magnetic coil of wire, which operates a switch. Each switch is connected to ground through one or more resistors. The coil of wire responds directly to system voltage. When the voltage reaches the required level, the magnetic field created by the winding of wire closes the switch and inserts a resistance into the generator field circuit, thus reducing the output. The contacts of the switch cycle open and close many times each second to precisely control voltage.

While alternators are self-limiting as far as maximum current is concerned, DC generators employ a current regulating circuit which responds directly to the total amount of current flowing through the generator circuit rather than to the output voltage. The current regulator is similar to the voltage regulator except that all system current must flow through the energizing coil on its way to the various accessories.

Battery and Starting System

The battery is the first link in the chain of mechanisms which work together to provide cranking of the automobile engine. In most modern cars, the battery is a lead-acid electrochemical device consisting of six two-volt (2 V) subsections connected in series so the unit is capable of producing approximately 12 V of electrical pressure. Each subsection, or cell, consists of a series of positive and negative plates held a short distance apart in a solution of sulfuric acid and water. The two types of plates are of dissimilar metals. This causes a chemical reaction to be set up, and it is this reaction which produces current flow from the battery when its positive and negative terminals are connected to an electrical appliance such as a lamp or motor. The continued transfer of electrons would eventually convert the sulfuric acid in the electrolyte to water, and make the two plates identical in chemical composition. As electrical energy is removed from the battery, its voltage output tends to drop. Thus, measuring battery voltage and battery electrolyte composition are two ways of checking the ability of the unit to supply power. During the starting of the

engine, electrical energy is removed from the battery. However, if the charging circuit is in good condition and the operating conditions are normal, the power removed from the battery will be replaced by the generator (or alternator) which will force electrons back through the battery, reversing the normal flow, and restoring the battery to its original chemical state.

The battery and starting motor are linked by very heavy electrical cables designed to minimize resistance to the flow of current. Generally, the major power supply cable that leaves the battery goes directly to the starter, while other electrical system needs are supplied by a smaller cable. During starter operation, power flows from the battery to the starter and is grounded through the car's frame and the battery's negative ground strap.

The starting motor is a specially designed, direct current electric motor capable of producing a great amount of power for its size. One thing that allows the motor to produce a great deal of power is its tremendous rotating speed. It drives the engine through a tiny pinion gear (attached to the starter's armature), which drives the very large flywheel ring gear at a greatly reduced speed. Another factor allowing it to produce so much power is that only intermittent operation is required of it. Thus, little allowance for air circulation is required, and the windings can be built into a very small space.

The starter solenoid is a magnetic device which employs the small current supplied by the starting switch circuit of the ignition switch. This magnetic action moves a plunger which mechanically engages the starter and electrically closes the heavy switch which connects it to the battery. The starting switch circuit consists of the starting switch contained within the ignition switch, a transmission neutral safety switch or clutch pedal switch, and the wiring necessary to connect these in series with the starter solenoid or relay.

A pinion, which is a small gear, is mounted to a one-way drive clutch. This clutch is splined to the starter armature shaft. When the ignition switch is moved to the "start" position, the solenoid plunger slides the pinion toward the flywheel ring gear via a collar and spring. If the teeth on the pinion and flywheel match properly, the pinion will engage the flywheel immediately. If the gear teeth butt one another, the spring will be compressed and will force the gears to mesh as soon as the starter turns far enough to allow them to do so. As the solenoid plunger reaches the end of its travel, it closes the contacts that connect the battery and starter and then the engine is cranked.

As soon as the engine starts, the flywheel ring gear begins turning fast enough to drive the pinion at an extremely high rate of speed. At this point, the one-way clutch begins allowing the pinion to spin faster than the starter shaft so that the starter will not operate at excessive speed. When the ignition switch is released from the starter position, the solenoid is de-energized, and a spring contained within the solenoid assembly pulls the gear out of mesh and interrupts the current flow to the starter.

Some starters employ a separate relay, mounted away from the starter, to switch the motor and solenoid current on and off. The relay thus replaces the solenoid electrical switch, but does not eliminate the need for a solenoid mounted on the starter used to mechanically engage the starter drive gears. The relay is used to reduce the amount of current the starting switch must carry.

High Energy Ignition (HEI) System

The General Motors HEI system is a pulse-triggered, transistored-controlled, inductive discharge ignition system. Except on inline four- and six-cylinder models, the entire HEI system is contained within the distributor cap. All 140 cu. four-cylinders have an external coil. Otherwise, the systems are the same.

The distributor, in addition to housing the mechanical and vacuum advance mechanisms, contains the ignition coil (except on four and inline six engines), the electronic control module, and the magnetic triggering device. The magnetic pick-up assembly contains a permanent magnet, a pole piece with internal "teeth," and a pick-up coil (not to be confused with the ignition coil).

In the HEI system, as in other electronic ignition systems, the breaker points have been replaced with an electronic switch—a transistor—which is located *within* the control module. This switching transistor performs the same function the points did in a conventional ignition system; it simply turns coil primary current on and off at the correct time. Essentially then, electronic and conventional ignition systems operate on the same principle.

The module which houses the switching transistor is controlled (turned on and off) by a magnetically generated impulse induced in the pick-up coil. When the teeth of the rotating timer align with the teeth of the pole piece, the induced voltage in the pick-up coil signals the electronic module to open the coil primary circuit. The primary current then decreases, and a high voltage is induced in the ignition coil secondary windings which is then directed through the rotor and high voltage leads (spark plug wires) to fire the spark plugs.

In essence then, the pick-up coil module system simply replaces the conventional breaker points and condenser. The condenser found within the distributor is for radio suppression purposes only and has nothing to do with the ignition process. The module automatically controls the dwell period, increasing it with increasing engine speed. Since dwell is automatically controlled, it cannot be adjusted. The module itself is non-adjustable and non-repairable and must be replaced if found defective.

HEI SYSTEM PRECAUTIONS

Before going on to troubleshooting, it might be a good idea to take note of the following precautions:

Timing Light Use

Inductive pick-up timing lights are the best kind to use if your car is equipped with HEI. Timing lights which connect between the spark plug and the spark plug wire occasionally (not always) give false readings.

Spark Plug Wires

The plug wires used with HEI systems are of a different construction than conventional wires. When replacing them, make sure you get the correct wires, since conventional wires won't carry the voltage. Also, handle them carefully to avoid cracking or splitting them and *never* pierce them.

Tachometer Use

Not all tachometers will operate or indicate correctly when used on a HEI system. While some tachometers may give a reading, this does not necessarily mean the reading is correct. In addition, some tachometers hook up differently from others. If you can't figure out whether or not your tachometer will work on your car, check with the tachometer manufacturer. Dwell readings, of course, have no significance at all.

HEI System Testers

Instruments designed specifically for testing HEI systems are available from several tool manufacturers. Some of these will even test the module itself. However, the tests given in the following section will require only an ohmmeter and a voltmeter.

TROUBLESHOOTING THE HEI SYSTEM

The symptoms of a defective component within the HEI system are exactly the same as those you would encounter in a conventional system. Some of these symptoms are:

• Hard or no starting
• Rough idle
• Poor fuel economy
• Engine misses under load or while accelerating

If you suspect a problem in your ignition system, there are certain preliminary checks which you should carry out before you begin to check the electronic portions of the system. First, it is extremely important to make sure the vehicle battery is in a good state of charge. A defective or poorly charged battery will cause the various components of the ignition system to read incorrectly when they are being tested. Second, make sure all wiring connections are clean and tight, not only at the battery, but also at the distributor cap, ignition coil, and at the electronic control module.

Since the only change between electronic and conventional ignition systems is in the distributor component area, it is imperative to check the secondary ignition circuit first. If the secondary circuit checks out properly, then the engine condition is probably not the fault of the ignition system. To check the secondary ignition system, perform a simple spark test. Remove one of the plug wires and insert some sort of extension in the plug socket. An old spark plug with the ground electrode removed makes a good extension. Hold the wire and extension about ¼ in. away from the block and crank the engine. If a normal spark occurs, then the problem is most likely *not* in the ignition system. Check for fuel system problems, or fouled spark plugs.

If, however, there is no spark or a weak spark, then further ignition system testing will have to be done. Troubleshooting tech-

niques fall into two categories, depending on the nature of the problem. The categories are (1) Engine cranks, but won't start or (2) Engine runs, but runs rough or cuts out. To begin with, let's consider the first case.

Engine Fails to Start

If the engine won't start, perform a spark test as described earlier. This will narrow the problem area down considerably. If no spark occurs, check for the presence of normal battery voltage at the battery (BAT) terminal in the distributor cap. The ignition switch must be in the "on" position for this test. Either a voltmeter or a test light may be used for this test. Connect the test light wire to ground and the probe end to the BAT terminal at the distributor. If the light comes on, you have voltage to the distributor. If the light fails to come on, this indicates an open circuit in the ignition primary wiring leading to the distributor. In this case, you will have to check wiring continuity back to the ignition switch using a test light. If there is battery voltage at the BAT terminal, but no spark at the plugs, then the problem lies within the distributor assembly. Go on to the distributor components test section.

Engine Runs, But Runs Rough or Cuts Out

1. Make sure the plug wires are in good shape first. There should be no obvious cracks or breaks. You can check the plug wires with an ohmmeter, but *do not* pierce the wires with a probe. Check the chart for the correct plug wire resistance.

HEI Plug Wire Resistance Chart

Wire Length	Minimum	Maximum
0–15 inches	3,000 ohms	10,000 ohms
15–25 inches	4,000 ohms	15,000 ohms
25–35 inches	6,000 ohms	20,000 ohms
Over 35 inches		25,000 ohms

2. If the plug wires are OK, remove the cap assembly, and check for moisture, cracks, chips, or carbon tracks, or any other high voltage leaks or failures. Replace the cap if you find any defects. Make sure the timer wheel rotates when the engine is cranked. If everything is all right so far, go on to the distributor components test section.

Distributor Components Testing

If the trouble has been narrowed down to the units within the distributor, the following tests can help pinpoint the defective component. An ohmmeter with both high and low ranges should be used. These tests are made with the cap assembly removed and the battery wire disconnected.

1. Connect an ohmmeter between the Tach and Bat terminals in the distributor cap. The primary coil resistance should be less than one ohm.

2. To check the coil secondary resistance, connect an ohmmeter between the rotor button and either the BAT or Tach terminals. The resistance should be between 6,000 and 30,000 ohms.

3. Replace the coil *only* if the readings in step one and two are infinite.

NOTE: *These resistance checks will not disclose shorted coil windings. This condition can only be detected with scope analysis or a suitably designed coil tester. If these instruments are unavailable, replace the coil with a known good coil as a final coil test.*

4. To test the pick-up coil, first disconnect the white and green module leads. Set the ohmmeter on the high scale and connect it between a ground and either the white or green lead. Any resistance measurement *less* than infinity requires replacement of the pick-up coil.

5. Pick-up coil continuity is tested by connecting the ohmmeter (on low range) between the white and green leads. Normal resistance is between 650 and 850 ohms. Move the vacuum advance arm while performing this test. This will detect any break in coil continuity. Such a condition can cause intermittent misfiring. Replace the pick-up coil if the reading is outside the specified limits.

6. If no defects have been found at this time, and you still have a problem, then the module will have to be checked. If you do not have access to a module tester, the only possible alternative is a substitution test. If the module fails the substitution test, replace it.

Distributor

REMOVAL

1. Mark the location of the No. 1 (front) spark plug wire on the side of the distributor with chalk.

2. Remove the cap hold-down screws and move the cap out of the way. Disconnect the spark plug wires if necessary.

3. Disconnect the distributor primary wire (the one from the side of the distributor) from the coil (1971–74 models only). Disconnect the vacuum line.

4. Place a ¾ in. socket on the crankshaft pulley nut and turn the engine until the distributor rotor (the metal end) points to the chalk mark made in Step 1 and the points start to open. This is easier if the spark plugs have been removed.

5. Mark the relationship of the distributor to the engine.

6. Remove the hold-down bolt and clamp and remove the distributor.

7. The procedure for installation varies depending on whether or not the engine was turned while the distributor was out.

INSTALLATION, ENGINE NOT TURNED

1. Turn the rotor about one-eighth turn past the chalk mark.

2. Align the distributor locating marks and push the distributor into place. The rotor should turn back to the chalk mark as the unit seats. Wiggle the rotor slightly to start the gear in mesh if necessary.

3. Tighten the clamp bolt and reconnect the primary wire and the vacuum line. Replace the cap.

4. Check the ignition timing as explained in Chapter 2.

INSTALLATION, ENGINE TURNED

This procedure is necessary to install a new distributor or if the engine has been turned while the distributor was out.

1. Locate the No. 1 cylinder in firing position by turning the engine with a finger held over the No. 1 spark plug hole. When compression is felt, turn the engine to align the correct mark on the timing pointer with the notch on the crankshaft pulley.

2. Hold the distributor with the vacuum control unit pointing to the front of the engine and turn the distributor drive gear to align the punch mark on the gear with the No. 1 distributor cap terminal location.

3. Turn the distributor body counterclockwise about one-eighth turn and set it into place in the engine. Wiggle the rotor slightly to start the gear in mesh if necessary.

4. When the distributor is in place, turn it slightly so that the points are just starting to

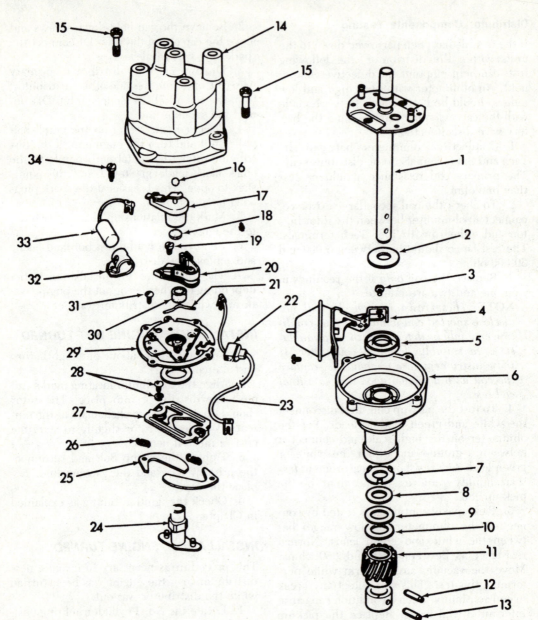

1. Mainshaft, distributor w/weight plate
2. Washer, distributor gear
3. Screw, distr vacuum control attaching
4. Control assy, distributor vacuum
5. Seal, distributor housing oil
6. Housing assy.
7. Washer, distributor gear
8. Washer, distr. mainshaft cplg.
9. Washer, distributor shim (.005)
10. Shim, distr. M/Shf.
11. Gear unit
12. Pin
13. Pin
14. Cap assy.
15. Screw (8-32x¾)
16. Part #14
17. Rotor asm, distr.
18. Lubricator unit, rotor wick
19. Screw (8-32x⁵/₁₆)
20. Point unit, distr.
21. Spring, breaker plate set
22. Grommet, distr. terminal
23. Lead, distr. terminal
24. Cam, distributor w/weight plate
25. Weight, distributor
26. Spring, distributor weight
27. Plate, distributor weight hold down
28. Screw (8-32 x ¼)
29. Plate and support asm., distr. circ. brkr.
30. Lubrication unit, cam
31. Screw
32. Bracket, condenser
33. Condenser, spade type terminal
34. Screw

Disassembled view of conventional distributor—1971-74

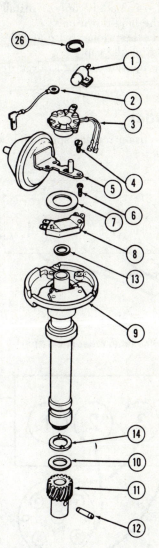
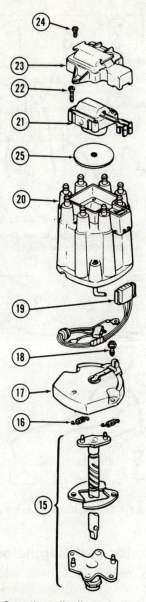

1. Capacitor, distributor
2. Lead assy., distributor terminal/grd.
3. Pole piece, w/plate
4. Screw
5. Control assy., distributor vacuum
6. Screw
7. Shield, distributor housing splash
8. Module, distributor
9. Housing assy., distributor
10. Washer
11. Gear
12. Pin
13. Seal, dis. housing
14. Washer, tang
15. Shaft
16. Spring, distributor weight
17. Rotor assy., distributor
18. Screw, distributor module attach.
19. Harness, module to coil
20. Cap, distributor
21. Coil, ignition
22. Screw, ignition coil attach.
23. Cover, distributor cap
24. Screw
25. Seal, dis. ignition coil
26. Retainer

Disassembled view of V6 and V8 HEI distributor—1975 and later

open (1971–74 models only). Install the clamp and the hold-down bolt.

5. Connect the primary wire and the vacuum line. Install the cap.

6. Set the ignition timing as described in Chapter 2.

Firing Order

To avoid confusion replace spark plug wires one at a time.

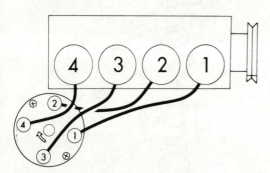

4 cyl. 140 engine firing order (1-3-4-2)

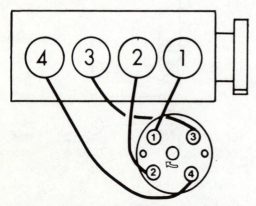

4 cyl. 151 engine—1977–78 firing order (1-3-4-2)

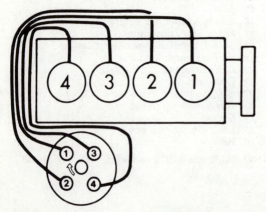

4 cyl. 151 engine—1979 and later firing order (1-3-4-2)

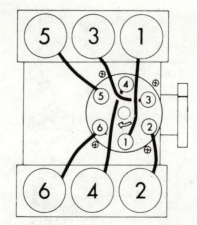

V6 196, 231 engine, firing order (1-6-5-4-3-2), distributor rotation clockwise

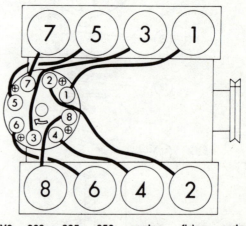

V8 262, 305, 350 engine, firing order (1-8-4-3-6-5-7-2), distributor rotation clockwise

Alternator and Regulator

The alternator contains the sealed voltage regulator which needs no adjustment and has no provision for adjustment. The alternator itself requires no lubrication or adjustments except for drive belt tension. Alternator output is stamped on the frame of the unit. Certain safety precautions should be observed concerning the alternator.

1. Do not polarize the unit.

2. Do not short across or ground any of the terminals.

3. Never operate the unit with the output terminal disconnected.

4. Make sure that the battery is installed with the correct polarity.

5. When connecting a booster battery, always connect positive terminal to positive terminal and negative terminal to negative terminal.

BELT TENSION ADJUSTMENTS

On 1971 models, the alternator drive belt is also used to drive the power steering unit. On 1972 and later models, this belt drives the alternator and power steering unit or air pump. In both arrangements, belt tension is adjusted by loosening the adjusting nut in the slot on the alternator and prying the alternator outward. The air conditioning compressor is driven by a separate belt. If a belt tension gauge is available, the correct tension is as follows:

Belt	Tension (new belt)	Tension (used belt)	Min Tension
Alternator	120–130 lbs	70–80 lbs	50 lbs
Compressor	135–144 lbs	90–100 lbs	65 lbs

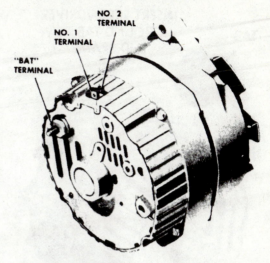

Alternator connections

If a bent tension gauge is not available, the following rule of thumb may be applied for adjustments:

Distance Between Pulley Centers	Belt Deflection
13–16 in.	½ in.
10–13 in.	⅜ in.
7–10 in.	¼ in.

The belt deflection is measured under moderate thumb pressure midway between the pulleys.

REMOVAL AND REPLACEMENT

1. Disconnect the battery negative cable.
2. Disconnect the alternator leads.
3. Remove the alternator brace bolt and drive belt.
4. Remove the alternator mounting bolt and remove the alternator.
5. Reverse the procedure for installation.
6. Adjust the drive belt.

TESTING

Undercharging

1. Check the drive belt tension.
2. Have the battery fully charged and checked for ability to take and hold a charge.
3. Check all wiring connections.
4. Turn the ignition switch on and connect a voltmeter from the alternator BAT terminal to a ground, then from the No. 1 terminal to a ground, and then from the No. 2 terminal to a ground. A zero reading indicates an open circuit between the voltmeter connection and the battery.
5. If the trouble has not yet been found, proceed as follows:

   a. Disconnect the battery ground cable.

   b. Connect an ammeter in the circuit at the BAT terminal.

   c. Connect the battery ground cable.

   d. Turn on the radio, windshield wipers, high-beam lights, and high-speed blower. Connect a carbon pile rheostat across the battery terminals.

   e. Run the engine at about 1500–2000 rpm and adjust the carbon pile to obtain the maximum current output.

   f. If the output is within 10% of the rated output stamped on the alternator frame, the unit is acceptable.

   g. If the output is not sufficient, ground the field winding by inserting a screwdriver into the test hole on the back of the alternator. There is a tab ¾ in. inside the hole. Ground this to the case. Be very careful not to insert the screwdriver more than 1 in.

   h. Repeat Step e. If the output is now within 10% of the rated output, the regulator is defective and must be replaced.

   i. If the output is still not within 10% of the rated output, the unit will have to be disassembled for further testing.

   j. Remove the ammeter and turn all the accessories off.

Overcharging

1. Perform steps 1–3 under Undercharging.
2. Connect a voltmeter from the No. 2 alternator terminal to a ground. If the reading is zero, the No. 2 lead circuit is open.
3. Any further testing requires disassembly.

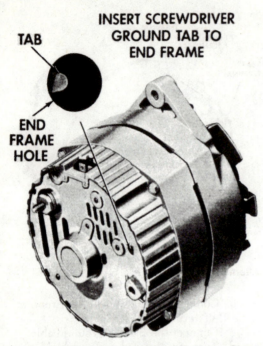

TAB

INSERT SCREWDRIVER
GROUND TAB TO
END FRAME

END
FRAME
HOLE

Alternator grounding procedures (Courtesy Chevrolet Motor Division)

ALTERNATOR PRECAUTIONS

To prevent damage to the alternator and regulator, the following precautions should be taken when working with the electrical system.

1. Never reverse the battery connections.

2. Booster batteries for starting must be connected properly—positive-to-positive and negative-to-negative.

3. Disconnect the battery cables before using a fast charger; the charger has a tendency to force current through the diodes in the opposite direction for which they were designed. This burns out the diodes.

4. Never use a fast charger as a booster for starting the vehicle.

5. Never disconnect the voltage regulator while the engine is running.

6. Avoid long soldering times when replacing diodes or transistors. Prolonged heat is damaging to AC generators.

7. Do not use test lamps of more than 12 volts (V) for checking diode continuity.

8. Do not short across or ground any of the terminals on the AC generator.

9. The polarity of the battery, generator, and regulator must be matched and considered before making any electrical connections within the system.

10. Never operate the alternator on an open circuit. Make sure that all connections within the circuit are clean and tight.

11. Disconnect the battery terminals when performing any service on the electrical system. This will eliminate the possibility of accidental reversal of polarity.

12. Disconnect the battery ground cable if arc welding is to be done on any part of the car.

Starter

No maintenance is required on the starter between overhauls. Rebuilt units are available on an exchange basis.

REMOVAL AND INSTALLATION

1. Disconnect the battery ground cable.

2. Disconnect the wires at the solenoid terminals. Reinstall each nut as the wire is disconnected so as to avoid mixing them.

3. Loosen the front bracket. Remove the two mounting bolts.

4. Remove the front bracket bolt. Turn the bracket out of the way. Remove the starter.

5. When installing the starter, tighten the mounting bolts first, then install the brace.

STARTER OVERHAUL

Drive Replacement

1. Disconnect the field coil straps from the solenoid.

2. Remove the through bolts, and separate commutator end frame, field frame assembly, drive housing, and armature assembly from each other.

3. Slide the two piece thrust collar off the end of the armature shaft.

4. Slide a suitably sized metal cylinder, such as a standard half-inch pipe coupling, or an old pinion, on the shaft so that the end of the coupling or pinion butts up against the edge of the pinion retainer.

5. Support the lower end of the armature securely on a soft surface, such as a wooden block, and tap the end of the coupling or pinion, driving the retainer towards the armature end of the snap ring.

6. Remove the snap ring from the groove in the armature shaft with a pair of pliers. Then, slide the retainer and starter drive from the shaft.

7. To reassemble, lubricate the drive end of the armature shaft with silicone lubricant, and then slide the starter drive onto shaft *with pinion facing outward*. Slide the re-

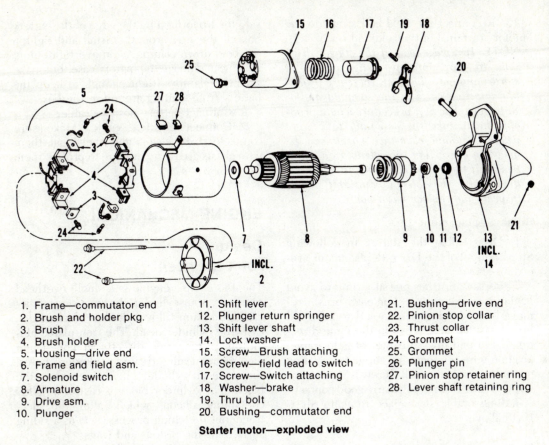

Starter motor—exploded view

1. Frame—commutator end
2. Brush and holder pkg.
3. Brush
4. Brush holder
5. Housing—drive end
6. Frame and field asm.
7. Solenoid switch
8. Armature
9. Drive asm.
10. Plunger
11. Shift lever
12. Plunger return springer
13. Shift lever shaft
14. Lock washer
15. Screw—Brush attaching
16. Screw—field lead to switch
17. Screw—Switch attaching
18. Washer—brake
19. Thru bolt
20. Bushing—commutator end
21. Bushing—drive end
22. Pinion stop collar
23. Thrust collar
24. Grommet
25. Grommet
26. Plunger pin
27. Pinion stop retainer ring
28. Lever shaft retaining ring

tainer onto the shaft *with cupped surface facing outward.*

8. Again support the armature on a soft surface, with the pinion at upper end. Center the snap ring on the top of the shaft (use a new snap ring if the original was damaged during removal). Gently place a block of wood flat on top of the snap ring so as not to move it from a centered position. Tap the wooden block with a hammer in order to force the snap ring around the shaft. Then, slide the ring down into the snap ring groove.

9. Lay the armature down flat on the surface you're working on. Slide the retainer close up on to the shaft and position it and the thrust collar next to the snap ring. Using two pairs of pliers on opposite sides of the shaft, squeeze the thrust collar and the retainer together until the snap ring is forced into the retainer.

10. Lube the drive housing bushing with a silicone lubricant. Then, install armature and clutch assembly into drive housing, engaging the solenoid shift lever with the clutch, and positioning front end of armature shaft into bushing.

11. Apply a sealing compound approved

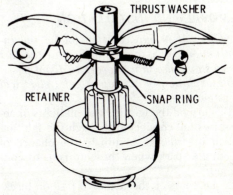

Installing snap ring

for this application onto the drive housing; then position field frame around armature shaft and against the drive housing. *Work slowly and carefully to prevent damaging the starter brushers.*

12. Lubricate the bushing in the commutator end frame with a silicone lubricant, place leather brake washer onto the armature shaft, and then slide the commutator end frame over the shaft and into position against the field frame. Line up bolt holes, and then install and tighten through bolts.

13. Reconnect the field coil straps to the "motor" terminal of the solenoid..

NOTE: *If replacement of the starter drive fails to cure improper engagement of starter pinion to flywheel, there are probably defective parts in the solenoid and/or shift lever. The best procedure would probably be to take the assembly to a shop where a pinion clearance check can be made by energizing the solenoid on a test bench. If the pinion clearance is incorrect, disassemble the solenoid and shift lever, inspect, and replace worn parts.*

Brush Replacement

1. Disassemble the starter by following Steps 1 and 2 of the Drive Replacement procedure above.

2. Replace brushes one at a time to avoid having to mark wiring. For each brush: remove brush holding screw; and remove old brush position new brush in the same direction (large end toward center of field frame; position wire connector on top of brush, line up holes, and reinstall screw. Make sure screw is snug enough to ensure good contact.

3. Reassemble starter according to Steps 10-13 above.

Battery

REMOVAL AND INSTALLATION

NOTE: *It is important to follow the instructions of Steps 1 and 2, and the last two steps carefully in order to avoid possible explosion or damage to the electrical system.*

1. Turn off the ignition and all lights or accessories not connected through the ignition switch in order to eliminate the chance of creating a spark when the battery is disconnected.

2. Disconnect the negative ("-" or black) terminal at the battery. On conventional connectors located on top of the battery, this may be easier if you pry the two jaws of the connector apart after loosening the through bolt.

3. Then, disconnect the positive connector in the same way.

4. Loosen the hold down clamp, and remove the battery.

5. Before installing, check to make sure the battery box is free of foreign matter in the bottom so the battery will sit flat and secure. Also, tighten the battery box mounting bolts.

6. To install, position the battery with terminals to the rear. Make sure battery is in-side the lip formed by the edge of the battery box all the way around. Install and tighten the hold down clamp. Avoid overtightening, which can damage the battery case, but make sure the clamp is tight enough to keep the battery from shifting around in the box.

7. Connect battery positive cable.

8. Connect negative cable. Make sure connectors are clean, and then coat them with chasis grease or vaseline to protect them from corrosion.

ENGINE MECHANICAL

Design
FOUR CYLINDER

The 140 cu. in. engine is a single overhead camshaft, four-cylinder design using a die-cast aluminum alloy cylinder block and a cast-iron cylinder head. The iron-plated aluminum pistons ride directly in honed and electrochemically treated cylinder bores; there are no cylinder liners inserted in the block. The cylinder block is cast of an alloy containing silicon, which, after the electrochemical etching process, acts as a riding surface for the pistons and rings.

The valve train, including the camshaft, tappets, and valves, is contained entirely in the cylinder head. The camshaft is driven by a toothed, flexible timing belt which is driven by a sprocket on the crankshaft. The water pump and fan assembly ride against the outside of the belt as an idler and are adjustable to correct belt tension.

Two versions of the engine are available: the standard unit with a single-barrel carburetor and a general performance camshaft, and an optional version with a two-barrel carburetor and a high performance camshaft.

In 1977 Pontiac introduced the 151 cu. in. engine to replace the 140 cu. in. engine and it was used the following year by Chevrolet. The 151 is a cast iron push rod type. It has overhead valves with very long connecting rods. Using a short stroke (3 in.) and long connecting rods minimizes roughness. In 1979, the 151 cylinder head configuration was changed to a crossflow design, and the distributor was moved to the rear left-hand side of the block.

V6 AND V8

The V6-196,231 engines and the V8-262,305,350 engines are very simular in design.

The nodular cast iron crankshaft is supported by five bearings (V8), four bearings (V6). The crankshaft is counterbalanced by weights cast integral with the crankshaft. Additional counterbalancing is obtained from the flywheel and harmonic balancer. The pistons are tin plated aluminum alloy and full skirts and are cam ground.

The camshaft is supported in the crankcase by five steel backed babbit lined bearings. It is driven from the crankshaft by sprockets and chain. The cylinder heads are cast iron. The V6 rocker arms are mounted on tubular steel shafts supported on the cylinder head by three pedestals. On the V8 engines the rocker arms are individually mounted. Hydraulic valve lifters and tubular push rods are used to operate the overhead rocker arms and valves of both banks of cylinders from a single camshaft. This system requires no lash adjustment.

Engine Removal and Installation

4 CYL. 140 ENGINE

1. Position the vehicle so that the underside will be accessible.

2. With the hood open, insert a bolt through the hold-open link to keep it open.

3. Disconnect the battery ground cable.

4. Disconnect the battery positive cable.

5. Drain the cooling system by using the petcock at the bottom of the radiator on 1971 models, or by removing the lower radiator hose on some late 1971 models and all 1972 models. 1973 and later models reverted to the petcock arrangement.

NOTE: *Do not start the siphoning action by mouth. Anti-freeze is poisonous.*

6. Disconnect both radiator hoses. Disconnect the heater hoses at the water pump and at the lower hose connection on the heater.

7. Disconnect the:

a. PCV hose from the cam cover,

b. the evaporation emission canister vacuum hose at the carburetor,

c. the PCV vacuum hose at the intake manifold, and

d. the bowl vent at the carburetor,

e. TCS hose in the rear of the carburetor.

8. Remove the radiator panel or shroud, depending on the installation, and the radiator, fan, and spacer.

9. Remove the air cleaner, disconnecting the vent tube at the base.

10. Disconnect the electrical connections at the following items:

a. alternator

b. coil

c. starter solenoid

d. oil pressure switch

e. temperature switch

f. TSC switch at the transmission

g. TCS solenoid on the firewall

h. engine ground strap

11. Disconnect the following items:

a. Powerglide transmission throttle valve linkage or Turbo Hydra-Matic 250 detent cable

b. fuel line at the rubber hose behind the carburetor

c. automatic transmission vacuum modulator line and air conditioning vacuum line at the intake manifold

d. accelerator cable at the manifold bellcrank

12. Disconnect the air conditioning compressor at the front and rear supports and the rear lower bracket. Remove the drive belt. Move the compressor forward to rest on the forward frame brace and tie it out of the way.

NOTE: *Do not disconnect any air conditioning system lines or fittings. Refer to Chapter 1 for further details on air conditioning.*

13. Dismount the power steering pump and set it out of the way.

14. Disconnect the exhaust pipe at the manifold.

15. Remove the flywheel lower cover or the torque converter underpan.

16. On automatic transmissions:

a. Mark the relationship of the converter to the flywheel for reassembly.

b. Remove the converter to flywheel bolts and install a strap to prevent the converter from falling out.

c. Remove the converter housing to engine bolts.

d. Loosen the front engine mount retaining bolts at the frame.

e. Place a hydraulic floor jack under the transmission.

f. Attack lifting chains or cables to the lifting points on the right front and left rear of the engine.

g. Raise the engine slightly and remove the front engine mount bolts.

h. Pull the engine forward while slowly lifting it. Remove the engine.

17. On manual transmission, remove the clutch housing to engine bolts and then proceed with Step 16, parts d, e, f, g, and h.

General Engine Specifications

Year	Engine Displacement Cu In. (cc)	Carburetor Type	Horsepower (@rpm)	Torque @rpm (ft lbs)	Bore x Stroke (in.)	Compression Ratio	Oil Pressure @rpm (psi)
1971	4-140	1 bbl	90 @ 4600	136 @ 2400	3.50 x 3.625	8.0 : 1	40
	4.140	2 bbl	110 @ 4800	138 @ 3200	3.50 x 3.625	8.0 : 1	40
1972	4-140	1 bbl	80 @ 4800	121 @ 2800	3.50 x 3.625	8.0 : 1	40
	4-140	2 bbl	90 @ 4800	121 @ 3200	3.50 x 3.625	8.0 : 1	40
1973	4-140	1 bbl	75 @ 4400	115 @ 2400	3.50 x 3.625	8.0 : 1	40
	4-140	2 bbl	85 @ 4400	122 @ 2400	3.50 x 3.625	8.0 : 1	40
1974	4-140	1 bbl	75 @ 4400	115 @ 2400	3.50 x 3.625	8.0 : 1	40
	4-140	2 bbl	85 @ 4400	122 @ 2400	3.50 x 3.625	8.0 : 1	40
1975	4-140	1 bbl	78 @ 4200	120 @ 2000	3.50 x 3.625	8.0 : 1	40
	4-140	2 bbl	87 @ 4400	122 @ 2800	3.50 x 3.625	8.0 : 1	40
	4-140 Calif.	2 bbl	80 @ 4400	116 @ 2800	3.50 x 3.625	8.0 : 1	40
	6-231	2 bbl	110 @ 4000	175 @ 2000	3.800 x 3.400	8.0 : 1	37
	8-262	2 bbl	110 @ 3600	200 @ 2000	3.671 x 3.100	8.5 : 1	32–40
	8-350 Calif.	2 bbl	125 @ 3600	235 @ 2000	4.000 x 3.480	8.5 : 1	32–40
1976	4-140①	1 bbl	69 @ 4000	113 @ 2400	3.50 x 3.625	7.9 : 1	40
	4-140②	1 bbl	70 @ 4400	107 @ 2400	3.50 x 3.625	8.0 : 1	27–41
	4-140①	2 bbl	87 @ 4400	122 @ 2800	3.50 x 3.625	7.9 : 1	40
	4-140②	2 bbl	84 @ 4400	113 @ 3200	3.50 x 3.625	8.0 : 1	27–41
	6-231①	2 bbl	110 @ 4000	175 @ 2000	3.80 x 3.400	8.0 : 1	40
	6-231③	2 bbl	105 @ 3400	185 @ 2000	3.80 x 3.400	8.0 : 1	37
	8-262	2 bbl	110 @ 3600	200 @ 2000	3.671 x 3.100	8.5 : 1	32–40
	8-305	2 bbl	140 @ 3800	245 @ 2000	3.736 x 3.480	8.5 : 1	32–40
1977	4-140①	2 bbl	87 @ 4400	122 @ 2800	3.50 x 3.625	7.9 : 1	40
	4-140④	2 bbl	84 @ 4400	117 @ 2400	3.50 x 3.625	8.0 : 1	27–41

General Engine Specifications (cont.)

Year	Engine Displacement Cu In. (cc)	Carburetor Type	Horsepower (@rpm)	Torque @rpm (ft lbs)	Bore x Stroke (in.)	Compression Ratio	Oil Pressure @rpm (psi)
1977	4-151	2 bbl	8.7 @ 4400	128 @ 2400	4.000 x 3.000	8.3 : 1	36–41
	6-231	2 bbl	105 @ 3200	185 @ 2000	3.800 x 3.400	8.0 : 1	36–41
	8-305	2 bbl	145 @ 3800	245 @ 2400	3.736 x 3.480	8.5 : 1	32–40
	8-305 Calif.	2 bbl	135 @ 3800	240 @ 2000	3.736 x 3.480	8.5 : 1	32–40
1978	4-151⑤	2 bbl	85 @ 4400	123 @ 2800	4.000 x 3.000	8.3 : 1	36–41
	4-151⑥	2 bbl	87 @ 4400	128 @ 2400	4.000 x 3.000	8.3 : 1	36–41
	4-151⑦	2 bbl	90 @ 4400	130 @ 2400	4.000 x 3.000	8.3 : 1	40
	6-196	2 bbl	90 @ 3600	165 @ 2000	3.500 x 3.400	8.0 : 1	37
	6-231	2 bbl	105 @ 3400	185 @ 2000	3.800 x 3.400	8.0 : 1	37
	8-305	2 bbl	145 @ 3800	245 @ 2400	3.736 x 3.480	8.4 : 1	32–70
1979	4-151⑧	2 bbl	85 @ 4400	123 @ 2800	4.000 x 3.000	8.3 : 1	36–41
	4-151⑨	2 bbl	90 @ 4400	128 @ 2400	4.000 x 3.000	8.3 : 1	36–41
	4-196	2 bbl	105 @ 4000	160 @ 2000	3.500 x 3.400	8.0 : 1	37
	6-231	2 bbl	115 @ 3600	190 @ 2000	3.800 x 3.400	8.0 : 1	37
	8-305	2 bbl	130 @ 3200	245 @ 2400	3.736 x 3.480	8.4 : 1	45
1980	4-151	2 bbl	90 @ 4400⑩	128 @ 2400⑪	4.000 x 3.000	8.2 : 1	37–41
	6-231	2 bbl	110 @ 3800	190 @ 1600	3.800 x 3.400	8.0 : 1	37

① Astre, Sunbird
② Vega, Monza
③ Skyhawk, Starfire
④ Starfire, Monza
⑤ Monza
⑥ Sunbird
⑦ Starfire
⑧ All exc. Calif.—Starfire
⑨ All exc. Calif.—Monza, Sunbird
⑩ Calif.—85 @ 4400
⑪ Calif.—123 @ 2800

Valve Specifications

Year	Engine Displacement Cu In. (cc)	Seat Angle (deg)	Face Angle (deg)	Spring Test Pressure (lbs @ in.) (valve open)	Spring Installed Height (in.)	Stem to Guide Clearance (in.)		Stem Diameter (in.)	
						Intake	Exhaust	Intake	Exhaust
1971–74	4-140	46	45	190 @ 1.31	1¾	.0010–.0027	.0010–.0027	.3414	.3414
1975	4-140	46	45	190 @ 1.31	1¾	.0010–.0027	.0010–.0027	.3414	.3414
	6-231	45	45	164 @ 1.34 ①	1⁴⁷/₆₄	.0015–.0035	.0015–.0032	.3407	.3407
	8-262	46	45	200 @ 1.25	1.70 ②	.0010–.0027	.0010–.0027	.3414	.3414
	8-350	46	45	200 @ 1.25	1.70 ②	.0010–.0027	.0010–.0027	.3414	.3414
1976	4-140	46	45	190 @ 1.31	1¾	.0010–.0027	.0010–.0027	.3414	.3414
	6-231	45	45	164 @ 1.34 ①	1⁴⁷/₆₄	.0015–.0035	.0015–.0035	.3414	.3414
	8-262	46	45	200 @ 1.25	1.70 ②	.0010–.0027	.0010–.0027	.3414	.3414
1977	4-140	46	45	190 @ 1.31	1¾	.0010–.0027	.0010–.0027	.3414	.3414
	4-151	46	45	177 @ 1.25	1⁴³/₆₄	.0010–.0027	.0010–.0027	.3422	.3422
	6-231	45	45	164 @ 1.34	1⁴⁷/₆₄	.0015–.0035	.0015–.0032	.3407	.3407
	8-305	46	45	180 @ 1.25 ③	1.70 ②	.0010–.0027	.0010–.0027	.3414	.3414
1978–79	4-151	46	45	176 @ 1.25	1.69	.0010–.0027	.0010–.0027	.3414	.3414
	6-196	45	45	168 @ 1.327	1.727	.0015–.0032	.0015–.0032	.3408	.3408
	6-231	45	45	168 @ 1.327	1⁴⁷/₆₄	.0015–.0032	.0015–.0032	.3408	.3408
	8-305	46	45	180 @ 1.25 ③	1.70 ②	.0010–.0027	.0010–.0027	.3414	.3414
1980	4-151	46	45	176 @ 1.25	1.66	.0010–.0027	.0010–.0027	.3422	.3422
	6-231	45	45	180 @ 1.34	1.727	.0015–.0035	.0015–.0032	.3408	.3408

① Exhaust—182 @ 1.34   ② Exhaust—1.61   ③ Exhaust 190 @ 1.61

Crankshaft And Connecting Rod Specifications
All measurements are given in inches

Year	Engine	Crankshaft				Connecting Rod		
		Main Brg. Journal Dia	Main Brg Oil Clearance	Shaft End-Play	Thrust on No.	Journal Diameter	Oil Clearance	Side Clearance
1971	4-140	2.2983–2.2993	.0003–.0029	.002–.008	4	1.999–2.000	.0007–.0027	.0009–.014
1972	4-140	2.2983–2.2993	.0003–.002	.002–.008	4	1.999–2.000	.0007–.0027	.0009–.014
1973–74	4-140	2.2983–2.2993	.0003–.002 ①	.002–.008	4	1.999–2.000	.0007–.0038	.0085–.0135
1975	4-140	2.3004	.0003–.0029	.002–.008	4	1.999–2.000	.0007–.0029	.0009–.0013
	6-231	2.4995	.0004–.0015	.004–.008	2	2.000	.0005–.0026	.006–.014
	8-262	2.4502 ②	③	.002–.007	5	2.098–2.099	.0013–.0035	.008–.014
	8-350	2.4502 ②	③	.002–.007	5	2.098–2.099	.0013–.0035	.008–.014
1976	4-140	2.3004	.0003–.0029	.002–.008	4	1.999–2.000	.0007–.0029	.0009–.0013
	6-231	2.4995	.0004–.0015	.004–.008	2	2.000	.0005–.0026	.006–.014
	8-262	2.4502 ②	③	.002–.007	5	2.098–2.099	.0013–.0035	.008–.014
	8-305	2.4502 ②	③	.002–.007	5	2.098–2.099	.0013–.0035	.008–.014
1977	4-140	2.3004	.0003–.0029	.002–.008	4	1.999–2.000	.0007–.0029	.0009–.0013
	4-151	2.30	.0002–.0022	.0035–.0085	5	2.000	.0005–.0026	.006–.022
	6-231	2.4995	.0004–.0015	.004–.008	2	2.000	.005–.0026	.006–.027
	8-305	2.4502 ②	③	.002–.008	5	2.098–2.099	.0013–.0035	.008–.014
1978–79	4-151	2.30	.0002–.0022	.0035–.0085	5	2.000	.0005–.0026	.006–.022
	6-196	2.4995	.0003–.0017	.004–.008	2	2.2487–2.2495	.0005–.0026	.006–.027
	6-231	2.4995	.0003–.0017	.004–.008	2	2.2487–2.2495	.0005–.0026	.006–.027
	8-305	④	③	.002–.006	5	2.0988–2.0998	.0013–.0035	.008–.014
1980	4-151	2.30	.0002–.0022	.0035–.0085	5	2.000	.0005–.0026	.006–.022
	6-231	2.4995	.0003–.0018	.003–.009	2	2.2487–2.2495	.0005–.0026	.006–.023

① 0.003–0.0027 for No. 2, 3, 4, 5
② No. 5—2.4508
③ No. 1—.0008–.0020 in.
　No. 2, 3, 4—.0011–.0023 in.
　No. 5—.0017–.0033 in.

④ No. 1—24484–2.4493
　No. 2, 3, 4—2.4481–2.4490
　No. 5—2.4479–2.4488

Ring Gap
All measurements are given in inches

Year	Engine No. Cyl Displacement (cu in.)	Top Compression	Bottom Compression	Oil Control
1971–77	4-140	.015–.025	.009–.019	.010–.030
1977–78	4-151	.010–.020	.010–.020	.010–.020
1979–80	4-151	.015–.025	.009–.019	.015–.055
1978	6-196	.010–.020	.010–.020	.015–.035
1979	6-196	.013–.023	.013–.023	.015–.035
1975–80	6-231	.010–.020	.010–.020	.015–.035
1975	8-262	.010–.020	.013–.025	.010–.025
1976	8-262	.010–.020	.010–.020	.010–.025
1976–79	8-305	.010–.020	.010–.025	.015–.055
1975	8-350	.010–.020	.010–.020	.015–.055

Ring Side Clearance
All measurements are given in inches

Year	Engine	Top Compression	Bottom Compression	Oil Control
1971–77	4-140	.0012–.0027	.0012–.0027	.000–.005
1977–80	4-151	.0025–.0033	.0025–.0033	.0025–.0033
1978–79	6-196	.003–.005	.003–.005	.0035 Max.
1975–80	6-231	.0030–.0050	.0030–.0050	.0035 Max.
1975–76	8-262	.0012–.0032	.0012–.0027	.000–.005
1976–77	8-305	.0012–.0032	.0012–.0032	.000–.001
1978–79	8-305	.0012–.0032	.0012–.0032	.002–.007
1975	8-350	.0012–.0032	.0012–.0027	.000–.005

Piston Clearance

Year	Engine No. Cyl. Displacement (cu. in.)	Piston to Bore Clearance (in.)
1971–77	4-140	.0018–.0028 ①
1977–80	4-151	.0025–.0033 ②
1978–79	6-196	.0008–.0020
1975–80	6-231	.0008–.0020
1975–76	8-262	.0008–.0018 ③
1976–79	8-305	.0007–.0017
1975	8-350	.0007–.0017

① Measured 1.50 in. from top of piston
② Measured 1.11 in. from top of piston
③ Measured 1.75 in. from top of piston

Torque Specifications
All readings in ft lbs

Year	Engine Displacement cu. in. (cc)	Cylinder Head Bolts	Rod Bearing Bolts	Main Bearing Bolts	Crankshaft Pulley Bolt	Flywheel-to-Crankshaft Bolts	Manifolds Intake	Manifolds Exhaust
1971–77	4-140	60	35	65	80	60 ①	30	30
1978–80	4-151	95	30	65	160	55	②	②
1978–79	6-196	80	40	100	225	60	45	25
1975	6-231	75	40	115	150	55	45	25
1976	6-231	75	40	115	150	60	45	25
1977	6-231	85	42	80 ③	310	60	40	25
1978–80	6-231	80	40	100	225	60	45	25
1975–76	8-262	65	45	70	60	60	30	20 ④
1976–79	8-305	65	45	80	60	60	30	20 ④
1975	8-350	65	45	75	60	60	30	20 ④

① 1975–77—65 ft lbs
② Bolt—40; nut—30
③ Rear main—120 ft lbs
④ Inside bolts—30 ft lbs

To replace the engine:

18. Install two guide pins into the upper bolt holes in the engine block. Guide pins can be fabricated by cutting the heads off two bolts and sawing screwdriver slots into them.

19. Lower the engine into place, aligning the engine with the transmission.

20. Install the front mount bolts loosely.

21. Install the converter or clutch housing to engine bolts, replacing the guide pins.

22. Remove the converter retaining strap.

23. Torque the clutch housing to engine bolts to 25 ft lbs and the converter housing to engine bolts to 35 ft lbs.

24. Tighten the front engine mounts after checking that they are aligned so as not to make metal to metal contact.

25. Align the converter and flywheel marks made in Step 16. Install the converter bolts, torquing to 35 ft lbs.

26. Replace the flywheel dust cover or torque converter underpan.

27. Connect the exhaust pipe at the manifold.

28. Install the air conditioning compressor and power steering pump. Adjust the belt as described under Alternator Belt Tension Adjustment.

29. Reconnect:
   a. the accelerator cable,
   b. the automatic transmission vacuum modulator line and the air conditioning vacuum line,
   c. the fuel line, and the TCS hose,
   d. the Powerglide transmission throttle valve linkage or the Turbo Hydra-Matic 250–350 detent cable.

30. Attach the following electrical connections:
   a. alternator
   b. coil
   c. starter solenoid
   d. oil pressure switch
   e. temperature switch
   f. TCS transmission switch
   g. TCS solenoid
   h. engine ground strap

31. Replace the air cleaner and install these hoses:
   a. vent tube at air cleaner base
   b. carburetor bowl vent
   c. PCV vacuum line
   d. vacuum canister hose

32. Install the radiator, radiator panel or shroud, spacer, and fan.

33. Connect the heater hoses and the radiator hoses. Fill the cooling system. Refer to the Anti-Freeze Charts in the Appendix and the Capacities Chart in Chapter 1.

34. Connect the battery cables. Start the engine, watching for leaks. Remember to remove the bolt from the hood hold-open link.

4 CYL. 151 ENGINE

1. Disconnect the negative battery cable. Remove the air cleaner assembly and heat pipe.

2. Scribe the outline of the hood hinges on the hood and remove the hood.

3. Drain the cooling system and disconnect the radiator and heater hoses from the engine.

4. Disconnect the engine ground strap from the cylinder head. Remove the fan shroud.

5. Disconnect and tag all vacuum lines and electrical leads from the engine.

6. Disconnect the throttle linkage. Disconnect the fuel line from the fuel pump. Remove the clutch equalizer on manual transmission cars.

7. If the car is equipped with an automatic transmission, disconnect the cooler lines from the radiator. If equipped with power steering or air conditioning, remove the pump and bracket or compressor and bracket from the engine without disconnecting the lines.

CAUTION: *Disconnecting the air conditioner lines could result in personal injury.*

8. Remove the radiator. Remove the fan, if necessary to gain working clearance. Raise the car and drain the enging oil.

9. Disconnect the exhaust pipe from the manifold.

10. On models with A/C, remove the converter cover, the three retaining bolts and slide the converter to the rear. On models with manual transmission, disconnect the clutch linkage and remove the clutch cross shaft.

11. Remove the four lower bell housing bolts.

12. Disconnect the transmission filler tube support and the starter wire harness.

13. Remove the front motor mount bolts and lower the car.

14. Using a jack, support the transmission. Support the engine using a drop chain.

15. Remove the remaining bell housing bolts and raise the transmission slightly.

16. Pull the engine forward and upward to remove.

17. Reverse the above to install.

V8 AND V6

1. Disconnect the negative battery cable. Remove the air cleaner assembly and heat pipe.

2. Scribe the outline of the hood hinges on the hood and remove the hood.

3. Drain the cooling system and disconnect the radiator and heater hoses from the engine.

4. Drain the engine oil and transmission fluid.

5. Disconnect the exhaust pipes at the manifold.

6. Remove the flywheel or converter underpan.

7. On automatic transmissions, remove the converter-to-flywheel retaining bolts and install a converter retaining strap.

8. Remove the accessible converter housing or flywheel housing-to-engine bolts.

9. Remove the transmission cooler lines from the retaining clips on the side of the engine.

10. Remove the engine front mounting bolts at the frame brackets and lower the car.

11. Remove the radiator panel or shroud.

12. Remove the radiator and fan.

13. Disconnect the heater hose from the water pump and manifold.

14. Remove the air cleaner.

15. Disconnect the electrical leads from:
• alternator
• distributor
• starter solenoid
• oil pressure switch
• engine temperature switch
• temperature gauge switch
• choke secondary pull-off solenoid

16. Unclip the wiring harness from the rocker cover and position it out of the way.

17. Disconnect the automatic transmission vacuum modulator and air conditioning vacuum line from the manifold.

18. Disconnect the rubber fuel line at the rear of the engine.

19. Disconnect the following:
• canister vacuum hose at the carburetor
• accelerator at the carburetor and manifold bracket
• air conditioning blower delay lead at the rear of the engine.

20. On air conditioned cars, remove the compressor from its mount. Do not disconnect any fittings. Secure the compressor to the fender.

21. Disconnect the power steering pump and lay it aside.

22. Install a floor jack under the transmission.

23. Install a hoist on the engine and raise the engine slightly to take the weight off the engine mounts. Remove the remaining engine to transmission bolts.

24. Remove the engine from the car.

To install the engine:

25. Install transmission-to-engine guide pins, made from ⅜ in. bolts with the heads cut off, into the engine.

26. Install the engine, aligning the engine with the transmission housing.

27. Align the engine mounts with the frame brackets and lower the engine onto the brackets. Loosely install the engine mount bolts.

28. Remove the guide pins and install the engine-to-housing bolts. Remove the lifting equipment.

29. Remove the support from the transmission and raise and support the car.

30. Remove the converter retaining strap and install and tighten the engine-to-housing bolts.

31. Tighten the engine front mount bolts.

32. Install the converter to the flywheel.

33. Install the flywheel cover or converter underpan.

34. Install the transmission cooler lines in the clips on the side of the block.

35. Connect the exhaust pipe at the manifold and lower the car.

36. Install the air conditioning compressor and power steering pump. Adjust the drive belts.

37. Connect the following:
• canister vacuum hose to carburetor
• Accelerator cable to carburetor and manifold bracket
• air conditioning blower delay lead at side of engine
• Fuel line to rubber hose at rear of engine
• air conditioning vacuum line.

38. Install the electrical harness in the clip in the rocker cover and connect the following:
• alternator
• distributor
• starter solenoid
• oil pressure switch

- engine temperature switch
- temperature gauge switch
- choke secondary pull-off solenoid.

39. Connect the heater hose at the water pump and at the manifold.

40. Install the radiator, fan, radiator panel or shroud, fill the cooling system, add engine oil and fill the transmission.

41. Install the air cleaner.

42. Connect the battery cables, start the engine and check for leaks.

Cylinder Head

REMOVAL AND INSTALLATION

4 cyl. 140 Engine

1. Remove the timing belt cover and the camshaft cover.

2. Drain or siphon out the coolant.

3. Remove the timing belt and camshaft timing sprocket.

4. Remove the intake and exhaust manifolds.

5. Disconnect the upper radiator hose.

6. Unbolt the ten cylinder-head bolts and remove the head. If the head sticks, operate the starter to loosen it by compression or rap it upward with a soft hammer. Do not force anything between the head and block.

7. Do not place the head upright after it is removed; the valves may be damaged.

8. If a valve job is to be done, remove the camshaft as described later in this Chapter. After this, procedures are similar to those for any cast-iron cylinder head. Refer to the Engine Rebuilding Section.

9. Install the new gasket with the smooth side up.

10. Guide the cylinder head into place.

11. Coat the head bolt threads with anti-seize compound. Install them finger tight with the lifting bracket under the second bolt from the front on the spark plug side. The shorter bolts belong on the spark plug side.

12. Tighten the head bolts in the sequence shown in several stages until the correct torque is reached. The bolts should be torqued again after the first 500 miles or so.

13. Replace the radiator hose and install the manifolds.

14. Replace the timing belt and sprocket, engine front cover, and camshaft cover with a new gasket.

15. Refill the cooling system.

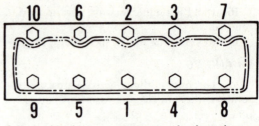

Cylinder head torque sequence—4 cyl. engines

4 Cyl. 151 eng.

1. Drain the cooling system.

2. Disconnect the accelerator cable at the bellcrank, and the manifold vacuum and fuel lines at the carburetor.

3. Remove the intake and exhaust manifolds.

4. Remove the alternator and power steering pump.

5. Disconnect all electrical connectors at the head.

6. Disconnect the radiator and heater hoses, and the battery ground strap.

7. Remove the spark plugs.

8. Remove the rocker arm cover, rocker arms, and push rods.

9. Unbolt and remove the cylinder head.

10. Clean the gasket surfaces thoroughly.

11. Install a new gasket over the dowels and position the cylinder head.

12. Coat the head bolt threads with sealer and install finger tight.

13. Tighten the bolts in sequence, in three equal steps to the specified torque.

14. Install all parts in the reverse of removal.

V6 engines

1. Disconnect the battery.

2. Drain the coolant.

3. Remove the air cleaner.

4. Remove the air conditioning compressor, *but do not disconnect any lines*. Disconnect the AIR hose at the check valve.

5. Remove the intake manifold.

6. When removing the right cylinder head, loosen the alternator belt, disconnect the wiring and remove the alternator. If equpped with A/C, remove the compressor from the mounting bracket and position it out of the way. Do not disconnect any of the hoses.

7. When removing the left cylinder head, except Skylark, remove the dipstick, power steering pump and air pump if so equipped.

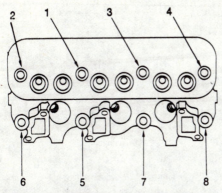

Cylinder head torque sequence—V6 engines

8. Disconnect and label the plug wires.

9. Disconnect exhaust manifold from the head being removed.

10. Remove the rocker arm cover and rocker shaft assembly. Lift out the push rods. Be extremely careful to avoid getting dirt into the valve lifters. Keep the pushrods in order; they must be returned to their original positions.

12. Remove the cylinder head bolts.

13. Remove the cylinder head and gasket.

14. Reverse the above steps to install. Torque the head bolts to specifications in three steps.

V8 Engines

1. Drain the coolant.

2. Remove the intake manifold.

3. Remove the exhaust manifolds.

4. Back off the rocker arm nuts and pivot the rocker arms out of the way so that the pushrods can be removed. Identify the pushrods so that they can be reinstalled in their original locations.

5. Remove the cylinder head bolts and cylinder heads.

6. Install using new gaskets. The head gasket is installed with the bead up.

NOTE: *Coat a steel gasket on both sides with sealer. If a steel/asbestos gasket is used, do not apply sealer. Clean the bolt*

threads, *apply sealing compound and install the bolts finger tight.*

7. Tighten the head bolts a little at a time in the sequence illustrated.

8. Install the exhaust and intake manifolds as described previously.

9. Adjust the rocker arms for zero lash. Crank the engine until the No. 1 piston is at TDC of its compression stroke (the compression can be felt by placing a finger over the spark plug hole or by feeling the valves as the timing mark passes "0"—if the valves don't move, the No. 1 piston is at the top of its compression stroke). With the crankshaft in this position the following valves may be adjusted:

Exhaust—1, 3, 4, 8

Intake—1, 2, 5, 7

Rotate the crankshaft one full revolution until the timing pointer is again aligned with the "0." With the crankshaft thus in No. 6 cylinder firing position, the following valves may be adjusted:

Exhaust—2, 5, 6, 7

Intake—3, 4, 6, 8

10. Turn the adjusting nut until all lash is removed from the valve train. This can be determined by checking pushrod side-play while turning the adjustment. When all play has been removed, turn the adjusting nut one more turn except n '76 and '77 engines. On these, turn the nut ¾ turn. This will place the lifter plunger in the center of its travel.

Valve Guides

Valve guides are integral with the cylinder head on all engines. Valve guide bores may be reamed to accommodate oversize valves. If wear permits, valve guides can be knurled to allow the retention of standard valves. Maximum allowable valve stem-to-guide bore clearances are listed under valve specifications.

Overhaul

For cylinder head overhaul procedures, see "Engine Rebuilding" following this chapter.

Rocker Arm and Shaft
REMOVAL AND INSTALLATION
V6 Engines

NOTE: *All of the V6 engines use rocker arm shafts, while the other engines use separate rocker arms mounted on studs.*

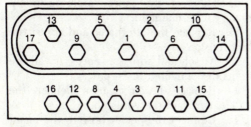

Cylinder head torque sequence—V8 engines

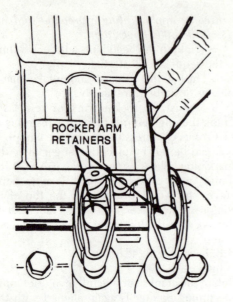

Removing the nylon rocker arm retainer—V6 engines

Intake manifold bolts and roll pins—4 cyl. 140 engine

1. Remove the rocker arm cover.
2. Remove the rocker arm shaft assembly bolts and the assembly.
3. Remove the nylon arm retainers by prying them out.
4. Remove the rocker arms.
5. Install the rocker arms on the shaft and lubricate them with oil.
6. Center each arm on the ¼ in. hole in the shaft. Install new nylon rocker arm retainers in the holes using a ½ in. drift.
7. Locate the push rods in the rocker arms and insert the shaft-to-cylinder head bolts. Tighten the bolts a little at a time until they are tightened to 30 ft lbs.
8. Install the rocker cover and use a new gasket.

Intake Manifold

REMOVAL AND INSTALLATION

4 cyl. 140 Engine

1. Disconnect the battery ground cable. Remove the clamps holding the EGR tube to the intake and exhaust manifolds. Remove the end of the tube in the exhaust manifold and try to twist the tube free. If this is impossible, use a drift to force it loose.
2. Drain or siphon out the coolant.
3. Disconnect the heater hose from the intake manifold.
4. Disconnect the vent tube and remove the air cleaner.
5. Remove the bolt holding the air

cleaner silencer to the heat stove tube and remove the silencer.
6. Disconnect:
 a. the choke rod from the carburetor,
 b. the PCV valve from the camshaft cover,
 c. the fuel line from the carburetor,
 d. the carburetor bowl vent line,
 e. the throttle linkage, and
 f. the Powerglide transmission throttle valve linkage or the Turbo Hydra-Matic 250.
7. Disconnect the power steering pump brace from the manifold. Remove the bolt holding (the alternator to the thermostat housing (radiator hose connection), loosen the swivel bolt and move the alternator out of the way.
8. Remove the four bolts and remove the manifold and carburetor.
9. Clean off the gasket surfaces before installation.
10. Place a new gasket over the locating dowels and replace the manifold. Install and tighten the bolts to 30 ft lbs. On the standard engine, the third bolt may be replaced by a stud.
11. Connect the power steering pump brace to the manifold.
12. Replace the alternator and adjust the belt tension.
13. Attach and adjust as necessary all the items disconnected in Step 6.
14. Replace the air cleaner silencer, the air cleaner, and the vent tube.
15. Connect the heater hose to the manifold. Raise the vehicle and from underneath

using a brass drift, install the EGR tube, then install the clamps on the ends of the tube.

16. Refill the cooling system. Refer to the Anti-Freeze Charts in the Appendix and the Capacities Chart in Chapter 1.

17. Connect the battery ground cable.

18. Start the engine and check for leaks.

V6 Engines

1. Disconnect the negative battery cable and drain the radiator.

2. Remove the air cleaner.

3. Disconnect the upper radiator hose and the heater hose at the manifold.

4. Disconnect the accelerator linkage at the carburetor and the linkage bracket at the manifold. Remove the cruise control chain, if so equipped.

5. Remove the fuel line from the carburetor and the booster vacuum pipe from the manifold.

6. On 1975–76 models, disconnect the choke pipe at the choke housing.

7. Disconnect and label the transmission vacuum modulator line, idle stop solenoid wire (if so equipped), distributor wires and the temperature sending unit wire.

8. Disconnect and mark the vacuum hoses at the distributor and the carburetor.

9. Disconnect the coolant bypass hose at the manifold.

10. On six cylinder models, remove the distributor cap and wires to gain access to the Torx® head bolt. Remove the bolt.

11. Remove the throttle linkage springs.

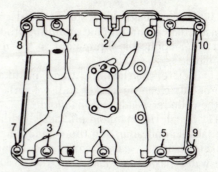

Intake manifold torque sequence—V6 engines

On 1975–76 models, remove the spark plug wires.

12. Remove the A/C compressor top bracket, if so equipped.

13. Remove the manifold.

14. Use a new gasket to install. Use sealer on the ends of the rubber gasket seals. Carefully guide the manifold onto the engine block dowel pin. Tighten the bolts in sequence, as illustrated. Reverse the removal procedure to install.

V8 Engines

1. Remove the air cleaner.

2. Drain the radiator.

3. Disconnect:

a. Battery cables at the battery.

b. Upper radiator and heater hoses at the manifold.

c. Crankcase ventilation hoses as required.

d. Fuel line at the rubber hose.

e. Accelerator linkage at the pedal lever.

f. Vacuum hose at the distributor.

g. Power brake hose at the accelerator bracket.

h. Ignition coil and temperature sending switch wires.

i. Air diverter valve line.

j. Choke pull-off lead.

k. Air conditioning bracket or power steering brace.

l. Choke hot and cold air pipes.

4. Remove the distributor cap and scribe the rotor position relative to distributor body.

5. Remove the distributor.

6. If applicable, remove the Delcotron upper bracket.

7. Remove the air pump.

8. Remove the manifold to head attaching bolts, then remove the manifold and carburetor as an assembly.

TORX® HEAD BOLT

TORX® head bolt—V6 engine

9. If the manifold is to be replaced, transfer the carburetor (and mounting studs), and other applicable equipment to the new manifold.

10. Before installing the manifold, thoroughly clean the gasket and seal surfaces of the cylinder heads and manifold.

11. Install the manifold end seals, folding the tabs if applicable, and the manifold/head gaskets, using a sealing compound around the water passages. Make sure the gaskets are firmly cemented in place before installing the manifold.

12. When installing the manifold, care should be taken not to dislocate the end seals, it is helpful to use a pilot in the distributor opening. Tighten the manifold bolts to the proper torque in the sequence illustrated.

13. Install the distributor with the rotor in its original location as indicated by the scribe line. If the engine has been disturbed, refer to Distributor Removal and Installation.

14. If applicable, install the Delcotron upper bracket and adjust the belt tension.

15. Install the air pump. Adjust all drive belts.

16. Connect all components disconnected in Step 3 above.

17. Fill the cooling system, start the engine, check for leaks and adjust the ignition timing and carburetor idle speed and mixture.

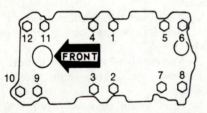

Intake manifold torque sequence—V8 engines

4 Cyl. 151 Engine

1977–78

NOTE: *In 1977 and 1978 the intake and exhaust manifolds were fastened together to utilized exhaust heat for intake and carburetor warm up.*

1. Remove the air cleaner and ducts.
2. Disconnect the fuel and vacuum lines.
3. Disconnect the electrical connectors.
4. Disconnect the carburetor linkage and remove the carburetor and heat shield.
5. Disconnect the exhaust pipe from the manifold.

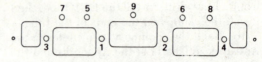

BOLT TORQUE 35 LB.FT.

Manifold torque sequence—151 engine (1977–78)

6. Unbolt and remove the manifold assembly from the head.

7. Disconnect the EGR pipe and remove the four manifold attaching bolts.

8. Installation is the reverse of removal. When assembling the manifolds for installation, do the following:

   a. position the two manifolds together and loosely install the four bolts.

   b. place the manifolds on a straight, flat surface.

   c. Hold the manifolds securely while tightening the bolts. Failure to follow this procedure could result in stress cracking.

NOTE: *The perforated side of the gasket always faces the intake manifold.*

1979 AND LATER

1. Remove the air cleaner. Drain the cooling system.

2. Disconnect and label the fuel line, all vacuum lines and electrical connectors from the carburetor, insulator and the intake manifold.

3. Disconnect the throttle linkage.

4. Remove the carburetor and insulator.

5. Remove the alternator rear support bracket from the manifold.

6. Remove the intake manifold bolts and remove the manifold.

7. To install, place a new gasket against the cylinder head, then install the manifold in place by starting all bolts finger tight.

8. Torque the intake manifold bolts to 25 ft lbs in two stages, using the torque sequence shown. The rest of installation is the reverse of removal.

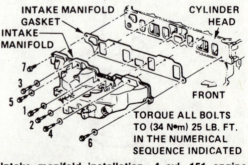

Intake manifold installation—4 cyl. 151 engine (1979 and later)

Exhaust Manifold

REMOVAL AND INSTALLATION

4 cyl. 140 engine

1. Disconnect the exhaust pipe from the manifold.

2. Remove the intake manifold.

3. Disconnect the oil dipstick bracket.

4. Remove the eight bolts and the manifold.

5. The longer bolts belong on the bottom; the first and fourth bolts are selflocking. Transfer the heat shroud.

6. Bolt the manifold in place, torquing the bolts to 30 ft lbs.

7. Connect the exhaust pipe.

8. Connect the dipstick bracket.

9. Replace the intake manifold.

4 Cyl 151 Engine

1977–1978

NOTE: *In 1977 and 1978 the intake and exhaust manifolds were fastened together. Follow the procedure given for Intake Manifold Removal and Installation.*

1979 AND LATER

1. Remove the air cleaner and the hot air tube.

2. Disconnect the exhaust pipe from the manifold at the flange. Spray the bolts first with penetrating lubricant, if necessary.

3. Remove the engine oil dipstick bracket bolt.

4. Remove the exhaust manifold bolts and remove the manifold from the head.

5. To install, place a new gasket against

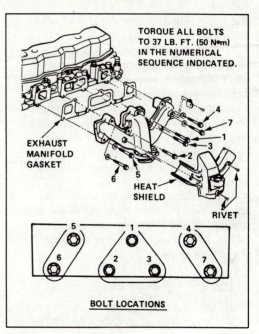

TORQUE ALL BOLTS TO 37 LB. FT. (50 N•m) IN THE NUMERICAL SEQUENCE INDICATED.

EXHAUST MANIFOLD GASKET

HEAT SHIELD

RIVET

BOLT LOCATIONS

Exhaust manifold installation—4 cyl. 151 engine

the cylinder head, then install the exhaust manifold over it. Start all the bolts into the head finger tight.

6. Torque the exhaust manifold bolts to 37 ft lbs in two stages, using the torque sequence illustrated.

7. The remainder of installation is the reverse of removal.

V6 Engines

1. Jack up the car and support with axle stands.

2. Remove the crossover pipe.

3. When removing the right side manifold disconnect the choke pipe.

4. When removing the left side manifold disconnect the EFE pipe.

5. Remove the exhaust manifold bolts and remove the manifold.

6. To install reverse the above procedure and torque the bolts to specifications.

V8 Engines

RIGHT SIDE

1. Disconnect the negative battery cable.

2. On air conditioned cars, remove the emission vapor canister. Without disconnecting any lines, remove the air conditioning compressor and place it out of the way.

3. Raise the car and disconnect the exhaust pipe from the manifold. Remove the

EXHAUST MANIFOLD BOLTS - 30 FT. LBS.

Exhaust manifold bolts—4 cyl. 140 engine

engine mount-to-frame bolts and slide the engine to the left.

4. Lower the car and disconnect the spark plug wires and temperature sender wire. Remove the alternator and alternator bracket from the exhaust manifold.

5. Remove No. 6 and 8 spark plugs and the six manifold attaching bolts. Remove the spark plug shields from the brackets and bend the brackets upward.

6. Remove the exhaust manifold and EFE valve as an assembly.

7. Installation is the reverse of removal. On installation, be sure to clean the mating surfaces of the manifold and cylinder head, adjust belt tension where necessary, and align the engine.

LEFT SIDE

1. Disconnect the negative battery cable.

2. Raise the car and disconnect the exhaust pipe from the manifold.

3. Remove the engine mount-to-frame bolts and slide the engine to the right.

4. Remove the two rear manifold bolts, then raise the engine and place a 6 in. piece of 2 x 4 wood block under the left engine mount.

5. Lower the car, remove the air cleaner and dipstick tube bracket nut, and move the dipstick tube aside.

6. Remove the remaining attaching bolts and remove the manifold.

7. To install, clean the mating surfaces of the manifold and cylinder head, install the manifold and the front four attaching bolts, and start the two rear bolts.

8. Install the dipstick tube bracket and air cleaner. Raise the car and remove the block from under the left engine mount.

9. Tighten the two rear manifold attaching bolts and connect the exhaust pipe to the manifold. Align and install the engine mount-to-frame bolts.

10. Lower the car and connect the negative battery cable.

Timing Belt Cover—4 cyl 140 eng.

The timing belt cover is divided into three sections: the front cover, the cover behind the camshaft sprocket, and the cover in front of the crankshaft sprocket. 1972 and later models have additional shields attached to the front cover.

REMOVAL AND INSTALLATION
Front Cover

1. Disconnect the battery ground cable.

2. Remove the fan and spacer.

3. Remove the upper bolt and loosen the two lower bolts.

4. Remove the cover.

5. Reverse the procedure for installation, torquing the fan bolts to 20 ft lbs for safety.

Camshaft Sprocket Cover

1. Remove the front cover, timing belt, and camshaft sprocket.

2. Remove the three bolts, the seal, and the cover assembly.

3. If the seal is worn, pry it from the retainer and install a new one flush with the retainer.

4. Place a new gasket over the end of the camshaft.

5. Replace the cover assembly. Torque the bolts to 15 ft lbs.

6. Replace the camshaft sprocket, timing belt, and front cover.

Crankshaft Sprocket Cover

1. Disconnect the battery ground cable.

2. Loosen and remove the accessory drive belts.

3. Remove the crankshaft pulley bolt, the four sprocket-to-pulley bolts, and remove the pulley (or torsional damper) and washer.

4. Remove the two bolts holding the front cover to the crankshaft sprocket cover. Remove the two bolts holding the sprocket cover and remove the sprocket cover.

5. When replacing the sprocket cover, use an anti-seize compound on the bolts.

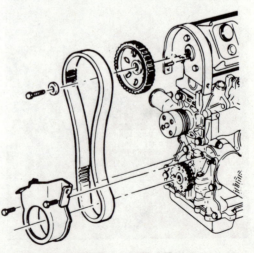

Timing belt installation—4 cyl. 140 eng.

6. Bolt the front cover to the sprocket cover.

7. Position the pulley and washer (or damper) to the sprocket, aligning the pulley tang with the crankshaft keyway. Insert the locating dowel on the damper in the locating hole in the sprocket.

8. Install the four bolts, then the crankshaft bolt. Torque the four bolts to 15 ft lbs and the crankshaft bolt to 80 ft lbs.

9. Replace and adjust the accessory drive belts.

10. Connect the battery ground cable.

Timing Belt—4 cyl. 140 eng

The timing belt does not require periodic adjustments. However, it must be adjusted whenever the belt has been slackened or removed for any reason.

CHECKING AND ADJUSTMENT

1. Loosen the two lower front cover bolts and remove the two upper bolts.

2. Tilt the front cover forward at the top to allow access to the belt.

3. The adjustment must be checked with a belt tension gauge. The correct tension is 100–140 lbs.

4. If the belt needs adjustment, drain or siphon the cooling system and remove the front cover.

5. Loosen the four water pump bolts.

6. A special tool is available to make this adjustment. This device is rotated with a torque wrench. It fits into the round hole in the square lug to the upper right (facing) of the water pump and bears against the water pump housing midway between the bolt holes. If the special tool is used, apply a

torque of 15 ft lbs against the water pump (and the belt). If the special tool is not available, apply a force to the pump in a similar manner. Tighten the pump bolts to 15 ft lbs.

7. Recheck the belt tension.

8. Replace the front cover and refill the cooling system.

NOTE: *Belt resonance at 650–700 rpm produces a sound very similar to that caused by a noisy water pump bearing. The sound is aggravated by excessive belt tension.*

REMOVAL AND INSTALLATION

1. Remove the front cover and the crankshaft sprocket cover, as previously described.

2. Drain or siphon the coolant.

3. Loosen the water pump bolts to relieve belt tension.

4. Remove the belt.

5. Align the camshaft sprocket mark with the notch in the camshaft sprocket cover (directly below the sprocket). Align the crankshaft sprocket mark with the tab on the oil pump casting (above the sprocket).

6. Place the belt on the crankshaft sprocket, align it in the water pump track, then install it to the camshaft sprocket. Make sure that both sprockets are still aligned.

7. Replace the crankshaft sprocket cover.

8. Check and adjust the belt tension, as previously described.

9. Refill the cooling system.

10. Replace the front cover.

NOTE: *On 1972 and later models, there is a hole in the back of the camshaft sprocket cover and in the back of the sprocket. Valve timing may be checked without removing the timing belt cover, by inserting a dowel into the hole in the cover and*

Belt adjustment—4 cyl. 140 eng.

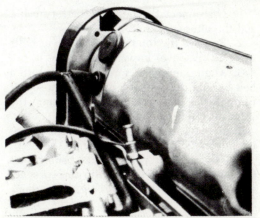

Hole for checking valve timing—4 cyl. 140 eng.

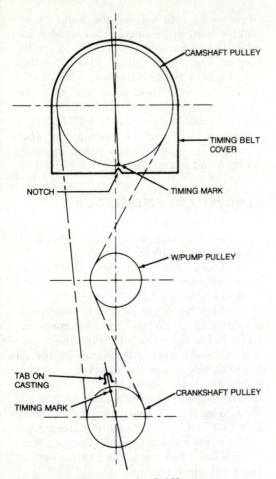

Timing belt alignment—4 cyl. 140 eng.

sprocket. The crankshaft timing mark should then be at TDC (0°).

SPROCKET REMOVAL AND INSTALLATION

Camshaft

1. Disconnect the negative battery cable and the alternator belt.

2. Remove the top timing belt cover bolts and pull the cover forward to remove it.

3. Align one of the sprocket holes with a bolt behind the sprocket and insert a socket through the hole onto the bolt to keep the sprocket from turning.

4. Remove the camshaft sprocket retaining bolt and pull the sprocket from the cam.

5. Replace the sprocket and timing belt *together*. Make sure the pin in the sprocket aligns in the camshaft hub hole, then check for proper belt alignment on the water pump.

6. Reinstall the timing belt cover and al-

ternator belt. Following this procedure, it is *not* necessary to adjust timing belt tension.

Crankshaft

1. Remove the front cover and the crankshft sprocket cover, as previously described. Remove the alternator/air conditioner pulley by first removing their drive belts, then removing the crankshaft-to-pulley bolt and the four sprocket-to-pulley bolt and the four sprocket-to-pully bolt and the four sprocket-to-pully bolts. After this the pulleys can be removed.

2. Remove the timing belt as previously described.

3. Bolt holes are provided in the sprocket for purposes of attaching a puller. Install a puller and remove the sprocket.

4. On installation, align the crankshaft key and make sure that the sprocket timing mark is facing out.

5. Force the sprocket into position with a nut and washer installed on the crankshaft pulley bolt.

6. Follow the procedure for timing belt installation. Proper torques are given under Crankshaft Sprocket Cover Installation. When installing the pulleys make sure that you align the tang on the pulley with the slot on the crankshaft sprocket.

Timing Gear Cover and Seal—4 Cyl. 151 Engine

REMOVAL AND INSTALLATION

1. Remove the crankshaft hub.

3. Remove the oil pan-to-front cover screws.

4. Remove the front cover-to-block screws.

5. Pull the cover slightly forward, just enough to allow cutting of the oil pan front seal flush with the block on both sides.

6. Remove the front cover and attached portion of the pan seal.

7. Clean the gasket surfaces thoroughly.

8. Cut the tabs from the new oil pan front seal.

9. Install the seal on the front cover, pressing the tips into the holes provided.

10. Coat the new gasket with sealer and position it on the front cover.

11. Apply an ⅛ in. bead of silicone sealer to the joint formed at the oil pan and block.

12. Align the front cover seal with a centering tool and install the front cover. Tighten the screws. Install the hub.

Timing Gear—4 Cyl. 151 Engine
REMOVAL AND INSTALLATION

NOTE: *Removal of the camshaft gear requires a special adapter #J-971 and the use of a press.*

1. Place the adapter on the press and place the camshaft through the opening.
2. Press the shaft out of the gear using a socket or other suitable tool.

CAUTION: *The thrust plate must be in position so that the woodruff key does not damage the gear when the shaft is pressed out.*

3. To install the gear firmly support the shaft at the back of the front journal in an arbor press using press plate adapters.
4. Place the gear spacer ring and thrust plate over the end of the shaft, and install the woodruff key in the shaft keyway.
5. Install the camshaft gear and press it onto the shaft until it bottoms against the gear spacer ring. The end clearance of the thrust plate should be .0015" to .0050". If less than .0015", the spacer ring should be replaced. If more than .0050", the thrust plate should be replaced.

Timing Chain, Cover Oil Seal, and Cover—V6 Engines
REMOVAL

1. Drain the cooling system.
2. Remove the radiator, fan, pulley and belt.
3. Remove the fuel pump and alternator.
4. Remove the distributor. If the timing chain and sprockets will not be disturbed, note the position of the distributor for installation in the same position.
5. Remove the thermostat bypass hose.
6. Remove the harmonic balancer.
7. Remove the timing chain-to-crankcase bolts.
8. Remove the oil pan-to-timing chain cover bolts and remove the timing chain cover.
9. Using a punch, drive out the old seal and the shedder toward the rear of the seal.
10. Coil the new packing around the opening so the ends are at the top. Drive in the shedder using a punch. Properly size the packing by rotating a hammer handle around the packing until the balancer hub can be inserted through the opening.
11. Align the timing marks on the sprockets.

12. Remove the camshaft sprocket bolt without changing the position of the sprocket. Remove the oil pan.
13. Remove the front crankshaft oil slinger.
14. Remove the camshaft sprocket bolts.
15. Using two large screwdrivers, carefully pry the camshaft sprocket and the crankshaft sprocket forward until they are free. Remove the sprockets and the chain.

INSTALLATION

1. Make sure, with sprockets temporarily installed, that No. 1 piston is at top dead center and the camshaft sprocket O-mark is straight down and on the centerline of both shafts.
2. Remove the camshaft sprocket and assemble the timing chain on both sprockets. Then slide the sprockets-and-chain assembly on the shafts with the O-marks in their closest together position and on a centerline with the sprocket hubs.
3. Assemble the slinger on the crankshaft with I.D. against the sprocket, (concave side toward the front of engine). Install the oil pan, if removed.
4. Install the camshaft sprocket bolts.
5. Install the distributor drive gear.
6. Install the drive gear and eccentric bolt and retaining washer. Torque to 40–55 ft lbs.
7. Install the timing case cover. Install a new seal by lightly tapping it in place. The lip of the seal faces inward. Pay particular attention to the following points.

   A. Remove the oil pump cover and pack the space around the oil pump gears completely full of petroleum jelly. There must be no air space left inside the pump. Reinstall the pump cover using a new gasket.

   B. The gasket surface of the block and timing chain cover must be clean and smooth. Use a new gasket correctly positioned.

   C. Install the chain cover being certain the dowel pins engage the dowel pin holes before starting the attaching bolts.

   D. Lube the bolt threads before installation and install them.

   E. If the car has power steering, the front pump bracket should be installed at this time.

   F. Lube the O.D. of the harmonic balancer hub before installation to prevent damage to the seal when starting the engine.

Timing Cover and Seal—V8 Engines

REMOVAL AND INSTALLATION

NOTE: *The timing case cover oil seal may be replaced without removing the case cover.*

After gaining access to the oil seal, pry the old seal out of the cover with a screwdriver. Then, lubricate the new seal and drive it into place with a seal installer tool.

1. Remove the fan belt, fan, and pulley.
2. Remove the radiator and shroud.
3. Remove the accessory drive pulley and the torsional damper retaining bolt.
4. Remove the damper from the crankshaft.
5. Remove the water pump.
6. Remove the front cover bolts and remove the front cover and gasket.
7. Clean the gasket mating surfaces.
8. Remove any oil pan gasket material that may still be adhering to the oil pan-engine block joint face.
9. Apply ⅛ in. bead of silicone sealant or the equivalent to the joint formed by the oil pan and cylinder block, as well as to the entire oil pan front lip.
10. Coat the cover gasket with gasket sealer and install it on the front cover.
11. Loosely install the front cover on the block. Install the 4 top bolts loosely (about 3 turns). Install two ¼-20x½ in. screws in the hole at each side of the front cover and apply a bead of sealant on the bottom of the seal and install it on the cover.
12. Tighten the screws evenly while aligning the dowel pins and holes in the front cover.
13. Remove the ¼-20x½ in. screws and install the rest of the cover screws.
14. Further installation is the reverse of removal. Refill the engine with oil.

Timing Chain—V8 Engines

REMOVAL AND INSTALLATION

1. Remove the harmonic balancer and timing gear cover as outlined above.
2. Crank the engine until the zero marks punched on both sprockets are closest to one another and in line between the shaft centers.
3. Remove the three bolts holding the camshaft sprocket to the camshaft. The gear will come off easily by tapping it with a rubber hammer.

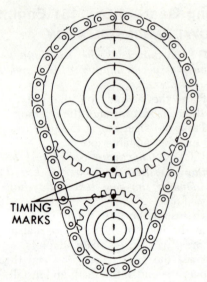

V8 timing marks

4. The chain can now be removed with the gear.
5. If the crankshaft gear is bad, it can be removed with a puller.
6. If removed, install the crankshaft gear but don't disturb the position of the crankshaft.
7. Install the timing chain on the camshaft gear and align the marks on the camshaft and crankshaft gears.
8. Install the camshaft gear and chain onto the camshaft, making sure that the locating dowel in the camshaft is inserted in the dowel hole in the gear. Tighten the three mounting bolts.

NOTE: *Do not hammer the camshaft gear into place or you may dislodge the plug at the rear of the camshaft.*

9. Lubricate the timing chain with engine oil.
10. Install the timing gear cover and harmonic balancer as outlined under Timing Cover and Seal-V-8 Engines Removal and Installation.

Camshaft

REMOVAL AND INSTALLATION

4 cyl 140 Engine

A special tool is required to remove the camshaft from the cylinder head. The camshaft can be removed with the engine in the car only if the front of the engine is raised and blocks are placed between the engine mounts and the body. The hood must also be removed.

1. Remove the hood if the engine is in

Camshaft removal tool in place—4 cyl. 140 eng.

Camshaft bearing replacement—4 cyl. 140 eng.

the car. The procedure is given in Chapter 10.

2. Remove the camshaft sprocket and camshaft sprocket cover as previously described.

3. Remove the air cleaner and camshaft cover.

4. Disconnect the carburetor fuel line and remove the idle solenoid from its bracket.

5. Remove the carburetor choke coil, cover, and rod assembly.

6. Remove the distributor.

7. Disconnect the front motor mounts and raise the front of the engine, being careful not to distort the oil pan. Place 1½ in. thick blocks between the mounts and the body.

8. Install the camshaft removal tool as follows:

    a. Align the attaching holes to the lower camshaft cover attaching holes.

    b. Align the tool tappet depressing lever so that each lever will depress both valves for each cylinder. Fit the levers into the notches between the tappets.

    c. Make sure that the bolts in the bottom of the tool are backed off.

    d. Bolt the tool in place firmly. Set the timing marks 90 degrees apart to make sure that none of the pistons are at TDC. This is important to prevent the valves from contacting the pistons.

    e. Lubricate the ball ends of the tool bolts and tighten them to depress the tappets. Use a torque wrench. If more than 10 ft lbs of force is required, check for correct tool installation, then continue carefully.

9. Carefully guide the camshaft out of the head.

10. If the camshaft bearings are to be replaced, they can be pulled or driven out. The oil holes in the three rear bearings must be aligned with the oil holes in the head. The oil

holes in the two front bearings must be placed in the 11 o'clock position (facing) and the oil groove in the front bearing must be toward the front of the engine.

11. Guide the camshaft into the head, being careful not to damage the bearings.

12. Install a new gasket and the camshaft retainer plate. Torque the bolts to 15 ft lbs.

13. Attach a dial indicator to the cylinder head and measure the camshaft end-play.

14. If end-play was not 0.004–0.012 in., a new retainer must be installed to allow correct end-play. Retainers are available in increments of 0.004 in., ranging from 0.226–0.238 in. This measurement is the thickness of the camshaft locator on the back of the retainer.

15. Release the tappet depressing levers and then remove the special tool.

16. Install the camshaft sprocket cover, the camshaft sprocket, and the timing belt as previously described.

17. Install the distributor as previously described.

18. Adjust the valve lash on mechanical lifters as detailed in Chapter 2. Place the hydraulic lifters in a can of clean oil before installation to coat them thoroughly.

19. Install the camshaft cover with a new gasket. Replace the choke assembly, idle solenoid, air cleaner, and fuel line.

20. Raise the front of the engine, being careful not to distort the oil pan. Remove the blocks and replace the engine mounts, making sure that no metal to metal contact is made. Replace the hood.

21. After the job is completed, check and adjust the ignition timing.

4 Cyl. 151 Engine

1. Drain the cooling system.
2. Remove the radiator.
3. Remove the fan and water pump pulley.

4. Remove the grille on Astre and Sunbird.

5. Remove the rocker cover, rocker arms, and pushrods.

6. Remove the distributor, spark plugs, and fuel pump.

7. Remove the pushrod cover and gasket. Remove the lifters.

8. Remove the crankshaft hub and timing gear cover.

9. Remove the two camshaft thrust plate screws by working through the holes in the gear.

10. Remove the camshaft and gear assembly by pulling it through the front of the block. Take care not to damage the bearings.

11. Install in the reverse order. Torque the thrust plate screws to 75 in. lbs.

V6 Engines

1. Drain the cooling system.

2. Remove the radiator, fan, and water pump pulley. If equipped with air conditioning, unbolt the condenser and position out of the way, without disconnecting any of the hoses. If this is not possible, have the system discharged by a mechanic trained in A/C work. Remove the grille.

3. Remove the intake manifold.

4. Remove the valve covers, rocker shaft assemblies, and pushrods. Keep these parts in order. They must be returned to their original positions.

5. Remove the distributor and fuel pump.

6. Remove the harmonic balancer, timing chain cover, timing chain and sprockets. Align the marks on the sprkcets before removal to avoid any damage to the camshaft upon removal.

7. Remove the hydraulic lifters, keeping them in order for installation.

8. Slide the camshaft forward, out of the bearing bores. Do this carefully, to avoid damage to the bearing surfaces and bearings.

9. Reverse to install. Clean all gasket surfaces thoroughly and use new gaskets. Lubricate the camshaft lobes with heavy oil before installation, and be careful not to contact any of the bearings with the cam lobes. Make sure that the camshaft timing marks are aligned with the crankshaft marks.

V8 Engines

1. Drain the cooling system and remove the radiator. Remove the hood.

2. Remove the water pump and the timing case cover.

3. Turn the crankshaft until the timing marks on the camshaft and crankshaft sprockets are aligned.

4. Remove the valve covers and loosen each rocker arm nut enough to turn the rocker to the side and remove the pushrods. Keep the pushrods in order when they are removed from the engine.

5. Remove the distributor cap and mark the position of the rotor relative to the distributor body and the position of the distributor body relative to the engine. Remove the distributor.

6. Remove the intake manifold, then remove the valve lifters from the engine. Keep the lifters in order when they are removed from the engine.

7. Remove the fuel pump.

8. Remove the timing chain and sprockets from the engine.

9. Install two $5/16$ in.-18x4 bolts in the holes in the front of the cam and carefully slide it out of the engine.

NOTE: *On some engine and model combinations it will be necessary to disconnect the motor mounts and jack up the front of the engine or remove the grille from the car in order to gain adequate clearance in front of the engine to get the camshaft out of the engine.*

10. Installation is the reverse of removal.

Pistons and Connecting Rods

Removal and installation procedures are covered in the engine rebuilding section at the end of the chapter. On all engines the letter F, or the notches in the edge of the piston, goes toward the front of the engine.

On the 151 4 cylinder engine the notch on the connecting rod should be opposite the notch on the piston. On the V6 engines the camfered corners of the bearing caps should face toward the front on the left bank and toward the rear on the rightbank. The boss on the connecting rod should face towards the front of the engine for the right bank and toward the rear of the engine on the left bank. On the V8 engines the tang on the connecting rod bearing faces away from the camshaft.

Be sure that the pistons and rods are installed in their original location. It is always a good idea to mark the cylinder number on all pistons, connecting rods and caps on removal.

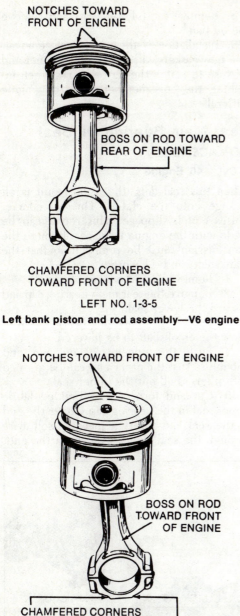

Left bank piston and rod assembly—V6 engine

Right bank piston and rod assembly—V6 engine

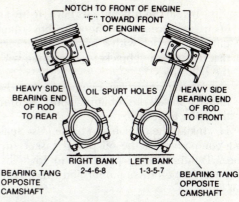

Piston-to-rod relationship—V8 engine

ENGINE LUBRICATION

Oil Pan

REMOVAL AND INSTALLATION

4 Cyl. 140 Engine

1. Raise and support the vehicle with jackstands under the lower control arms and rear axle. Drain the engine oil. Raise the front of the engine slightly to take the weight off the mounts, being careful not to distort the pan.

2. Support the engine with a jack and remove the frame crossmember and both front crossmember braces.

3. Disconnect the steering idler arm at the frame side rail. On vehicles with air conditioning, disconnect the idler arm at the relay rod.

4. Mark the position of the steering linkage pitman arm to the steering gear pitman shaft and remove the pitman arm.

NOTE: *Do not rotate the steering gear pitman shaft while the linkage is disconnected, because the steering wheel alignment will be changed.*

5. Remove the flywheel lower cover or converter underpan.

6. Remove the oil pan bolts, tap the oil pan to break the seal, then remove the pan.

7. Disconnect the exhaust pipe from the manifold and move it out of the way.

8. Remove the pick-up screen-to-support retaining bolt and the pick-up screen-to-baffle support bolts, then remove the support from the baffle.

9. Remove the bolt which secures the oil drain back tube to the baffle, then rotate the baffle 90° toward the left side of the car and remove the baffle from the pick-up screen.

10. The oil pump screen and pick up tube may be removed as follows:

a. Remove the two self-locking mounting bolts (in block).

b. Lightly tap on the U section of the pick-up tube to remove the tube from the casting.

c. If damaged, the tube and screen assembly are replaced as a unit.

d. Apply sealing compound to the pick-up tube sealing surface.

e. Install the tube into its bore, using an open end wrench on the tube boss, tapping the wrench with a mallet. Make sure that the retaining brackets are aligned with the bolt holes.

f. Using anti-seize compound on the threads, install the retaining bolts. Tighten the bolts to 25 ft lbs.

11. Install the oil pan and baffle. Use sealing compound on the oil pump gasket surface. Tighten the oil pan bolts to 15 ft lbs. Tighten frame crossmember and brace bolts to 35 ft lbs.

4 Cyl. 151 Engine

1. Disconnect the battery ground cable.
2. Drain the oil.
3. Remove the rear section of the crossmember.
4. Disconnect the exhaust pipe at the manifold and loosen the hanger bracket.
5. Remove the starter.
6. Remove the flywheel housing inspection cover.
7. Disconnect the steering linkage at the steering gear and idler arm support.
8. Remove the pan retaining bolts and remove the pan.
9. Thoroughly clean the gasket surfaces and install the pan in the reverse order of removal. The bolts into the timing gear cover should be installed last.

V6 Engines

1. Raise the car and drain the oil.
2. Remove the flywheel cover.
3. Remove the exhaust crossover pipe.
4. Remove the oil pan attaching bolts and remove the oil pan.
5. Thoroughly clean the gasket surfaces and install the pan in the reverse order of removal.

V8 Engines

1. Disconnect the battery.
2. Raise the car and drain the oil.
3. Disconnect the exhaust crossover pipe.
4. Remove the converter housing underpan and splash shield.
5. Scribe marks on each side of the frame crossmember and support the engine. Remove the frame crossmember.
6. Disconnect the steering idler arm at the frame side rail.
7. Disconnect the starter brace and remove the starter.

8. Remove the oil pan bolts and remove the oil pan.
9. Installation is the reverse of removal. Use new gaskets with sealer as a retainer and be sure to match the scribe marks when installing the crossmember. Fill the engine with oil.

Rear Main Bearing Oil Seal
REPLACEMENT
4 Cyl. 140 Engine

When this seal fails, the usual result is oil leakage onto the clutch. This, of course, causes clutch slippage. This repair can be made with the engine in place, although the transmission must be removed so that the crankshaft can be lowered.

1. Remove the oil pan and baffle.
2. Remove the rear main bearing cap and discard the lower seal.
3. Loosen the remaining bearing caps to allow the crankshaft to be lowered.
4. Push the upper seal on one end enough so that the other end can be grasped with pliers. Pull out the upper seal.
5. Cut and form a new braided fabric upper seal in the bearing cap. Taper the end of the seal and insert a piece of soft wire through the seal about ¼ in. from the end.

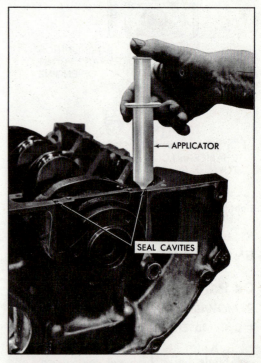

Applying the rear main bearing cap side sealant with a plunger applicator

Wrap the wire around the seal to form a secure attachment.

6. Thread the wire through the upper seal groove, then start the seal and pull it into position.

7. Tighten all the bearing caps except the rear cap to 65 ft lbs.

8. Cut the seal flush to $1/64$ in. below the bearing edge, making a clean cut and leaving no raveled edges.

9. Install and cut a seal in the rear main bearing cap.

10. Install the rear main bearing cap and measure the clearance with Plastigage, tightening the cap bolts to 65 ft lbs. If the bearing clearance is within specifications, the seal is properly seated.

11. Install the bearing cap, tightening to 65 ft lbs.

12. Install rear main bearing cap side sealant. This is available in a kit, with a plunger applicator. Force the compound firmly into place to ensure that there are no air bubbles.

13. Install the oil pan and baffle.

4 Cyl. 151 Engine
1977–78

1. Remove the oil pan.

2. Remove the rear bearing cap.

3. Remove the oil seal from its groove by prying at the bottom with a small screwdriver.

4. Clean and oil the crankshaft surface.

5. Coat a new seal with clean engine oil and insert it in the bearing cap groove. Take care to keep oil off the rear edge, since it is treated with sealant. Gradually push the seal into place with a hammer handle.

6. The upper seal half may be removed by tapping it out of its groove with a hammer and blunt punch.

7. Push the new seal into place with the lip toward the front of the engine.

8. Install the bearing cap with the bolts loose.

9. Move the crankshaft first to the rear and then to the front with a rubber mallet. This will correctly position the thrust bearing.

10. Torque the cap bolts to 65 ft lbs.

11. Install the oil pan.

1979 AND LATER

The rear main oil seal is a one piece unit, and is removed or installed without removal of the oil pan or crankshaft.

1. Remove the transmission, flywheel or torque converter bellhousing, and the flywheel or flex plate.

2. Remove the rear main oil seal with a screw driver. Be extremely careful not to scratch the crankshaft.

3. Oil the lips of the new seal with clean engine oil. Install the new seal by hand onto the rear crankshaft flange. The helical lip side of the seal should face the engine. Make sure the seal is firmly and evenly installed.

4. Replace the flywheel or flexplate, bellhousing and transmission.

V6 Engines
LOWER HALF

1. Remove the oil pan and rear main bearing cap.

2. Remove the old seal from the bearing cap and place a new seal in the groove with both ends projecting above the parting surface of the cap.

3. Force the seal into the groove by rubbing down with a hammer handle or smooth tool, until the seal projects above the groove not more than $1/16$ in. Cut the ends off flush with the surface of the cap. Use a razor blade.

4. Place new neoprene seals in the grooves in the sides of the bearing cap after soaking the seals in kerosene for a minute or two.

NOTE: *The neoprene composition seals will swell up once exposed to the oil and heat. It is normal for the seals to leak for a short time, until they become properly seated. The seals must not be cut to fit.*

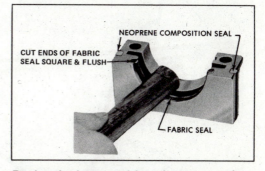

Forcing the lower seal into the groove using a smooth object such as a hammer handle

UPPER HALF

Although the factory recommends removing the crankshaft to replace the top half of the oil seal, the following procedure can be used without removing the crankshaft.

1. Remove the oil pan and rear main bearing cap.

2. Loosen the rest of the crankshaft main bearings and allow the crankshaft to drop about $1/16$ in.

3. Remove the old upper half of the oil seal.

4. Wrap some soft copper wire around the end of the new seal and leave about 12 in. on the end. Generously lubricate the new seal with oil.

5. Slip the free end of the copper wire into the oil seal groove and around the crankshaft. Pull the wire until the seal protrudes an equal amount on each side. Rotate the crankshaft as the seal is pulled into place.

6. Remove the wire. Push any excess seal that may be protruding back into the groove.

7. Before tightening the crankshaft bearing caps, visually check the bearings to make sure they are in place. Torque the bearing cap bolts to specifications. Make sure there is no oil on the parting surfaces.

8. Replace the oil pan. Run the engine slowly for the first few minutes of operation.

V8 Engines

The rear main bearing seal may be replaced without removing the crankshaft. Seals should only be replaced as a pair. Fabrication of a seal installation tool will prevent damaging the bead on the cylinder block. The seal lips should face the front of the engine when properly installed.

1. Remove the oil pan and pump, and remove the rear main bearing cap.

2. Pry the lower seal out of the bearing cap with a screwdriver, being careful not to gouge the cap surface.

3. Remove the upper seal by lightly tapping on one end with a brass pin punch until the other end can be grasped and pulled out with pliers.

4. Clean the bearing cap, cylinder block, and crankshaft mating surfaces with solvent. Inspect all these surfaces for gouges, nicks, and burrs.

5. Apply light engine oil to the seal lips and bead, but keep the seal ends clean.

6. Insert the tip of the installation tool between the crankshaft and the seal seat of the cylinder block. Place the seal between the tip of the tool and the crankshaft, so that the bead contacts the tip of the tool.

7. Be sure that the seal lip is facing the front of the engine, and work the seal around the crankshaft, using the installation tool to protect the seal from the corner of the cylinder block.

NOTE: *Do not remove the tool until the opposite end of the seal is flush with the cylinder block surface.*

8. Remove the installation tool, being careful not to pull the seal out at the same time.

9. Using the same procedure, install the lower seal into the bearing cap. Use your finger and thumb to lever the seal into the cap.

10. Apply sealer to the cylinder block only where the cap mates to the surface. Do not apply sealer to the seal ends.

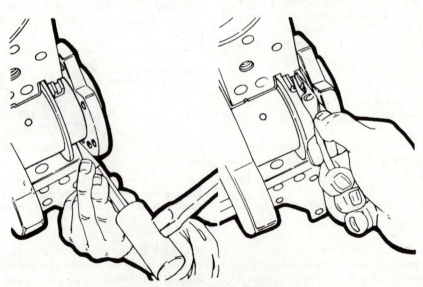

Rear main seal removal—V8 engines

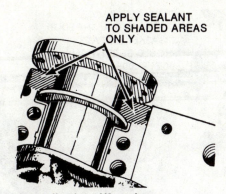

APPLY SEALANT
TO SHADED AREAS
ONLY

Sealant application—V8 engines

11. Install the rear cap and torque the bolts to specifications. Install the oil pan and pump.

Oil Pump

REMOVAL AND INSTALLATION

4 Cyl. 140 Engine

The oil pump casting also serves as the front cover of the crankcase. When running oil pressure drops below a safe level (2 psi), safety switch cuts off the current to the electric fuel pump, thus preventing engine damage.

1. Remove the following items as described earlier in this chapter:
   a. front cover and accessory drive pulleys
   b. crankshaft pulley
   c. timing belt
   d. crankshaft sprocket cover
   e. crankshaft sprocket
   f. oil pan and baffle

2. Remove the bolts and stud and remove the oil pump.

3. Clean all parts in a safe solvent and blow out the oil passages.

4. Remove the pressure regulating valve assembly from the top of the pump and check that it works freely.

5. Check the pump clearances. If the pump is worn, replace the entire unit as service parts are not available.

Measuring point	Clearance (in.)
Between outside of drive gear and pump case	0.0038–0.0068
Between outside of drive gear and crescent	0.0023–0.0093
Between inside of drive gear and crescent	0.0068–0.0148
Gear end clearance in case	0.0009–0.0023

6. If necessary, replace the seal as de-

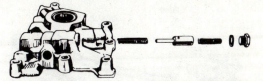

Oil pump pressure regulator—4 cyl. 140 engine

scribed under Crankcase Front Seal Removal and Installation.

7. Clean off the gasket surface on the engine block.

8. Lubricate the gears and the oil seal with engine oil.

9. Install the pump drive key in the crankshaft, align the pump driven gear with the key, and install the pump. Coat the bolt and stud threads with anti-seize compound. The stud belongs in the upper right (facing) hole. Torque the bolts to 15 ft lbs and the stud to 30 ft lbs.

10. Replace the baffle and oil pan.

11. Replace the rest of the parts removed in Step 1.

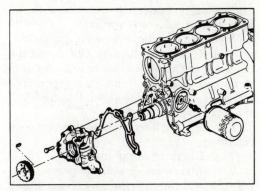

Oil pump-to-cylinder block—4 cyl. 140 engine

4 Cyl. 151 Engine

1. Remove the engine oil pan.

2. Remove pump attaching screws and carefully lower the pump.

3. Reinstall in reverse order. To ensure immediate oil pressure on start-up, the oil pump gear cavity should be packed with petroleum jelly.

V6 Engines

On the V6 and V8, the oil pump is located in the left side of the timing chain cover, where it is connected by a drilled passage in the cylinder crankcase to an oil screen housing and standpipe assembly.

1. Remove the oil filter.

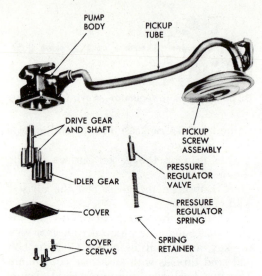

PUMP BODY
PICKUP TUBE
DRIVE GEAR AND SHAFT
PICKUP SCREW ASSEMBLY
PRESSURE REGULATOR VALVE
IDLER GEAR
PRESSURE REGULATOR SPRING
COVER
COVER SCREWS
SPRING RETAINER

Exploded view of oil pump—4 cyl. 151 engine

2. Unbolt the pump cover assembly from the timing chain cover.

3. Remove the cover assembly and slide out the pump gears.

4. Remove the oil pressure relief valve cap, spring, and valve. Do not remove the oil filter by-pass valve and spring.

5. Check that the relief valve spring isn't worn on its side or collapsed. Check that the relief valve is no more than an easy slip fit in its bore in the cover. If there is any perceptible sideplay, replace the valve. If there is still side-play, replace the cover.

6. Check the filter by-pass valve for good condition.

    To assemble the pump:

7. Lubricate and install the pressure relief valve and spring in the cover bore. Install the gasket and cap, torquing the cap to 35 ft lbs.

8. Install the gears and check that gear-to-cover end clearance is between 0.002–0.006 in. If the clearance is less, check the timing cover gear pocket for wear.

9. Remove the gears and pack the gear pocket full of petroleum jelly. Don't use grease.

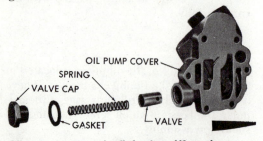

OIL PUMP COVER
SPRING
VALVE CAP
GASKET
VALVE

Oil pump cover and relief valve—V6 engine

CHECK CLEARANCE BETWEEN STRAIGHT EDGE & GASKET SURFACE SHOULD BE BETWEEN .002″ & .006″

Checking oil pump clearance—V6 engine

NOTE: *Unless the pump is primed this way, it won't produce any oil pressure when the engine is started.*

10. Install the gears. Install a new gasket and the cover. Torque the bolts evenly to 10 ft lbs. Replace the filter.

V8 Engines

1. Remove the oil pan.

2. Remove the bolt holding the oil pump to the rear main bearing cap.

3. Remove the pump and the extension shaft.

4. Installation is the reverse of removal. Align the slot on the top of the extension shaft with the drive tang on the lower end of the distributor driveshaft. The installed posi-

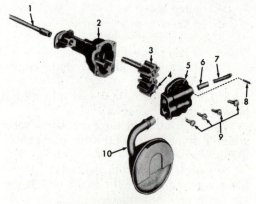

1. Shaft Extension
2. Pump body
3. Drive gear and shaft
4. Idler gear
5. Pump cover
6. Pressure regulator valve
7. Pressure regulator spring
8. Retaining pin
9. Screws
10. Pickup screen and pipe

Exploded view of oil pump—V8 engine

tion of the oil pump screen should be parallel to the oil pan rails.

To prime the oil pump, fill the gear cavity with engine oil. Do not use grease.

ENGINE COOLING

Radiator

REMOVAL AND INSTALLATION

All Models

1. Drain or siphon the coolant.
2. Remove the fan shroud on heavy duty cooling installation.
3. Disconnect the radiator hoses.
4. Remove the two bolts holding the radiator fan guard panel or the two radiator support bracket bolts on the heavy duty cooling system.
5. Lift the radiator up and out of the lower supports, being careful not to damage it.
6. Reverse the procedure for installation.

Water Pump

REMOVAL AND INSTALLATION

4 Cyl. 140 Engine

The pump bearings are permanently lubricated during manufacture and do not require periodic maintenance other than keeping the air vent (top of housing) and drain holes (bottom of housing) free of dirt and grease.

The pump components cannot be serviced separately and, in the event of pump failure, the complete assembly must be replaced as a unit, as follows:

1. Raise and support the hood.
2. Disconnect the negative battery cable.
3. Remove the fan.
4. Loosen, but do not remove, the two lower timing belt cover retaining screws. The holes in the cover are slotted so that the cover is easily removed.
5. Remove the two upper timing belt cover retaining screws and remove the cover.
6. Drain the coolant.
7. Loosen the water pump bolts to relieve the tension on the timing belt.
8. Remove the hoses from the water pump.
9. Remove the water pump bolts, pump and gasket.
10. Thoroughly clean the old gasket material from the pump and block.
11. To install, position the water pump on the block using a new gasket and loosely in-

Timing belt adjustment gauge hole—4 cyl. 140 engine

stall the water pump bolts. Make sure that the V grooves of the belt are aligned with the grooves in the water pump.

NOTE: *Use an anti-seize compound on the water pump bolt threads.*

12. A special tool is available to adjust the timing belt. It fits into the round hole in the square lug to the upper right (facing) of the water pump and bears against the pump housing midway between the bolt holes. If this tool is available, apply 15 ft lbs of torque against the water pump (and belt). If the tool is not available, apply a force to the pump in a similar manner. Tighten the pump bolts to 15 ft lbs.
13. Install the radiator and heater hoses to the pump.
14. Install the timing belt cover, lowering the cover lower screw slots over the screws. Loosely tighten the screws against the cover.
15. Install the two upper timing cover screws, then tighten the upper and lower screws to 50 in lbs.
16. Install the fan, tightening the bolts to 20 ft lbs.
17. Fill the cooling system, connect the battery negative cable, start the engine and check for leaks.

All Except 4 Cyl. 140 Engine

1. Drain the coolant from the radiator.
2. Loosen the fan pulley bolts.
3. If necessary, remove the alternator with the drive belt and brackets.
4. If necessary, remove the air pump with the drive belt and brackets.
5. Disconnect the lower radiator hose and the heater hose at the water pump.

6. Remove the fan and pulley.

7. Remove the pump-to-cylinder block and power steering-to-pump bolts and remove the water pump and old gasket.

8. Installation is the reverse of removal. Use a new gasket coated with sealer. Adjust the alternator and air pump drive belt tension. Fill the cooling system, run the engine and check for leaks.

Thermostat

REMOVAL AND INSTALLATION

The 4-140 and 4-151 thermostat is located in a housing at the cylinder head water outlet adjacent to the intake manifold. On the V6 and V8 engines, the thermostat is in the water outlet housing in the front of the intake manifold.

4 Cyl 140 Engine

1. Drain the cooling system.

2. Disconnect the upper radiator hose at the engine.

3. On models with the alternator attached to the water outlet, remove the retaining bolt and adjusting bolt, and position the alternator out of the way.

4. Unbolt the housing and remove the housing, gasket, and thermostat.

5. Replace the thermostat and housing, using a new gasket.

6. Install the alternator retaining bolt in the water outlet housing. (Use anti-sieze compound on the bolt threads). Install the alternator drive belt and adjust as outlined in the Charging System Section.

7. Replace the radiator hose, fill the cooling system, start the engine, and check for leaks.

All Except 4 Cyl. 140 Engine

1. Drain the coolant to a level below that of the water outlet housing.

2. Remove the radiator upper hose.

3. Remove the housing bolts and remove the water outlet housing and gasket.

4. Remove the thermostat.

5. Installation is the reverse of removal. Use a new gasket.

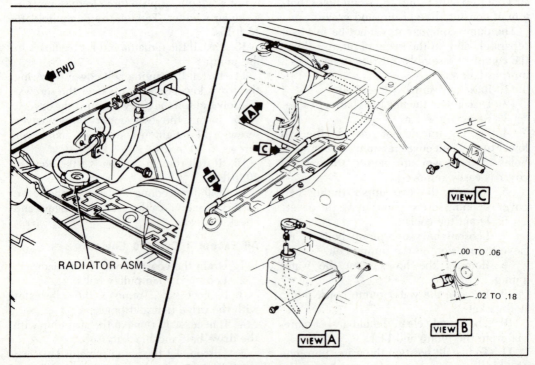

Typical coolant recovery systems

ENGINE REBUILDING

Most procedures involved in rebuilding an engine are fairly standard, regardless of the type of engine involved. This section is a guide to accepted rebuilding procedures. Examples of standard rebuilding practices are illustrated and should be used along with specific details concerning your particular engine, found earlier in this chapter.

The procedures given here are those used by any competent rebuilder. Obviously some of the procedures cannot be performed by the do-it-yourself mechanic, but are provided so that you will be familiar with the services that should be offered by rebuilding or machine shops. As an example, in most instances, it is more profitable for the home mechanic to remove the cylinder heads, buy the necessary parts (new valves, seals, keepers, keys, etc.) and deliver these to a machine shop for the necessary work. In this way you will save the money to remove and install the cylinder head and the mark-up on parts.

On the other hand, most of the work involved in rebuilding the lower end is well within the scope of the do-it-yourself mechanic. Only work such as hot-tanking, actually boring the block or Magnafluxing (invisible crack detection) need be sent to a machine shop.

Tools

The tools required for basic engine rebuilding should, with a few exceptions, be those included in a mechanic's tool kit. An accurate torque wrench, and a dial indicator (reading in thousandths) mounted on a universal base should be available. Special tools, where required, are available from the major tool suppliers. The services of a competent automotive machine shop must also be readily available.

Precautions

Aluminum has become increasingly popular for use in engines, due to its low weight and excellent heat transfer characteristics. The following precautions must be observed when handling aluminum (or any other) engine parts:
—Never hot-tank aluminum parts.
—Remove all aluminum parts (identification tags, etc.) from engine parts before hot-tanking (otherwise they will be removed during the process).

—Always coat threads lightly with engine oil or anti-seize compounds before installation, to prevent seizure.
—Never over-torque bolts or spark plugs in aluminum threads. Should stripping occur, threads can be restored using any of a number of thread repair kits available (see next section).

Inspection Techniques

Magnaflux and Zyglo are inspection techniques used to locate material flaws, such as stress cracks. Magnaflux is a magnetic process, applicable only to ferrous materials. The Zyglo process coats the matrial with a fluorescent dye penetrant, and any material may be tested using Zyglo. Specific checks of suspected surface cracks may be made at lower cost and more readily using spot check dye. The dye is sprayed onto the suspected area, wiped off, and the area is then sprayed with a developer. Cracks then will show up brightly.

Overhaul

The section is divided into two parts. The first, Cylinder Head Reconditioning, assumes that the cylinder head is removed from the engine, all manifolds are removed, and the cylinder head is on a workbench. The camshaft should be removed from overhead cam cylinder heads. The second section, Cylinder Block Reconditioning, covers the block, pistons, connecting rods and crankshaft. It is assumed that the engine is mounted on a work stand, and the cylinder head and all accessories are removed.

Procedures are identified as follows:

Unmarked—Basic procedures that must be performed in order to successfully complete the rebuilding process.

Starred (*)—Procedures that should be performed to ensure maximum performance and engine life.

Double starred (**)—Procedures that may be performed to increase engine performance and reliability.

When assembling the engine, any parts that will be in frictional contact must be pre-lubricated, to provide protection on initial start-up. Any product specifically formulated for this purpose may be used. NOTE: *Do not use engine oil. Where semi-permanent* (locked but removable) installation of bolts or nuts is desired, threads should be cleaned and located with Loctite ® or a similar product (non-hardening).

Repairing Damaged Threads

Several methods of repairing damaged threads are available. Heli-Coil® (shown here), Keenserts® and Microdot® are among the most widely used. All involve basically the same principle—drilling out stripped threads, tapping the hole and installing a pre-wound insert—making welding, plugging and oversize fasteners unnecessary.

Two types of thread repair inserts are usually supplied—a standard type for most Inch Coarse, Inch Fine, Metric Coarse and Metric Fine thread sizes and a spark plug type to fit most spark plug port sizes. Consult the individual manufacturer's catalog to determine exact applications. Typical thread repair kits will contain a selection of pre-wound threaded inserts, a tap (corresponding to the outside diameter threads of the insert) and an installation tool. Spark plug inserts usually differ because they require a tap equipped with pilot threads and a combined reamer/tap section. Most manufacturers also supply blister-packed thread repair inserts separately in addition to a master kit containing a variety of taps and inserts plus installation tools.

Before effecting a repair to a threaded hole, remove any snapped, broken or damaged bolts or studs. Penetrating oil can be used to free frozen threads; the offending item can be removed with locking pliers or with a screw or stud extractor. After the hole is clear, the thread can be repaired, as follows:

Drill out the damaged threads with specified drill. Drill completely through the hole or to the bottom of a blind hole

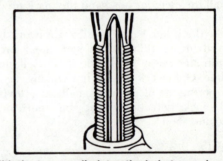

With the tap supplied, tap the hole to receive the thread insert. Keep the tap well oiled and back it out frequently to avoid clogging the threads

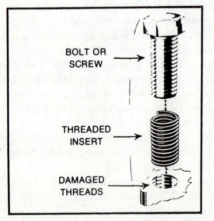

BOLT OR SCREW →

THREADED INSERT →

DAMAGED THREADS →

Damaged bolt holes can be repaired with thread repair inserts

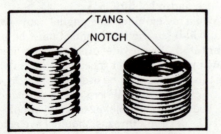

TANG
NOTCH

Standard thread repair insert (left) and spark plug thread insert (right)

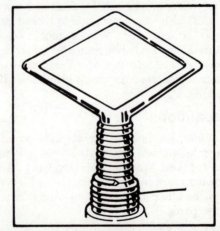

Screw the threaded insert onto the installation tool until the tang engages the slot. Screw the insert into the tapped hole until it is ¼–½ turn below the top surface. After installation break off the tang with a hammer and punch

Standard Torque Specifications and Fastener Markings

The Newton-metre has been designated the world standard for measuring torque and will gradually replace the foot-pound and kilogram-meter. In the absence of specific torques, the following chart can be used as a guide to the maximum safe torque of a particular size/grade of fastener.

- There is no torque difference for fine or coarse threads.
- Torque values are based on clean, dry threads. Reduce the value by 10% if threads are oiled prior to assembly.
- The torque required for aluminum components or fasteners is considerably less.

U. S. BOLTS

SAE Grade Number	1 or 2			5			6 or 7		

Bolt Markings

Manufacturer's marks may vary—number of lines always 2 less than the grade number.

Usage	Frequent			Frequent			Infrequent		
Bolt Size (inches)—(Thread)	Maximum Torque			Maximum Torque			Maximum Torque		
	Ft-Lb	kgm	Nm	Ft-Lb	kgm	Nm	Ft-Lb	kgm	Nm
1/4—20	5	0.7	6.8	8	1.1	10.8	10	1.4	13.5
—28	6	0.8	8.1	10	1.4	13.6			
5/16—18	11	1.5	14.9	17	2.3	23.0	19	2.6	25.8
—24	13	1.8	17.6	19	2.6	25.7			
3/8—16	18	2.5	24.4	31	4.3	42.0	34	4.7	46.0
—24	20	2.75	27.1	35	4.8	47.5			
7/16—14	28	3.8	37.0	49	6.8	66.4	55	7.6	74.5
—20	30	4.2	40.7	55	7.6	74.5			
1/2—13	39	5.4	52.8	75	10.4	101.7	85	11.75	115.2
—20	41	5.7	55.6	85	11.7	115.2			
9/16—12	51	7.0	69.2	110	15.2	149.1	120	16.6	162.7
—18	55	7.6	74.5	120	16.6	162.7			
5/8—11	83	11.5	112.5	150	20.7	203.3	167	23.0	226.5
—18	95	13.1	128.8	170	23.5	230.5			
3/4—10	105	14.5	142.3	270	37.3	366.0	280	38.7	379.6
—16	115	15.9	155.9	295	40.8	400.0			
7/8— 9	160	22.1	216.9	395	54.6	535.5	440	60.9	596.5
—14	175	24.2	237.2	435	60.1	589.7			
1— 8	236	32.5	318.6	590	81.6	799.9	660	91.3	894.8
—14	250	34.6	338.9	660	91.3	849.8			

METRIC BOLTS

NOTE: *Metric bolts are marked with a number indicating the relative strength of the bolt. These numbers have nothing to do with size.*

Description	Torque ft-lbs (Nm)			
Thread size x pitch (mm)	Head mark—4		Head mark—7	
6 x 1.0	2.2–2.9	(3.0–3.9)	3.6–5.8	(4.9–7.8)
8 x 1.25	5.8–8.7	(7.9–12)	9.4–14	(13–19)
10 x 1.25	12–17	(16–23)	20–29	(27–39)
12 x 1.25	21–32	(29–43)	35–53	(47–72)
14 x 1.5	35–52	(48–70)	57–85	(77–110)
16 x 1.5	51–77	(67–100)	90–120	(130–160)
18 x 1.5	74–110	(100–150)	130–170	(180–230)
20 x 1.5	110–140	(150–190)	190–240	(160–320)
22 x 1.5	150–190	(200–260)	250–320	(340–430)
24 x 1.5	190–240	(260–320)	310–410	(420–550)

NOTE: *This engine rebuilding section is a guide to accepted rebuilding procedures. Typical examples of standard rebuilding procedures are illustrated. Use these procedures along with the detailed instructions earlier in this chapter, concerning your particular engine.*

Cylinder Head Reconditioning

Procedure	Method
Remove the cylinder head:	See the engine service procedures earlier in this chapter for details concerning specific engines.
Identify the valves:	Invert the cylinder head, and number the valve faces front to rear, using a permanent felt-tip marker.
Remove the rocker arms (OHV engines only):	Remove the rocker arms with shaft(s) or balls and nuts. Wire the sets of rockers, balls and nuts together, and identify according to the corresponding valve.
Remove the camshaft (OHC engines only):	See the engine service procedures earlier in this chapter for details concerning specific engines.
Remove the valves and springs:	Using an appropriate valve spring compressor (depending on the configuration of the cylinder head), compress the valve springs. Lift out the keepers with needlenose pliers, release the compressor, and remove the valve, spring, and spring retainer. See the engine service procedures earlier in this chapter for details concerning specific engines.

Cylinder Head Reconditioning

Procedure	Method

Check the valve stem-to-guide clearance:

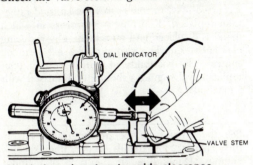

Check the valve stem-to-guide clearance

Clean the valve stem with lacquer thinner or a similar solvent to remove all gum and varnish. Clean the valve guides using solvent and an expanding wire-type valve guide cleaner. Mount a dial indicator so that the stem is at 90° to the valve stem, as close to the valve guide as possible. Move the valve off its seat, and measure the valve guide-to-stem clearance by rocking the stem back and forth to actuate the dial indicator. Measure the valve stems using a micrometer, and compare to specifications, to determine whether stem or guide wear is responsible for excessive clearance.
NOTE: *Consult the Specifications tables earlier in this chapter.*

De-carbon the cylinder head and valves:

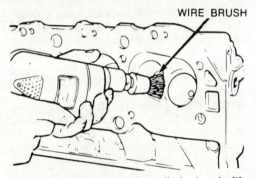

Remove the carbon from the cylinder head with a wire brush and electric drill

Chip carbon away from the valve heads, combustion chambers, and ports, using a chisel made of hardwood. Remove the remaining deposits with a stiff wire brush.
NOTE: *Be sure that the deposits are actually removed, rather than burnished.*

Hot-tank the cylinder head (cast iron heads only):
CAUTION: *Do not hot-tank aluminum parts.*

Have the cylinder head hot-tanked to remove grease, corrosion, and scale from the water passages.
NOTE: *In the case of overhead cam cylinder heads, consult the operator to determine whether the camshaft bearings will be damaged by the caustic solution.*

Degrease the remaining cylinder head parts:

Clean the remaining cylinder head parts in an engine cleaning solvent. Do not remove the protective coating from the springs.

Check the cylinder head for warpage:

Check the cylinder head for warpage

Place a straight-edge across the gasket surface of the cylinder head. Using feeler gauges, determine the clearance at the center of the straight-edge. If warpage exceeds .003″ in a 6″ span, or .006″ over the total length, the cylinder head must be resurfaced.
NOTE: *If warpage exceeds the manufacturer's maximum tolerance for material removal, the cylinder head must be replaced.* When milling the cylinder heads of V-type engines, the intake manifold mounting position is altered, and must be corrected by milling the manifold flange a proportionate amount.

Cylinder Head Reconditioning

Procedure	Method

*Knurl the valve guides:

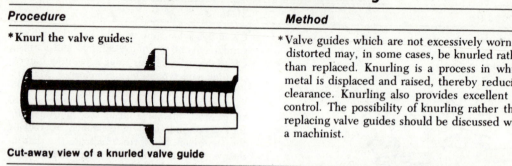

Cut-away view of a knurled valve guide

*Valve guides which are not excessively worn or distorted may, in some cases, be knurled rather than replaced. Knurling is a process in which metal is displaced and raised, thereby reducing clearance. Knurling also provides excellent oil control. The possibility of knurling rather than replacing valve guides should be discussed with a machinist.

Replace the valve guides:
NOTE: *Valve guides should only be replaced if damaged or if an oversize valve stem is not available.*

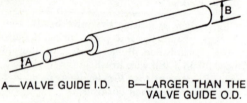

A—VALVE GUIDE I.D.   B—LARGER THAN THE VALVE GUIDE O.D.

WASHERS

A—VALVE GUIDE I.D.   B—LARGER THAN THE VALVE GUIDE O.D.

Valve guide installation tool using washers for installation

See the engine service procedures earlier in this chapter for details concerning specific engines. Depending on the type of cylinder head, valve guides may be pressed, hammered, or shrunk in. In cases where the guides are shrunk into the head, replacement should be left to an equipped machine shop. In other cases, the guides are replaced using a stepped drift (see illustration). Determine the height above the boss that the guide must extend, and obtain a stack of washers, their I.D. similar to the guide's O.D., of that height. Place the stack of washers on the guide, and insert the guide into the boss.
NOTE: *Valve guides are often tapered or beveled for installation.* Using the stepped installation tool (see illustration), press or tap the guides into position. Ream the guides according to the size of the valve stem.

Replace valve seat inserts:

Replacement of valve seat inserts which are worn beyond resurfacing or broken, if feasible, must be done by a machine shop.

Resurface (grind) the valve face:

FOR DIMENSIONS, REFER TO SPECIFICATIONS

CHECK FOR BENT STEM

DIAMETER

VALVE FACE ANGLE

1/32" MINIMUM   THIS LINE PARALLEL WITH VALVE HEAD

Critical valve dimensions

Using a valve grinder, resurface the valves according to specifications given earlier in this chapter.
CAUTION: *Valve face angle is not always identical to valve seat angle.* A minimum margin of

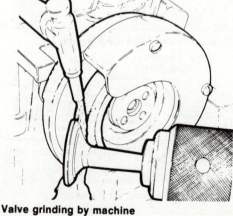

Valve grinding by machine

Cylinder Head Reconditioning

Procedure	Method

Method (continued)

$^1/_{32}$" should remain after grinding the valve. The valve stem top should also be squared and resurfaced, by placing the stem in the V-block of the grinder, and turning it while pressing lightly against the grinding wheel.

NOTE: *Do not grind sodium filled exhaust valves on a machine. These should be hand lapped.*

Resurface the valve seats using reamers or grinder:

Valve seat width and centering

Reaming the valve seat with a hand reamer

Select a reamer of the correct seat angle, slightly larger than the diameter of the valve seat, and assemble it with a pilot of the correct size. Install the pilot into the valve guide, and using steady pressure, turn the reamer clockwise.

CAUTION: *Do not turn the reamer counterclockwise.* Remove only as much material as necessary to clean the seat. Check the concentricity of the seat (following). If the dye method is not used, coat the valve face with Prussian blue dye, install and rotate it on the valve seat. Using the dye marked area as a centering guide, center and narrow the valve seat to specifications with correction cutters.

NOTE: *When no specifications are available, minimum seat width for exhaust valves should be $^5/_{64}$", intake valves $^1/_{16}$".*

After making correction cuts, check the position of the valve seat on the valve face using Prussian blue dye.

To resurface the seat with a power grinder, select a pilot of the correct size and coarse stone of the proper angle. Lubricate the pilot and move the stone on and off the valve seat at 2 cycles per second, until all flaws are gone. Finish the seat with a fine stone. If necessary the seat can be corrected or narrowed using correction stones.

Check the valve seat concentricity:

Check the valve seat concentricity with a dial gauge

Coat the valve face with Prussian blue dye, install the valve, and rotate it on the valve seat. If the entire seat becomes coated, and the valve is known to be concentric, the seat is concentric.

---

* Install the dial gauge pilot into the guide, and rest of the arm on the valve seat. Zero the gauge, and rotate the arm around the seat. Run-out should not exceed .002".

Cylinder Head Reconditioning

Procedure	Method

*Lap the valves:
NOTE: *Valve lapping is done to ensure efficient sealing of resurfaced valves and seats.*

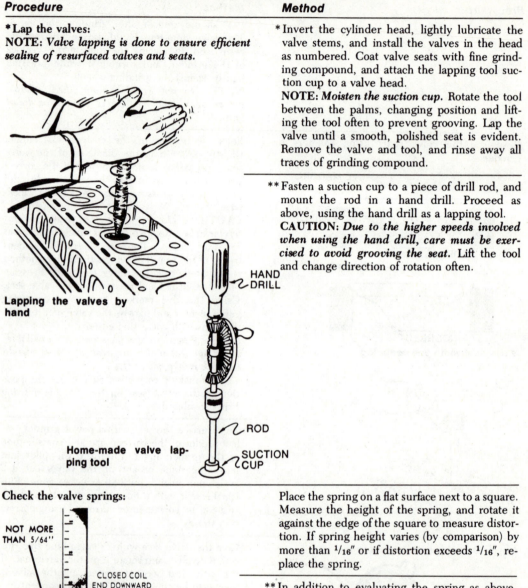

Lapping the valves by hand

Home-made valve lapping tool

HAND DRILL

ROD

SUCTION CUP

*Invert the cylinder head, lightly lubricate the valve stems, and install the valves in the head as numbered. Coat valve seats with fine grinding compound, and attach the lapping tool suction cup to a valve head.

NOTE: *Moisten the suction cup.* Rotate the tool between the palms, changing position and lifting the tool often to prevent grooving. Lap the valve until a smooth, polished seat is evident. Remove the valve and tool, and rinse away all traces of grinding compound.

**Fasten a suction cup to a piece of drill rod, and mount the rod in a hand drill. Proceed as above, using the hand drill as a lapping tool.

CAUTION: *Due to the higher speeds involved when using the hand drill, care must be exercised to avoid grooving the seat.* Lift the tool and change direction of rotation often.

Check the valve springs:

NOT MORE THAN 5/64"

CLOSED COIL END DOWNWARD

Check the valve spring free length and squareness

Check the valve spring test pressure

Place the spring on a flat surface next to a square. Measure the height of the spring, and rotate it against the edge of the square to measure distortion. If spring height varies (by comparison) by more than $1/16''$ or if distortion exceeds $1/16''$, replace the spring.

**In addition to evaluating the spring as above, test the spring pressure at the installed and compressed (installed height minus valve lift) height using a valve spring tester. Springs used on small displacement engines (up to 3 liters) should be $\mp$ 1 lb of all other springs in either position. A tolerance of $\mp$ 5 lbs is permissible on larger engines.

Cylinder Head Reconditioning

Procedure	Method
*Install valve stem seals: 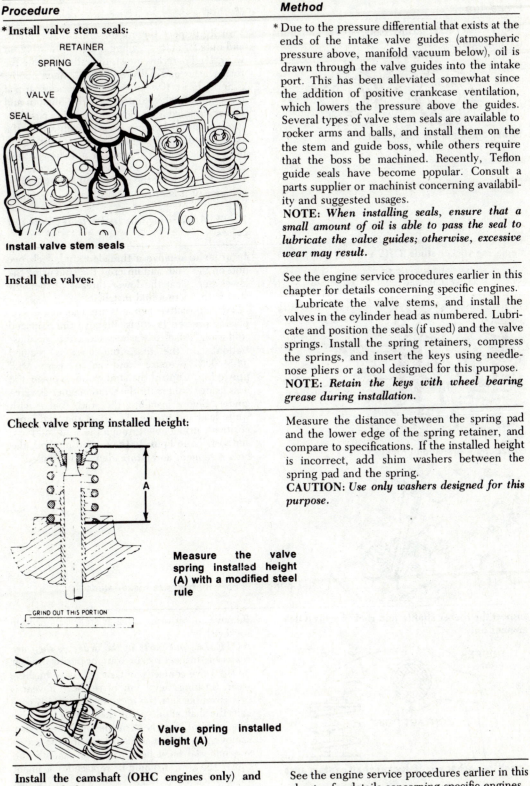 Install valve stem seals	* Due to the pressure differential that exists at the ends of the intake valve guides (atmospheric pressure above, manifold vacuum below), oil is drawn through the valve guides into the intake port. This has been alleviated somewhat since the addition of positive crankcase ventilation, which lowers the pressure above the guides. Several types of valve stem seals are available to rocker arms and balls, and install them on the the stem and guide boss, while others require that the boss be machined. Recently, Teflon guide seals have become popular. Consult a parts supplier or machinist concerning availability and suggested usages. **NOTE:** *When installing seals, ensure that a small amount of oil is able to pass the seal to lubricate the valve guides; otherwise, excessive wear may result.*
Install the valves:	See the engine service procedures earlier in this chapter for details concerning specific engines. Lubricate the valve stems, and install the valves in the cylinder head as numbered. Lubricate and position the seals (if used) and the valve springs. Install the spring retainers, compress the springs, and insert the keys using needlenose pliers or a tool designed for this purpose. **NOTE:** *Retain the keys with wheel bearing grease during installation.*
Check valve spring installed height: Measure the valve spring installed height (A) with a modified steel rule GRIND OUT THIS PORTION Valve spring installed height (A)	Measure the distance between the spring pad and the lower edge of the spring retainer, and compare to specifications. If the installed height is incorrect, add shim washers between the spring pad and the spring. **CAUTION:** *Use only washers designed for this purpose.*
Install the camshaft (OHC engines only) and check end-play:	See the engine service procedures earlier in this chapter for details concerning specific engines.

Cylinder Head Reconditioning

Procedure	Method
Inspect the rocker arms, balls, studs, and nuts (OHV engines only):	Visually inspect the rocker arms, balls, studs, and nuts for cracks, galling, burning, scoring, or wear. If all parts are intact, liberally lubricate the rocker arms and balls, and install them on the cylinder head. If wear is noted on a rocker arm at the point of valve contact, grind it smooth and square, removing as little material as possible. Replace the rocker arm if excessively worn. If a rocker stud shows signs of wear, it must be replaced (see below). If a rocker nut shows stress cracks, replace it. If an exhaust ball is galled or burned, substitute the intake ball from the same cylinder (if it is intact), and install a new intake ball. NOTE: *Avoid using new rocker balls on exhaust valves.*

SMALL FRACTURES

Stress cracks in the rocker nuts

Procedure	Method
Replacing rocker studs (OHV engines only):	In order to remove a threaded stud, lock two nuts on the stud, and unscrew the stud using the lower nut. Coat the lower threads of the new stud with Loctite, and install. Two alternative methods are available for replacing pressed in studs. Remove the damaged stud using a stack of washers and a nut (see illustration). In the first, the boss is reamed .005–.006″ oversize, and an oversize stud pressed in. Control the stud extension over the boss using washers, in the same manner as valve guides. Before installing the stud, coat it with white lead and grease. To retain the stud more positively drill a hole through the stud and boss, and install a roll pin. In the second method, the boss is tapped, and a threaded stud installed.

AS STUB BEGINS TO PULL UP, IT WILL BE NECESSARY TO REMOVE THE NUT AND ADD MORE WASHERS

⅜″ NUT

FLAT WASHERS

Extracting a pressed-in rocker stud

Ream the stud bore for oversize rocker studs

Procedure	Method
Inspect the rocker shaft(s) and rocker arms (OHV engines only)	Remove rocker arms, springs and washers from rocker shaft. NOTE: *Lay out parts in the order as they are removed.* Inspect rocker arms for pitting or wear on the valve contact point, or excessive bushing wear. Bushings need only be replaced if wear is excessive, because the rocker arm normally contacts the shaft at one point only. Grind the valve contact point of rocker arm smooth if necessary, removing as little material as possible. If excessive material must be removed to smooth and square the arm, it should be replaced. Clean out all oil holes and passages in rocker shaft. If shaft is grooved or worn, replace it. Lubricate and assemble the rocker shaft.

ROCKER ARM

SHAFT

CONTACT POINT

Check the rocker arm-to-rocker shaft contact area

Cylinder Head Reconditioning

Procedure	Method
Inspect the pushrods (OHV engines only):	Remove the pushrods, and, if hollow, clean out the oil passages using fine wire. Roll each pushrod over a piece of clean glass. If a distinct clicking sound is heard as the pushrod rolls, the rod is bent, and must be replaced.
	*The length of all pushrods must be equal. Measure the length of the pushrods, compare to specifications, and replace as necessary.
Inspect the valve lifters (OHV engines only): CHECK FOR CONCAVE WEAR ON FACE OF TAPPET USING TAPPET FOR STRAIGHT EDGE **Check the lifter face for squareness**	Remove lifters from their bores, and remove gum and varnish, using solvent. Clean walls of lifter bores. Check lifters for concave wear as illustrated. If face is worn concave, replace lifter, and carefully inspect the camshaft. Lightly lubricate lifter and insert it into its bore. If play is excessive, an oversize lifter must be installed (where possible). Consult a machinist concerning feasibility. If play is satisfactory, remove, lubricate, and reinstall the lifter.
*Testing hydraulic lifter leak down (OHV engines only):	Submerge lifter in a container of kerosene. Chuck a used pushrod or its equivalent into a drill press. Position container of kerosene so pushrod acts on the lifter plunger. Pump lifter with the drill press, until resistance increases. Pump several more times to bleed any air out of lifter. Apply very firm, constant pressure to the lifter, and observe rate at which fluid bleeds out of lifter. If the fluid bleeds very quickly (less than 15 seconds), lifter is defective. If the time exceeds 60 seconds, lifter is sticking. In either case, recondition or replace lifter. If lifter is operating properly (leak down time 15–60 seconds), lubricate and install it.

Cylinder Block Reconditioning

Procedure	Method
Checking the main bearing clearance: 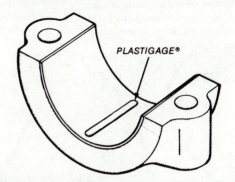 PLASTIGAGE® **Plastigage® installed on the lower bearing shell**	Invert engine, and remove cap from the bearing to be checked. Using a clean, dry rag, thoroughly clean all oil from crankshaft journal and bearing insert. NOTE: *Plastigage® is soluble in oil; therefore, oil on the journal or bearing could result in erroneous readings.* Place a piece of Plastigage along the full length of journal, reinstall cap, and torque to specifications. NOTE: *Specifications are given in the engine specifications earlier in this chapter.* Remove bearing cap, and determine bearing clearance by comparing width of Plastigage to the scale on Plastigage envelope. Journal taper is determined by comparing width of the Plastigage strip near its ends. Rotate crankshaft 90° and retest, to determine journal eccentricity. NOTE: *Do not rotate crankshaft with Plastigage*

Cylinder Block Reconditioning

Procedure	Method
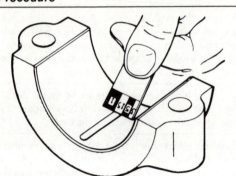 **Measure Plastigage® to determine main bearing clearance**	*installed.* If bearing insert and journal appear intact, and are within tolerances, no further main bearing service is required. If bearing or journal appear defective, cause of failure should be determined before replacement.
	* Remove crankshaft from block (see below). Measure the main bearing journals at each end tiwce (90° apart) using a micrometer, to determine diameter, journal taper and eccentricity. If journals are within tolerances, reinstall bearing caps at their specified torque. Using a telescope gauge and micrometer, measure bearing I.D. parallel to piston axis and at 30° on each side of piston axis. Subtract journal O.D. from bearing I.D. to determine oil clearance. If crankshaft journals appear defective, or do not meet tolerances, there is no need to measure bearings; for the crankshaft will require grinding and/or undersize bearings will be required. If bearing appears defective, cause for failure should be determined prior to replacement.
Check the connecting rod bearing clearance:	Connecting rod bearing clearance is checked in the same manner as main bearing clearance, using Plastigage. Before removing the crankshaft, connecting rod side clearance also should be measured and recorded.
	* Checking connecting rod bearing clearance, using a micrometer, is identical to checking main bearing clearance. If no other service is required, the piston and rod assemblies need not be removed.
Remove the crankshaft: 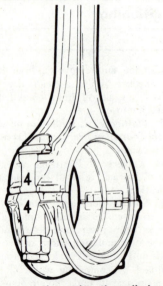 **Match the connecting rod to the cylinder with a number stamp**	Using a punch, mark the corresponding main bearing caps and saddles according to position (i.e., one punch on the front main cap and saddle, two on the second, three on the third, etc.). Using number stamps, identify the corresponding connecting rods and caps, according to cylinder (if no numbers are present). Remove the main and connecting rod caps, and place sleeves of plastic tubing or vacuum hose over the connecting rod bolts, to protect the journals as the crankshaft is removed. Lift the crankshaft out of the block. 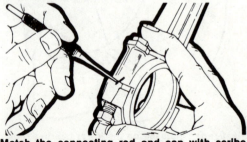 **Match the connecting rod and cap with scribe marks**

Cylinder Block Reconditioning

Procedure	Method
Remove the ridge from the top of the cylinder: 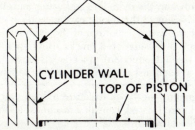 **Cylinder bore ridge**	In order to facilitate removal of the piston and connecting rod, the ridge at the top of the cylinder (unworn area; see illustration) must be removed. Place the piston at the bottom of the bore, and cover it with a rag. Cut the ridge away using a ridge reamer, exercising extreme care to avoid cutting too deeply. Remove the rag, and remove cuttings that remain on the piston. **CAUTION:** *If the ridge is not removed, and new rings are installed, damage to rings will result.*
Remove the piston and connecting rod: 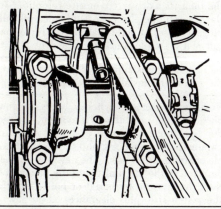 **Push the piston out with a hammer handle**	Invert the engine, and push the pistons and connecting rods out of the cylinders. If necessary, tap the connecting rod boss with a wooden hammer handle, to force the piston out. **CAUTION:** *Do not attempt to force the piston past the cylinder ridge (see above).*
Service the crankshaft:	Ensure that all oil holes and passages in the crankshaft are open and free of sludge. If necessary, have the crankshaft ground to the largest possible undersize.
	** Have the crankshaft Magnafluxed, to locate stress cracks. Consult a machinist concerning additional service procedures, such as surface hardening (e.g., nitriding, Tuftriding) to improve wear characteristics, cross drilling and chamfering the oil holes to improve lubrication, and balancing.
Removing freeze plugs:	Drill a small hole in the middle of the freeze plugs. Thread a large sheet metal screw into the hole and remove the plug with a slide hammer.
Remove the oil gallery plugs:	Threaded plugs should be removed using an appropriate (usually square) wrench. To remove soft, pressed in plugs, drill a hole in the plug, and thread in a sheet metal screw. Pull the plug out by the screw using pliers.
Hot-tank the block: NOTE: *Do not hot-tank aluminum parts.*	Have the block hot-tanked to remove grease, corrosion, and scale from the water jackets. **NOTE:** *Consult the operator to determine whether the camshaft bearings will be damaged during the hot-tank process.*

Cylinder Block Reconditioning

Procedure	Method

Check the block for cracks:	Visually inspect the block for cracks or chips. The most common locations are as follows:
	  Adjacent to freeze plugs.
	  Between the cylinders and water jackets.
	  Adjacent to the main bearing saddles.
	  At the extreme bottom of the cylinders.
	Check only suspected cracks using spot check dye (see introduction). If a crack is located, consult a machinist concerning possible repairs.

	** Magnaflux the block to locate hidden cracks. If cracks are located, consult a machinist about feasibility of repair.
Install the oil gallery plugs and freeze plugs:	Coat freeze plugs with sealer and tap into position using a piece of pipe, slightly smaller than the plug, as a driver. To ensure retention, stake the edges of the plugs. Coat threaded oil gallery plugs with sealer and install. Drive replacement soft plugs into block using a large drift as driver.
	* Rather than reinstalling lead plugs, drill and tap the holes, and install threaded plugs.
Check the bore diameter and surface:	Visually inspect the cylinder bores for roughness, scoring, or scuffing. If evident, the cylinder bore must be bored or honed oversize to eliminate imperfections, and the smallest possible oversize piston used. The new pistons should be given to the machinist with the block, so that the cylinders can be bored or honed exactly to the piston size (plus clearance). If no flaws are evident, measure the bore diameter using a telescope gauge and micrometer, or dial gauge, parallel and perpendicular to the engine centerline, at the top (below the ridge) and bottom of the bore. Subtract the bottom measurements from the top to determine taper, and the parallel to the centerline measurements from the perpendicular measurements to determine eccentricity. If the measurements are not within specifications, the cylinder must be bored or honed, and an oversize piston installed. If the measurements are within specifications the cylinder may be used as is, with only finish honing (see below).

Measure the cylinder bore with a dial gauge

CAUTION: *The 4 cyl. 140 eng. cylinder walls are impregnated with silicone. Boring or honing can be done only by a shop with the proper equipment.*

CENTERLINE OF ENGINE

A—AT RIGHT ANGLE TO CENTERLINE OF ENGINE
B—PARALLEL TO CENTERLINE OF ENGINE

Cylinder bore measuring points

TELESCOPE GAUGE 90° FROM PISTON PIN

Measure the cylinder bore with a telescope gauge

TELESCOPE GAUGE

MICROMETER

Measure the telescope gauge with a micrometer to determine the cylinder bore

Cylinder Block Reconditioning

Procedure	Method
	NOTE: *Prior to submitting the block for boring, perform the following operation(s).*
Check the cylinder block bearing alignment: **Check the main bearing saddle alignment**	Remove the upper bearing inserts. Place a straightedge in the bearing saddles along the centerline of the crankshaft. If clearance exists between the straightedge and the center saddle, the block must be alignbored.
*Check the deck height:	The deck height is the distance from the crankshaft centerline to the block deck. To measure, invert the engine, and install the crankshaft, retaining it with the center main cap. Measure the distance from the crankshaft journal to the block deck, parallel to the cylinder centerline. Measure the diameter of the end (front and rear) main journals, parallel to the centerline of the cylinders, divide the diameter in half, and subtract it from the previous measurement. The results of the front and rear measurements should be identical. If the difference exceeds .005″, the deck height should be corrected. NOTE: *Block deck height and warpage should be corrected at the same time.*
Check the block deck for warpage:	Using a straightedge and feeler gauges, check the block deck for warpage in the same manner that the cylinder head is checked (see Cylinder Head Reconditioning). If warpage exceeds specifications, have the deck resurfaced. NOTE: *In certain cases a specification for total material removal (Cylinder head and block deck) is provided. This specification must not be exceeded.*
Clean and inspect the pistons and connecting rods: RING EXPANDER **Remove the piston rings**	Using a ring expander, remove the rings from the piston. Remove the retaining rings (if so equipped) and remove piston pin. NOTE: *If the piston pin must be pressed out, determine the proper method and use the proper tools; otherwise the piston will distort.* Clean the ring grooves using an appropriate tool, exercising care to avoid cutting too deeply. Thoroughly clean all carbon and varnish from the piston with solvent. CAUTION: *Do not use a wire brush or caustic solvent on pistons.* Inspect the pistons for scuffing, scoring, cracks, pitting, or excessive ring groove wear. If wear is evident, the piston must be replaced. Check the connecting rod length by measuring the rod from the inside of the large end to the

Cylinder Block Reconditioning

Procedure	Method

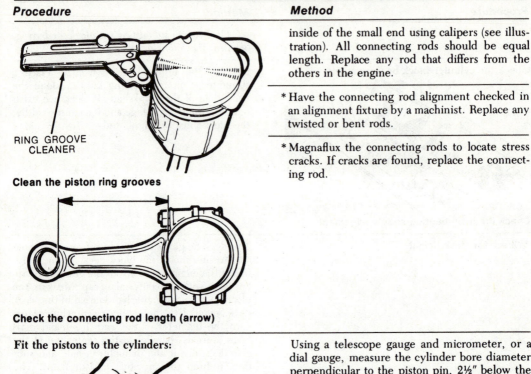

RING GROOVE CLEANER

Clean the piston ring grooves

inside of the small end using calipers (see illustration). All connecting rods should be equal length. Replace any rod that differs from the others in the engine.

* Have the connecting rod alignment checked in an alignment fixture by a machinist. Replace any twisted or bent rods.

* Magnaflux the connecting rods to locate stress cracks. If cracks are found, replace the connecting rod.

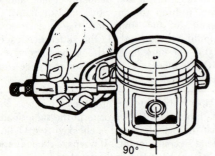

Check the connecting rod length (arrow)

Fit the pistons to the cylinders:

Using a telescope gauge and micrometer, or a dial gauge, measure the cylinder bore diameter perpendicular to the piston pin, 2½″ below the deck. Measure the piston perpendicular to its pin on the skirt. The difference between the two measurements is the piston clearance. If the clearance is within specifications or slightly below (after boring or honing), finish honing is all that is required. If the clearance is excessive, try to obtain a slightly larger piston to bring clearance within specifications. Where this is not possible, obtain the first oversize piston, and hone (or if necessary, bore) the cylinder to size.

CAUTION: *The 4 cyl. 140 eng. cylinders are impregnated with silicone; honing can be performed only by a shop with the proper equipment.*

90°

Measure the piston prior to fitting

Assemble the pistons and connecting rods:

Inspect piston pin, connecting rod small end bushing, and piston bore for galling, scoring, or excessive wear. If evident, replace defective part(s). Measure the I.D. of the piston boss and connecting rod small end, and the O.D. of the piston pin. If within specifications, assemble piston pin and rod.

CAUTION: *If piston pin must be pressed in, determine the proper method and use the proper tools; otherwise the piston will distort.*

Install the lock rings; ensure that they seat properly. If the parts are not within specifications, determine the service method for the type of engine. In some cases, piston and pin are serviced as an assembly when either is defective. Others specify reaming the piston and connecting rods for an oversize pin. If the connecting

Install the piston pin lock-rings (if used)

Cylinder Block Reconditioning

Procedure	Method

rod bushing is worn, it may in many cases be replaced. Reaming the piston and replacing the rod bushing are machine shop operations.

Clean and inspect the camshaft:

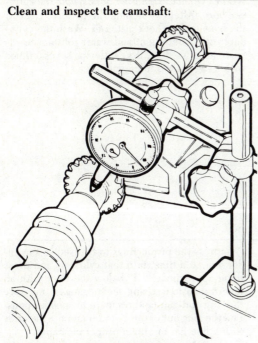

Check the camshaft for straightness

Degrease the camshaft, using solvent, and clean out all oil holes. Visually inspect cam lobes and bearing journals for excessive wear. If a lobe is questionable, check all lobes as indicated below. If a journal or lobe is worn, the camshaft must be reground or replaced.

NOTE: *If a journal is worn, there is a good chance that the bushings are worn.* If lobes and journals appear intact, place the front and rear journals in V-blocks, and rest a dial indicator on the center journal. Rotate the camshaft to check straightness. If deviation exceeds .001″, replace the camshaft.

* Check the camshaft lobes with a micrometer, by measuring the lobes from the nose to base and again at 90° (see illustration). The lift is determined by subtracting the second measurement from the first. If all exhaust lobes and all intake lobes are not identical, the camshaft must be reground or replaced.

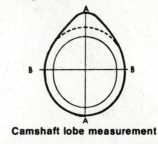

Camshaft lobe measurement

Replace the camshaft bearings (OHV engines only):

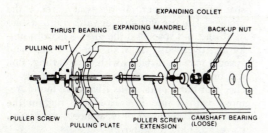

Camshaft bearing removal and installation tool (OHV engines only)

If excessive wear is indicated, or if the engine is being completely rebuilt, camshaft bearings should be replaced as follows: Drive the camshaft rear plug from the block. Assemble the removal puller with its shoulder on the bearing to be removed. Gradually tighten the puller nut until bearing is removed. Remove remaining bearings, leaving the front and rear for last. To remove front and rear bearings, reverse position of the tool, so as to pull the bearings in toward the center of the block. Leave the tool in this position, pilot the new front and rear bearings on the installer, and pull them into position: Return the tool to its original position and pull remaining bearings into position.

NOTE: *Ensure that oil holes align when installing bearings.* Replace camshaft rear plug, and stake it into position to aid retention.

Finish hone the cylinders:

Chuck a flexible drive hone into a power drill, and insert it into the cylinder. Start the hone,

Cylinder Block Reconditioning

Procedure	Method

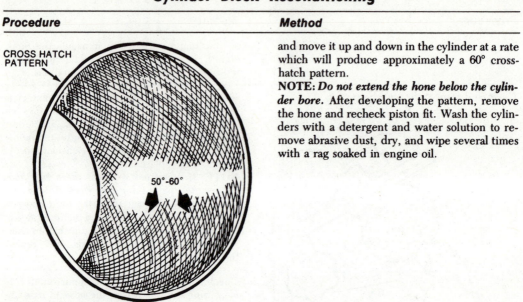

CROSS HATCH PATTERN

50°-60°

Cylinder bore after honing

and move it up and down in the cylinder at a rate which will produce approximately a 60° cross-hatch pattern.

NOTE: *Do not extend the hone below the cylinder bore.* After developing the pattern, remove the hone and recheck piston fit. Wash the cylinders with a detergent and water solution to remove abrasive dust, dry, and wipe several times with a rag soaked in engine oil.

Check piston ring end-gap:

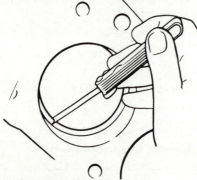

Check the piston ring end gap

Compress the piston rings to be used in a cylinder, one at a time, into that cylinder, and press them approximately 1″ below the deck with an inverted piston. Using feeler gauges, measure the ring end-gap, and compare to specifications. Pull the ring out of the cylinder and file the ends with a fine file to obtain proper clearance.

CAUTION: *If inadequate ring end-gap is utilized, ring breakage will result.*

Install the piston rings:

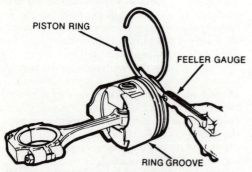

PISTON RING

FEELER GAUGE

RING GROOVE

Check the piston ring side clearance

Inspect the ring grooves in the piston for excessive wear or taper. If necessary, recut the grooves(s) for use with an overwidth ring or a standard ring and spacer. If the groove is worn uniformly, overwidth rings, or standard rings and spacers may be installed without recutting. Roll the outside of the ring around the groove to check for burrs or deposits. If any are found, remove with a fine file. Hold the ring in the groove, and measure side clearance. If necessary, correct as indicated above.

NOTE: *Always install any additional spacers above the piston ring.*

The ring groove must be deep enough to allow the ring to seat below the lands (see illustration). In many cases, a "go-no-go" depth gauge will be provided with the piston rings. Shallow grooves may be corrected by recutting, while deep grooves require some type of filler or expander behind the piston. Consult the piston ring sup-

Cylinder Block Reconditioning

Procedure	Method
	plier concerning the suggested method. Install the rings on the piston, lowest ring first, using a ring expander. NOTE: *Position the ring as specified by the manufacturer.* Consult the engine service procedures earlier in this chapter for details concerning specific engines.
Install the camshaft (OHV engines only):	Liberally lubricate the camshaft lobes and journals, and install the camshaft. CAUTION: *Exercise extreme care to avoid damaging the bearings when inserting the camshaft.* Install and tighten the camshaft thrust plate retaining bolts. See the engine service procedures earlier in this chapter for details concerning specific engines.
Check camshaft end-play (OHV engines only): **Check the camshaft end-play with a feeler gauge** DIAL INDICATOR CAMSHAFT **Check the camshaft end-play with a dial indicator**	Using feeler gauges, determine whether the clearance between the camshaft boss (or gear) and backing plate is within specifications. Install shims behind the thrust plate, or reposition the camshaft gear and retest endplay. In some cases, adjustment is by replacing the thrust plate. See the engine service procedures earlier in this chapter for details concerning specific engines. * Mount a dial indicator stand so that the stem of the dial indicator rests on the nose of the camshaft, parallel to the camshaft axis. Push the camshaft as far in as possible and zero the gauge. Move the camshaft outward to determine the amount of camshaft endplay. If the endplay is not within tolerance, install shims behind the thrust plate, or reposition the camshaft gear and retest. See the engine service procedures earlier in this chapter for details concerning specific engines.
Install the rear main seal:	See the engine service procedures earlier in this chapter for details concerning specific engines.
Install the crankshaft: INSTALLING BEARING SHELL REMOVING BEARING SHELL **Remove or install the upper bearing insert using a roll-out pin**	Thoroughly clean the main bearing saddles and caps. Place the upper halves of the bearing inserts on the saddles and press into position. NOTE: *Ensure that the oil holes align.* Press the corresponding bearing inserts into the main bearing caps. Lubricate the upper main bearings, and lay the crankshaft in position. Place a strip of Plastigage on each of the crankshaft journals, install the main caps, and torque to specifications. Remove the main caps, and compare the Plastigage to the scale on the Plastigage envelope. If clearances are within tolerances, remove the Plastigage, turn the crankshaft 90°, wipe off all oil and retest. If all clearances are correct, re-

Cylinder Block Reconditioning

Procedure	Method

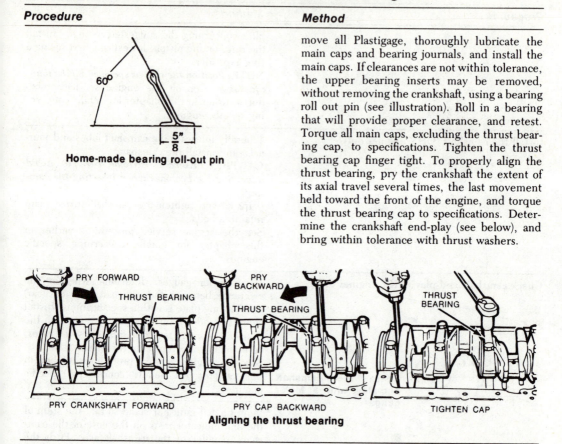

Home-made bearing roll-out pin

move all Plastigage, thoroughly lubricate the main caps and bearing journals, and install the main caps. If clearances are not within tolerance, the upper bearing inserts may be removed, without removing the crankshaft, using a bearing roll out pin (see illustration). Roll in a bearing that will provide proper clearance, and retest. Torque all main caps, excluding the thrust bearing cap, to specifications. Tighten the thrust bearing cap finger tight. To properly align the thrust bearing, pry the crankshaft the extent of its axial travel several times, the last movement held toward the front of the engine, and torque the thrust bearing cap to specifications. Determine the crankshaft end-play (see below), and bring within tolerance with thrust washers.

Aligning the thrust bearing

Measure crankshaft end-play:

Mount a dial indicator stand on the front of the block, with the dial indicator stem resting on the nose of the crankshaft, parallel to the crankshaft axis. Pry the crankshaft the extent of its travel rearward, and zero the indicator. Pry the crankshaft forward and record crankshaft end-play.
NOTE: *Crankshaft end-play also may be measured at the thrust bearing, using feeler gauges (see illustration).*

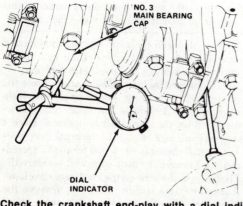

Check the crankshaft end-play with a dial indicator

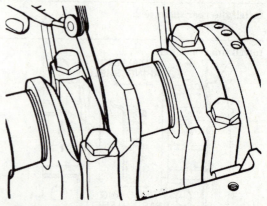

Check the crankshaft end-play with a feeler gauge

Cylinder Block Reconditioning

Procedure	Method

Install the pistons:

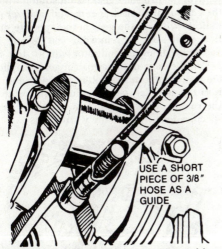

USE A SHORT PIECE OF 3/8″ HOSE AS A GUIDE

Use lengths of vacuum hose or rubber tubing to protect the crankshaft journals and cylinder walls during piston installation

RING COMPRESSOR

Install the piston using a ring compressor

Press the upper connecting rod bearing halves into the connecting rods, and the lower halves into the connecting rod caps. Position the piston ring gaps according to specifications (see car section), and lubricate the pistons. Install a ring compresser on a piston, and press two long (8″) pieces of plastic tubing over the rod bolts. Using the tubes as a guide, press the pistons into the bores and onto the crankshaft with a wooden hammer handle. After seating the rod on the crankshaft journal, remove the tubes and install the cap finger tight. Install the remaining pistons in the same manner. Invert the engine and check the bearing clearance at two points (90° apart) on each journal with Plastigage.

NOTE: *Do not turn the crankshaft with Plastigage installed.* If clearance is within tolerances, remove *all* Plastigage, thoroughly lubricate the journals, and torque the rod caps to specifications. If clearance is not within specifications, install different thickness bearing inserts and recheck.

CAUTION: *Never shim or file the connecting rods or caps.* Always install plastic tube sleeves over the rod bolts when the caps are not installed, to protect the crankshaft journals.

Check connecting rod side clearance:

Check the connecting rod side clearance with a feeler gauge

Determine the clearance between the sides of the connecting rods and the crankshaft, using feeler gauges. If clearance is below the minimum tolerance, the rod may be machined to provide adequate clearance. If clearance is excessive, substitute an unworn rod, and recheck. If clearance is still outside specifications, the crankshaft must be welded and reground, or replaced.

Inspect the timing chain (or belt):

Visually inspect the timing chain for broken or loose links, and replace the chain if any are found. If the chain will flex sideways, it must be replaced. Install the timing chain as specified. Be sure the timing belt is not stretched, frayed or broken.

NOTE: *If the original timing chain is to be reused, install it in its original position.*

Cylinder Block Reconditioning

Procedure	Method
Check timing gear backlash and runout (OHV engines):	Mount a dial indicator with its stem resting on a tooth of the camshaft gear (as illustrated). Rotate the gear until all slack is removed, and zero the indicator. Rotate the gear in the opposite direction until slack is removed, and record gear backlash. Mount the indicator with its stem resting on the edge of the camshaft gear, parallel to the axis of the camshaft. Zero the indicator, and turn the camshaft gear one full turn, recording the runout. If either backlash or runout exceed specifications, replace the worn gear(s).

Check the camshaft gear backlash

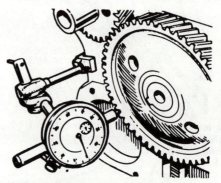

Check the camshaft gear run-out

Completing the Rebuilding Process

Following the above procedures, complete the rebuilding process as follows:

Fill the oil pump with oil, to prevent cavitating (sucking air) on initial engine start up. Install the oil pump and the pickup tube on the engine. Coat the oil pan gasket as necessary, and install the gasket and the oil pan. Mount the flywheel and the crankshaft vibration damper or pulley on the crankshaft. NOTE: *Always use new bolts when installing the flywheel*. Inspect the clutch shaft pilot bushing in the crankshaft. If the bushing is excessively worn, remove it with an expanding puller and a slide hammer, and tap a new bushing into place.

Position the engine, cylinder head side up. Lubricate the lifters, and install them into their bores. Install the cylinder head, and torque it as specified. Insert the pushrods (where applicable), and install the rocker shaft(s) (if so equipped) or position the rocker arms on the pushrods. Adjust the valves.

Install the intake and exhaust manifolds, the carburetor(s), the distributor and spark plugs. Adjust the point gap and the static ignition timing. Mount all accessories and install the engine in the car. Fill the radiator with coolant, and the crankcase with high quality engine oil.

Break-in Procedure

Start the engine, and allow it to run at low speed for a few minutes, while checking for leaks. Stop the engine, check the oil level, and fill as necessary. Restart the engine, and fill the cooling system to capacity. Check the point dwell angle and adjust the ignition timing and the valves. Run the engine at low to medium speed (800–2500 rpm) for approximately ½ hour, and retorque the cylinder head bolts. Road test the car, and check again for leaks.

Follow the manufacturer's recommended engine break-in procedure and maintenance schedule for new engines.

Emission Controls and Fuel System

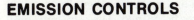

4

EMISSION CONTROLS

Positive Crankcase Ventilation (PCV)

This system draws crankcase vapors that are formed through normal combustion into the intake manifold and subsequently into the combustion chamber to be burned. Fresh air is introduced to the crankcase by way of a hose connected to the carburetor air cleaner. Manifold vacuum is used to draw the vapors from the crankcase through a PCV valve and into the intake manifold. See Chapter 1, "General Information and Maintenance" for information on checking and replacing the PCV valve.

Controlled Combustion System (CCS)

The Controlled Combustion System (CCS) is used on all models. Essentially the CCS increases combustion efficiency through carburetor and distributor calibrations and by increasing engine operating temperatures.

Carburetors are calibrated leaner and initial ignition timing is retarded. The vacuum advance curve is also altered to decrease emissions.

The CCS also incorporates a higher engine

operation temperature. A 195° thermostat is used. Engines that run hotter provide more complete vaporation of fuel and reduce quench area in the combustion chamber. Quench area is the relatively cool area near the cylinder wall and combustion chamber surfaces. Fuel in these areas does not burn properly because of the lower temperatures. This incomplete burning increases emissions.

The CCS uses a thermostatically controlled air cleaner called the Auto-Therm air cleaner. It is designed to keep the temperature of the air entering the carburetor at approximately 100° F. This allows the lean carburetor to work properly, minimizes carburetor icing, and improves engine warmup characteristics. A sensor unit located on the clean air side of the air filter senses the temperature of the air passing over it and regulates the vacuum supplied to a vacuum diaphragm in the inlet tube of the air cleaner. The colder the air, the greater the amount of vacuum supplied to the vacuum diaphragm. The vacuum diaphragm, depending on the vacuum supplied to it, opens or closes a damper door in the inlet tube of the air cleaner. If the door is open it allows air from the engine compartment to go to the carburetor. If the door is closed, air flows from the heat stove located on the exhaust manifold

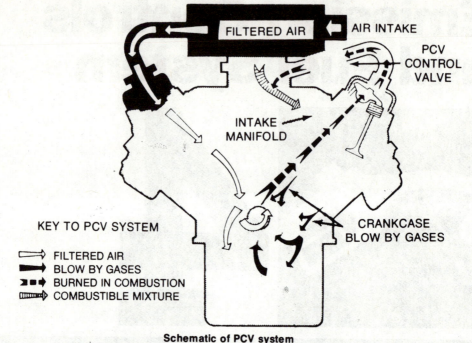

KEY TO PCV SYSTEM

⇨ FILTERED AIR
➡ BLOW BY GASES
➤➤➤ BURNED IN COMBUSTION
⟼ COMBUSTIBLE MIXTURE

Schematic of PCV system

into the carburetor. In this way, heated air is supplied to the carburetor during cold days and when first starting the engine and warming it up.

Since the only extra component added with a CCS system is the thermostatically controlled air cleaner, there is no additional maintenance required; however, tune-up adjustments such as idle speed, ignition timing, and dwell become much more critical. Care must be taken to make certain that these settings are correct, both for trouble-free operation and a low emission level.

Evaporative Control System (ECS)

This system is designed to prevent gasoline vapors from escaping into the atmosphere. Float bowl emissions are controlled by internal carburetor modifications. Redesigned bowl vents, reduced bowl capacity, heat shields, and improved intake manifold-to-carburetor insulation serve to reduce vapor loss into the atmosphere. The venting of fuel tank vapors into the air has been eliminated. Fuel vapors are now directed through lines to a canister containing an activated charcoal filter. Unburned vapors are trapped here until the engine is running, the canister is purged by air drawn in by manifold vacuum.

The air and fuel vapors are then directed into the engine to be burned. The canister should be replaced at recommended intervals. These intervals and the replacement procedure are covered in Chapter 1, "General Information and Maintenance."

Transmission Controlled Spark System

The function of TCS is to prevent full distributor vacuum spark advance in any transmission gears other than the following:

Transmission	Gear
3-Speed	3rd
4-Speed	3rd, 4th
Torque Drive	2nd
Powerglide	2nd
Turbo Hydra-Matic 250, 350	reverse, 3rd
1972–75 California automatic transmission models	none

This is accomplished by a transmission-operated switch which governs the action of a solenoid-operated vacuum valve. This valve connects the distributor vacuum advance unit either to the normal vacuum source when de-energized, or to the carburetor air intake, where normal atmospheric pressure exists, when energized. The system is overridden when engine temperature is below

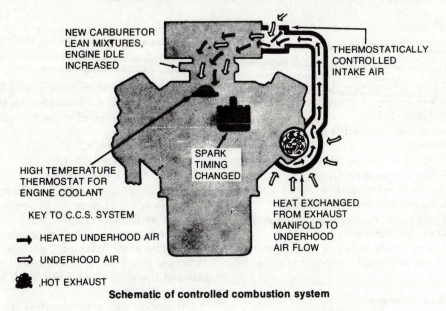

NEW CARBURETOR LEAN MIXTURES, ENGINE IDLE INCREASED

THERMOSTATICALLY CONTROLLED INTAKE AIR

SPARK TIMING CHANGED

HIGH TEMPERATURE THERMOSTAT FOR ENGINE COOLANT

HEAT EXCHANGED FROM EXHAUST MANIFOLD TO UNDERHOOD AIR FLOW

KEY TO C.C.S. SYSTEM

HEATED UNDERHOOD AIR

UNDERHOOD AIR

HOT EXHAUST

Schematic of controlled combustion system

82°F to provide good starting and warmup. A temperature switch opens the system relay, de-energizing the solenoid to provide the override. The system is of the fail-safe type; that is, if the circuit to the solenoid vacuum valve should be broken, full vacuum advance in all gear positions would be allowed. The idle stop solenoid is de-energized when the ignition switch is turned off. This allows the solenoid plunger to retract, letting the carburetor throttle plates close beyond the normal idle position. Thus the engine is prevented from running on, or dieseling.

TCS Component	Location
Idle stop solenoid	At carburetor throttle level
Solenoid vacuum valve	On left-side of firewall
Relay	1972–75—left-side of firewall 1971—right fender
Temperature switch	Integrated with cylinder head temperature sending unit, between spark plugs No. 2 and 3
Transmission switch	Right-side of transmission

1973–74

Distributor vacuum advance is allowed only in High gear except for cars with four-speed transmissions, these are also allowed vacuum advance in Third gear. The advance is regulated by a solenoid located in the vacuum line between the distributor and the carburetor. When the solenoid is *energized*, there is vacuum advance. When de-energized, there is

none. This is the opposite of the system used in 1971–72. The solenoid receives its current from the ignition switch and the circuit is completed to ground through a temperature switch or transmission switch.

The temperature switch turns on the vacuum solenoid below 93° F, allowing vacuum advance in all gears. The temperature switch is built into the same sending unit that turns on the red temperature warning light on the instrument panel. On cars with a temperature gauge, the temperature switch may be a single unit.

The transmission switch turns on the vacuum solenoid by grounding the circuit. The transmission switch is on the outside of the transmission on all models.

1976 W/1bbL-140 Engine

The TCS system used for 1976 is basically the same as the one used in 1973–74. The only difference is that both a temperature switch and a transmission switch are used.

TESTING

If there is a TCS system malfunction, first connect a vacuum gauge in the hose between the solenoid valve and the distributor vacuum unit. Drive the vehicle or raise it on a frame lift and observe the vacuum gauge. Full vacuum should be available only in the gears indicated in the chart earlier in this section. If full vacuum is available in all gears, check for the following:

1. Blown fuse.

2. Disconnected wire at solenoid-operated vacuum valve.

3. Disconnected wire at transmission switch.

4. Temperature override switch energized due to low engine temperature.

5. Solenoid failure.

If no vacuum is available in any gear, check the following:

1. Normal condition for 1972–75 California automatic transmission car.

2. Solenoid valve vacuum lines switched.

3. Clogged solenoid vacuum valve.

4. Distributor or manifold vacuum lines leaking or disconnected.

5. Transmission switch or wire grounded.

Tests for individual components are as follows:

Idle Stop Solenoid

This unit may be checked simply by observing it while an assistant switches the ignition on and off. It should extend further with the current switched on. The unit is not repairable.

Vacuum Solenoid

1971–72

Turn the ignition switch on, but do not start the engine. You should be able to hear the solenoid click on.

If not, unplug the double connector from the solenoid and use a voltmeter or non-powered test light to check for current at the wires connected to the solenoid with the ignition on. Only one of the wires will have current. If there is no current, check the wiring, the ignition switch or the fuse.

With the plug disconnected from the solenoid, run a hot jumper wire from the battery to one of the solenoid terminals.

Connect the other terminal to ground. The solenoid should click when the wire is grounded. If not, replace the solenoid.

CAUTION: *Do not hot wire the solenoid with the connector in place. There is a danger of damaging the transmission switch if you do. Remove the double connector and place it safely away from any hot wires.*

1973–76

Unplug the electrical connector at the vacuum solenoid and run a hot jumper wire from the battery positive post to one of the terminals on the solenoid.

Use another jumper wire to ground the other terminal on the solenoid. It should click. If not, the solenoid is defective.

Coolant Temperature Switch

When the temperature switch completes the circuit to ground, it allows vacuum advance. The switch is grounded at the following temperatures:

• 1971–72: Below 82° F
• 1973–76: Below 93° F

NOTE: *The engine must be cold (below the temperatures listed above) or the temperature switch will have to be removed and cooled in ice water.*

The temperature switch on models with a red temperature warning light on the instrument panel has two terminals and is located at the right side of the block between No. 1 and 2 spark plugs.

On models with a temperature gauge, the gauge sending unit may be screwed into a coolant passage at the front of the intake manifold. On some cars, the positions of the gauge sending unit and the TCS temperature switch may be reversed. To find the TCS temperature switch, turn the ignition switch on and ground the wire to the switch. If you have the correct wire, the vacuum solenoid will click.

Once you have located the TCS temperature switch terminal, use a penlight-powered test light between the switch terminal and ground. On a cold engine (below the temperatures listed above) the test light should go on when you hook it up. Start the engine and, as it warms up, the test light should go off. If not, the temperature switch is defective.

Transmission Switch

1971–72

Disconnect the wire connector at the transmission and connect a penlight-powered test light between the terminal on the transmission and ground. On a Powerglide car, support the rear wheels in the air so that the transmission can be operated. Block the front wheels.

CAUTION: *Do not use the car battery to test the switch. Use a penlight-powered test light to avoid running too much current through the switch and damaging it.*

Position the test light so that you can see it from the driver's seat. Make sure manual transmission cars are in Neutral. When the light is connected, it should come on. It not, the transmission switch is defective.

On a manual transmission, put the transmission in Third and Fourth gear. The light should go off in both gears.

On a Powerglide, start the engine, put the transmission in Drive and accelerate the engine slowly until the transmission upshifts. The light should go off except on 1972 Calif. cars.

On a Torque Drive, start the engine and put the transmission in High. The light should go off, except on 1972 Calif. cars.

On a Turbo Hydra-Matic, start the engine, hold your foot on the brake and put the transmission in Reverse. The light should go off, except on 1972 Calif. cars.

1972 Calif. automatic transmission cars do not allow vacuum advance in any gear. The light should stay on in all gears.

If the transmission switch does not work correctly, it must be replaced.

1973–76

Disconnect the wire connector at the transmission and connect a penlight-powered test light between the terminal on the transmission and ground.

CAUTION: *Do not use the car battery to test the switch. Use a penlight-powered test light to avoid running too much current through the switch and damaging it.*

Position the test light so that you can see it from the driver's seat. Make sure the transmission is in Neutral. When the light is connected, it should stay off. If not, the switch is defective.

Put the transmission in High gear. The light should come on. If the transmission switch does not work correctly, it must be replaced.

Relay

1971–72

NOTE: *This relay has 3 terminals plus a short stub terminal. The part No. is 3961573.*

Connect a penlight-powered test light between the two regular length terminals at one end of the relay. The light should go on when it is connected. If not, the relay is defective.

Connect a 12-volt battery positive post to the regular length terminal at the other end of the relay. Connect the battery negative post to the small stub terminal. The test light should go out. If not, the relay is defective.

Thermal Check and Delay Valve

NOTE: *This procedure applies to the following models: 1974—All auto. trans. cars. 1975—(49 states) All two-barrel engine, auto. trans. cars; (Calif.) All two-barrel engine cars.*

To test the thermal check and delay valve for cold operation, it must be cooled below 40° F. Connect a vacuum gauge to the distributor side of the valve, and a hand vacuum pump to the CARB nozzle of the valve. Operate the pump, and there should be no delay in the readings between the two gauges. If there is a delay, the valve is clogged or defective.

To make the warm test (above 50° F.) use the same connections, with a vacuum gauge on the distributor nozzle, and a pump on the CARB nozzle. Operate the pump quickly to create a vacuum of about 20 in. Hg. The pump gauge will rise immediately, but the gauge connected to the TVS nozzle should hesitate, rising slowly. After you stop pumping, the pump gauge should drop slightly, and take 3 or 4 seconds to balance with the vacuum gauge connected to the distributor nozzle. If you don't get the hesitation and balancing of readings, the valve is defective.

Remove the gauge from the distributor nozzle and plug the nozzle with your finger. Pump up 15 in. Hg. vacuum. This vacuum should hold and not leak down. If it leaks down, the valve is defective. Remove your finger. The pump gauge should drop slowly to zero. If it drops quickly, the valve is defective.

Air Injection Reactor System

AIR is used on all 1973–74 models except non-California cars with single-barrel carburetors. 1975 California cars with the 140 cu. in. engine, and Monza V8 also use an air pump. 1976 49 states 1 bbl four cylinder engines and California 2 bbl four cylinder engines also have air injection. Both 1977 engines use air injection. California V6 and V8 engines for 1978 use AIR. All 1979–80 V8 engines and California V6 engines use AIR.

The Air Injection Reactor (AIR) system is used to treat exhaust emissions. It consists of an air pump, a diverter valve, and tubes and hoses used to inject the air into the exhaust manifolds. The pump, driven by the engine, compresses air which is routed to the exhaust port of each cylinder. The air provides oxygen to further burn any unburned gases that

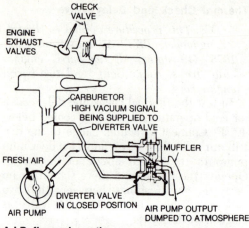

CHECK VALVE
ENGINE EXHAUST VALVES
CARBURETOR
HIGH VACUUM SIGNAL BEING SUPPLIED TO DIVERTER VALVE
MUFFLER
FRESH AIR
DIVERTER VALVE IN CLOSED POSITION
AIR PUMP
AIR PUMP OUTPUT DUMPED TO ATMOSPHERE

A.I.R. flow schematic

are left over from the combustion process.

The diverter valve closes during engine overrun and deceleration and dumps the output from the air pump to the atmosphere. This prevents backfire due to air being injected when an overly rich mixture is present in the exhaust port.

TESTING

Check Valve

To test the check valve, disconnect the hose at the diverter valve. Blow into the hose and suck on it. Air should flow only into the engine.

Diverter Valve

Pull off the vacuum line to the top of the valve with the engine running. There should be vacuum in the line. Replace the line. No air should be escaping with the engine running at a steady idle. Open and quickly close the throttle. A blast of air should come out of the valve muffler for at least one second. If the valve must be replaced, use a new gasket at the valve mounting on the pump and torque the bolts to 85 in. lbs.

Air Pump

Disconnect the hose from the diverter valve. Start the engine and accelerate it to about 1,500 rpm. The airflow should increase as the engine is accelerated. If no airflow is noted or it remains constant, check the following:

1. Drive belt tension.
2. Listen for a leaking pressure relief valve. If it is defective, replace the whole relief/diverter valve.
3. Foreign matter in pump filter open-

ings. If the pump is defective or excessively noisy, it must be replaced.

AIR PUMP REMOVAL AND INSTALLATION

1. Disconnect the output hose.
2. Hold the pump from turning by squeezing the drive belt.
3. Loosen the pulley bolts.
4. Loosen the alternator so the belt can be removed.
5. Remove the pulley.
6. Remove the pump mounting bolts and the pump.
7. Install the pump with the mounting bolts loose.
8. Install the pulley and tighten the bolts finger-tight.
9. Install and adjust the drive belt as explained under Alternator Belt Tension Adjustment in Chapter 3.
10. Squeeze the drive belt to prevent the pump from turning.
11. Torque the pulley bolts to 25 ft lbs. Tighten the pump mountings.
12. Check and adjust the belt tension again, if necessary.
13. Connect the hose.
14. If any hose leaks are suspected, pour soapy water over the suspected area with the engine running. Bubbles will form wherever air is escaping.

Pulse Air Injection Reactor System

On 1977 models with 140 cu in. engines the Pulse Air system replaces the AIR system previously used on California engines and the CCS system used on 49 states engines.

The Pulse Air system, like AIR, injects air into the exhaust system to burn hydrocarbons and carbon monoxide. Pulse Air takes advantage of the fact that exhaust gases flow in pulses: after each exhaust valve closes there is a specific time interval and area in the exhaust ports when pressures drop below the surrounding atmosphere. A series of air injection tubes fed by an air valve chamber directs atmospheric flow at the right time and place in the exhaust system. The air chamber contains a set of four high-frequency check valves which regulate airflow and prevent exhaust gas from escaping.

The Pulse Air system is simpler and lighter (by 15 lbs), than AIR. It offers improved driveability and increased fuel economy while producing a small horsepower increase.

Exhaust Gas Recirculation (EGR)

The exhaust gas recirculation (EGR) is used on all models. The valve is mounted on the intake manifold and connected to the exhaust manifold by a "U"-shaped tube. The valve is operated by a ported vacuum through a hose connected to the carburetor. A spring in the valve keeps it closed when there is no ported vacuum to open it. The EGR valve is closed at idle, blocking off the exhaust gas recirculation. It is open at part throttle, which allows exhaust gas to enter the intake manifold.

TESTING

Put the transmission in Park or Neutral with the parking brake on, and connect a tachometer to the engine.

Start the engine and set the throttle so that the engine runs at exactly 2,000 rpm. The engine must be at normal operating temperature with the choke fully open.

Disconnect the vacuum hose at the EGR valve. The engine speed should increase at least 100 rpm.

If the engine speed does not increase, use your finger to check for vacuum at the end of the hose. If there is no vacuum, look for a plugged hose or carburetor port.

If the vacuum is okay, hook the hose back up to the valve and watch or feel with your hand under the valve to find out if the diaphragm moves to the open position. If the diaphragm does not move, the valve is stuck or defective.

If the valve moves to the open position, but has no effect on engine speed at 2,000 rpm, either the valve or the passageway underneath it are plugged. The valve will have

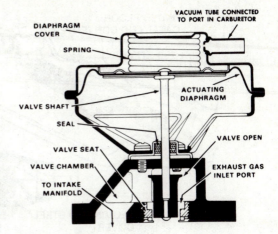

EGR valve sectional view

to be removed and either cleaned or replaced.

NOTE: *Do not open the EGR valve while the engine is idling, to see if the valve is recirculating exhaust gas. Some engines recirculate such a small amount of exhaust gas that opening the valve at idle will make so small a change in rpm that you can't detect it. The test must be performed at 2,000 rpm.*

CLEANING THE EGR VALVE

Cleaning of the valve is recommended. Do not use any kind of solvent or cleaning fluids. They will damage the valve diaphragm. The base of the valve can be cleaned with a wire brush.

1. Remove the EGR valve and tap lightly on the sides and end with a plastic hammer to remove the exhaust deposits. Do not clamp it in a vise for this.

2. Using a wire wheel, buff the exhaust deposits from the mounting surface and around the valve.

3. Depress the valve disphragm and check the valve seating area through the valve outlet and check the seating area for cleanliness.

4. If there are any deposits around the outlet, clean them with a small screwdriver.

5. Clean the mounting surfaces and reinstall using a new gasket.

Catalytic Converter

All 1975 and later models have an underfloor oxidizing catalytic converter used to control hydrocarbon and carbon monoxide emissions. Control is accomplished by placing a catalyst in the exhaust system in such a way as to enable all exhaust gas flow from the

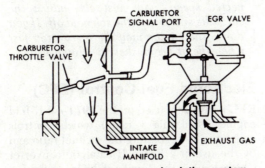

Schematic of exhaust gas recirculation system

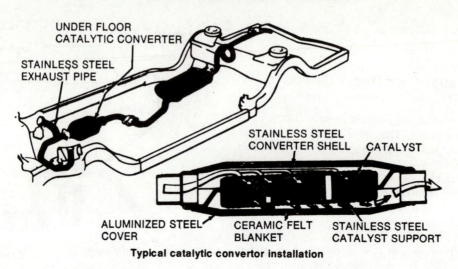

Typical catalytic convertor installation

engine to pass through it and undergo a chemical reaction before passing into the atmosphere. The chemical reaction involved is the oxidizing of hydrocarbons and carbon monoxide into water vapor and carbon dioxide.

NOTE: *Unleaded fuel must be used with catalytic converters.*

In addition to the catalytic converters, a restricted fuel inlet is used, which will only accept the smaller fuel nozzles used to dispense unleaded fuel.

Anti-Dieseling Solenoid

This solenoid is called a deceleration assist solenoid by Chevrolet, but it is actually just an anti-dieseling solenoid. The only difference is in what it is called, and the method of setting the idle mixture on the carburetor. Normally, a carburetor with an anti-dieseling solenoid, sometimes called an idle stop solenoid, has its normal curb idle set with the solenoid adjustment. This is the "solenoid connected" speed. The idle mixture settings are made at that speed. The "solenoid disconnected" speed is set with the throttle screw or the allen screw in the middle of the solenoid. This is the way the settings have been made for years.

On 1975 manual transmission cars equipped with a solenoid, the mixture setting is made at the "solenoid disconnected" speed, just as if the solenoid wasn't there. After the mixture setting is made, the idle speed is 700 rpm, and this is the normal curb idle speed. Then the solenoid is connected, and the idle speed should rise to 1200 rpm.

Because of the difference in procedure, the solenoid was renamed the "deceleration assist solenoid." The term comes from the dropping of the idle rpm when the clutch is disengaged, which "assists" in shifting into gear without clashing. The clutch switch that turns the solnoid off is nothing new. It has always been on every manual transmission car with an anti-dieseling solenoid.

TESTING

The solenoid stem should extend against the throttle lever whenever the ignition switch is on. The solenoid does not have enough power to push the throttle open. If the throttle is opened by stepping on the gas pedal, the solenoid will extend fully and hold the throttle at the solenoid connected speed.

Stepping on the clutch pedal should turn the solenoid off, and the engine speed should drop to a normal curb idle.

CAUTION: *On the 1-bbl carburetor, moving the body of the solenoid to make the solenoid-connected speed will change the curb idle speed when the solenoid is off. If at any time you adjust the solenoid-connected speed, you must also adjust the curb idle speed with the solenoid off. If you don't, the engine may die or run too fast when the driver pushes the clutch pedal.*

Electronic Fuel Control (EFC)

EFC is a system used on the 1979–80 151cid engine (California version) which controls emissions by regulating the air/fuel ratio and by the use of a Phase II catalytic converter which lowers the levels of NOx, hydrocar-

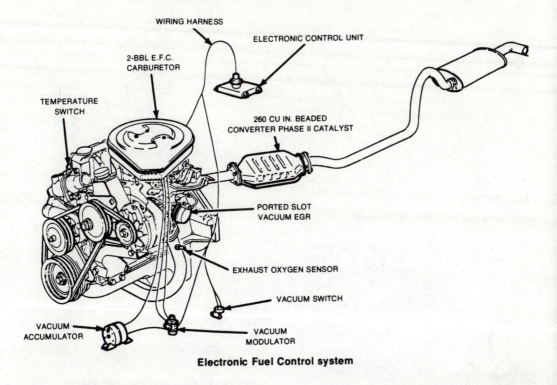

Electronic Fuel Control system

bons and carbon monoxide. The chief components are an exhaust gas oxygen sensor, an electronic control unit, a vacuum modulator, a controlled air/fuel ratio carburetor, and a Phase II catalytic converter. Briefly, the system senses the amount of oxygen present in the exhaust gas stream and varies the ratio of the air/fuel mixture at the carburetor to keep the oxygen content of the exhaust within a specified level.

All cars equipped with EFC have a small rectangular slot on the speedometer face. When the oxygen sensor is in need of replacement, the word SENSOR will appear in the slot. This is a reminder to take the car to a trained technician and have the sensor replaced. Once the sensor has been replaced, the flag should be reset. If that has not been done, you can do it yourself.

1. Remove the speedometer trimplate and lens, by removing the attaching screws (8 on the trim plate, 4 on the lens).

2. Viewing the slot on an angle from the right side, insert a small awl into the toothed wheel on the upper left corner of the slot. Rotate the SENSOR flag downward. When all the way down, the wheel will rotate no further and a black mark on the edge of the wheel will appear centered and slightly to the left.

Remember, the flag should be reset ONLY

AFTER the sensor has been replaced. If the sensor is not replaced, engine fuel mixture will not be monitored, resulting in poor driveability and high fuel consumption.

Early Fuel Evaporation (EFE)

Early fuel evaporation is used on all V8 models and all 1977–80 models. The system consists of an EFE valve at the exhaust manifold flange, an actuator and a thermal vacuum switch (TVS). The TVS is mounted in the

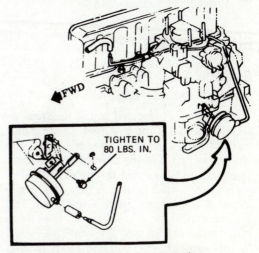

Heat valve and actuator—4 cyl. engine

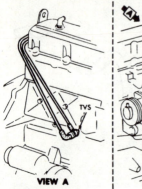

Heat valve and actuator—V6 engine

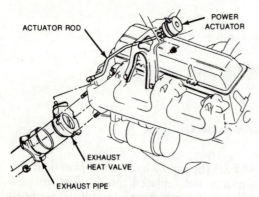

Heat valve and actuator V8 engine

water outlet housing and directly controls vacuum in response to coolant temperatures.

The actuator closes the EFE valve when coolant temperatures are below 180° F, routing hot gases to the base of the carburetor. When coolant temperatures reach 180° F, vacuum to the actuator is cut off releasing an internal spring in the actuator and opening the EFE valve.

FUEL SYSTEM

Electric Fuel Pump

All Exc 4 Cyl. 151 Eng.

The fuel pump is located in the fuel tank as an integral part of the tank level sending unit assembly. The pump is activated when the ignition switch is in the Start of On position. Pump current is carried through an oil pressure safety switch which breaks the pump circuit if oil pressure drops below 2 psi. The fuel tank must be removed from the car to remove the fuel pump. The unit is serviced by replacement. Fuel pump fuses are located

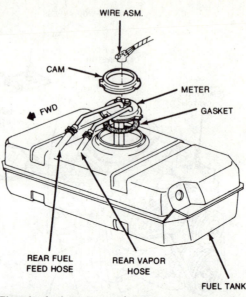

Electric fuel meter and pump—except station wagon and hatchback coupe

in the vehicle fuse block. See Chapter 5 for details.

REMOVAL AND INSTALLATION

1. Remove the fuel tank from the car, using the procedure given later in this chapter. The battery ground cable must be disconnected.

2. Use the special spanner wrench or a suitable substitute to unscrew the retaining cam ring. Be very careful and avoid making any sparks. Do not strike any part with a metal object or hammer.

3. Remove the sending unit and pump assembly.

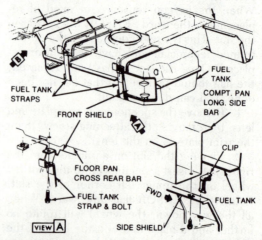

Electric fuel meter and pump—station wagon and hatchback coupe

4. Remove the flat wire conductor from the plastic clip on the fuel tube.

5. Squeeze the clamp and pull the pump straight back about ½ in.

6. Remove the two nuts, lockwashers, and wires from the pump terminals.

7. Squeeze the clamp and pull the pump straight back to remove it from the sending unit, being careful not to bend the circular support bracket.

8. Slide the new pump through the circular support bracket until it rests against the rubber coupling. Make sure that the pump has the rubber isolator and the saran strainer supplied in the service package attached.

9. Attach the two wires to the pump terminals, using lockwashers and nuts. Make sure that the flat conductor is on the terminal away from the float arm.

10. Squeeze the clamp and push the pump into the rubber coupling.

11. Replace the flat wire conductor in the plastic clip on the fuel tube.

12. Place the unit in the tank opening. Tighten the cam ring.

13. Replace the fuel tank in the car.

Mechanical Fuel Pump

4 Cyl. 151 Engine

All four cylinder 151 engines use a mechanical fuel pump which is mounted on the right front side of the engine.

REMOVAL

1. Disconnect the negative battery cable.

2. Disconnect the fuel inlet hose from the pump.

3. Disconnect the vapor return hose, if so equipped.

4. Disconnect the fuel outlet pipe.

5. Remove the two ½" hex head bolts, using a ⅜" drive deep socket and ratchet handle.

6. Remove the fuel pump.

INSTALLATION

1. Position the new pump using a new gasket.

2. Install the two ½" hex head bolts and tighten evenly.

3. Install the fuel outlet pipe.

NOTE: *If you have difficulty starting the fitting on the outlet pipe it might make it easier if you disconnect the upper end of the pipe from the carburetor then hold the fuel pump nut with a wrench and tighten the fitting securely. Reconnect and tighten the fitting at the carburetor.*

4. Install the fuel inlet hose.

5. Install the vapor return hose, if so equipped.

6. Connect the negative battery cable.

7. Start the engine and check for leaks.

Carburetors

The one barrel carburetors used by the GM Sub-Compacts are manufactured by Rochester. The two barrels are made by either Rochester or Holley. Below is a carburetor model application chart. The chart was made from the latest factory sources however it is possible that your model may differ due to changes made during vehicle production. To be positive check the model and identification number which are either on a tag attached to the carburetor or stamped on the carburetor housing. The following adjustments are divided by carburetor models. For adjustment specifications refer to the Carburetor Specification Chart following the model adjustments. The carburetors are listed by model, year and identification number.

REMOVAL AND INSTALLATION

1. Remove the air cleaner and gasket.

2. Disconnect the fuel and vacuum lines.

3. Disconnect the choke rod, or on an early model two-barrel, remove the choke water cover by removing the three attaching screws. Disconnect all electrical connections.

4. Disconnect the accelerator linkage.

5. Disconnect the Powerglide throttle valve linkage or Turbo Hydra-Matic detent cable.

6. Unbolt the carburetor and remove the carburetor and solenoid assembly.

7. Remove the insulator gasket, air cleaner bracket, and flange gasket.

8. Before installation, make sure that the carburetor and manifold sealing surfaces are clean.

NOTE: *To reduce the possibility of back-firing fill the carburetor bowl with a small amount of fuel.*

9. Install a new carburetor base gasket.

10. Install the air cleaner brace and the insulator.

11. Install the carburetor and start the fuel and vacuum lines.

12. Bolt down the carburetor evenly.

Carburetor Model Application Chart

Year	Engine No Cyl Displacement (cu in.)	No bbl	Models
VEGA, MONZA			
1971–72	4 cyl. 140	1	Rochester MV
		2	Rochester 2GV
1973–74	4 cyl. 140	1	Rochester MV
		2	Holley 5210C
1975–76	4 cyl. 140	1	Rochester MV
		2	Holley 5210C
	V8 262,305,350	2	Rochester 2GC
1978	4 cyl. 151	2	Holley 5210C,6510C
	V6 196,231	2	Rochester 2GC,2GE
	V8 305	2	Rochester 2GC,2GE
1979	4 cyl. 151(Calif.)	2	Holley 6510C
	4 cyl. 151(Fed.)	2	Rochester 2SE
	V6 196,231	2	Rochester M2ME/M2MC
	V8 305	2	Rochester M2ME/M2MC
1980	4 cyl. 151	2	Rochester 2SE
	V6 231	2	Rochester M2ME/M2MC
ASTRE, SUNBIRD			
1975	4 cyl. 140	2	Holley 5210C
1976	4 cyl. 140	1	Rochester MV
		2	Holley 5210C
	V6 231	2	Rochester 2GC
1977	4 cyl. 140,151	2	Holley 5210C
	V6 231	2	Rochester 2GC,2GE
1978	4 cyl. 151	2	Holley 5210C,6510C
	V6 231	2	Rochester 2GE
1979	4 cyl. 151(Calif.)	2	Holley 5210C,6510C
	4 cyl. 151(Fed.)	2	Rochester 2SE
	V6 231	2	Rochester M2MC/M2ME
	V8 305	2	Rochester M2MC/M2ME
1980	4 cyl. 151	2	Rochester 2SE
	V6 231	2	Rochester M2MC/M2ME
STARFIRE			
1975–76	V6 231	2	Rochester 2GC
1973	4 cyl. 140	2	Holley 5210C
	V6 231	2	Rochester 2GC

Carburetor Model Application Chart (cont.)

Year	Engine No Cyl Displacement (cu in.)	No bbl	Models
1978	4 cyl. 151	2	Holley 5210C, 6510C
	V6 231	2	Rochester 2GC, 2GE
	V8 305	2	Rochester 2GC, 2GE
1979	4 cyl. 151	2	Holley 5210C
	V6 231	2	Rochester 2ME
	V8 305	2	Rochester M2MC/M2ME
1980	4 cyl. 151	2	Rochester 2SE
	V6 231	2	Rochester 2ME

SKYHAWK

Year	Engine No Cyl Displacement (cu in.)	No bbl	Models
1975–76	V6 231	2	Rochester 2GC
1977	V6 231	2	Rochester 2GC, 2GE
1978	V6 231	2	Rochester 2GE
1979–80	V6 231	2	Rochester 2ME

13. Tighten the fuel and vacuum lines.

14. Connect and adjust the accelerator and automatic transmission linkage. See Chapter 6 for details on the transmission linkage adjustments.

15. Connect the choke rod or water cover if so equipped.

Install the air cleaner. Adjust the idle speed as described in Chapter 2. Do not tamper with the idle mixture screw unless the carburetor has been repaired, overhauled, or replaced.

OVERHAUL

Whenever wear or dirt causes a carburetor to perform poorly, there are two possible solutions to the problem. The simplest is to trade in the old unit for a rebuilt one. The other cheaper alternative is to purchase a carburetor overhaul kit and rebuild the original unit. Some of the better overhaul kits contain complete step by step instructions along with exploded views and gauges. Other kits, probably intended for the professional, have only a few general overhaul hints. The second type can be moderately confusing to the novice, especially since a kit may have extra parts so that one kit can cover several variations of the same carburetor. In any event, it is inadvisable to dismantle any carburetor without at least replacing all the gaskets. The carburetor adjustments should all be checked after overhaul.

THROTTLE LINKAGE ADJUSTMENT

The throttle linkage is of the cable type. No adjustments are necessary. However, it is advisable to check that the throttle valve(s) open all the way when the accelerator pedal is held in the wide-open throttle position. If there is any binding, check that the cable is correctly routed and that the carpet is not interfering with the pedal.

ROCHESTER MODEL MV CARBURETOR ADJUSTMENTS

Float Level Adjustment

This adjustment requires that the top of the carburetor be removed. Incorrect float level can cause stalling or a highspeed miss.

1. Hold the float retaining pin (vertical) firmly in place in the carburetor body.

2. Push down on the end of the float arm to hold it against the needle valve.

3. Measure the vertical distance from the highest point at the end of the float to the bowl gasket surface, with the gasket re-

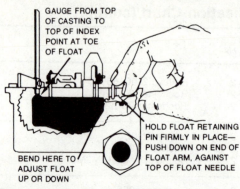

GAUGE FROM TOP OF CASTING TO TOP OF INDEX POINT AT TOE OF FLOAT

HOLD FLOAT RETAINING PIN FIRMLY IN PLACE— PUSH DOWN ON END OF FLOAT ARM, AGAINST TOP OF FLOAT NEEDLE

BEND HERE TO ADJUST FLOAT UP OR DOWN

Float level adjustment—model MV

moved. The measurement should be as shown in the "Carburetor Specifications" chart.

4. To adjust, bend the float arm up or down adjacent to the float.

Fast Idle Speed

The idle speed must be properly set before making this adjustment. The engine must be at normal operating temperature.

1. Disconnect the electrical lead from the TCS solenoid vacuum valve on the left-side of the firewall, if so equipped. Make sure that the choke is open, the EGR valve isn't hanging up, and the air conditioning is off. After this, connect a tach.

2. Let the engine idle in Neutral.

3. Place the fast idle cam so that the cam follower tang ('71–'74), or screw ('75–'76), is on the highest step.

4. Fast idle speed should be 2,400 rpm ('71–'72 manual trans.); 2,800 rpm ('71–'72 auto. trans. with TCS disconnected and connector off vacuum solenoid on the left-side of firewall); 2,000 rpm ('73–'75 manual trans.);

1,500 rpm ('76 manual trans.); 2,200 rpm ('73–'76 auto. trans. with no vacuum to the distributor).

5. If the fast idle speed is incorrect, insert a screwdriver in the slot on the follower tang and bend it carefully to adjust; if equipped with a screw, turn it in or out to adjust.

6. When finished, reconnect the electrical lead, if so equipped.

Choke Coil Rod Adjustment

1. Disconnect the thermostatic coil rod from the upper choke lever and hold the choke valve closed.

2. Push down on the coil rod to the end of its travel.

3. The top of the rod should be even with the bottom hole in the choke lever.

4. To make adjustments, bend the rod.

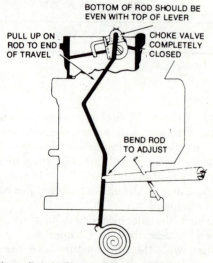

BOTTOM OF ROD SHOULD BE EVEN WITH TOP OF LEVER

PULL UP ON ROD TO END OF TRAVEL

CHOKE VALVE COMPLETELY CLOSED

BEND ROD TO ADJUST

Choke coil rod adjustment—model MV

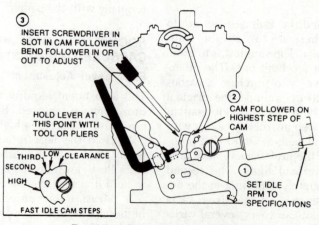

③ INSERT SCREWDRIVER IN SLOT IN CAM FOLLOWER BEND FOLLOWER IN OR OUT TO ADJUST

HOLD LEVER AT THIS POINT WITH TOOL OR PLIERS

② CAM FOLLOWER ON HIGHEST STEP OF CAM

THIRD LOW CLEARANCE
SECOND
HIGH

FAST IDLE CAM STEPS

① SET IDLE RPM TO SPECIFICATIONS

Fast idle adjustment—model MV

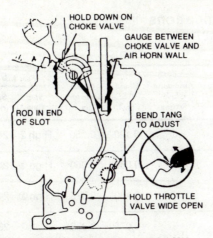

Choke unloader adjustment—model MV

Choke Unloader Adjustment

1. Apply pressure to the choke valve and hold it in the closed position.

2. Open the throttle valve to the wide open position.

3. Check the dimension between the lower edge (upper edge for 1976) of the choke plate and the air horn wall; if adjustment is needed, bend the unloader tang on the throttle lever.

Choke Rod (Fast Idle Cam) Adjustment

NOTE: *Adjust the fast idle before making choke rod adjustments.*

1. Place the fast idle cam follower on the second step of the fast idle cam and hold it firmly against the rise to the high step.

2. Rotate the choke valve in the direction of a closed choke by applying force to the choke coil lever.

3. Bend the choke rod to give the specified opening between the lower edge (upper edge for 1976) of the choke valve and the inside air horn wall.

NOTE: *Measurement must be made at the center of the choke valve.*

Choke Vacuum Break Adjustment

The adjustment of the vacuum break diaphragm unit insures correct choke valve opening after engine starting.

1. Remove the air cleaner on vehicles with Therm AC air cleaner; plug the sensor's vacuum take off port.

2. Using an external vacuum source, apply vacuum to the vacuum break diaphragm until the plunger is fully seated.

3. When the plunger is seated, push the choke valve toward the closed position.

4. Holding the choke valve in this position, place the specified gauge between the lower edge (upper edge for 1976) of the choke valve and the air horn wall.

5. If the measurement is not correct, bend the vacuum break rod.

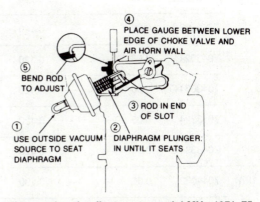

Vacuum break adjustment—model MV—1971–75

Choke Auxiliary Vacuum Break Adjustment (Beginning 1975)

This adjustment is required in addition to the preceding vacuum break adjustment beginning 1975.

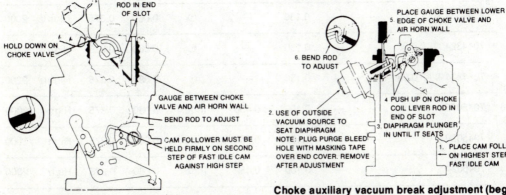

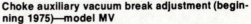

Choke rod (fast idle cam) adjustment—model MV

Choke auxiliary vacuum break adjustment (beginning 1975)—model MV

Carburetor Specifications
Rochester—1 BBL
Model—MV

Year	Carburetor Identification	Float Level (in.)	Float Drop (in.)	Pump Rod (in.)	Primary Vacuum Break (in.)	Secondary Vacuum Break (in.)	Automatic Choke Setting	Choke Rod (in.)	Choke Unloader (in.)	Fast Idle Step Cam	Fast Idle Spd. (rpm)
1971	7041023	1/16	—	—	0.200	—	①	0.120	0.350	High ②	2400
	7041024	1/16	—	—	0.140	—	①	0.080	0.350	High ②	2400
1972	7042023	1/8	—	—	0.200	—	①	0.130	0.375	High ②	2400
	7042024	1/16	—	—	0.120	—	①	0.070	0.375	High ②	2800
1973	7043023	0.06	—	—	0.140	—	①	0.110	0.375	High ③	2000
	7043033 ④	0.06	—	—	0.140	—	①	0.110	0.375	High ③	2200
	7043323	0.06	—	—	0.140	—	①	0.110	0.375	High ③	2000
	7043333 ④	0.06	—	—	0.140	—	①	0.110	0.375	High ③	2200
	7043024	0.06	—	—	0.120	—	①	0.085	0.375	High ③	2000
	7043034 ④	0.06	—	—	0.120	—	①	0.085	0.375	High ③	2200
	7043324	0.06	—	—	0.120	—	①	0.085	0.375	High ③	2000
	7043334 ④	0.06	—	—	0.120	—	①	0.085	0.375	High ③	2200
1974	7044023	0.06	—	—	0.130	—	①	0.080	0.375	High ③	2000
	7044033	0.06	—	—	0.130	—	①	0.080	0.375	High ③	2000
	7044323	0.06	—	—	0.130	—	①	0.080	0.375	High ③	2200
	7044333 ④	0.06	—	—	0.130	—	①	0.080	0.375	High ③	2200
	7044024 ④	0.06	—	—	0.130	—	①	0.080	0.375	High ③	2000
	7044034 ④	0.06	—	—	0.130	—	①	0.080	0.375	High ③	2000
	7044324	0.06	—	—	0.130	—	①	0.080	0.375	High ③	2200
	7044334 ④	0.06	—	—	0.130	—	①	0.080	0.375	High ③	2200
1975	7045025	1/8	—	—	0.100	0.450	Index	0.080	0.375	High	2000
	7045029	1/8	—	—	0.100	0.450	Index	0.080	0.375	High	2000
	7045024	1/8	—	—	0.100	0.450	Index	0.080	0.375	High	2000

Carburetor Specifications (cont.)
Rochester—1 BBL
Model—MV

Year	Carburetor Identification	Float Level (in.)	Float Drop (in.)	Pump Rod (in.)	Primary Vacuum Break (in.)	Secondary Vacuum Break (in.)	Automatic Choke Setting	Choke Rod (in.)	Choke Unloader (in.)	Fast Idle Step Cam	Fast Idle Spd. (rpm)
	7045028	⅛	—	—	0.100	0.450	Index	0.080	0.375	High	2000
1976	17056023	⅛	—	—	0.060	0.450	①	0.045	0.215	High ⑤	2200
	17056027	⅛	—	—	0.060	0.450	①	0.045	0.215	High ⑤	2200
	17056022	⅛	—	—	0.060	0.450	①	0.045	0.215	High ⑤	2200
	17056026	⅛	—	—	0.060	0.450	①	0.045	0.215	High ⑤	2200

① Hold the choke valve completely open after disconnecting the upper end of the coil rod. Push down on the rod to the end of travel. Top of the rod should be even with the bottom of the hole in the lever. Bend the rod to adjust
② With TCS solenoid disconnected
③ With no vacuum to distributor
④ With hot idle compensator for air conditioning installation
⑤ Adjust with A.C. off

1. Using an external source of vacuum, apply vacuum to the auxiliary vacuum break diaphram until the plunger is seated fully.

2. Place the cam follower on the highest step of the fast idle cam.

3. With the diaphragm seated, insert the specified gauge between the upper edge of the choke valve and the inner air horn wall.

4. To adjust the clearance, bend the link between the vacuum break and the choke lever.

NOTE: *The auxiliary vacuum break diaphragm is on the same side of the carburetor as the throttle stop solenoid.*

ROCHESTER MODEL 2GC, 2GV, 2GE CARBURETOR ADJUSTMENTS

Float Level

With the air horn assembly upside down, measure the distance from the air horn gasket to the lip at the toe of the float. Bend the float arm to adjust to specifications.

Float Drop

Holding the air horn assembly upright, measure the distance from the gasket to the lip or notch at the toe of the float. If correction is necessary, bend the float tang at the rear, next to the needle and seat.

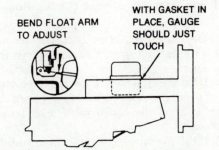

BEND FLOAT ARM TO ADJUST

WITH GASKET IN PLACE, GAUGE SHOULD JUST TOUCH

Float level measurement—model 2GC, 2GV, 2GE

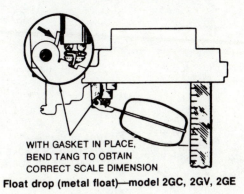

WITH GASKET IN PLACE, BEND TANG TO OBTAIN CORRECT SCALE DIMENSION

Float drop (metal float)—model 2GC, 2GV, 2GE

Fast Idle Adjustment

The fast idle is set automatically when the curb idle and mixture is set.

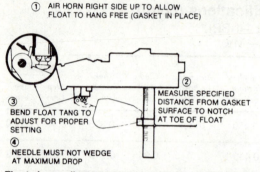

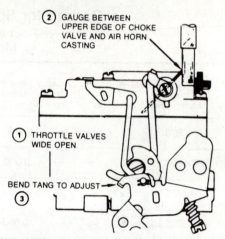

① AIR HORN RIGHT SIDE UP TO ALLOW
FLOAT TO HANG FREE (GASKET IN PLACE)

③ BEND FLOAT TANG TO
ADJUST FOR PROPER
SETTING

② MEASURE SPECIFIED
DISTANCE FROM GASKET
SURFACE TO NOTCH
AT TOE OF FLOAT

④ NEEDLE MUST NOT WEDGE
AT MAXIMUM DROP

Float drop adjustment (plastic float) model 2GC, 2GV, 2 GE

② GAUGE BETWEEN
UPPER EDGE OF CHOKE
VALVE AND AIR HORN
CASTING

① THROTTLE VALVES
WIDE OPEN

BEND TANG TO ADJUST →

③

Choke unloader adjustment—Models 2GC, 2GE, 2GV

Choke Unloader Adjustment

1. Hold the throttle valves wide open and use a rubber band to hold the choke valve toward the closed position.

2. Measure the distance between the upper edge of the choke valve and the air horn wall.

3. If this measurement is not within specifications, bend the unloader tang on the throttle lever to correct it.

Fast Idle Cam Adjustment (Choke Rod In.)

1. Turn the idle screw onto the second step of the fast idle cam, abutting against the top step.

2. Hold the choke valve toward the closed position and check the clearance between the upper edge of the choke valve and the air horn wall.

3. If this measurement varies from specifications, bend the tang on the choke lever.

Model 2GV Choke Coil Rod Adjustment—1971

1. Hold the choke valve completely open.

2. Disconnect the thermostat coil rod from the upper lever and push downward on the rod to the end of travel.

3. The top of the rod should cover ½ diameter of the hole.

Model 2GV Choke Coil Rod Adjustment—1972

1. Hold the choke valve completely open.

2. Disconnect the thermostatic coil rod from the upper lever.

3. Push downward on the coil rod to the end of travel.

4. The top of the pin on the adjustable

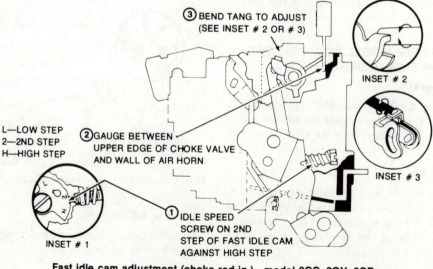

③ BEND TANG TO ADJUST
(SEE INSET # 2 OR # 3)

INSET # 2

INSET # 3

L—LOW STEP
2—2ND STEP
H—HIGH STEP

② GAUGE BETWEEN
UPPER EDGE OF CHOKE VALVE
AND WALL OF AIR HORN

① IDLE SPEED
SCREW ON 2ND
STEP OF FAST IDLE CAM
AGAINST HIGH STEP

INSET # 1

Fast idle cam adjustment (choke rod in.)—model 2GC, 2GV, 2GE

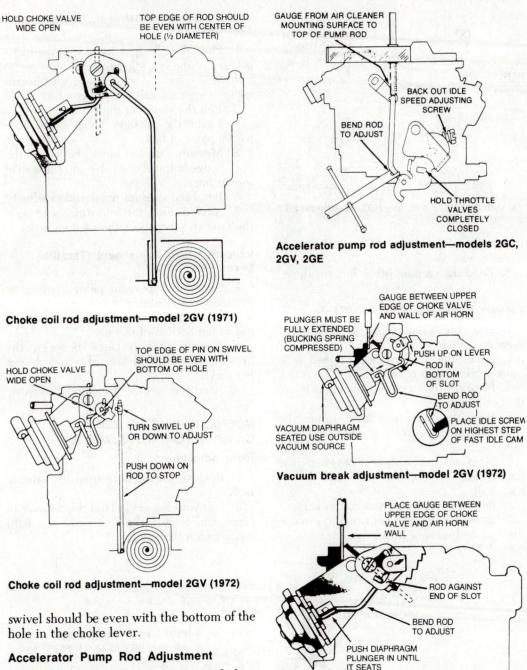

HOLD CHOKE VALVE WIDE OPEN

TOP EDGE OF ROD SHOULD BE EVEN WITH CENTER OF HOLE (½ DIAMETER)

Choke coil rod adjustment—model 2GV (1971)

GAUGE FROM AIR CLEANER MOUNTING SURFACE TO TOP OF PUMP ROD

BACK OUT IDLE SPEED ADJUSTING SCREW

BEND ROD TO ADJUST

HOLD THROTTLE VALVES COMPLETELY CLOSED

Accelerator pump rod adjustment—models 2GC, 2GV, 2GE

HOLD CHOKE VALVE WIDE OPEN

TOP EDGE OF PIN ON SWIVEL SHOULD BE EVEN WITH BOTTOM OF HOLE

TURN SWIVEL UP OR DOWN TO ADJUST

PUSH DOWN ON ROD TO STOP

Choke coil rod adjustment—model 2GV (1972)

GAUGE BETWEEN UPPER EDGE OF CHOKE VALVE AND WALL OF AIR HORN

PLUNGER MUST BE FULLY EXTENDED (BUCKING SPRING COMPRESSED)

PUSH UP ON LEVER

ROD IN BOTTOM OF SLOT

BEND ROD TO ADJUST

PLACE IDLE SCREW ON HIGHEST STEP OF FAST IDLE CAM

VACUUM DIAPHRAGM SEATED USE OUTSIDE VACUUM SOURCE

Vacuum break adjustment—model 2GV (1972)

PLACE GAUGE BETWEEN UPPER EDGE OF CHOKE VALVE AND AIR HORN WALL

ROD AGAINST END OF SLOT

BEND ROD TO ADJUST

PUSH DIAPHRAGM PLUNGER IN UNTIL IT SEATS

Vacuum break adjustment—model 2GV (1971)

swivel should be even with the bottom of the hole in the choke lever.

Accelerator Pump Rod Adjustment

1. Back out the idle stop screw and close the throttle valves in their bores.
2. Measure the distance from the top of the air horn to the top of the pump rod.
3. Bend the pump rod at angle to correct this dimension.

Vacuum Break Adjustment—1971–72

1. Seat the vacuum break diaphragm plunger using an outside vacuum source.
2. Rotate the choke valve towards the closed choke position so that the vacuum link is at the bottom of the slot in the choke shaft lever and the spring loaded plunger is fully compressed.
3. Place the idle screw on the highest step of the fast idle cam.
4. Measure the distance between the

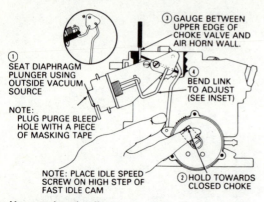

Vacuum break adjustment—1975–76—model 2GV

upper edge of the choke valve and the inside air horn wall.

5. Bend the vacuum break link to adjust.

Vacuum Break Adjustment—1975–76

1. Seat the vacuum break diaphragm using an outside vacuum source.

2. Cover the vacuum break bleed hole using a small piece of tape.

3. Place the idle screw on the high step of the fast idle cam.

4. Hold the choke coil lever inside the choke housing towards the closed choke position.

5. Measure the distance between the upper edge of the choke valve and the air horn wall.

6. Bend the vacuum break rod to adjust.

7. After making the adjustment remove the tape and reconnect the vacuum hose.

Vacuum Break Adjustment (Choke Side) 1977–78

1. Place the idle speed screw on the highest step of the fast idle cam.

2. Seat the vacuum break diaphragm using an outside vacuum source.

3. Pull the stem out until seated.

4. Cover the vacuum break bleed hole with a piece of tape.

5. Measure the distance between the upper edge of the choke valve and the wall of the air horn.

6. Bend the vacuum break rod to adjust.

7. After making the adjustments remove the tape and reconnect the vacuum hose.

Vacuum Break Adjustment (Throttle Lever Side) 1978

1. Seat the diaphragm plunger using an outside vacuum source.

2. Hold the choke valve closed with the rod in the bottom of the slot.

3. Measure the distance between the upper edge of the choke valve and the air horn wall.

4. Bend the vacuum break link to adjust.

ROCHESTER MODEL 2SE CARBURETOR ADJUSTMENTS

Float Adjustment

1. Remove the air horn from the throttle body.

2. Use your fingers to hold the retainer in place, and to push the float down into light contact with the needle.

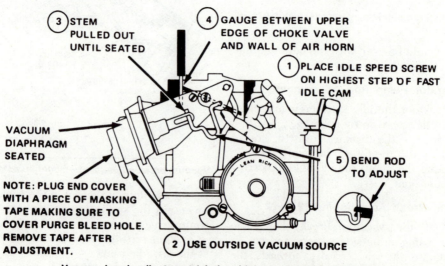

Vacuum break adjustment (choke side)—model 2GC—1977–78

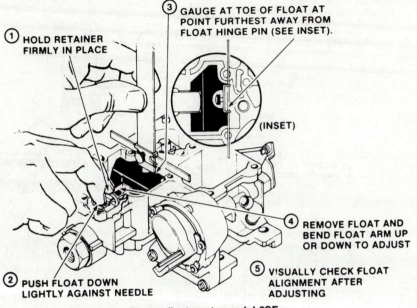

③ GAUGE AT TOE OF FLOAT AT POINT FURTHEST AWAY FROM FLOAT HINGE PIN (SEE INSET).

(INSET)

① HOLD RETAINER FIRMLY IN PLACE

④ REMOVE FLOAT AND BEND FLOAT ARM UP OR DOWN TO ADJUST

⑤ VISUALLY CHECK FLOAT ALIGNMENT AFTER ADJUSTING

② PUSH FLOAT DOWN LIGHTLY AGAINST NEEDLE

Float adjustment—model 2SE

NOTE: ON MODELS USING A CLIP TO RETAIN PUMP ROD IN PUMP LEVER, NO PUMP ADJUSTMENT IS REQUIRED. ON MODELS USING THE "CLIPLESS" PUMP ROD, THE PUMP ADJUSTMENT SHOULD NOT BE CHANGED FROM ORIGINAL FACTORY SETTING UNLESS GAUGING SHOWS OUT OF SPECIFICATION. THE PUMP LEVER IS MADE FROM HEAVY DUTY, HARDENED STEEL MAKING BENDING DIFFICULT. DO NOT REMOVE PUMP LEVER FOR BENDING UNLESS ABSOLUTELY NECESSARY.

② GAUGE FROM AIR HORN CASTING SURFACE TO TOP OF PUMP STEM. DIMENSION SHOULD BE AS SPECIFIED.

① THROTTLE VALVES COMPLETELY CLOSED. MAKE SURE FAST IDLE SCREW IS OFF STEPS OF FAST IDLE CAM.

③ IF NECESSARY TO ADJUST, REMOVE PUMP LEVER RETAINING SCREW AND WASHER AND REMOVE PUMP LEVER BY ROTATING LEVER TO REMOVE FROM PUMP ROD. PLACE LEVER IN A VISE, PROTECTING LEVER FROM DAMAGE, AND BEND END OF LEVER (NEAREST NECKED DOWN SECTION).

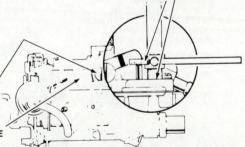

⑤ OPEN AND CLOSE THROTTLE VALVES CHECKING LINKAGE FOR FREEDOM OF MOVEMENT AND OBSERVING PUMP LEVER ALIGNMENT.

④ REINSTALL PUMP LEVER, WASHER AND RETAINING SCREW. RECHECK PUMP ADJUSTMENT ① AND ②. TIGHTEN RETAINING SCREW SECURELY AFTER THE PUMP ADJUSTMENT IS CORRECT.

NOTE: DO NOT BEND LEVER IN A SIDEWAYS OR TWISTING MOTION.

Pump adjustment—model 2SE

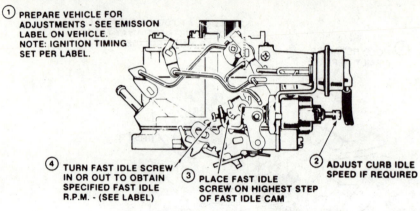

① PREPARE VEHICLE FOR ADJUSTMENTS - SEE EMISSION LABEL ON VEHICLE. NOTE: IGNITION TIMING SET PER LABEL.

④ TURN FAST IDLE SCREW IN OR OUT TO OBTAIN SPECIFIED FAST IDLE R.P.M. - (SEE LABEL)

③ PLACE FAST IDLE SCREW ON HIGHEST STEP OF FAST IDLE CAM

② ADJUST CURB IDLE SPEED IF REQUIRED

Fast idle adjustment—model 2SE

3. Measure the distance from the toe of the float (furthest from the hinge) to the top of the carburetor (gasket removed).

4. To adjust, remove the float and gently bend the arm to specification. After adjustment, check the float alignment in the chamber.

Pump Adjustment

1. With the throttle closed and the fast idle screw off the steps of the fast idle cam, measure the distance from the air horn casting to the top of the pump stem.

2. To adjust, remove the retaining screw and washer and remove the pump lever. Bend the end of the lever to correct the stem height. Do not twist the lever or bend it sideways.

3. Install the lever, washer and screw and check the adjustment. When correct, open and close the throttle a few times to check the linkage movement and alignment.

Fast Idle Adjustment

1. Set the ignition timing and curb idle speed, and disconnect and plug hoses as directed on the emission control decal.

2. Place the fast idle screw on the highest step of the cam.

3. Start the engine and adjust the engine speed to specification with the fast idle screw.

Choke Coil Lever Adjustment

1. Remove the three retaining screws and remove the choke cover and coil. On models with a riveted choke cover, drill out the three rivets and remove the cover and choke coil.

NOTE: *A choke stat cover retainer kit is required for reassembly.*

2. Place the fast idle screw on the high step of the cam.

3. Close the choke by pushing in on the intermediate choke lever. On front wheel

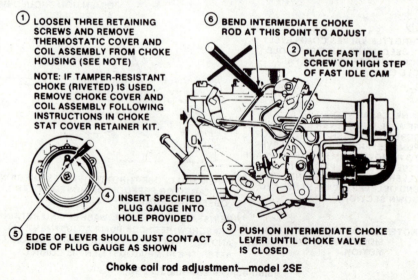

① LOOSEN THREE RETAINING SCREWS AND REMOVE THERMOSTATIC COVER AND COIL ASSEMBLY FROM CHOKE HOUSING (SEE NOTE)

NOTE: IF TAMPER-RESISTANT CHOKE (RIVETED) IS USED, REMOVE CHOKE COVER AND COIL ASSEMBLY FOLLOWING INSTRUCTIONS IN CHOKE STAT COVER RETAINER KIT.

⑥ BEND INTERMEDIATE CHOKE ROD AT THIS POINT TO ADJUST

② PLACE FAST IDLE SCREW ON HIGH STEP OF FAST IDLE CAM

④ INSERT SPECIFIED PLUG GAUGE INTO HOLE PROVIDED

⑤ EDGE OF LEVER SHOULD JUST CONTACT SIDE OF PLUG GAUGE AS SHOWN

③ PUSH ON INTERMEDIATE CHOKE LEVER UNTIL CHOKE VALVE IS CLOSED

Choke coil rod adjustment—model 2SE

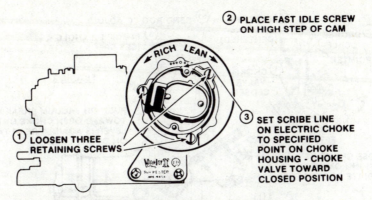

② PLACE FAST IDLE SCREW
ON HIGH STEP OF CAM

① LOOSEN THREE
RETAINING SCREWS

③ SET SCRIBE LINE
ON ELECTRIC CHOKE
TO SPECIFIED
POINT ON CHOKE
HOUSING - CHOKE
VALVE TOWARD
CLOSED POSITION

Electric choke setting—model 2SE

drive V6 models, the intermediate choke lever is behind the choke vacuum diaphragm.

4. Insert a drill or gauge of the specified size into the hole in the choke housing. The choke lever in the housing should be up against the side of the gauge.

5. If the lever does not just touch the gauge, bend the intermediate choke rod to adjust.

Electric Choke Setting

This procedure is only for those carburetors with choke covers retained by screws. Riveted choke covers are present and nonadjustable.

1. Loosen the three retaining screws.
2. Place the fast idle screw on the high step of the cam.
3. Rotate the choke cover to align the cover mark with the specified housing mark.

Primary Side Vacuum Break Adjustment

1. Follow Steps 1–4 of the Fast Idle Cam Adjustment.
2. Seat the choke vacuum diaphragm with an outside vacuum source.
3. Push in on the intermediate choke lever to close the choke valve, and hold closed during adjustment.
4. Adjust by bending the vacuum break rod until the bubble is centered.

Fast Idle Cam (Choke Rod) Adjustment

NOTE: *A special angle gauge should be used.*

1. Adjust the choke coil lever and fast idle first.
2. Rotate the degree scale until it is zeroed.
3. Close the choke and install the degree scale onto the choke plate. Center the leveling bubble.

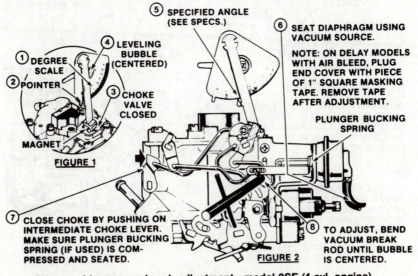

⑤ SPECIFIED ANGLE
(SEE SPECS.)

① DEGREE SCALE
② POINTER
④ LEVELING BUBBLE (CENTERED)
③ CHOKE VALVE CLOSED
MAGNET
FIGURE 1

⑥ SEAT DIAPHRAGM USING VACUUM SOURCE.

NOTE: ON DELAY MODELS WITH AIR BLEED, PLUG END COVER WITH PIECE OF 1" SQUARE MASKING TAPE. REMOVE TAPE AFTER ADJUSTMENT.

PLUNGER BUCKING SPRING

⑦ CLOSE CHOKE BY PUSHING ON INTERMEDIATE CHOKE LEVER. MAKE SURE PLUNGER BUCKING SPRING (IF USED) IS COMPRESSED AND SEATED.

⑧ TO ADJUST, BEND VACUUM BREAK ROD UNTIL BUBBLE IS CENTERED.

FIGURE 2

Primary side vacuum break adjustment—model 2SE (4 cyl. engine)

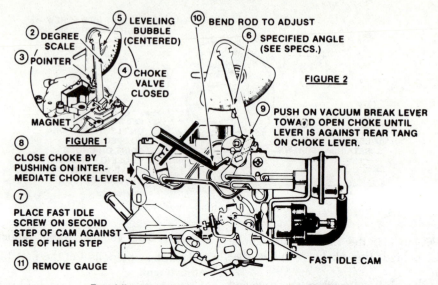

Fast idle cam (choke rod) adjustment—model 2SE

4. Rotate the scale so that the specified degree is opposite the scale pointer.

5. Place the fast idle screw on the second step of the cam (against the high step). Close the choke by pushing in the intermediate lever.

6. Push on the vacuum break lever in the direction of opening choke until the lever is against the rear tang on the choke lever.

7. Bend the fast idle cam rod at the U to adjust angle to specifications.

Choke Unloader Adjustment

1. Follow Steps 1–4 of the Fast Idle Cam Adjustment.

2. Install the choke cover and coil, if removed, aligning the marks on the housing and cover as specified.

3. Hold the primary throttle wide open.

4. If the engine is warm, close the choke valve by pushing in on the intermediate choke lever.

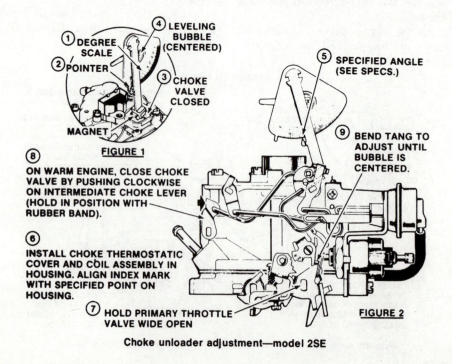

Choke unloader adjustment—model 2SE

5. Bend the unloader tang until the bubble is centered.

ROCHESTER MODEL 2MC, 2ME CARBURETOR ADJUSTMENTS

Float Level Adjustment

See the illustration for float level adjustments.

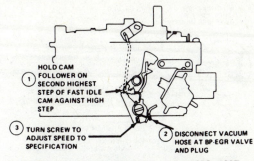

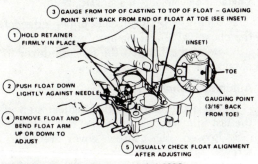

Float level adjustment—model 2MC

Fast Idle Speed

1. Place the fast idle lever on the high step of the fast idle cam.

2. Turn the fast idle screw out until the throttle valves are closed.

3. Turn the screw in to contact the lever, then turn it in two more turns. Check this preliminary setting against the sticker figure.

Fast Idle Cam (Choke Rod) Adjustment

1. Adjust the fast idle speed.

2. Place the cam follower lever on the second step of the fast idle cam, holding it firmly against the rise of the high step.

3. Close the choke valve by pushing upward on the choke coil lever inside the choke housing.

4. Gauge between the upper edge of the

Fast idle speed adjustment—model 2MC, 2ME

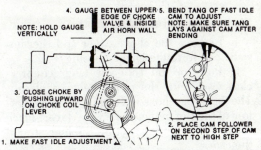

Fast idle cam (choke rod) adjustment—model 2MC, 2ME

choke valve and the inside of the air horn wall.

5. Bend the tang on the fast idle cam to adjust.

Pump Adjustment

1. With the fast idle cam follower off the steps of the fast idle cam, back out the idle speed screw until the throttle valves are completely closed.

2. Place the pump rod in the proper hole of the lever.

3. Measure from the top of the choke valve wall, next to the vent stack, to the top of the pump stem.

4. Bend the pump lever to adjust.

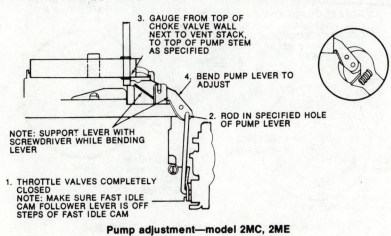

Pump adjustment—model 2MC, 2ME

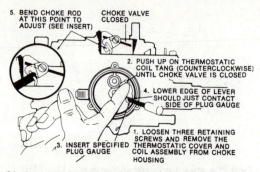

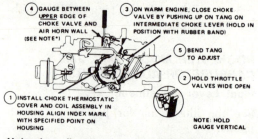

Choke coil lever adjustment—model 2MC, 2ME

Unloader adjustment—model 2MC, 2ME

Choke Coil Lever Adjustment

1. Remove the choke cover and thermostatic coil from the choke housing.

2. Push up on the coil tang (counterclockwise) until the choke valve is closed. The top of the choke rod should be at the bottom of the slot in the choke valve lever. Place the fast idle cam follower on the high step of the cam.

3. Insert a 0.120 in. plug gauge in the hole in the choke housing.

4. The lower edge of the choke coil lever should just contact the side of the plug gauge.

5. Bend the choke rod to adjust.

Unloader Adjustment

1. With the choke valve completely closed, hold the throttle valves wide open.

2. Measure between the upper edge of the choke valve and air horn wall.

3. Bend the tang on the fast idle lever to obtain the proper measurement.

Automatic Choke Setting

1. Place the lever on the highest step of the fast idle cam.

2. Loosen the three cover retaining screws.

3. Rotate the cover and coil assembly counter-clockwise until the choke valve just closes.

4. Align the mark on the cover to the specified point on the housing listed in the Carburetor Specifications Chart.

5. Tighten the three cover retaining screws.

Front/Rear Vacuum Break Adjustment

1. Seat the front diaphragm, using an outside vacuum source. If there is an air bleed hole on the diaphragm, tape it over.

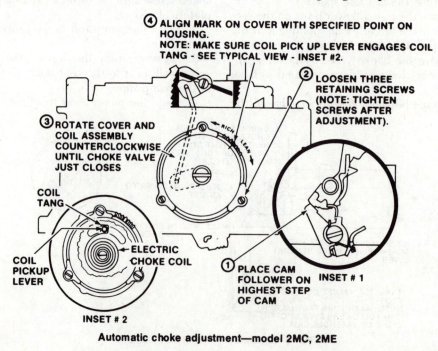

Automatic choke adjustment—model 2MC, 2ME

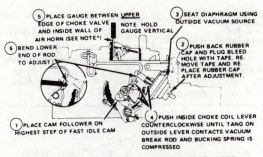

Vacuum break adjustment—model 2MC, 2ME

2. Remove the choke cover and coil. Rotate the inside coil lever counterclockwise.

3. Check that the specified gap is present between the top of the choke valve and the air horn wall.

4. Turn the front vacuum break adjusting screw to adjust.

5. To adjust the rear vacuum break diaphragm, perform Steps 1–3 on the rear diaphragm, but make sure that the plunger bucking spring is compressed and seated in Step 2. Adjust by bending the link at the bend nearest the diaphragm.

Air Conditioning Idle Speed-Up Solenoid Adjustment

1. With the engine at normal operating temperature and the air conditioning turned on but the compressor clutch lead disconnected, the solenoid should be electrically energized (plunger stem extended).

2. Adjust the plunger screw to obtain the specified idle speed.

3. Turn off the air conditioner. The solenoid plunger should move away from the tang on the throttle lever.

4. Adjust the curb idle speed with the idle speed screw, if necessary.

HOLLEY MODEL 5210C CARBURETOR ADJUSTMENTS

Float Level

1. With the carburetor air horn inverted, and the float tang resting lightly on the inlet needle, insert the specified gauge between the air horn and the float.

2. Bend the float tang if an adjustment is needed.

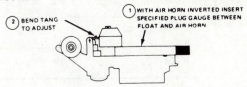

Float level adjustment—model 5210C

Float Drop

1. With the air horn right side up, measure between the air horn and the top of the float.

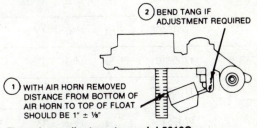

Float drop adjustment—model 5210C

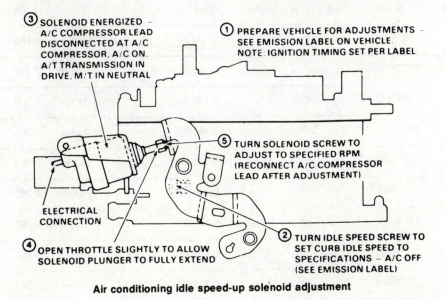

Air conditioning idle speed-up solenoid adjustment

Carburetor Specifications
Rochester—2 BBL
Models—2GV, 2GC, 2GE, 2SE, 2MC, 2ME

Year	Carburetor Identification ①	Float Level (in.)	Float Drop (in.)	Pump Rod (in.)	Primary Vacuum Break (in.)	Secondary Vacuum Break (in.)	Automatic Choke Setting	Choke Rod (in.)	Choke Unloader (in.)
Vega, Monza									
1971	7041181	$5/8$	$1\,3/4$	$1\,3/8$	0.120	—	②	0.080	0.180
	7041182	$5/8$	$1\,3/4$	$1\,3/8$	0.120	—	②	0.080	0.180
1972	7042106	$19/32$	$1\,7/8$	$1\,1/16$	0.085	—	③	0.060	0.215
	7042107	$19/32$	$1\,7/8$	$1\,1/16$	0.100	—	③	0.080	0.215
	7042826	$19/32$	$1\,7/8$	$1\,1/16$	0.085	—	③	0.060	0.215
	7042827	$19/32$	$1\,7/8$	$1\,1/16$	0.100	—	③	0.080	0.215
1975	7045105	$19/32$	$1\,7/32$	$1\,19/32$	0.130	—	Index	0.375	0.350
	7045405	$21/32$	$1\,7/32$	$1\,19/32$	0.130	—	Index	0.380	0.350
	7045106	$19/32$	$1\,7/32$	$1\,19/32$	0.130	—	Index	0.375	0.350
	7045406	$21/32$	$1\,7/32$	$1\,19/32$	0.130	—	Index	0.380	0.350
1976	17056101	$17/32$	$1\,9/32$	$1\,5/8$	0.130	—	Index	0.260	0.350
	17056102	$17/32$	$1\,9/32$	$1\,5/8$	0.130	—	Index	0.260	0.325
	17056104	$17/32$	$1\,5/32$	$1\,5/8$	0.140	—	Index	0.260	0.325
	17056404	$9/16$	$1\,3/16$	$1\,21/32$	0.140	—	Index	0.260	0.325
1977	17057104	$7/16$	$1\,9/32$	$1\,21/32$	0.130 ⑤	—	Index	0.260	0.325
	17057105	$1/2$	$1\,9/32$	$1\,21/32$	0.150 ⑤	—	Index	0.260	0.325
	17057107	$7/16$	$1\,9/32$	$1\,5/8$	0.130 ⑤	—	Index	0.260	0.325
	17057109	$1/2$	$1\,9/32$	$1\,21/32$	0.160 ⑤	—	Index	0.260	0.325
	17057404	$1/2$	$1\,9/32$	$1\,21/32$	0.160 ⑤	—	1 Lean	0.260	0.325
	17057405	$1/2$	$1\,9/32$	$1\,21/32$	0.160 ⑤	—	$1/2$ Lean	0.260	0.325
1978	17058102	$15/32$	$1\,9/37$	$1\,17/32$	0.150 ⑤	—	Index	0.260	0.325
	17058103	$15/32$	$1\,9/32$	$1\,17/32$	0.150 ⑤	—	Index	0.260	0.325
	17058104	$15/32$	$1\,9/32$	$1\,21/32$	0.160 ⑤	—	Index	0.260	0.325

Carburetor Specifications (cont'd)
Rochester—2 BBL
Models—2GV, 2GC, 2GE, 2SE, 2MC, 2ME

Year	Carburetor Identification ①	Float Level (in.)	Float Drop (in.)	Pump Rod (in.)	Primary Vacuum Break (in.)	Secondary Vacuum Break (in.)	Automatic Choke Setting	Choke Rod deg./lin.	Choke Unloader deg./lin.
1978	17058107	$15/32$	$19/32$	$1^{17}/32$	0.160 ⑤	—	Index	0.260	0.325
	17058109	$15/32$	$19/32$	$1^{17}/32$	0.160 ⑤	—	Index	0.260	0.325
	17058404	$1/2$	$19/32$	$1^{21}/32$	0.160 ⑤	—	$1/2$ Lean	0.260	0.325
	17058405	$1/2$	$19/32$	$1^{21}/32$	0.160 ⑤	—	Index	0.260	0.325
	17058447	$7/16$	$15/32$	$1^{5}/8$	0.110 ⑤	0.150 ⑥	1 Rich	0.080	0.140
	17058143	$7/16$	$15/32$	$1^{5}/8$	0.040 ⑤	0.110 ⑥	1 Rich	0.080	0.140
	17058147	$7/16$	$15/32$	$1^{5}/8$	0.100 ⑤	0.140 ⑥	1 Rich	0.080	0.140
	17058144	$7/16$	$15/32$	$1^{5}/8$	0.060 ⑤	0.110 ⑥	1 Rich	0.080	0.140
1979	17059675	$13/64$	—	$1/2$	0.117	—	1 Rich	0.120	32/.195
	17059677	$13/64$	—	$17/32$	0.117	—	1 Rich	0.120	32/.195
	17059674	$13/64$	—	$1/2$	0.103	—	2 Rich	0.120	32/.195
	17059676	$13/64$	—	$17/32$	0.103	—	2 Rich	0.120	32/.195
	17059193	$13/32$	—	$1/4$ ④	0.103 ⑦	0.090 ⑧	1 Lean	—	0.220
	17059194	$11/32$	—	$1/4$ ④	0.103 ⑦	0.090 ⑧	1 Lean	—	0.220
	17059184	$11/32$	—	$1/4$ ④	0.103 ⑦	0.090 ⑧	1 Lean	—	0.220
	17059491	$11/32$	—	$9/32$ ④	—	0.117	1 Lean	—	—
	17059498	$11/32$	—	$9/32$ ④	—	0.117	1 Lean	—	—
	17059196	$11/32$	—	$1/4$ ④	0.129	0.117	1 NCCW	0.139	0.277
	17059135	$13/32$	—	$1/4$ ④	0.157	—	1 Lean	0.243	0.243
	17059134	$13/32$	—	$1/4$ ④	0.157	—	1 Lean	0.243	0.243
	17059136	$13/32$	—	$1/4$ ④	0.157	—	1 Lean	0.243	0.243
	17059430	$9/32$	—	$1/4$ ④	0.157	—	1 Lean	0.243	0.243
	17059432	$9/32$	—	$1/4$ ④	0.157	—	1 Lean	0.243	0.243
1980	17080674	$3/16$	—	$1/2$	—	—	—	18/.120	32/.195

Carburetor Specifications (cont.)
Rochester—2 BBL
Models—2GV, 2GC, 2GE, 2SE, 2MC, 2ME

Year	Carburetor Identification ①	Float Level (in.)	Float Drop (in.)	Pump Rod (in.)	Primary Vacuum Break (in.)	Secondary Vacuum Break (in.)	Automatic Choke Setting	Choke Rod deg./in.	Choke Unloader deg./in.
1980	17080676	3/16	—	1/2	—	—	—	18/.120	32/.195
	17080675	3/16	—	1/2	—	—	—	18/.120	32/.195
	17080677	3/16	—	1/2	—	—	—	18/.120	32/.195
	17080195	9/32	—	1/4 ④	.103 ⑦	.090 ⑧	—	24.5/.139	38/.243
	17080197	9/32	—	1/4 ④	.103 ⑦	.090 ⑧	—	24.5/.139	38/.243
	17080191	11/32	—	1/4 ④	.096 ⑦	.096 ⑧	—	24.5/.139	38/.243
	17080496	5/16	—	3/8	.117 ⑦	.203 ⑧	—	24.5/.139	38/.243
	17080498	5/16	—	3/8	.117 ⑦	.203 ⑧	—	24.5/.139	38/.243
	17080491	—	—	3/8	.117 ⑦	— ⑧	—	24.5/.139	38/.243
	17059775	3/16	—	1/2	—	—	—	18/.096	32/.195
	17059777	3/16	—	1/2	—	—	—	18/.096	32/.195

① The carburetor identification number is stamped on the float bowl, next to the fuel inlet nut.
② Hold the choke valve completely open. Disconnect the thermostat coil rod from the upper lever and push downward on the rod to the end of travel. The top of the rod should cover 1/2 diameter of the hole.
③ Hold the choke valve completely open. Disconnect the thermostat coil rod from the upper lever and push downward on the rod to the end of travel. The top of the pin on the adjustable swivel should be even with the bottom of the hole in the choke lever.
④ Inner hole
⑤ Choke side of vacuum break
⑥ Throttle side of vacuum break
⑦ Front vacuum break
⑧ Rear vacuum break

Carburetor Specifications
Rochester—2 BBL
Models—2GC, 2GE, 2MC, 2ME, 2SE

Year	Carburetor Identification ①	Float Level (in.)	Float Drop (in.)	Pump Rod (in.)	Primary Vacuum Break (in.)	Secondary Vacuum Break (in.)	Automatic Choke Setting	Choke Rod deg./in.	Choke Unloader deg./in.
Astre, Sunbird									
1976	17056149	7/16	19/32	1 19/32	0.120	0.100	1 Rich	0.080	0.140
	17056447	7/16	19/32	1 19/32	0.110	0.100	1 Rich	0.080	0.140
	17056449	7/16	19/32	1 19/32	0.130	0.110	1 Rich	0.080	0.140

Carburetor Specifications (cont.)
Rochester—2 BBL
Models—2GC, 2GE, 2MC, 2ME, 2SE

Year	Carburetor Identification ①	Float Level (in.)	Float Drop (in.)	Pump Rod (in.)	Primary Vacuum Break (in.)	Secondary Vacuum Break (in.)	Automatic Choke Setting	Choke Rod deg./in.	Choke Unloader deg./in.
1977	17057143	$15/32$	$19/32$	$1^{11}/32$	0.140 ⑤	0.100 ④	Index	0.080	0.180
	17057145	$7/16$	$15/32$	$1^{19}/32$	0.110 ⑤	0.090 ④	1 Rich	0.080	0.140
	17057448	$7/16$	$15/32$	$1^{19}/32$	0.130 ⑤	0.110 ④	1 Rich	0.080	0.140
	17057447	$7/16$	$15/32$	$1^{19}/32$	0.130 ⑤	0.100 ④	1 Rich	0.080	0.140
	17057148	$7/16$	$15/32$	$1^{19}/16$	0.110 ⑤	0.090 ④	1 Rich	0.080	0.140
1978	17058145	$7/16$	$15/32$	$1^5/8$	0.110 ④	0.110 ⑤	1 Lean	0.080	0.160
	17058185	$7/16$	$15/32$	$1^{19}/32$	0.110 ④	0.110 ⑤	1 Rich	0.080	0.140
	17058187	$7/16$	$15/32$	$1^{19}/32$	0.110 ④	0.110 ⑤	1 Rich	0.080	0.140
1979	17059675	$13/64$	—	$17/32$	0.123	—	2 NCC	—	0.195
	17059676	$13/64$	—	$1/2$	0.123	—	2 NCC	—	0.195
	17059677	$13/64$	—	$17/32$	0.123	—	2 NCC	—	0.195
	17059674	$13/64$	—	$1/2$	0.123	—	2 NCC	—	0.195
	17059492	$11/32$	—	$9/32$	0.129	0.117	2 NCC	—	0.277
	17059191	$11/32$	—	$1/4$	0.103	0.090	2 NCC	—	0.243
	17059491	$11/32$	—	$9/32$	0.129 ②	0.117 ③	1 NCC	—	0.277
	17059190	$11/32$	—	$1/4$	0.103 ②	0.090 ③	2 NCC	—	0.243
	17059180	$11/32$	—	$1/4$	0.103 ②	0.090 ③	2 NCC	—	0.243
	17059498	$11/32$	—	$9/32$	0.129 ②	0.117 ③	2 NCC	—	0.277
	17059196	$11/32$	—	$1/4$	0.129 ②	0.117 ③	1 NCC	—	0.277
1980	17080674	$3/16$	—	$1/2$	—	—	—	18/.120	32/.195
	17080676	$3/16$	—	$1/2$	—	—	—	18/.120	32/.195
	17080675	$3/16$	—	$1/2$	—	—	—	18/.120	32/.195
	17080677	$3/16$	—	$3/16$	—	—	—	18/.120	32/.195
	17080191	$11/32$	—	$1/4$ ④	.096 ②	.096 ③	—	24.5/.139	38/.243

Carburetor Specifications (cont.)
Rochester—2 BBL
Models—2GC, 2GE, 2MC, 2ME, 2SE

Year	Carburetor Identification ①	Float Level (in.)	Float Drop (in.)	Pump Rod (in.)	Primary Vacuum Break (in.)	Secondary Vacuum Break (in.)	Automatic Choke Setting	Choke Rod deg./in.	Choke Unloader deg./in.
1980	17080195	$9/32$	—	$1/4$ ④	.103 ②	.090 ③	—	24.5/.139	38/.243
	17080197	$9/32$	—	$1/4$ ④	.103 ②	.090 ③	—	24.5/.139	38/.243
	17080496	$5/16$	—	$3/8$	.117 ②	.203 ③	—	24.5/.139	38/.243
	17080498	$5/16$	—	$3/8$	.117 ②	.203 ③	—	24.5/.139	38/.243
	17080491	—	—	$3/8$	.117 ②	— ③	—	24.5/.139	38/.243
	17059775	$3/16$	—	$1/2$	—	—	—	18/.096	32/.195
	17059777	$3/16$	—	$1/2$	—	—	—	18/.096	32/.195

① The carburetor identification number is stamped on the float bowl, next to the fuel inlet nut.
② Front vacuum break
③ Rear vacuum break
④ Choke side vacuum break
⑤ Throttle lever side vacuum break

Carburetor Specifications
Rochester—2 BBL
Models—2GC, 2GE, 2ME, 2MC

Year	Carburetor Identification ①	Float Level (in.)	Float Drop (in.)	Pump Rod (in.)	Primary Vacuum Break (in.)	Secondary Vacuum Break (in.)	Automatic Choke Setting	Choke Rod deg./in.	Choke Unloader deg./in.
Starfire									
1975	7045147	$7/16$	$19/32$	$1^{19}/32$	0.120	0.120	1 Lean	0.080	0.140
	7045149	$7/16$	$19/32$	$1^{19}/32$	0.120	0.120	1 Rich	0.080	0.140
	7045449	$7/16$	$19/32$	$1^{19}/32$	0.120	0.120	1 Lean	0.080	0.140
1976	17056145	$7/16$	$15/32$	$1^{19}/32$	0.110	0.100	1 Rich	0.080	0.140
	17056149	$7/16$	$15/32$	$1^{19}/32$	0.120	0.100	1 Rich	0.080	0.140
	17056447	$7/16$	$15/32$	$1^{19}/32$	0.130	0.110	1 Rich	0.080	0.140
	17056449	$7/16$	$15/32$	$1^{19}/32$	0.130	0.110	1 Rich	0.080	0.140

Carburetor Specifications (cont'd)
Rochester—2 BBL
Models—2GC, 2GE, 2ME, 2MC

Year	Carburetor Identification ①	Float Level (in.)	Float Drop (in.)	Pump Rod (in.)	Primary Vacuum Break (in.)	Secondary Vacuum Break (in.)	Automatic Choke Setting	Choke Rod deg./in.	Choke Unloader deg./in.
1977	17057148	7/16	15/32	1 19/32	0.090 ④	0.110 ⑤	1 Rich	0.080	0.140
	17057143	7/16	15/32	1 19/32	0.100 ④	0.130 ⑤	1 Rich	0.080	0.140
	17057447	7/16	15/32	1 19/32	0.100 ④	0.130 ⑤	1 Rich	0.080	0.140
	17057448	7/16	15/32	1 19/32	0.110 ④	0.130 ⑤	1 Rich	0.080	0.140
	17057145	7/16	15/32	1 19/32	0.090 ④	0.110 ⑤	1 Rich	0.080	0.140
1978	17058140	7/16	15/32	1 19/32	0.070 ④	0.110 ⑤	1 Rich	0.080	0.140
	17058145	7/16	15/32	1 19/32	0.060 ④	0.110 ⑤	1 Rich	0.080	0.160
	17058147	7/16	15/32	1 19/32	0.100 ④	0.140 ⑤	1 Rich	0.080	0.140
	17058182	7/16	15/32	1 19/32	0.080 ④	0.110 ⑤	1 Rich	0.080	0.140
	17058185	7/16	15/32	1 19/32	0.050 ④	0.110 ⑤	1 Rich	0.080	0.140
	17058448	7/16	15/32	1 19/32	0.110 ④	0.150 ⑤	1 Rich	0.080	0.140
	17058447	7/16	15/32	1 9/16	0.100 ④	0.140 ⑤	1 Rich	0.080	0.140
1979	17059180	11/32	—	1/4	0.103 ②	0.090 ③	2 Rich	—	0.243
	17059190	11/32	—	1/4	0.103 ②	0.090 ③	2 Rich	—	0.243
	17059191	11/32	—	9/32	0.103 ②	0.090 ③	2 Rich	—	0.243
	17059196	11/32	—	1/4	0.129 ②	0.117 ③	1 Rich	—	0.277
	17059498	11/32	—	9/32	0.129 ②	0.117 ③	1 Rich	—	0.277
	17059491	11/32	—	9/32	0.129 ②	0.117 ③	1 Rich	—	0.277
1980	17080676	3/16	—	1/2	—	—	—	18/.120	32/.195
	17080675	3/16	—	1/2	—	—	—	18/.120	32/.195
	17080677	3/16	—	3/16	—	—	—	18/.120	32/.195
	17080191	11/32	—	1/4 ⑥	.096 ②	.096 ③	—	24.5/.139	38/.243
	17080195	9/32	—	1/4 ⑥	.103 ②	.090 ③	—	24.5/.139	38/.243

Carburetor Specifications (cont.)
Rochester—2 BBL
Models—2GC, 2GE, 2ME, 2MC

Year	Carburetor Identification ①	Float Level (in.)	Float Drop (in.)	Pump Rod (in.)	Primary Vacuum Break (in.)	Secondary Vacuum Break (in.)	Automatic Choke Setting	Choke Rod deg./in.	Choke Unloader deg./in.
1980	17080197	9/32	—	1/4 ⑥	.103 ②	.090 ③	—	24.5/.139	38/.243
	17059775	3/16	—	1/2	—	—	—	18/.096	32/.195
	17059777	3/16	—	1/2	—	—	—	18/.096	32/.195

① The carburetor identification number is stamped on the float bowl, next to the fuel inlet nut.
② Front vacuum break
③ Rear vacuum break
④ Choke side vacuum break
⑤ Throttle lever side vacuum break
⑥ Inner hole

Carburetor Specifications
Rochester—2 BBL
Models—2GC, 2ME, 2GE

Year	Carburetor Identification ①	Float Level (in.)	Float Drop (in.)	Pump Rod (in.)	Primary Vacuum Break (in.)	Secondary Vacuum Break (in.)	Automatic Choke Setting	Choke Rod deg./in.	Choke Unloader deg./in.
Skyhawk									
1975	7045145	15/32	19/32	1 15/32	0.120	0.120	Index	0.080	0.120
	704149	15/32	19/32	1 15/32	0.120	0.120	1 Rich	0.080	0.120
	7045449	15/32	19/32	1 15/32	0.120	0.120	1 Lean	0.080	0.120
1976	17056447	7/16	19/32	1 19/32	0.130 ③	0.100 ④	1 Rich	0.080	0.140
	17056145	13/32	19/32	1 3/4	0.110 ③	0.100 ④	1 Rich	0.080	0.140
	17056149	7/16	19/32	1 19/32	0.120 ③	0.100 ④	1 Rich	0.080	0.140
	17056449	7/16	19/32	1 19/32	0.130 ③	0.110 ④	1 Rich	0.080	0.140
1977	17057143	7/16	15/32	1 17/32	0.130 ⑥	0.100 ⑤	1 Rich	0.080	0.140
	17057148	7/16	15/32	1 17/32	0.130 ⑥	0.100 ⑤	1 Rich	0.080	0.140
	17057448	7/16	15/32	1 1/2	0.130 ⑥	0.110 ⑤	1 Rich	0.080	0.140
	17057447	7/16	15/32	1 1/2	0.130 ⑥	0.100 ⑤	1 Rich	0.080	0.140
1978	17058141	7/16	15/32	1 19/32	0.100	0.140	1 Rich	0.080	0.140
	17058447	7/16	15/32	1 19/32	0.110	0.150	1 Rich	0.080	0.140

Carburetor Specifications (cont.)
Rochester—2 BBL
Models—2GC, 2ME, 2GE

Year	Carburetor Identification ①	Float Level (in.)	Float Drop (in.)	Pump Rod (in.)	Primary Vacuum Break (in.)	Secondary Vacuum Break (in.)	Automatic Choke Setting	Choke Rod deg./in.	Choke Unloader deg./in.
1978	17058448	$7/16$	$1^5/32$	$1^9/16$	0.100	0.140	1 Rich	0.080	0.140
1979	17059191	$11/32$	—	$9/32$ ②	0.103	0.090	2 Rich	0.139	0.243
	17059180	$11/32$	—	$9/32$ ②	0.103	0.090	2 Rich	0.139	0.243
	17059190	$11/32$	—	$9/32$ ②	0.103	0.090	2 Rich	0.139	0.243
	17059491	$11/32$	—	$9/32$ ②	0.129	0.117	1 Rich	0.139	0.277
	17059492	$11/32$	—	$9/32$ ②	0.129	0.117	1 Rich	0.139	0.277
	17059498	$11/32$	—	$9/32$ ②	0.129	0.117	1 Rich	0.139	0.277
	17059196	$11/32$	—	$1/4$ ②	0.129	0.117	1 Rich	0.139	0.277
1980	17080195	$9/32$	—	$1/4$ ②	.103 ③	.090 ④	—	24.5/.139	38/.243
	17080197	$9/32$	—	$1/4$ ②	.103 ③	.090 ④	—	24.5/.139	38/.243
	17080191	$11/32$	—	$1/4$ ②	.096 ③	.096 ④	—	24.5/.139	38/.243

① The carburetor identification number is stamped on the float bowl, next to the fuel inlet nut
② Inner hole
③ Front vacuum break
④ Rear vacuum break
⑤ Choke side vacuum break
⑥ Throttle lever side vacuum break

2. Bend the float tang if an adjustment is needed.

Fast Idle Cam Adjustment

1. Place the fast idle screw on the second step of the fast idle cam and against the shoulder of the high step.
2. Place the specified drill or gauge on the down side of the choke plate.
3. To adjust, bend the choke lever tang.

Choke Plate Pulldown (Vacuum Break) Adjustment

1. Remove the three hex headed screws and ring which retain the choke cover.
NOTE: *Do not remove the choke water housing screw if adjusting on the car. Pull the choke water housing and bimetal cover assembly back out of the way.*
2. Push the diaphragm shaft against the stop. Push the coil lever clockwise.

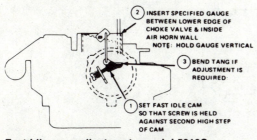

Fast idle cam adjustment—model 5210C

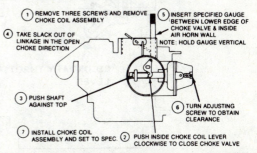

Choke plate pull down adjustment—model 5210C

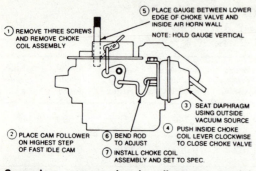

① REMOVE THREE SCREWS AND REMOVE CHOKE COIL ASSEMBLY

⑤ PLACE GAUGE BETWEEN LOWER EDGE OF CHOKE VALVE AND INSIDE AIR HORN WALL
NOTE: HOLD GAUGE VERTICAL

③ SEAT DIAPHRAGM USING OUTSIDE VACUUM SOURCE

② PLACE CAM FOLLOWER ON HIGHEST STEP OF FAST IDLE CAM

⑥ BEND ROD TO ADJUST

④ PUSH INSIDE CHOKE COIL LEVER CLOCKWISE TO CLOSE CHOKE VALVE

⑦ INSTALL CHOKE COIL ASSEMBLY AND SET TO SPEC.

Secondary vacuum break adjustment—model 5210C

3. Insert the specified size gauge on the down side of the primary choke plate.

4. Take the slack out of the linkage and turn the adjusting screw with a $5/32$ in. Allen wrench.

Secondary Vacuum Break Adjustment

1. Remove the three screws and the choke coil assembly.

2. Place the cam follower on the highest step of the fast idle cam.

3. Seat the diaphragm by applying an outside source of vacuum.

4. Push the inside choke coil lever counterclockwise through 1977; clockwise for 1978 and later, to close the choke valve.

5. Place a gauge of the size specified in the chart between the lower edge of the choke valve and the air horn wall.

6. Bend the vacuum break rod to adjust.

7. Replace and adjust the choke.

Choke Unloader Adjustment

1. Position the throttle lever at the wide open position.

② INSERT SPECIFIED GAUGE BETWEEN LOWER EDGE OF CHOKE VALVE & INSIDE AIR HORN WALL

NOTE: HOLD GAUGE VERTICAL

③ BEND TANG AT EXISTING RADIUS TO ADJUST

① POSITION THROTTLE LEVER TO WIDE–OPEN

Secondary throttle stop screw adjustment—model 5210C

2. Insert a gauge of the size specified in the chart between the lower edge of the choke valve and the air horn wall.

3. Bend the unloader tang for adjustment.

Secondary Throttle Stop Screw Adjustment

1. Back off the screw until it doesn't touch the throttle lever.

2. Turn the screw in until it touches the secondary throttle lever. Turn it in ¼ turn more.

Fast Idle Speed Adjustment

THROUGH 1975

1. Engine temperature must be normal with the air cleaner off. Disconnect and plug

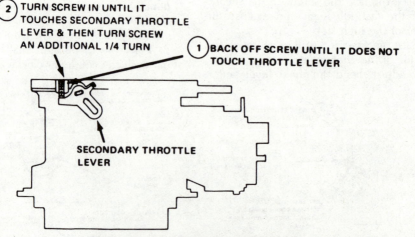

② TURN SCREW IN UNTIL IT TOUCHES SECONDARY THROTTLE LEVER & THEN TURN SCREW AN ADDITIONAL 1/4 TURN

① BACK OFF SCREW UNTIL IT DOES NOT TOUCH THROTTLE LEVER

SECONDARY THROTTLE LEVER

Choke unloader adjustment—model 5210C

CHILTON'S
FUEL ECONOMY
& TUNE-UP TIPS

55 WAYS TO IMPROVE FUEL ECONOMY

Tune-up • Spark Plug Diagnosis • Emission Controls

Fuel System • Cooling System • Tires and Wheels

General Maintenance

CHILTON'S FUEL ECONOMY & TUNE-UP TIPS

Fuel economy is important to everyone, no matter what kind of vehicle you drive. The maintenance-minded motorist can save both money and fuel using these tips and the periodic maintenance and tune-up procedures in this Repair and Tune-Up Guide.

There are more than 130,000,000 cars and trucks registered for private use in the United States. Each travels an average of 10-12,000 miles per year, and, and in total they consume close to 70 billion gallons of fuel each year. This represents nearly ⅔ of the oil imported by the United States each year. The Federal government's goal is to reduce consumption 10% by 1985. A variety of methods are either already in use or under serious consideration, and they all affect you driving and the cars you will drive. In addition to "down-sizing", the auto industry is using or investigating the use of electronic fuel delivery, electronic engine controls and alternative engines for use in smaller and lighter vehicles, among other alternatives to meet the federally mandated Corporate Average Fuel Economy (CAFE) of 27.5 mpg by 1985. The government, for its part, is considering rationing, mandatory driving curtailments and tax increases on motor vehicle fuel in an effort to reduce consumption. The government's goal of a 10% reduction could be realized — and further government regulation avoided — if every private vehicle could use just 1 less gallon of fuel per week.

How Much Can You Save?

Tests have proven that almost anyone can make at least a 10% reduction in fuel consumption through regular maintenance and tune-ups. When a major manufacturer of spark plugs sur-

TUNE-UP

1. Check the cylinder compression to be sure the engine will really benefit from a tune-up and that it is capable of producing good fuel economy. A tune-up will be wasted on an engine in poor mechanical condition.

2. Replace spark plugs regularly. New spark plugs alone can increase fuel economy 3%.

3. Be sure the spark plugs are the correct type (heat range) for your vehicle. See the Tune-Up Specifications.

Heat range refers to the spark plug's ability to conduct heat away from the firing end. It must conduct the heat away in an even pattern to avoid becoming a source of pre-ignition, yet it must also operate hot enough to burn off conductive deposits that could cause misfiring.

The heat range is usually indicated by a number on the spark plug, part of the manufacturer's designation for each individual spark plug. The numbers in bold-face indicate the heat range in each manufacturer's identification system.

Periodically, check the spark plugs to be sure they are firing efficiently. They are excellent indicators of the internal condition of your engine.

Manufacturer	Typical Designation
AC	R **45** TS
Bosch (old)	WA **145** T30
Bosch (new)	HR **8** Y
Champion	RBL **15** Y
Fram/Autolite	4**15**
Mopar	P-**62** PR
Motorcraft	BRF-**42**
NGK	BP **5** ES-15
Nippondenso	W **16** EP
Prestolite	14GR **5** 2A

On AC, Bosch (new), Champion, Fram/Autolite, Mopar, Motorcraft and Prestolite, a higher number indicates a hotter plug. On Bosch (old), NGK and Nippondenso, a higher number indicates a colder plug.

4. Make sure the spark plugs are properly gapped. See the Tune-Up Specifications in this book.

5. Be sure the spark plugs are firing efficiently. The illustrations on the next 2 pages show you how to "read" the firing end of the spark plug.

6. Check the ignition timing and set it to specifications. Tests show that almost all cars have incorrect ignition timing by more than 2°.

veyed over 6,000 cars nationwide, they found that a tune-up, on cars that needed one, increased fuel economy over 11%. Replacing worn plugs alone, accounted for a 3% increase. The same test also revealed that 8 out of every 10 vehicles will have some maintenance deficiency that will directly affect fuel economy, emissions or performance. Most of this mileage-robbing neglect could be prevented with regular maintenance.

Modern engines require that all of the functioning systems operate properly for maximum efficiency. A malfunction anywhere wastes fuel. You can keep your vehicle running as efficiently and economically as possible, by being aware of your vehicle's operating and performance characteristics. If your vehicle suddenly develops performance or fuel economy problems it could be due to one or more of the following:

PROBLEM	POSSIBLE CAUSE
Engine Idles Rough	Ignition timing, idle mixture, vacuum leak or something amiss in the emission control system.
Hesitates on Acceleration	Dirty carburetor or fuel filter, improper accelerator pump setting, ignition timing or fouled spark plugs.
Starts Hard or Fails to Start	Worn spark plugs, improperly set automatic choke, ice (or water) in fuel system.
Stalls Frequently	Automatic choke improperly adjusted and possible dirty air filter or fuel filter.
Performs Sluggishly	Worn spark plugs, dirty fuel or air filter, ignition timing or automatic choke out of adjustment.

Check spark plug wires on conventional point type ignition for cracks by bending them in a loop around your finger.

Be sure that spark plug wires leading to adjacent cylinders do not run too close together. (Photo courtesy Champion Spark Plug Co.)

7. If your vehicle does not have electronic ignition, check the points, rotor and cap as specified.

8. Check the spark plug wires (used with conventional point-type ignitions) for cracks and burned or broken insulation by bending them in a loop around your finger. Cracked wires decrease fuel efficiency by failing to deliver full voltage to the spark plugs. One misfiring spark plug can cost you as much as 2 mpg.

9. Check the routing of the plug wires. Misfiring can be the result of spark plug leads to adjacent cylinders running parallel to each other and too close together. One wire tends to

pick up voltage from the other causing it to fire "out of time".

10. Check all electrical and ignition circuits for voltage drop and resistance.

11. Check the distributor mechanical and/or vacuum advance mechanisms for proper functioning. The vacuum advance can be checked by twisting the distributor plate in the opposite direction of rotation. It should spring back when released.

12. Check and adjust the valve clearance on engines with mechanical lifters. The clearance should be slightly loose rather than too tight.

SPARK PLUG DIAGNOSIS

Normal

APPEARANCE: This plug is typical of one operating normally. The insulator nose varies from a light tan to grayish color with slight electrode wear. The presence of slight deposits is normal on used plugs and will have no adverse effect on engine performance. The spark plug heat range is correct for the engine and the engine is running normally.

CAUSE: Properly running engine.

RECOMMENDATION: Before reinstalling this plug, the electrodes should be cleaned and filed square. Set the gap to specifications. If the plug has been in service for more than 10-12,000 miles, the entire set should probably be replaced with a fresh set of the same heat range.

Oil Deposits

APPEARANCE: The firing end of the plug is covered with a wet, oily coating.

CAUSE: The problem is poor oil control. On high mileage engines, oil is leaking past the rings or valve guides into the combustion chamber. A common cause is also a plugged PCV valve, and a ruptured fuel pump diaphragm can also cause this condition. Oil fouled plugs such as these are often found in new or recently overhauled engines, before normal oil control is achieved, and can be cleaned and reinstalled.

RECOMMENDATION: A hotter spark plug may temporarily relieve the problem, but the engine is probably in need of work.

Incorrect Heat Range

APPEARANCE: The effects of high temperature on a spark plug are indicated by clean white, often blistered insulator. This can also be accompanied by excessive wear of the electrode, and the absence of deposits.

CAUSE: Check for the correct spark plug heat range. A plug which is too hot for the engine can result in overheating. A car operated mostly at high speeds can require a colder plug. Also check ignition timing, cooling system level, fuel mixture and leaking intake manifold.

RECOMMENDATION: If all ignition and engine adjustments are known to be correct, and no other malfunction exists, install spark plugs one heat range colder.

Photos Courtesy Fram Corporation

Carbon Deposits

APPEARANCE: Carbon fouling is easily identified by the presence of dry, soft, black, sooty deposits.

CAUSE: Changing the heat range can often lead to carbon fouling, as can prolonged slow, stop-and-start driving. If the heat range is correct, carbon fouling can be attributed to a rich fuel mixture, sticking choke, clogged air cleaner, worn breaker points, retarded timing or low compression. If only one or two plugs are carbon fouled, check for corroded or cracked wires on the affected plugs. Also look for cracks in the distributor cap between the towers of affected cylinders.

RECOMMENDATION: After the problem is corrected, these plugs can be cleaned and reinstalled if not worn severely.

MMT Fouled

APPEARANCE: Spark plugs fouled by MMT (Methycyclopentadienyl Maganese Tricarbonyl) have reddish, rusty appearance on the insulator and side electrode.

CAUSE: MMT is an anti-knock additive in gasoline used to replace lead. During the combustion process, the MMT leaves a reddish deposit on the insulator and side electrode.

RECOMMENDATION: No engine malfunction is indicated and the deposits will not affect plug performance any more than lead deposits (see Ash Deposits). MMT fouled plugs can be cleaned, regapped and reinstalled.

High Speed Glazing

APPEARANCE: Glazing appears as shiny coating on the plug, either yellow or tan in color.

CAUSE: During hard, fast acceleration, plug temperatures rise suddenly. Deposits from normal combustion have no chance to fluff-off; instead, they melt on the insulator forming an electrically conductive coating which causes misfiring.

RECOMMENDATION: Glazed plugs are not easily cleaned. They should be replaced with a fresh set of plugs of the correct heat range. If the condition recurs, using plugs with a heat range one step colder may cure the problem.

Ash (Lead) Deposits

APPEARANCE: Ash deposits are characterized by light brown or white colored deposits crusted on the side or center electrodes. In some cases it may give the plug a rusty appearance.

CAUSE: Ash deposits are normally derived from oil or fuel additives burned during normal combustion. Normally they are harmless, though excessive amounts can cause misfiring. If deposits are excessive in short mileage, the valve guides may be worn.

RECOMMENDATION: Ash-fouled plugs can be cleaned, gapped and reinstalled.

Detonation

APPEARANCE: Detonation is usually characterized by a broken plug insulator.

CAUSE: A portion of the fuel charge will begin to burn spontaneously, from the increased heat following ignition. The explosion that results applies extreme pressure to engine components, frequently damaging spark plugs and pistons.

Detonation can result by over-advanced ignition timing, inferior gasoline (low octane) lean air/fuel mixture, poor carburetion, engine lugging or an increase in compression ratio due to combustion chamber deposits or engine modification.

RECOMMENDATION: Replace the plugs after correcting the problem.

Photos Courtesy Champion Spark Plug Co.

EMISSION CONTROLS

13. Be aware of the general condition of the emission control system. It contributes to reduced pollution and should be serviced regularly to maintain efficient engine operation.

14. Check all vacuum lines for dried, cracked or brittle conditions. Something as simple as a leaking vacuum hose can cause poor performance and loss of economy.

15. Avoid tampering with the emission control system. Attempting to improve fuel econ-

FUEL SYSTEM

Check the air filter with a light behind it. If you can see light through the filter it can be reused.

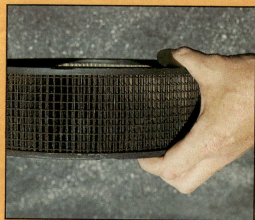

Extremely clogged filters should be discarded and replaced with a new one.

18. Replace the air filter regularly. A dirty air filter richens the air/fuel mixture and can increase fuel consumption as much as 10%. Tests show that ⅓ of all vehicles have air filters in need of replacement.

19. Replace the fuel filter at least as often as recommended.

20. Set the idle speed and carburetor mixture to specifications.

21. Check the automatic choke. A sticking or malfunctioning choke wastes gas.

22. During the summer months, adjust the automatic choke for a leaner mixture which will produce faster engine warm-ups.

COOLING SYSTEM

29. Be sure all accessory drive belts are in good condition. Check for cracks or wear.

30. Adjust all accessory drive belts to proper tension.

31. Check all hoses for swollen areas, worn spots, or loose clamps.

32. Check coolant level in the radiator or expansion tank.

33. Be sure the thermostat is operating properly. A stuck thermostat delays engine warm-up and a cold engine uses nearly twice as much fuel as a warm engine.

34. Drain and replace the engine coolant at least as often as recommended. Rust and scale

TIRES & WHEELS

38. Check the tire pressure often with a pencil type gauge. Tests by a major tire manufacturer show that 90% of all vehicles have at least 1 tire improperly inflated. Better mileage can be achieved by over-inflating tires, but never exceed the maximum inflation pressure on the side of the tire.

39. If possible, install radial tires. Radial tires deliver as much as ½ mpg more than bias belted tires.

40. Avoid installing super-wide tires. They only create extra rolling resistance and decrease fuel mileage. Stick to the manufacturer's recommendations.

41. Have the wheels properly balanced.

omy by tampering with emission controls is more likely to worsen fuel economy than improve it. Emission control changes on modern engines are not readily reversible.

16. Clean (or replace) the EGR valve and lines as recommended.

17. Be sure that all vacuum lines and hoses are reconnected properly after working under the hood. An unconnected or misrouted vacuum line can wreak havoc with engine performance.

23. Check for fuel leaks at the carburetor, fuel pump, fuel lines and fuel tank. Be sure all lines and connections are tight.

24. Periodically check the tightness of the carburetor and intake manifold attaching nuts and bolts. These are a common place for vacuum leaks to occur.

25. Clean the carburetor periodically and lubricate the linkage.

26. The condition of the tailpipe can be an excellent indicator of proper engine combustion. After a long drive at highway speeds, the inside of the tailpipe should be a light grey in color. Black or soot on the insides indicates an overly rich mixture.

27. Check the fuel pump pressure. The fuel pump may be supplying more fuel than the engine needs.

28. Use the proper grade of gasoline for your engine. Don't try to compensate for knocking or "pinging" by advancing the ignition timing. This practice will only increase plug temperature and the chances of detonation or pre-ignition with relatively little performance gain.

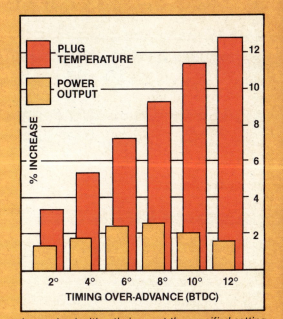

Increasing ignition timing past the specified setting results in a drastic increase in spark plug temperature with increased chance of detonation or preignition. Performance increase is considerably less. (Photo courtesy Champion Spark Plug Co.)

that form in the engine should be flushed out to allow the engine to operate at peak efficiency.

35. Clean the radiator of debris that can decrease cooling efficiency.

36. Install a flex-type or electric cooling fan, if you don't have a clutch type fan. Flex fans use curved plastic blades to push more air at low speeds when more cooling is needed; at high speeds the blades flatten out for less resistance. Electric fans only run when the engine temperature reaches a predetermined level.

37. Check the radiator cap for a worn or cracked gasket. If the cap does not seal properly, the cooling system will not function properly.

42. Be sure the front end is correctly aligned. A misaligned front end actually has wheels going in differed directions. The increased drag can reduce fuel economy by .3 mpg.

43. Correctly adjust the wheel bearings. Wheel bearings that are adjusted too tight increase rolling resistance.

Check tire pressures regularly with a reliable pocket type gauge. Be sure to check the pressure on a cold tire.

GENERAL MAINTENANCE

Check the fluid levels (particularly engine oil) on a regular basis. Be sure to check the oil for grit, water or other contamination.

A vacuum gauge is another excellent indicator of internal engine condition and can also be installed in the dash as a mileage indicator.

44. Periodically check the fluid levels in the engine, power steering pump, master cylinder, automatic transmission and drive axle.

45. Change the oil at the recommended interval and change the filter at every oil change. Dirty oil is thick and causes extra friction between moving parts, cutting efficiency and increasing wear. A worn engine requires more frequent tune-ups and gets progressively worse fuel economy. In general, use the lightest viscosity oil for the driving conditions you will encounter.

46. Use the recommended viscosity fluids in the transmission and axle.

47. Be sure the battery is fully charged for fast starts. A slow starting engine wastes fuel.

48. Be sure battery terminals are clean and tight.

49. Check the battery electrolyte level and add distilled water if necessary.

50. Check the exhaust system for crushed pipes, blockages and leaks.

51. Adjust the brakes. Dragging brakes or brakes that are not releasing create increased drag on the engine.

52. Install a vacuum gauge or miles-per-gallon gauge. These gauges visually indicate engine vacuum in the intake manifold. High vacuum = good mileage and low vacuum = poorer mileage. The gauge can also be an excellent indicator of internal engine conditions.

53. Be sure the clutch is properly adjusted. A slipping clutch wastes fuel.

54. Check and periodically lubricate the heat control valve in the exhaust manifold. A sticking or inoperative valve prevents engine warm-up and wastes gas.

55. Keep accurate records to check fuel economy over a period of time. A sudden drop in fuel economy may signal a need for tune-up or other maintenance.

Carburetor Specifications
Holley Model 5210-C

Year	Carb. Part No. ①②	Float Level (Dry) (in.)	Float Drop (in.)	Pump Position	Fast Idle Cam (in.)	Choke Plate Pulldown * (in.)	Secondary Vacuum Break (in.)	Fast Idle Setting (rpm)	Choke Unloader (in.)	Choke Setting
Vega, Monza										
1973	R-6477A	0.420	1	#3	0.140	0.300	—	2000	—	1 Rich
	R-6478A	0.420	1	#2	0.140	0.300	—	2200	—	2 Rich
	R-6580A	0.420	1	#2	0.140	0.300	—	2200	—	2 Rich
	R-6581A	0.420	1	#3	0.140	0.300	—	2000	—	1 Rich
1974	338179	0.420	1	#3	0.140	0.300	—	2000 ⑥	—	2½ Rich
	338181	0.420	1	#3	0.140	0.300	—	2000 ⑥	—	2½ Rich
	338168	0.420	1	#2	0.140	0.300	—	2200 ⑥	—	3½ Rich
	338170	0.420	1	#2	0.140	0.300	—	2200 ⑥	—	3½ Rich
1975	348659, 348663,	0.420	1	#2	0.110	0.325	—	1600 ⑥	—	3 Rich
	348661, 348665	0.420	1	#2	0.110	0.275	—	1600 ⑥	—	3 Rich
	348660, 348664	0.420	1	#2	0.110	0.300	—	1600 ⑥	—	4 Rich
	348662, 348666	0.420	1	#2	0.110	0.275	—	1600 ⑥	—	4 Rich
1976	366829, 366831	0.420	1	#3	0.320	0.313	—	2200	0.375	2 Rich
	366833, 366841	0.420	1	#3	0.320	0.268	—	2200	0.375	2 Rich
	366830, 366832	0.420	1	#2	0.320	0.288	—	2200	0.375	3 Rich
	366834, 366840	0.420	1	#2	0.320	0.268	.400	2200	0.375	3 Rich
1977	458103, 458105	0.420	1	#2	0.120	0.250	.400	2500	0.350	3 Rich
	458107, 458109	0.420	1	#2	0.120	0.275	.400	2500	0.400	3 Rich
	458102, 458104	0.420	1	#1	0.085	0.250	.400	2500	0.350	3 Rich
	458106, 458108	0.420	1	#1	0.120	0.275	.400	2500	0.400	3 Rich
	458110, 458112	0.420	1	#1	0.120	0.300	.400	2500	0.400	3 Rich
1978	see notes	.520	1	—	.150	⑦	.400	2500	.350	⑧

Carburetor Specifications (cont'd)
Holley Model 5210-C

Year	Carb. Part No. ①②	Float Level (Dry) (in.)	Float Drop (in.)	Pump Position	Fast Idle Cam (in.)	Choke Plate Pulldown * (in.)	Secondary Vacuum Break (in.)	Fast Idle Setting (rpm)	Choke Unloader (in.)	Choke Setting
Astre, Sunbird										
1975	Manual	0.420	1	#3	0.140	0.300	—	2000 ⑥	—	2½ Rich
	Automatic	0.420	1	#2	0.140	0.400	—	2200 ⑥	—	3½ Rich
1976	Manual	0.410	1	#3	0.420	0.313 ③	—	2200 ⑥	0.375	2 Rich
	Automatic	0.410	1	#2	0.320	0.288 ③	—	2200 ⑥	0.375	3 Rich
1977	458102, 458103, 458104, 458105	0.420	1	④	0.085	0.250	— 0.400	2500	0.350	3 Rich
	458107, 458109	0.420	1	④	0.125	0.275	0.400	2500	0.350	3 Rich
	458110, 458112	0.420	1	④	0.120	0.300	0.400	2500	0.350	3 Rich
1978	see notes	.520	1	—	.150	⑫	—	⑬	.350	⑭
Starfire										
1976	Manual	0.420	1	#3	0.320	0.313 ③	—	2200	0.375	2 Rich
	Automatic	0.420	1	#2	0.320	0.288 ③	—	2200	0.375	3 Rich
1977	458102, 458104	0.420	1	④	0.085	0.250	0.400	2500	0.350	3 Rich
	458103, 458105	0.420	1	④	0.120	0.250	0.400	2500	0.350	3 Rich
	458106, 458107, 458108, 458109	0.420	1	④	0.120	0.275	0.400	2500	0.400	3 Rich
	458110, 458112	0.420	1	④	0.120	0.300	0.400	2500	0.400	3 Rich
1978	see notes	.520	1	—	.150	⑨	—	⑩	.350	⑪

① Located on tag attached to the carburetor, or on the casting or choke plate
② Beginning 1974, GM identification numbers are used in place of the Holley numbers
③ 0.268 in California
④ #1 manual, #2 automatic
⑤ Not used
⑥ With no vacuum to the distributor
*Vacuum break initial choke valve clearance on AMC
⑦ Part #10001048, 10001050: .300
  #10001047, 10001049, 10001052, 10001054: .325
⑧ Part #10001047, 10001049: 1 Rich
  #10001048, 10001050, 10001052, 10001054: 2 Rich

⑨ Part #10001047, 10001049: .325
  #10004048, 10004049: .300
⑩ Part #10001047, 10001049: 2200
  #10004048, 10004049: 2400
⑪ Part #10001047, 10001049: 1 Rich
  #10004048, 10004049: 2 Rich
⑫ Part #10001047, 10001049: .325
  #10004048, 10004049: .300
⑬ Part #10001047, 10001049: 2200
  #10004048, 10004049: 2400
⑭ Part #10001047, 10001049: 1 Rich
  #10004048, 10004049: 2 Rich

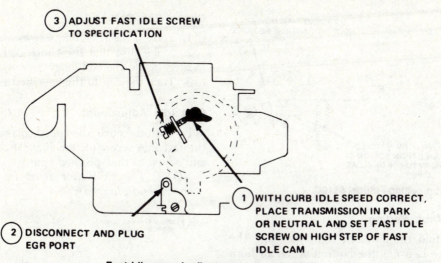

③ ADJUST FAST IDLE SCREW TO SPECIFICATION

② DISCONNECT AND PLUG EGR PORT

① WITH CURB IDLE SPEED CORRECT, PLACE TRANSMISSION IN PARK OR NEUTRAL AND SET FAST IDLE SCREW ON HIGH STEP OF FAST IDLE CAM

Fast idle speed adjustment—model 6510C

the vacuum advance line to the distributor.

2. Position the fast idle screw on the top step (second step for 1975) of the fast idle cam.

3. Adjust the fast idle speed to specifications.

4. Adjustments are made by turning the fast idle screw in or out.

1976 AND LATER

1. The engine must be at normal operating temperature with the air cleaner off.

2. With the engine running, position the fast idle screw on the high step of the cam for GM cars, or on the second step against the shoulder of the high step for AMC cars. Plug the EGR Port on the carburetor.

3. Adjust the speed by turning the fast idle screw.

HOLLEY MODEL 6510C CARBURETOR ADJUSTMENTS

Float Level Adjustment

1. Remove and invert the air horn.

2. Place the specified gauge between the air horn and the float.

3. If necessary, bend the float arm tang to adjust.

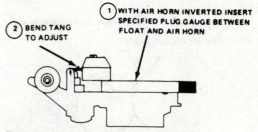

① WITH AIR HORN INVERTED INSERT SPECIFIED PLUG GAUGE BETWEEN FLOAT AND AIR HORN

② BEND TANG TO ADJUST

Float level adjustment—model 6510C

Holley Model 6510-C
All Models

Year	Part Number	Vacuum Break Adjustment (in.)	Fast Idle Cam Adjustment (in.)	Unloader Adjustment (in.)	Fast Idle Adjustment (rpm)	Float Level Adjustment (in.)	Choke Setting
1978	10001056, 10001058	.325	.150	.350	2400	.520	1 Rich
1979	10008489, 10008490	.250	.150	.350	2400	.520	1 Rich
	10008491, 10008492	.250	.150	.350	2200	.520	2 Rich
	10009973, 10009974	.275	.150	.350	2400	.520	2 Rich

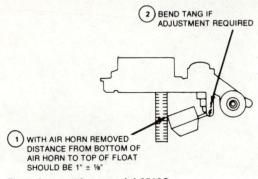

② BEND TANG IF ADJUSTMENT REQUIRED

① WITH AIR HORN REMOVED DISTANCE FROM BOTTOM OF AIR HORN TO TOP OF FLOAT SHOULD BE 1" ± ⅛"

Float drop setting—model 6510C

Float Drop Setting

1. Hold the air horn right side up. The distance between the bottom of the air horn and the top of the float should be 1 inch.

2. If necessary, bend the tang on the side of the float arm support, to adjust.

Unloader Adjustment

1. Place the throttle in the wide open position.

2. Insert a .350 inch gauge between the lower edge of the choke valve and the air horn wall.

3. Bend the tang on the choke arm to adjust.

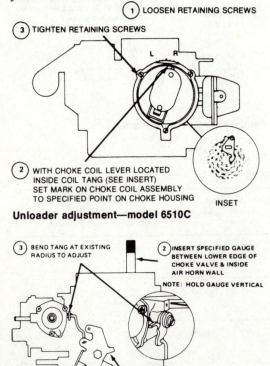

① LOOSEN RETAINING SCREWS

③ TIGHTEN RETAINING SCREWS

L R

② WITH CHOKE COIL LEVER LOCATED INSIDE COIL TANG (SEE INSERT) SET MARK ON CHOKE COIL ASSEMBLY TO SPECIFIED POINT ON CHOKE HOUSING

INSET

Unloader adjustment—model 6510C

③ BEND TANG AT EXISTING RADIUS TO ADJUST

② INSERT SPECIFIED GAUGE BETWEEN LOWER EDGE OF CHOKE VALVE & INSIDE AIR HORN WALL

NOTE: HOLD GAUGE VERTICAL

① POSITION THROTTLE LEVER TO WIDE-OPEN

Choke cap setting—model 6510C

Choke Cap Setting

1. Loosen the retaining screws.

2. Make sure that the choke coil lever is located inside the coil tang.

3. Turn the cap to the specified setting.

Fast Idle Adjustment

1. With the curb idle speed correct, place the fast idle screw on the highest cam step and adjust to the specified rpm.

NOTE: *The EGR line must be disconnected and plugged.*

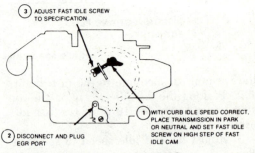

③ ADJUST FAST IDLE SCREW TO SPECIFICATION

① WITH CURB IDLE SPEED CORRECT, PLACE TRANSMISSION IN PARK OR NEUTRAL AND SET FAST IDLE SCREW ON HIGH STEP OF FAST IDLE CAM

② DISCONNECT AND PLUG EGR PORT

Fast idle adjustment—model 6510C

Secondary Throttle Stop Screw Adjustment

1. Back off the screw until it does not touch the lever.

2. Turn the screw in until it touches the lever, then turn it and additional ¼ turn.

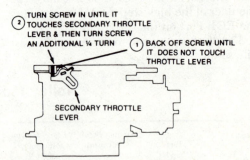

② TURN SCREW IN UNTIL IT TOUCHES SECONDARY THROTTLE LEVER & THEN TURN SCREW AN ADDITIONAL ¼ TURN

① BACK OFF SCREW UNTIL IT DOES NOT TOUCH THROTTLE LEVER

SECONDARY THROTTLE LEVER

Secondary throttle stop screw adjustment—model 6510C

Vacuum Break Adjustment.

1. Remove the choke coil assembly.

2. Push the choke coil lever clockwise to close the choke valve.

3. Push the choke shaft against its stop.

4. Take the slack out of the linkage, in the open direction.

5. Insert the specified gauge between the lower edge of the choke plate and the air

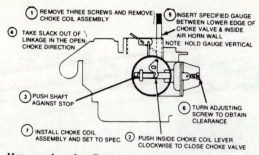

Vacuum break adjustment—model 6510C

① REMOVE THREE SCREWS AND REMOVE CHOKE COIL ASSEMBLY
④ TAKE SLACK OUT OF LINKAGE IN THE OPEN CHOKE DIRECTION
⑤ INSERT SPECIFIED GAUGE BETWEEN LOWER EDGE OF CHOKE VALVE & INSIDE AIR HORN WALL
NOTE: HOLD GAUGE VERTICAL
③ PUSH SHAFT AGAINST STOP
⑥ TURN ADJUSTING SCREW TO OBTAIN CLEARANCE
⑦ INSTALL CHOKE COIL ASSEMBLY AND SET TO SPEC.
② PUSH INSIDE CHOKE COIL LEVER CLOCKWISE TO CLOSE CHOKE VALVE

horn wall. Turn the adjusting screw on the diaphragm housing to adjust.

Fast Idle Adjustment

1. Set the fast idle cam so that the screw is on the second highest step of the fast idle cam.

2. Insert the specified gauge between the lower edge of the choke valve and the air horn wall.

3. Bend the tang on the arm to adjust.

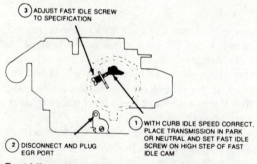

③ ADJUST FAST IDLE SCREW TO SPECIFICATION
② DISCONNECT AND PLUG EGR PORT
① WITH CURB IDLE SPEED CORRECT, PLACE TRANSMISSION IN PARK OR NEUTRAL AND SET FAST IDLE SCREW ON HIGH STEP OF FAST IDLE CAM

Fast idle cam adjustment—model 6510C

FUEL TANK

REMOVAL AND INSTALLATION

1. Disconnect the battery ground cable to prevent any chance of sparks.

2. Siphon out the contents of the tank.

3. Disconnect the meter (fuel gauge) and pump wires at the rear wiring harness connector. Raise and support the vehicle safely.

4. Disconnect the fuel line hose at the gauge unit connection.

5. On 1971 models, disconnect the tank vent lines to the vapor separator, which is mounted on top of the tank. On later models, disconnect the tank vent line to the vapor separator, which is mounted in the tank.

6. Remove the gauge wire ground screw from the floorpan.

7. Remove the tank strap bolts and carefully lower the tank.

8. The cam holding the meter unit in place in the top of the tank is normally removed with a special spanner wrench tool, shaped like a very large socket. If an attempt is made to remove this without the special tool, do not strike it with a steel hammer or use a steel drift. This could cause sparks, resulting in an explosion of gas fumes. See Chapter 4 for information on the electrical fuel pump.

9. It is advisable to rinse out the tank thoroughly while it is off the car. This cannot be done with the tank in place, since no drain plug is provided.

10. Reverse the procedure to install the tank.

Chassis Electrical

HEATER

Blower Motor

REMOVAL AND INSTALLATION

All except 1975-76 Starfire with Air Conditioning

The heater blower may have to be removed in case of excessive motor noise or electrical failure. The unit is removed from inside the engine compartment.

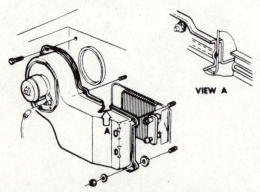

Heater blower motor—all models without A/C

1. Disconnect the battery ground cable.
2. Disconnect the blower motor lead wire.
3. Mark the position of the blower flange with respect to the case. Unscrew the blower assembly from the case and remove, prying gently if the flange is stuck on by sealant.

4. Remove the retaining nut and separate the motor and the blower wheel. When replacing the wheel on the motor, make sure that the open end of the wheel is facing away from the motor.

5. To replace, line up the marks made in Step 3, replace the bolts, and connect the lead wire. Replace the battery ground cable and check that the blower operates when the ignition switch is turned on.

1975-76 Starfire With Air Conditioning

NOTE: *This procedure requires discharging and charging the A/C system. Do not attempt it unless you have the special tools and knowledge necessary to perform this task. Escaping refrigerant can cause serious injury.*

1. Disconnect the battery.
2. Disconnect the blower relay.
3. Carefully discharge the refrigerant from the system. There may be enough clearance to get the blower motor by the A/C line on 1976 and later models. If so, discharging is not necessary.
4. Disconnect the O-ring and the A/C lines.
5. Remove the screws securing the blower motor. Remove the motor.

6. Installation is the reverse of removal. Apply a bead of sealer to the flange before installing the blower motor. Recharge the A/C system.

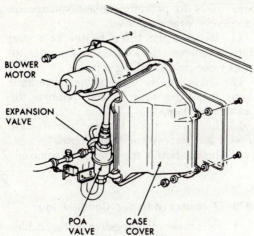

BLOWER MOTOR

EXPANSION VALVE

POA VALVE

CASE COVER

Blower and evaporator case assembly—1971–72

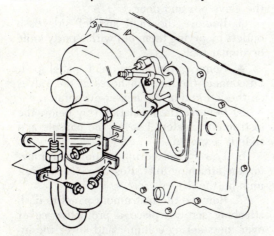

Blower and evaporator case assembly with accumulator—1973–74 all models and 1975 and later station wagon

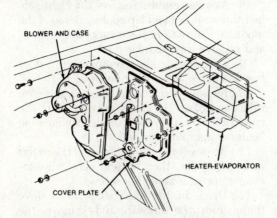

BLOWER AND CASE

HEATER-EVAPORATOR

COVER PLATE

Blower and evaporator case assembly 1975 and later except station wagon

Core

REMOVAL AND INSTALLATION

All Models Without Air Conditioning

The heater core may have to be removed for repair in case of clogging or coolant leakage. Repair service can usually be obtained at radiator repair shops. The unit is removed from inside the engine compartment.

1. Disconnect the battery ground cable and blower motor lead wire.

2. Prepare for some coolant spillage by placing a pan under the heater core inlet and outlet hoses.

3. Disconnect the hoses and raise them above the engine to prevent further coolant loss. The hoses will often stick to the core inlet and outlet tubes. If this is the case, cut the hoses off. Do not twist or pull on the core tubes; core damage will result.

4. Unbolt the ignition coil from the firewall and move it aside.

5. Remove the bolts and nuts holding the blower duct to the firewall. Remove the blower duct and motor as an assembly.

6. The core is retained by straps held in place by bolts. Remove these bolts and the core.

7. Before installing a repaired or new heater core, it would be wise to make a quick check for leakage by filling the unit with water.

8. Reverse the removal procedure to install the core, using new hoses if the old ones had to be cut off or are soft or cracked. Screw type hose clamps should be used if they are not already installed. Refill the cooling system, run the engine with the heater in the Hot position for ten minutes, and recheck the coolant level.

1971–75 Vega, 1975 Monza With Air Conditioning

1. Disconnect the battery ground cable.

2. Disconnect the heater hoses at the core and plug them.

3. Remove the firewall selector stud nuts.

4. Disconnect the left-side flexible dash outlet hose from the center distributor duct.

5. Remove the right-side dash outlet assembly.

6. Remove the instrument bezel and center outlet as an assembly.

7. Remove the ash tray and retainer.

8. Remove the radio.

9. Remove the control-to-dash screws and lower the control assembly.

10. Remove the cigarette lighter. Remove the screw retaining the right side of the dash reinforcement.

11. Pry out the center duct-to-dash clip. Remove the center duct-to-selector duct screws and remove the center duct. Turn the duct clockwise and pull down and to the left to remove.

12. Remove the defroster duct-to-selector duct screw. Remove the remaining selector duct-to-dash screws and pull the duct back far enough to allow the electrical and vacuum lines to be disconnected.

13. Disconnect the lines and the control cable and remove the selector duct assembly.

14. Pry off the temperature door bell-crank, being careful not to bed the arm or damage the selector case.

15. Remove the temperature door. Remove the backing plate and temperature door cable retainer screws.

16. Remove the heater core and backing plate as an assembly. Remove the core retaining straps and withdraw the core.

17. Reverse the removal procedure to install the core.

1976–77 Monza with Air Conditioning

1. Disconnect the negative battery cable.

2. Remove the floor outlet duct. Remove the glove box and door.

3. Remove the right and left-side dash outlets by prying them out with a putty knife or similar tool.

4. Remove the instrument panel pad. Disconnect the vacuum hoses at the valves on the left end of the heater-evaporator.

5. Remove the insulation tray below the instrument cluster. Loosen the console and slide it rearward.

6. Lower the steering column by removing the attaching nuts. Rest the steering column on the driver's seat.

7. Remove the instrument panel-to-dash attaching screws, place a protective cover over the steering column, and lower the instrument panel onto the steering column. Disconnect the speedometer cable, radio electrical leads, and control head connectors.

8. As an assembly, remove the right-side instrument panel and lap cooler. Remove the modular duct-to-heater-evaporator screw and remove the modular duct.

9. Disconnect the temperature door bowden cable and wiring harness.

10. Remove the heater hoses at the core tubes and place the hoses upright. Plug the core tubes to prevent coolant spillage on heater-evaporator removal.

11. Remove the three heater case stud nuts. Remove the heater core case-to-evaporator case attaching screws.

12. Drive on the case studs to remove them from the firewall and remove the heater core case.

13. Remove the heater core-to-case screws and remove the heater core.

14. Installation is the reverse of removal.

1976–77 Monza with Air Conditioning

1. Disconnect the negative battery cable.

2. Remove the floor outlet duct. Remove the glove box and door.

3. Remove the right and left-side dash outlets by prying them out with a putty knife or similar tool.

4. Remove the instrument panel pad. Disconnect the vacuum hoses at the valves on the left end of the heater-evaporator.

5. Remove the insulation tray below the instrument cluster. Loosen the console and slide it rearward.

6. Lower the steering column by removing the attaching nuts. Rest the steering column on the driver's seat.

7. Remove the instrument panel-to-dash attaching screws, place a protective cover over the steering column, and lower the instrument panel onto the steering column. Disconnect the speedometer cable, radio electrical leads, and control head connectors.

8. As an assembly, remove the right-side instrument panel and lap cooler. Remove the modular duct-to-heater-evaporator screw and remove the modular duct.

9. Disconnect the temperature door bowden cable and wiring harness.

10. Remove the heater hoses at the core tubes and place the hoses upright. Plug the core tubes to prevent coolant spillage on heater-evaporator removal.

11. Remove the three heater case stud nuts. Remove the heater core case-to-evaporator case attaching screws.

12. Drive in the case studs to remove them from the firewall and remove the heater core case.

13. Remove the heater core-to-case screws and remove the heater core.

14. Installation is the reverse of removal.

1978–80 Monza "S" Hatchback and Station Wagon with Air Conditioning

1. Disconnect the battery ground.

2. Disconnect the hoses at the core tubes and place in a raised position.

3. Remove the nuts from the selector duct studs in the engine compartment.

4. Remove the glove box and door.

5. Remove the right outlet to instrument panel screws and remove the outlet and hose.

6. Remove the intermediate duct leading to the left outlet.

7. Lower the steering column as described in Ignition Switch Removal and Installation.

8. Remove the instrument panel bezel. Remove the ashtray and retainer.

9. Remove the screws securing the A/C control head to the instrument panel.

10. Disconnect the radio leads and antenna wire.

11. Remove the instrument cluster screws and allow the entire cluster, including the radio, to rest on the steering column.

12. Disconnect the speedometer cable and remove the A/C control head.

13. Remove the center duct screws, then slide it first to the left, then to the right then remove it.

14. Remove the defroster duct and remaining selector ducts.

15. Disconnect all electrical and vacuum lines from the evaporator.

16. Disconnect the temperature door cables.

17. Pry off or punch out the temperature door bell crank.

18. Remove the temperature door.

19. Remove the screws securing the temperature door cable retainer and backing plate.

20. Remove the heater core and backing plate assembly assembly and remove the straps from the core.

21. Installation is the reverse of removal. When installing the ducts, make sure the firewall seals are positioned correctly. When installing the cluster, position the A/C control head and connect the speedometer cable before the cluster is secured. Adjust the temperature door at the selector duct attachment. With the temperature lever and door in the Off position, tighten the cable attaching screw.

1978–80 Monza (except Monza "S" and Station Wagon) with Air Conditioning

1. Disconnect the battery ground.

2. Remove the floor outlet duct.

3. Remove the glove box and door.

4. Remove the left and right dash outlets.

5. Remove the instrument panel pad.

6. Disconnect the vacuum hoses and electrical wires from the heater-evaporator case.

7. Remove the insulation tray below the instrument cluster and loosen the console and slide it rearward.

8. Lower the steering column assembly, following the instructions in Ignition Switch Removal and Installation.

9. Remove the instrument panel attaching screws and allow the instrument panel to rest on the steering column.

10. Disconnect the speedometer cable, radio wiring and control head wiring.

11. Remove the right side instrument panel and lap duct.

12. Remove the modular duct from the case.

13. Disconnect the temperature door cable and the wiring harness.

14. Remove the heater hoses from the core tubes and position them upright to avoid coolant loss.

15. Remove the three heater case stud nuts.

16. Remove the heater core case-to-evaporator core case screws.

17. Hammer on the studs, carefully, to break loose the heater core case.

18. Unbolt the core from the case.

19. Installation is the reverse of removal. Replace any damaged sealer.

Astre with Air Conditioning

1. Disconnect the battery ground cable.

2. Disconnect the heater hoses at the core and plug them.

3. Remove the firewall selector stud nuts, the glove box, and door.

4. Disconnect the left-side flexible dash outlet hose from the center distributor duct.

5. Remove the right-side dash outlet and hose assembly.

6. Remove the steering column lower plastic retainer, insulation, and screws. Remove the column instrument panel stud nuts and let the column rest on the seat.

NOTE: *Be extremely careful with the steering column. Never let it hang unsupported.*

7. Remove the instrument panel bezel, ash tray, and tray retainer.

8. Take out the air conditioning control panel screws.

9. Disconnect the radio and antenna leads.

10. Remove the instrument cluster to panel screws, cover the column to prevent scratches, and let the cluster rest on the column. Detach the speedometer cable.

11. Push the air conditioning controls forward and let them rest on the floor.

12. Remove the center distributor duct screws at the selector duct. Remove the duct to instrument panel upper retainer and remove the duct by sliding it to the left to clear the lower instrument panel to cluster tab, and then to the right.

13. Remove the defroster duct-to-selector duct screw. Remove the remaining selector duct-to-dash screws and pull the duct back far enough to allow the electrical and vacuum lines to be disconnected.

14. Disconnect the lines and the control cable and remove the selector duct assembly.

15. Pry off the temperature door bellcrank, being careful not to bend the arm or damage the selector case.

16. Remove the temperature door. Remove the backing plate and temperature door cable retainer screws.

17. Remove the heater core and backing plate as an assembly. Remove the core retaining straps and withdraw the core.

18. Reverse the removal procedure to install the core.

Sunbird with Air Conditioning.

1. Have the air conditioning system purged of refrigerant.

2. Disconnect the negative battery cable.

3. Disconnect the inlet and oulet lines and the oil bleed line from the VIR (receiver-dryer) assembly, on 1975–77 systems.

4. Remove the VIR to blower case strap screw, and remove the VIR unit on 1975–77 systems. Cap all the open connections immediately.

5. Remove the blower and case assembly.

6. Remove and plug the heater hoses at the core tubes and then hang them out of the way.

7. Remove the evaporator to firewall cover plate screws and remove the plate.

8. Remove (from inside the car), the floor outlet duct, the glove compartment assembly and the dash outlets on both sides. To remove the dash outlets, use a putty knife and pry them out.

9. Remove the eleven instrument panel pad screws and pry the pad off.

10. Remove the right side instrument panel to dash and kick pad screws, then loosen the left side instrument cluster to instrument panel screws.

11. Pull out on the right side of the instrument cluster to gain the necessary clearance to remove the right side instrument panel and lower duct.

12. Disconnect the vacuum hoses on the left side of the heater unit and tag them for later reinstallation.

13. Remove the modulator duct to heater unit screw, then pull the carpet and pad to the rear to make room for the heater unit removal.

14. Pull the heater unit toward you until the core tubes clear the firewall, then pull it to the right until there is enough clearance to disconnect the control cable.

15. After disconnecting the control cable, disconnect the wiring harness and remove the heater assembly.

16. Remove the screws and separate the heater case, then remove the core to case screws and remove the core.

17. Installation is the reverse of the above procedure, but before assembly, add 3 oz. of refrigerant oil to the evaporator core.

18. When installing the refrigerant lines, coat all the O-rings with refrigerant oil.

1975 Skyhawk with Air Conditioning

NOTE: *This procedure requires purging the air conditioning system of refrigerant and should not be attempted by anyone lacking the skill to perform the job properly. Serious injury may result.*

1. Disconnect the battery and purge the refrigerant from the air conditioning system.

2. Remove the glove compartment, the right side air outlet duct, the instrument bezel and pad, and air outlet duct on the left side.

3. Lower the steering column.

NOTE: *Make sure that the steering column*

is adequately supported when lowered to avoid major damage.

4. Remove the instrument panel assembly and heater-air conditioner control assembly from the instrument panel.

5. Remove the radio and the defroster duct.

6. Remove the large center distributor duct, and the heater hoses at the core pipes.

7. Clean the VIR (receiver vessel) of any dirt which may have accumulated on it. Disconnect the compressor inlet line, oil bleed line and condenser outlet line; cap all these lines.

8. Loosen the evaporator inlet and outlet lines; remove the accumulator mounting clamp and slide the accumulator off the evaporator, outlet line first.

9. Remove and discard all the old O-ring gaskets and plug all open lines to prevent contamination.

10. Remove the heater to cowl attaching nuts and remove the heater-distributor assembly, disconnect all electrical and vacuum connections.

11. Separate the heater case from the distributor assembly; separate the heater core from the heater case.

12. Installation is the reverse of removal, but when raising the steering column to its proper position, be careful not to damage any of its components. If the mounting bracket for the steering column is damaged, replace it.

1976–80 Skyhawk with Air Conditioning

NOTE: *This procedure requires purging the air conditioning system of refrigerant. Do not attempt this unless you are a qualified air conditioning technician.*

1. Have the air conditioning system purged of refrigerant.

2. Disconnect the negative battery cable.

3. Disconnect the inlet and outlet lines and the oil bleed line from the accumulator assembly.

4. Remove the accumulator to blower case strap screw, and remove the accumulator unit. Cap all the open connections immediately.

5. Remove the blower and case assembly.

6. Remove and plug the heater hoses at the core tubes and hang them out of the way.

7. Remove the evaporator to firewall cover plate screws and remove the plate.

8. Remove (from inside the car), the floor outlet duct, the glove compartment assembly and the dash outlets on both sides. Use a putty knife to pry out the dash outlets.

9. Remove the eleven instrument panel pad screws and pry the pad off.

10. Remove the right side instrument panel to dash and kick pad screws, then loosen the left side instrument cluster to instrument panel screws.

11. Pull out on the right side of the instrument cluster to gain the necessary clearance to remove the right side instrument panel and lower duct.

12. Disconnect the vacuum hoses on the left side of the heater unit and tag them for later reinstallation.

13. Remove the modulator duct to heater unit screw, then pull the carpet and pad to the rear to make room for the heater unit.

14. Pull the heater unit toward you until the core tubes clear the firewall, then pull it to the right until there is enough clearance to disconnect the control cable.

15. After disconnecting the control cable, disconnect the wiring harness and remove the heater assembly.

16. Remove the screws and separate the heater case, then remove the core to case screws and remove the core.

17. Installation is the reverse of the above procedure, but before assembly, add 3 oz. of refrigerant oil to the evaporator core.

18. When installing the refrigerant lines, coat all the O-rings with refrigerant oil.

1975 Starfire with Air Conditioning

NOTE: *This procedure requires discharging and charging the A/C system. Do not attempt it unless you have the special tools and knowledge necessary to perform this task. Serious personal injury could result from escaping refrigerant.*

1. Disconnect the battery.

2. Remove the glovebox.

3. Remove the right-hand air outlet duct.

4. Remove the instrument cluster bezel and the instrument panel crash pad.

5. Remove the left-hand air outlet deflector and feed duct.

6. Remove its retaining screws and lower the steering column so that it rests on the driver's seat.

7. Unfasten the instrument cluster screws, leads, speedometer cable, and remove the cluster. Remove the radio.

8. Remove the defroster and center distribution ducts.

9. Carefully discharge the refrigerant from the system.

10. Place a container beneath them and then remove the heater hoses from the core pipes. Plug the hoses.

11. Clean the external surfaces and fittings of the VIR assembly.

12. Disconnect the compressor intake line, oil bleed line, and condenser outlet line. Plug all open connections.

13. Loosen the evaporator intake and outlet connections. Remove the VIR mounting clamp screw and remove the clamp. Slide the VIR off the evaporator outlet line and then off the intake line. Remove and throw all the old O-rings away. Plug all open connections.

14. Remove the heater distributor/case stud-to-firewall nuts. Remove the distributor/case assembly after disconnecting all electrical leads and vacuum hoses from it.

15. Separate the heater case from the distributor and the core from the case.

16. Installation is the reverse of removal. Charge the A/C system and add coolant, as required.

1976–80 Starfire with Air Conditioning

1. Disconnect the battery ground cable.

2. Remove the three nuts from the engine compartment side of the cover plate.

3. Disconnect the heater hoses and fasten them in a raised position to prevent coolant loss. Plug the core tubes.

4. Remove the heater floor outlet.

5. Remove the glove box and door.

6. Remove the right and left air outlets.

7. Unscrew and move the console back.

8. Remove the instrument panel pad. Remove the column nuts and let the wheel rest on the seat. Remove the instrument panel screws and lower the panel onto the steering column.

9. Remove the right instrument panel and the lower outlet as an assembly.

10. Disconnect the vacuum hoses at the left end of the heater case.

11. Remove the modular duct to heater case screw and the two heater case to evaporator case screws. Pry off the retaining clips at the defroster outlets and move the duct back.

12. Pull the heater case away from the firewall until the core tubes clear, then disconnect the temperature cable.

13. Remove the core to case screws and remove the core.

14. Reverse the procedure for installation. Torque the steering column nuts to 25 ft lbs.

RADIO

REMOVAL AND INSTALLATION

1971–75

1. Disconnect the battery ground cable.

2. Remove the knobs, control wheels, nuts, and washers.

3. Unplug the antenna lead, power connector, and speaker connectors from the rear of the unit.

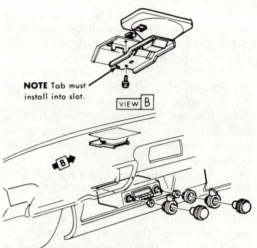

NOTE Tab must install into slot.

VIEW B

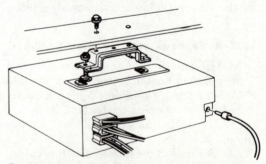

Radio and speaker mounting

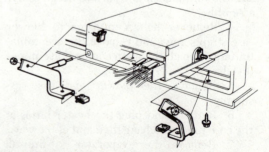

Receiver mounting—Monza S and station wagon

Receiver mounting—all except Monza S and station wagon

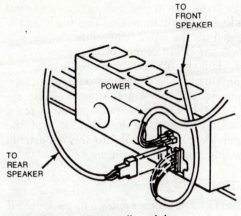

Receiver connections—all models

4. Remove the two screws holding the radio mounting bracket to the instrument panel. Lift out the unit.

5. To replace, reverse the removal procedure.

NOTE: *Make sure that the speakers are connected before energizing the radio. The output transistors will be ruined if the radio is operated without a speaker load.*

6. Set the antenna trimmer adjustment.

1976 and Later

1. Disconnect the negative battery cable.

2. Remove the knobs, bezels, nuts, and washers from the radio control shafts.

3. Remove the two screws attaching the radio to the instrument panel reinforcement.

4. With mounts still attached, lower the radio and disconnect the electrical leads.

5. Installation is the reverse of removal.

Speaker

REMOVAL AND INSTALLATION

Without Air Conditioning

1. Remove the nine screws and lift out the instrument panel.

2. Unplug the speaker connector behind the defroster duct.

3. Unbolt the speaker from the brace.

4. Reverse the procedure to install, observing the Note under Radio Removal and Installation.

With Air Conditioning

1. Disconnect the battery ground cable.

2. Remove the nine screws and the instrument panel bezel (trim) with the air conditioning outlet.

3. Remove the upper retainer and the two lower screws for the center air conditioning duct.

4. Remove the radio and lighter.

5. Push the air conditioning center duct down and rotate it to the left.

6. Reach through the instrument panel opening and remove the bolt holding the speaker to the brace. Unplug and remove the speaker.

7. Reverse the procedure to install, observing the Note under Radio Removal and Installation.

Antenna

The factory-installed radio utilizes an antenna embedded in the windshield. Dealers have a device for checking continuity in case of suspected failure.

LEAD ASSEMBLY INSTALLATION

When installing a radio in a Vega delivered without a radio but with a windshield antenna, an antenna lead assembly must be installed.

NOTE: *The lead assembly should be installed before the speaker or radio.*

1. Disconnect the battery ground cable.

2. Reach under the cowl air intake grille from under the hood and carefully pull the windshield antenna connector from the dummy socket. From under the instrument

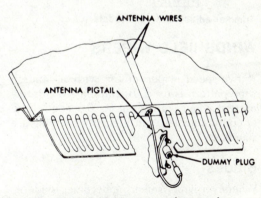

Location of windshield antenna dummy plug

panel, unbolt and remove the dummy socket.

3. Install the antenna lead assembly in place of the dummy socket.

4. Plug the windshield antenna connector into the lead assembly socket.

5. Install the speaker and radio, observing

the Note under Radio Removal and Installation.

6. Connect the battery ground cable.
7. Set the antenna trimmer adjustment.

TRIMMER ADJUSTMENT

The antenna trimmer adjustment should be made whenever the radio or antenna is replaced.

1. Remove the right-side radio control knobs.
2. Tune the radio to a weak station at about 1400 kc on the AM band and turn the volume up fully. If a telescoping antenna is being used, set it to the height desired for normal use.
3. Adjust the trimmer screw, just above the tuning knob shaft, for maximum volume.
4. Replace the knobs.

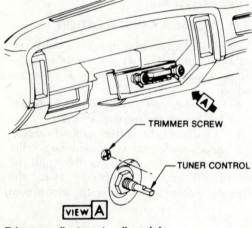

TRIMMER SCREW

TUNER CONTROL

VIEW A

Trimmer adjustment—all models

WINDSHIELD WIPERS

A two-speed wiper motor with a tandem wipe pattern is used. Beginning 1977, intermittent wipers providing ½-20 second delay or continuous low and highspeed wiping are standard.

Blades

Whenever wiper smearing becomes evident, the condition of the rubber blades should be checked. Smearing is often caused by a build up of road dirt on the blades. This can be prevented by cleaning the blade rubbing surfaces carefully each time the car is washed.

REMOVAL AND INSTALLATION

The factory-installed wiper blades are replaced as follows:

1. Press down on the wiper arm and blade tab simultaneously. The blade tab is located at the point where the wiper arm meets the blade connector.
2. Pull the blade away from the arm.
3. Simply snap the arm into the new blade connector. If the wiper arms must be removed, they can be carefully pulled or pried off. They should be installed so that the wiper blades are parallel to the windshield molding in the park position.

Motor

NOTE: *The wiper blades will park only if the wipers are operating at Low speed.*

REMOVAL AND INSTALLATION

1. Disconnect the battery ground cable.
2. Reach through the cowl opening under the hood to loosen the two wiper transmission drive link to crankarm attaching nuts.
3. Remove the transmission drive link from the motor crankarm.
4. Disconnect the motor wiring and remove the three attaching bolts. Disconnect the windshield washer hoses.
5. Remove the motor, guiding the crankarm.
6. Reverse the procedure to install.

INSTRUMENT CLUSTER

All instruments and gauges may be removed from the front of the cluster. Illumination and indicator bulbs can be removed from the rear of the cluster by turning the socket holder ¼ turn.

NOTE: *The temperature warning light sending unit will not function properly unless the coolant has at least 0°F antifreeze protection.*

REMOVAL AND INSTALLATION
Standard Models 1971–80

1. Disconnect the battery ground cable.
2. Remove the nine phillips screws from the bezel (trim). Remove the bezel.
3. Remove the clock stem set knob with a small screwdriver.
4. Remove the lens attaching screws. There may be four or six. Tip the lens out at the top and lift it off.

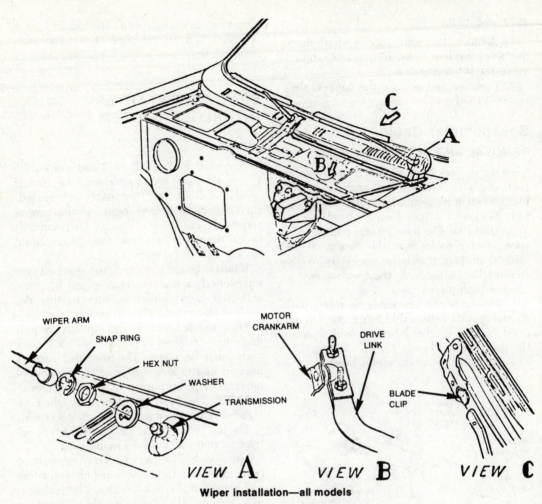

WIPER ARM
SNAP RING
HEX NUT
WASHER
TRANSMISSION

MOTOR CRANKARM
DRIVE LINK
BLADE CLIP

VIEW **A**   *VIEW* **B**   *VIEW* **C**

Wiper installation—all models

5. Remove the two screws and shield crossbar at the bottom of the cluster. The crossbar is not used on all models.

6. Remove the two screws at the bottom of the speedometer face and lift out the speedometer head assembly. The speedometer cable need not be removed.

7. To remove the fuel gauge from the cluster, remove the two screws, release the locking tab with a small screwdriver while rocking the gauge gently, pull the gauge straight out, and disconnect the electrical plug. The clock may be removed in the same way.

8. Reverse the procedure to install.

GT Option 1971–80

1. Disconnect the battery ground cable.

2. Remove the clock stem set knob with a small screwdriver.

3. Remove the six screws and the wood grain trim plate.

4. Remove the six screws and the lens light shield.

5. Remove the two screws (the tachometer has three) and disconnect the electrical plug to remove each instrument. The speedometer cable need not be removed.

6. Reverse the removal procedure to install.

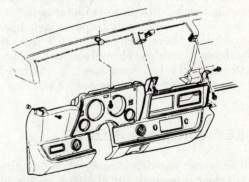

Standard instrument cluster—1977 and later except station wagons—typical

1977 and Later

1. Remove the four screws that attach the bezel and lens to the instrument, and remove the bezel and lens.

2. Unscrew and remove the gauges, then reinstall the bezel and lens.

Speedometer Cable

REMOVAL AND INSTALLATION

Clicking or jerky speedometer movement, particularly in cold weather, may be caused by a kinked or inadequately lubricated cable.

1. Remove the speedometer head.

2. Using needle nose pliers, pull out the speedometer cable from the casing. If the cable is broken, it may be necessary to disconnect the casing from the transmission to remove both pieces.

3. Lubricate the new cable sparingly with special speedometer cable lubricant. Do not overlubricate or the lubricant will damage the speedometer head.

4. Replace the speedometer head.

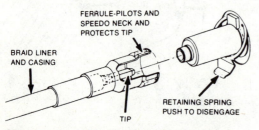

Speedometer cable attachment at the cluster

IGNITION SWITCH

Replacement of the ignition switch requires lowering of the energy-absorbing steering column. This unit can be damaged by its own weight if unsupported, or by any impact. It is recommended that this operation be left to qualified Chevrolet service personnel. Ignition lock cylinder, turn signal switch, and key warning buzzer switch replacement require steering wheel removal and are covered under Steering in Chapter 8.

KEY WARNING BUZZER

This buzzer sounds a warning when the driver's door is opened with the ignition key in the switch. The buzzer is combined with the horn relay in a single unit. The buzzer switch is connected to terminal 4 on the buzzer/relay unit.

SEAT BELT/STARTER INTERLOCK SYSTEM

1974–75

As required by law, all 1974 and some 1975 Chevrolet passenger cars cannot be started until the front seat occupants are seated, then fasten their seat belts. If the proper sequence is not followed, e.g., the occupants fasten their seat belts and then sit on them, the car cannot be started.

If, after the car is started, the seat belts are unfastened, a warning buzzer and light are activated in a similar manner to that described above for 1972–73 models.

The shoulder harness and lap belt are permanently fastened together, so that they both must be worn. The shoulder harness uses an inertia-lock reel to allow freedom of movement under normal driving conditions. NOTE: *This type of reel locks up when the car decelerates rapidly, as during a crash.*

The lap belts use the same ratchet-type retractors that the 1972–73 models use.

The switches for the interlock system have been removed from the lap belt retractors and placed in the belt buckles. The seat sensors remain the same as those used in 1972–73.

For ease of service, the car may be started from outside, by reaching in and turning the key, but without depressing the seat sensors.

In case of system failure, an override switch is located under the hood. This is a "one start" switch and it must be reset each time it is used.

DISABLING THE INTERLOCK SYSTEM

Since the requirement for the interlock system was dropped during the 1975 model year, those systems installed on cars built earlier may now be legally disabled. The seat belt warning light is still required.

1. Disconnect the negative battery cable.

2. Locate the interlock harness connector with orange, yellow and green leads under the left side of the instrument panel on or near the fuse block. 1974 Vegas have the connector under the parking brake cable cover.

3. Cut and tape the ends of the green wire on the body side of the connector.

4. Remove the buzzer from the fuse block or connector.

FLASHERS

Turn Signal

The turn signal flasher is located under the left side of the instrument panel. If the turn signals operate in only one direction, a bulb is probably burned out. If they operate in neither direction, a bulb on each side may be burned out, or the flasher may be defective.

REMOVAL AND INSTALLATION

1. Pull the flasher from its spring clip mounting.
2. Unplug and discard the flasher. Plug in the new flasher.
3. Replace the flasher in the spring clip and check operation.

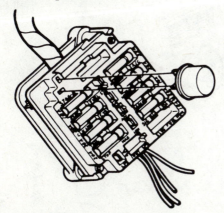

Fuse block with four way flasher

Four-Way Warning

This flasher is located in the fuse block just above the headlight dimmer floor switch. If the four-way flashers do not operate, but the turn signals do, the flasher is probably defective. It can be removed simply by pulling it from the fuse block. The flashers will not operate with the brake pedal depressed, since they use the stop-light filaments in the taillight bulbs.

FUSES

The fuse block is located beneath the instrument panel above the headlight dimmer floor switch. Fuse holders are labeled as to their service and the correct amperage.

Always replace blown fuses with new ones of the correct amperage. Otherwise electrical overloads and possible wiring damage will result.

Circuit Breaker

A circuit breaker is an electrical switch which breaks the circuit during an electrical overload. The circuit breaker will remain open until the short or overload condition in the circuit is corrected.

FUSIBLE LINKS

Fusible links are sections of wire, with special insulation, designed to melt under electrical overload. Replacements are simply spliced into the wire. There may be as many as five of these in the engine compartment wiring harnesses. These are:

1. Horn relay to fuse panel circuit—one link.

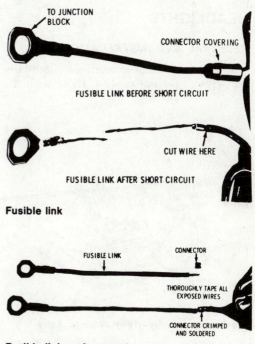

TO JUNCTION BLOCK

CONNECTOR COVERING

FUSIBLE LINK BEFORE SHORT CIRCUIT

CUT WIRE HERE

FUSIBLE LINK AFTER SHORT CIRCUIT

Fusible link

FUSIBLE LINK   CONNECTOR

THOROUGHLY TAPE ALL EXPOSED WIRES

CONNECTOR CRIMPED AND SOLDERED

Fusible link replacement

2. Charging circuit, from the starter solenoid to the horn relay—two links.
3. Starter solenoid to ammeter circuit—one link.

4. Horn relay to rear window defroster circuit—one link.

The fusible links are all two wire gauge sizes smaller than the wires they protect.

REPLACEMENT

1. Disconnect the battery ground cable.
2. Disconnect the fusible link from the junction block or starter solenoid.
3. Cut the harness directly behind the connector to remove the damaged fusible link.
4. Strip the harness wire approximately ½ in.
5. Connect the new fusible link to the harness wire using a crimp on connector. Soder the connection using rosin core solder.
6. Tape all exposed wires with plastic electrical tape.
7. Connect the fusible link to the junction block or starter solenoid and reconnect the battery ground cable.

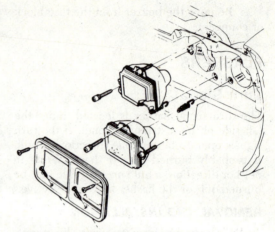

Dual headlamp system—Monza 2+2

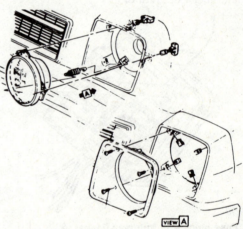

Single headlamp system except Vega and Astre

HEADLIGHTS

REMOVAL AND INSTALLATION

1. Remove the three headlight rim retaining screws. Do not confuse these with the

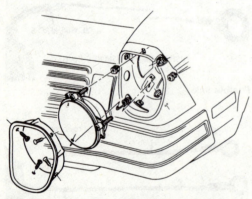

Headlamp assembly—1974–77 Vega, Astre

two headlight aiming screws which are located closer to the headlight.

2. Use a hook to pull the retaining spring aside to release the unit. Remove the rim.

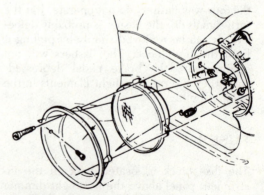

Headlamp assembly—1971–73

3. Rotate the right headlight clockwise, and rotate the left one counterclockwise to release them from the aiming pins.

4. Pull off the electrical connector.

5. Remove the retaining ring.

6. Reverse the removal procedure to install the new unit.

NOTE: *When aiming the headlights, each low beam should be 0 to 4 in. to the right and down of the headlight centerline, at a distance of 25 ft.*

WIRING DIAGRAMS

Wiring diagrams have been left out of this book. As cars have become more complex, and available with longer and longer option lists, wiring diagrams have grown in size and complexity also. It has become virtually impossible to provide a readable reproduction in a reasonable number of pages. Information on ordering wiring diagrams from the vehicle manufacturer can be found in the owner's manual.

Clutch and Transmission

MANUAL TRANSMISSION

Both the 1971–72 three-speed and the four-speed manual transmissions use metric threads throughout. Several metric spiral pins are used in the shifting mechanism. No drain plug is used, as the manufacturer states that the lubricant needs to be changed only after overhaul. The factory installed transmission lubricant contains an orange color, helpful in tracing leaks.

The Opel-made transmissions used in 1971–72 were replaced with fully synchronized Saginaw three and four-speed units in 1973.

A five-speed Borg-Warner T-50 transmission is optional on 1975 and later models. Fourth gear is direct drive with fifth gear an overdrive. The transmission is shifted by a single shift rail enclosed within the transmission. An unusual feature of this transmission is that it uses automatic transmission fluid for lubrication.

In 1976–77, the 70mm four-speed transmission was used on base models. This light weight transmission is also used in the Chevette. Gear shifting is done by an internal shifter shaft.

In 1978, the Saginaw four-speed, now called the 76mm, was reinstated as the standard four-speed.

The designation by millimeters refers to the measured distance between the centerlines of the transmission's mainshaft and countershaft.

REMOVAL AND INSTALLATION
1971–72

1. Place the shift lever in neutral and remove the boot trim screws. Pull the boot up.

2. Unhook the antirattle coil spring. Remove the shift finger (lower end of lever) pin retaining clip and pin. Remove the shift lever.

3. Raise and support the vehicle safely. Refer to Jacking in Chapter 1. Drain the transmission if it is to be disassembled. This requires removing the bottom pan, since there is no drain plug. Pan bolt torque is 48 in. lbs.

NOTE: *The magnet inside the pan should be cleaned thoroughly.*

4. Remove the driveshaft as described in Chapter 7.

5. Disconnect the speedometer cable,

TCS switch (right side), and backup light switch. The backup light switch is on the extension housing on the three-speed and on the right rear of the case on the four-speed.

7. Support the rear of the engine with suitable stands or wooden blocks. Support at the oil pan rail to prevent pan distortion.

8. Unbolt the crossmember from the frame and remove it.

9. Remove the transmission to clutch housing upper bolts and replace them with guide pins. Guide pins can be fabricated by cutting the heads off two bolts and sawing screwdriver slots into them.

NOTE: *It is possible to remove and install the transmission without using guide pins, but it may be rather difficult.*

10. Remove the lower bolts. Slide the transmission back on the guide pins and remove it, supporting it with a transmission jack or a safe substitute.

To install the transmission:

11. Check the throwout bearing support gasket located beneath the lip of the support on the clutch housing. Replace it if necessary.

12. Lightly lubricate the inside diameter of the clutch drive gear (transmission input shaft) seal and install the seal on the drive gear. Make sure that the splines are clean and dry.

13. Place a new gasket on the clutch housing. The gasket may temporarily be held in place by a small amount of grease.

14. Raise the transmission into place. Slide it forward on the guide pins. The clutch gear may have to be turned slightly to align the splines.

15. Install the lower bolts. Remove the guide pins and replace them with the upper bolts. Torque the bolts, in rotation, to 24 ft lbs.

16. Replace the crossmember. Torque the mounting bolts to 26 ft lbs and the frame bolts to 28 ft lbs.

NOTE: *Check that the engine is still properly aligned on its front mounts.*

17. Connect the speedometer cable, backup light switch, and TCS switch.

18. Replace the driveshaft. Lower the vehicle.

19. Fill the transmission to the proper level with the specified lubricant as described in Chapter 1.

20. Lubricate the ball end of the shift finger and the shift finger retaining pin. Install the lever, pin, and retaining clip.

21. Replace the coil spring on the shift lever. Install the rubber boot and trim.

REMOVAL AND INSTALLATION
1973 and Later 3 and 4 Speed

1. Raise vehicle and support on hoist or with jackstands.

2. Remove the driveshaft. Remove the damper assembly, the catalytic converter bracket and the torque arm bracket on 1976 and later models.

3. Disconnect the speedometer, TCS switch and backup lamp switch.

4. Disconnect the transmission control rod and level assemblies from the shifter shafts.

5. Remove the crossmember-to-transmission mounting bolts.

6. Support the engine with a jackstand and remove the crossmember-to-frame bolts. Remove the crossmember from the vehicle.

7. Remove the bolts retaining the transmission to the upper clutch housing. Install guide pins into holes.

8. Remove lower bolts and slide transmission back and down out of vehicle.

9. To install, position transmission-to-clutch housing and slide forward engaging the input shaft splines with the clutch and into the pilot bearing.

10. Install bolts and lockwashers retaining transmission-to-clutch housing. Torque to specifications.

11. Position crossmember to frame and loosely install retaining bolts. Install crossmember-to-transmission mounting bolts. Torque all bolts to specifications. Remove engine support stand.

12. Make sure that the engine mounts are aligned in front end of vehicle.

13. Position control rod and levers to shifter shafts. Install and torque retaining bolts.

5 Speed

1. Remove the boot retainer and slide the boot upward on the shift lever.

2. Remove the foam insulator over the control assembly bolts.

3. Remove the four control level bolts and remove the control lever.

4. Raise the car and remove the driveshaft.

5. Remove the damper assembly, the catalytic converter bracket, and the torque arm bracket.

6. Disconnect the speedometer cable and the back-up light switch.

7. Place a transmission jack under the transmission and remove the transmission support.

8. Remove the transmission-to-clutch housing bolts and slide the exhaust bracket forward, after this the transmission can be moved rearward and removed from the car.

9. Installation is the reverse of removal, but make sure that the main drive gear splines are clean and dry.

SHIFT MECHANISM ADJUSTMENT
1971–72 4 Speed

The reverse gearshift blocker adjustment can be made on the four-speed transmission only. This adjustment is made at the selector shaft on the left side of the transmission.

1. Shift into Second gear.

2. Adjust the selector ring so that the shift lever finger ball has equal clearance on both sides in the intermediate lever hole.

3. Back off the selector ring a quarter turn and tighten the locknut.

LINKAGE ADJUSTMENT
1973 and Later 3 and 4 Speed

1. With the ignition off, raise the vehicle and support on hoist or jackstands.

2. Loosen the locknuts at the swivels on the shift rods.

3. Set the transmission shift levers in Neutral.

4. Set the shift lever in Neutral. Align the control lever and insert a gauge pin into the levers and bracket.

5. Tighten the 1-R (1-2) shift rod nut against the swivel. Torque to 120 in. lbs.

6. Tighten the 2-3 (3-4) shift rod nut against the swivel. Torque to 120 in. lbs.

7. On 4 speed units, tighten the reverse shift control rod nut to 120 in. lbs.

8. Remove the gauge pin from the lever and check operation.

9. Lower the vehicle.

SHIFT LEVER LOCKOUT WIRE REPLACEMENT
1971–72 4 Speed

The procedure for replacing the reverse lockout wire inside the four-speed shift lever is as follows:

1. Remove the shift lever, following Steps 1 and 2 under Manual Transmission Removal and Installation.

2. Pull off the shift knob and loosen the allen head setscrew at top of the lever.

3. Drive out the two spiral pins at the bottom of the lever. Remove the shift finger.

4. Pull the wire out of the lever.

5. Oil the sliding surface of the stop sleeve on the shift finger tube.

6. Install the new wire and fasten it so that the cutout of the stop sleeve is to the left. Insert the long spiral pin.

7. Clamp the wire with the setscrew so that the lockout knob has about 1/16 in. free travel.

8. Install the short spiral pin and shift finger.

9. Replace the shift knob and make sure that the distance between the shift knob and lockout knob is 0.30 in.

CLUTCH

The clutch is of the diaphragm spring type, actuated by a cable and pulley arrangement. Periodic adjustment is required to maintain the proper pedal free-play. A safety switch attached to the clutch pedal arm prevents the engine from being started unless the pedal is depressed. This switch is self-aligning on installation and requires no adjustment.

REMOVAL AND INSTALLATION

The transmission must be removed to remove the clutch.

1. Raise and support the vehicle safely. Refer to Jacking in Chapter 1.

2. Remove the transmission as described under Manual Transmission Removal and Installation.

3. Remove the clutch fork cover (just behind the cable entry into the left side of the clutch housing). Disconnect the clutch return spring and control cable from the clutch fork.

4. Remove the main drive gear (transmission input shaft) oil seal from the clutch release bearing sleeve.

5. Remove the flywheel housing lower cover and flywheel housing.

6. To remove the release bearing from the clutch fork and sleeve, slide the fork end off the ball stud (adjustable pivot point) against spring tension.

7. If the assembly marks on the clutch

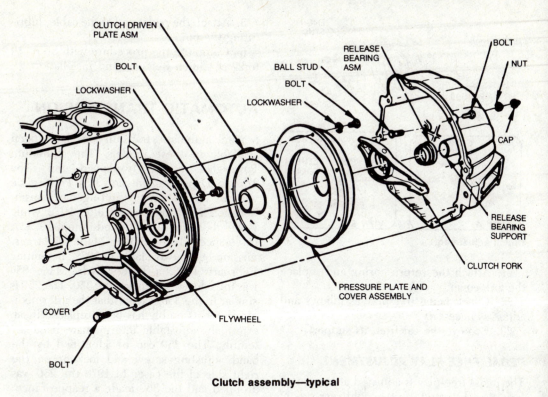

Clutch assembly—typical

and flywheel cannot be seen, mark the relationship between the clutch and flywheel with paint for reassembly.

8. Loosen the clutch cover attaching bolts one turn at a time, in rotation, until spring pressure is released. If this is not done, the cover will be warped.

9. Remove the bolts, pressure platecover assembly, and clutch driven plate.

10. Inspect all parts. Check that the flywheel and pressure plate are not scored. A scored pressure plate should be replaced. A scored flywheel can often be resurfaced by machining. Minor roughness can be cleaned up with fine emery cloth. If the driven plate has oil on it, check for evidence of engine or transmission leakage. Check the front face of the release bearing and the sleeve outside diameter for wear. Any parts that appear at all worn or damaged should be replaced to avoid future difficulty.

11. To install the clutch, place the driven plate on the pressure plate with the long end of the splined part forward.

12. Hold the clutch assembly against the flywheel, aligning the marks made in Step 7, and insert a dummy clutch gear shaft through the cover and the driven plate into the crankshaft pilot bearing. A dummy shaft for aligning the clutch can be made from an old trans-

mission input shaft or something similar.

13. Install the cover bolts finger tight. Then tighten the bolts evenly, in rotation, to avoid distortion. Torque the bolts to 18 ft lbs. Remove the dummy shaft.

14. Lubricate the clutch fork pivot ball socket and the diaphragm spring fingers with high melting point graphite grease. Also lightly lubricate the recess on the inside of the throwout bearing collar and the fork groove.

15. Install the clutch fork in the housing but not on the ball stud.

16. Install the throwout bearing on the sleeve, position the fork in the housing over the bearing, and slide the fork onto the ball stud.

17. Install the flywheel housing and lower cover and torque the bolts to 25 ft lbs.

18. Replace the transmission.

19. Place the clutch cable through the hole in the clutch fork. Pull the cable until the pedal is against the rubber bumper. Push the fork forward until the throwout bearing can be felt contacting the clutch spring fingers.

20. Screw the cross-pin onto the cable until it bottoms out on the clutch fork. Tighten the pin a quarter turn more and set it into the fork groove.

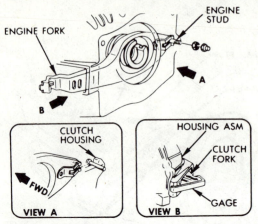

Clutch adjustment

21. Attach the return spring and replace the fork cover.

22. Check pedal free-play as follows and adjust as necessary.

23. Remove the car from its supports.

PEDAL FREE-PLAY ADJUSTMENT

The pedal free-play is adjusted at the clutch fork pivot ball stud, on the right rear side of the clutch housing. Free-play is the distance that the pedal travels from the free position to the point at which clutch spring pressure can be felt. Permissible free-play is 0.65–1.15 in. (1971–72 models) or 0.90± 0.25 in. (1973–80 models). This can be measured by placing a yardstick alongside the clutch pedal pad.

1. Remove the ball stud cap. Loosen the locknut.

2. Using a ¼ in. allen wrench, adjust the stud until the correct free-play is obtained. Turn counterclockwise to increase free-play, and clockwise to decrease.

3. Tighten locknut to 25 ft lbs and recheck free-play. Replace the stud cap.

CABLE REPLACEMENT

1. Remove the clutch fork cover (just behind the cable entry into the left side of the clutch housing). Disconnect the return spring and cable from the clutch fork.

2. Remove the clip and pin at the pedal end of the cable.

3. Pull out the old cable. The outer cable simply plugs into the firewall and clutch housing. There is an O-ring at the clutch housing end.

4. Install the new cable, follwing the old routing.

5. Attach the pedal end of the cable, lubricating the pin.

6. Complete the procedure with Steps 19 to 22 of Clutch Removal and Installation.

AUTOMATIC TRANSMISSION

Several automatic transmissions have been available in these models. The aluminum Powerglide is the two-speed unit. The Torque Drive transmission is a Powerglide without the automatic shifting mechanism. Torque Drive was dropped after 1972, while Powerglide was discontinued in mid-1973. A three-speed Turbo Hydra-Matic 350 transmission became available in 1972. Beginning February 1973, a Turbo Hydra-Matic 250 was introduced to replace the 350. The 250 is similar to the 350, except that the intermediate clutch assembly has been replaced by an externally adjustable intermediate band assembly. The 250 can be identified by the band adjusting screw and locknut on the right side of the case. In 1978 the 250 was dropped and the 350 made a reappearance. Starting 1976, a new three-speed transmission is offered: Turbo Hydra-Matic 200. The light weight Turbo Hydra-Matic 200 transmission can be identified by the use of metric fasteners throughout. The 200 has 10 pan-bolts and the 350 has 13.

No automatic transmission overhaul procedures are given in this book, as this work requires numerous specialized tools and procedures.

SHIFT LINKAGE ADJUSTMENT
1971–72 Powerglide, Torque Drive

The function of this adjustment is to provide about 0.05 in. overtravel for each shift position to make sure that it is fully engaged. If this is not done, the transmission may be only partially engaged in a range position. This would result in severe damage due to clutch slippage. The adjustment is made underneath the vehicle.

1. Loosen the two shift rod adjusting nuts at the swivel. The swivel is attached to the floorshift lever assembly lower lever.

2. Turn the shift lever on the transmission all the way clockwise. This is the Park detent position. Turn counterclockwise two detents to the neutral detent position.

3. Make sure that the floorshift lever is in the neutral position.

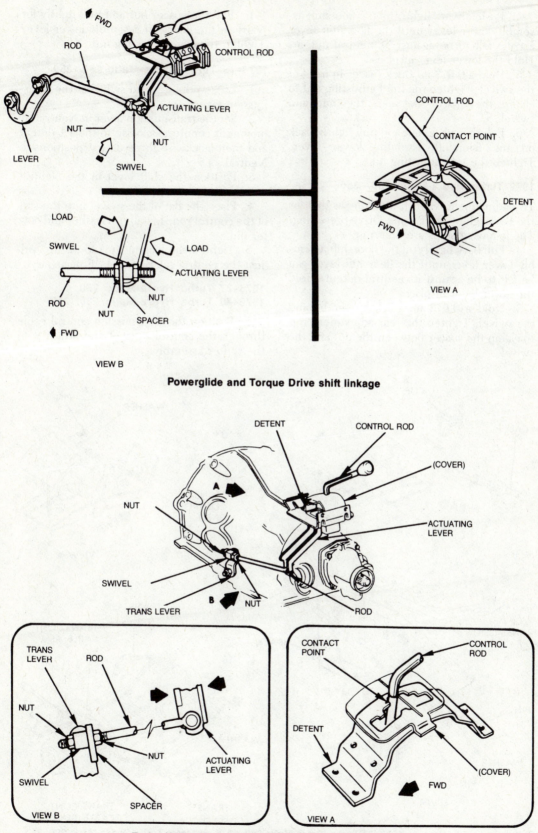

Powerglide and Torque Drive shift linkage

Turbo Hydra-Matic 250–350 shift linkage through 1975

4. Push forward lightly on the floorshift assembly lower lever until the floorshift lever can be felt to be against its neutral detent. Hold the lower lever in place.

5. Hold a 0.073 in. thick spacer in front of the swivel. Tighten the front adjusting nut to clamp the spacer between the nut and swivel.

6. Pull the spacer out and pull lightly back on the floorshift assembly lower lever. Tighten the rear adjusting nut.

1972 Turbo Hydra-Matic 250—350

This adjustment is much the same as that for the Powerglide and Torque Drive preceding. The following steps are different:

4. Pull back lightly on the floorshift assembly lower lever until the floorshift lever can be felt to be against its neutral detent. Hold the lower lever in place.

5. Hold a 0.073 in. thick spacer behind the swivel. Tighten the rear adjustment nut to clamp the spacer between the nut and the swivel.

6. Pull the spacer out and pull lightly forward on the floorshift assembly lower lever. Tighten the front adjusting nut.

1973–75 Turbo Hydra-Matic 250, 350

1. Loosen the nut and swivel at the transmission lever.

2. Set the transmission lever in Neutral by moving it counterclockwise to the L1 detent and then clockwise three detent positions to Neutral.

3. Position the shift level in the Neutral notch of the detent plate.

4. Place the flat of the swivel into the slot of the control rod. Install the washer and cotter pin.

5. Tighten the locknut to 120 in. lbs. Adjust the neutral safety switch, if necessary.

1976–77 Turbo Hydra-Matic 250
1976–80 Turbo Hydra-Matic 200, 250

1. Position the transmission control cable through the control bracket and attach it to the shifter assembly.

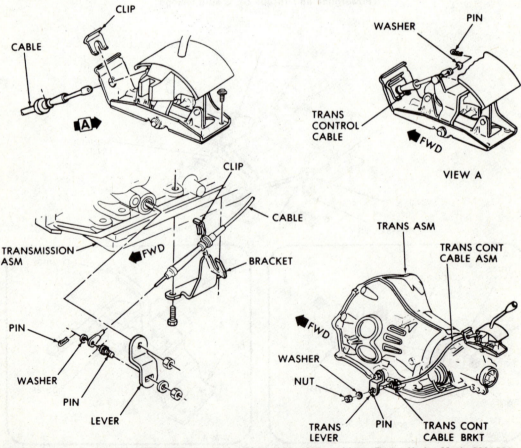

Shift linkage adjustment—1976–77 Turbo Hydra-Matic 250, 1976 and later Turbo Hydra-Matic 200, 350

2. Position the lever pin through the transmission lever and loosely install the washer and nut.

3. Place the shift lever on the transmission into the Neutral position.

4. Place the shift lever (inside car) into Neutral. You can find Neutral by moving the transmission lever counterclockwise to the L1 position, then clockwise through four positions to Neutral.

5. Tighten the transmission lever to 20 ft lbs.

NEUTRAL SAFETY AND BACK-UP SWITCH ADJUSTMENT

Powerglide, Torque Drive, Turbo Hydra-Matic 200, 250, 350

This switch prevents the engine from being started in any transmission position other than neutral or Park. It also activates the back-up lights. On installation, the switch is located by a plastic pin which is sheared off as soon as the floorshift lever is operated. The switch is contained within the floorshift console.

To replace the switch:

1. Remove the console unit.

2. Disconnect the electrical plugs. The neutral safety terminals are at the front; the back-up terminals are in the center.

3. Place the floorshift lever in Neutral.

4. Unscrew and remove the shift indicator plate and the curved cover.

5. Remove the two switch retaining screws from their slotted mounting brackets. These are hidden beneath the lever cover.

6. Tilt the switch to the right and lift it out.

7. Make sure that the lever is still in Neutral.

8. Install the switch, inserting the drive tang into the switch lever. If a used switch is being reinstalled, align the slot in the contact support with the service adjustment hole in the switch (next to the shear pin hole) and insert a $3/32$ in. diameter pin to hold the switch in place. The pin can be removed after the switch is fastened in place.

9. Install the switch retaining screws, curved cover, and shift indicator plate.

10. Shift out of Neutral to shear off the locating pin on the new switch.

11. Install the electrical connectors. Hold the footbrake while checking that the engine will start only in Neutral or Park. Check that the back-up lights operate only in Reverse. If the switch does not operate properly, it may have to be moved on its slotted mounting brackets.

12. Replace the console cover.

THROTTLE VALVE LINKAGE ADJUSTMENT

Powerglide

The throttle valve linkage causes the transmission to downshift when the accelerator is depressed to the wide open throttle position at speeds up to 60 to 65 mph. The linkage is on the left side of the engine and transmission, below and to the rear of the carburetor.

1. Hold the accelerator pedal all the way down.

2. Unclip and detach the rear end of the throttle valve control rod (the horizontal rod).

3. The bellcrank lever stud should be all the way forward in the slot at the front of the throttle valve control rod.

4. Hold the lever at the transmission against its internal stop.

5. If the rear end of the throttle valve control rod does not align with the hole in the lever, pull out the retaining clip from the sleeve in the center of the rod. Adjust the sleeve to lengthen or shorten the rod.

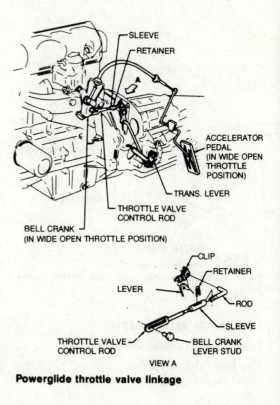

Powerglide throttle valve linkage

NOTE: *The sleeve can be adjusted only in increments of one turn.*

6. Install the throttle valve control rod in the lever hole and attach the clip.

DETENT CABLE ADJUSTMENT
Turbo Hydra-Matic 200, 250, 350

The detent cable causes the transmission to downshift when the accelerator is depressed to the wide open throttle position at speeds between 57 and 74 mph for Second gear, and 24 and 40 mph for First gear. The actual downshift speed range depends upon gearing, engine option, and tire size. The linkage is on the left side of the engine and transmission, below and to the rear of the carburetor.

1. Remove the carburetor air cleaner.
2. Insert a screwdriver on each side of the snap-lock on the bracket at the front of the transmission and pry up to release the lock.
3. Compress the locktabs and disconnect the snap-lock assembly from the bracket.
4. Position the carburetor lever in the wide open throttle position.
5. Hold the carburetor lever in position and push the snap-lock on the cable down until the top is flush with the cable.

NOTE: *The cable is not to be lubricated.*

6. Replace the air cleaner.

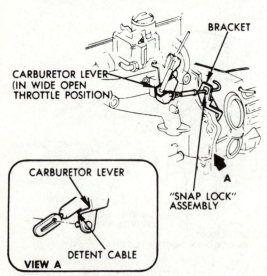

Turbo Hydra-Matic 200, 250, 350 detent cable linkage

LOW BAND ADJUSTMENT
Powerglide, Torque Drive

The low band should be adjusted after the initial 24,000 miles (12,000 miles under se-

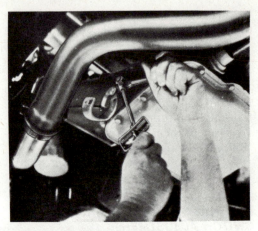

Adjusting Powerglide low band linkage

vere use) or whenever slippage is evident. The adjustment is made on the left side of the transmission, from underneath the car. This adjustment is possible only on these two transmissions.

1. Place the floorshift lever in neutral.
2. Remove the protective cap from the adjusting screw.
3. Loosen the locknut ¼ turn and hold it with a wrench during the entire adjusting procedure.
4. Tighten the adjusting nut to 70 in. lbs. using a $^{7}/_{32}$ in. allen wrench.
5. Back off the adjusting nut exactly three turns for a band used less than 6,000 miles. Back off exactly four turns for a band used 6,000 miles or more.
6. Torque the locknut to 15 ft lbs and replace the cap.

INTERMEDIATE BAND ADJUSTMENT
Turbo Hydra-Matic 250

1. Position the shift lever in Neutral.
2. Loosen the locknut ½ turn and tighten the adjusting screw to 30 in lbs.
3. Back the screw out three turns and then tighten the locknut to 15 ft lbs.

Pan, Fluid, and Filter
REMOVAL AND INSTALLATION

The fluid should be drained with the transmission warm.

1. Support the transmission at the vibration damper. If necessary, remove the crossmember.
2. Prepare a large pan to catch the transmission fluid.
3. Loosen all the pan screws, then pull one corner down to drain most of the fluid.

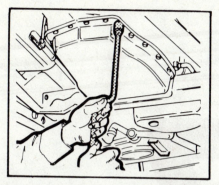

Loosen the pan screws and lower one corner to drain

4. Remove the pan screws and empty out the pan. The pan can be cleaned out with solvent but it must be dried thoroughly before replacement. Be very careful not to leave any lint or threads from rags in the pan.

5. Remove the filter or strainer retaining bolt (two on Turbo Hydra-Matic 200, 250, and 350). A reuseable strainer is used on two-speed transmissions and the Turbo Hydra-Matic 250. The strainer may be cleaned in solvent and air-dried thoroughly. Filters are to be replaced. Use a new gasket on all other models.

6. Install the new filter or cleaned strainer.

7. Install the pan with a new gasket. Tighten the bolts evenly (12 ft lbs) in a criss-cross pattern.

8. Replace the crossmembers if removed.

9. Add Dexron® or Dexron® II transmission fluid through the dipstick tube. Add 6 pints for Turbo Hydra-Matic 200; 5 pints for Turbo Hydra-Matic 250; and 3 pints for the 350, Torque Drive, and Powerglide.

10. Start the engine and let it idle. Do not race the engine. Shift through all the indicator positions, holding the brakes. Check the fluid level with the engine idling in Park. The level should be between the two dimples on the dipstick, about ¼ in. below the ADD mark. Add fluid as necessary.

11. Check the fluid level after the car has been driven enough to thoroughly warm up the transmission. The level should be at the FULL mark on the dipstick. If the transmission is overfilled, the excess must be drained off. Overfilling causes aerated fluid, resulting in transmission slippage and probable damage.

Drive Train

DRIVELINE

The driveshaft has sliding splines at the transmission end and two universal joints to allow for slight misalignments caused by suspension travel.

Driveshaft and U-Joints
REMOVAL AND INSTALLATION

1. Raise and support the vehicle.
2. Mark the relationship of the shaft to the rear axle flange with chalk or paint.
3. Remove the U-bolts at the rear universal (U-) joint. Tape the bearing cups onto the trunnion so that the roller bearings are not lost.
4. Remove the driveshaft to the rear. There may be some leakage from the rear of the transmission, so it is advisable to plug the opening.
5. Check that the seal in the rear of the transmission is in good condition. If necessary, replace the seal. Note that the front yoke of the driveshaft must be smooth to prevent rapid seal wear.
6. Insert the driveshaft front yoke into the rear of the transmission, aligning the splines.
7. Align the marks made in Step 2. Remove the tape holding the bearing cups, in-

stall the U-bolts to the rear axle flange, and torque them to 15 ft lbs.
8. Check the transmission lubricant level if there was much loss in Step 4.

U-JOINT OVERHAUL

Worn universal joints will cause a clanking noise on acceleration and deceleration.

1. Mark the front of the driveshaft tube with paint or chalk.
2. Remove all four lock-rings from the U-joint.
3. Place a piece of 1¼ in. inside diameter (I.D.) pipe against one side of the yoke.
4. Place a socket smaller than the bearing cup against the other side. Squeeze the pipe,

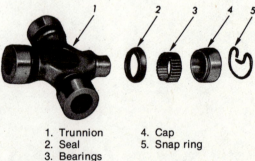

1. Trunnion
2. Seal
3. Bearings
4. Cap
5. Snap ring

U-joint repair kit

yoke, and socket in a vise until one bearing cup is forced out.

5. Reverse the arrangement to press out the opposite cup. Press out the other two cups on the front U-joint.

6. Clean all the parts in solvent. Check the condition of the trunnion, bearing rollers, and cups. Service kits are available to replace these parts.

7. Pack the bearings into their cups with high quality chassis grease. Pack the lubricant holes in the trunnion also.

8. Place the trunnion into the yoke. Place one bearing cup with rollers into the yoke. Position the other cup and squeeze the cups into place in the vise. Use the socket as before to press the cups in far enough to install the lockrings. Install the other yoke on the front U-joint.

NOTE: *The mark made in Step 1 must be at the front, or else imbalance will result.*

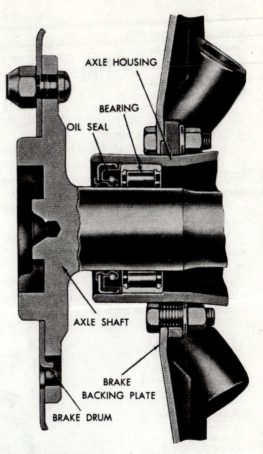

Axle housing details

REAR AXLE

All models use the C-lock type axle with C-locks retaining the axle shafts. All axles are hypoid type, semi-floating with an integral gear carrier, and a removable cover plate.

All of the models use either a 6½ in. or a 7½ in. diameter ring gear. The rear axle identification code letters are stamped on the right or left axle tube adjacent to the carrier.

Determining Axle Ratio

The drive axle of a car is said to have a certain axle ratio. This number (usually a whole number and a decimal fraction) is actually a comparison of the number of gear teeth on the ring gear and the pinion gear. For example, a 4.11 rear means that theoretically, there are 4.11 teeth on the ring gear and one tooth on the pinion gear or, put another way, the driveshaft must turn 4.11 times to turn the wheels once. Actually, on a 4.11 rear, there might be 37 teeth on the ring gear and 9 teeth on the pinion gear. By dividing the number of teeth on the pinion gear into the number of teeth on the ring gear, the numerical axle ratio (4.11) is obtained. This also provides a good method of ascertaining exactly which axle ratio one is dealing with.

Another method of determining gear ratio is to jack up and support the car so that both rear wheels are off the ground. Make a chalk mark on the rear wheel and the drive shaft. Put the transmission in neutral. Turn the rear wheel one complete turn and count the number of turns that the driveshaft makes. The number of turns that the driveshaft makes in one complete revolution of the rear wheel is an approximation of the rear axle ratio.

Axle Shaft
REMOVAL AND INSTALLATION

1. Raise and support the rear of the car safely.

2. Remove the wheel and the brake drum. If difficulty is experienced in removing the drum, refer to Chapter 9.

3. Clean the differential carrier cover area thoroughly. Remove the cover to drain the lubricant.

4. Back out the pinion shaft lockbolt and remove the differential pinion shaft.

5. Push the axle shaft in toward the differential. Remove the C-lock from the inner (button) end of the shaft.

6. Pull out the axle shaft, being careful not to damage the oil seal at the outer end of the axle housing.

7. Slide the shaft back into place, being careful of the oil seal. Turn the shaft slightly if the splines do not align.

8. Install the C-lock on the button end of the shaft. It is a good idea to use a new C-lock to avoid the chance of failure and serious damage. Pull the shaft out so that the C-lock seats in the counterbore in the differential side gear.

9. Replace the differential pinion shaft and its lockbolt. Torque the lockbolt to 125 in. lbs.

10. Install the differential carrier cover with a new gasket and torque the bolts in a criss-cross pattern to 20 ft lbs.

11. Fill the rear axle with lubricant as specified in Chapter 1.

12. Replace the brake drum and wheel. Lower the vehicle.

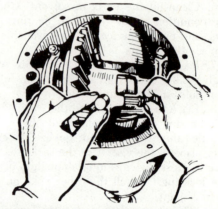

Removing or installing the differential pinion shaft lockpin

1. Companion flange
2. Deflector
3. Pinion oil seal
4. Pinion front bearing
5. Pinion bearing spacer
6. Differential carrier
7. Differential case
8. Shim
9. Gasket
10. Differential bearing
11. "C" lock
12. Pinion shaft lockbolt
13. Cover
14. Pinion shaft
15. Ring gear
16. Side gear

17. Bearing cap
18. Axle shaft
19. Thrust washer
20. Differential pinion
21. Shim
22. Pinion rear bearing
23. Drive pinion

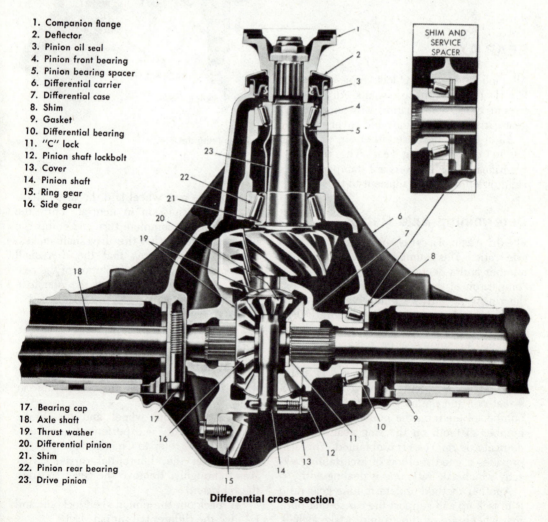

SHIM AND SERVICE SPACER

Differential cross-section

OIL SEAL REPLACEMENT

The oil seal needs replacement if lubricant leaks out onto the rear brakes.

1. Remove the axle shaft.

2. Use the button end of the axle shaft to pry the old seal out.

3. Pack the cavity between the lips of the new seal with wheel bearing grease. Tap the seal into place with a section of pipe, a socket of the correct size, or a seal installing tool.

4. Replace the axle shaft after checking that the part contacting the seal is smooth.

BEARING REPLACEMENT

1. Remove the axle shaft and oil seal.

2. Pull out the bearing with the aid of a slide hammer.

3. Lubricate the new bearing with rear axle lubricant. Tap the bearing into place with a section of pipe, a socket of the correct size, or a bearing installing tool.

NOTE: *Drive against the bearing outer race, not the inner race.*

4. Replace the oil seal and axle shaft.

Suspension and Steering

8

REAR SUSPENSION

All Vegas through 1975 and the 1975 Astre use a coil spring rear suspension with upper and lower control arms.

The Monza, Sunbird, Starfire, Skyhawk and all 1976 and later Vegas use a torque arm rear suspension. This suspension consists of lower control arms and a track bar to control lateral movement. A torque arm is used to control rear axle wind-up. A stabilizer bar is standard and the upper control arms have been eliminated.

Springs
REMOVAL AND INSTALLATION

NOTE: *Be extremely cautious when removing or installing coil springs.*

1. Raise the rear of the vehicle and support it safely.

2. Support the rear axle with a hydraulic

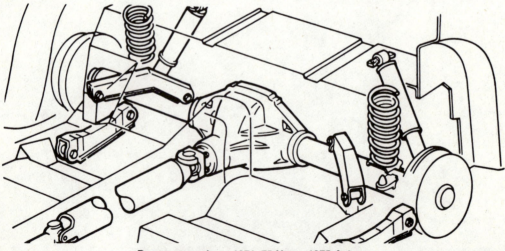

Rear suspension—1971–75 Vega, 1975 Astre

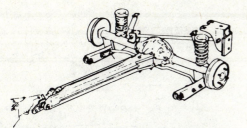

Rear suspension—Monza, Sunbird, Starfire

floor jack. Mark the positions of the spring ends at the upper and lower pads.

3. Disconnect the lower ends of both shock absorbers.

4. Lower the axle cautiously until the springs are fully extended. Be careful not to strain the brake hose.

5. Remove the springs and their insulators.

If the coil springs are to be replaced, they should be replaced in pairs to maintain an even ride height.

6. Place the insulators on the top and bottom of the springs. Replace the springs, locating the ends in the positions previously marked.

7. Raise the axle and connect the shock absorbers, torquing the bottom stud or bolt nuts to 80 in. lbs.

8. Lower the vehicle.

Shock Absorbers

TESTING

To test the shock absorbers, bounce the rear of the car up and down by hand a few times.

When released, the car should return to its normal ride height and stop bouncing immediately. If the shocks are worn, they should be replaced in pairs to provide equal damping.

REMOVAL AND INSTALLATION

1. Raise the rear of the car and support the rear axle. An alternate procedure is to place the car on a drive-on hoist or over a grease pit.

2. Remove the two upper attaching bolts from the floorpan.

3. Unbolt the lower attachment. Some 1971 models use a stud attachment. Later, a change was made to a horizontal thru-bolt, for greater ground clearance at this point.

To install:

4. On stud type shocks, install the upper retainer washer and the rubber grommet on the stud.

5. Put the shock in position and install the upper mounting bolts, torquing them to 18 ft lbs.

6. On the stud type, install the bottom rubber grommet, retainer washer, and nut. The proper torque is 80 in. lbs.

7. On the thru-bolt type, install the thru-bolt with a rubber grommet on each side of the shack eye. Torque the nut to 80 in. lbs.

Stabilizer Bar

The stabilizer bar can be readily installed on models on which this is an original equipment option if these models have the proper mounting holes in the lower control arms. The rear stabilizer bar should be used in conjunction with the front stabilizer bar. If only

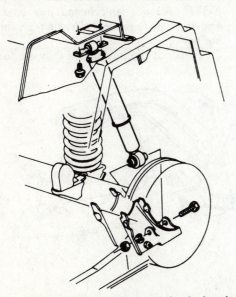

Late 1971 and 1972 and later rear shock absorber

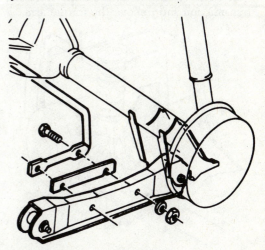

Rear stabilizer bar installation

the rear bar is installed, peculiar and dangerous handling characteristics will result.

INSTALLATION

1. Place the bar in position. It should form an inverted U-shape.

2. Place an equal number of shims between the bar and the lower control arm on each side.

3. Install the mounting bolts and torque them to 36 ft lbs.

NOTE: *The special mounting bolts must be used, and they must be tightened to the correct torque.*

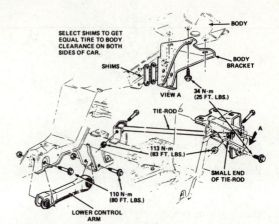

Track rod (tie rod) installation

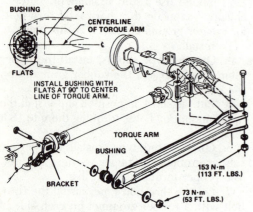

Torque arm installation

Torque Arm
REMOVAL AND INSTALLATION
All Except 1971–75 Vega, 1975 Astre

1. Raise the car and support the rear axle.

2. Remove the mounting bracket from the transmission, then remove the through bolt.

3. Remove the mounting bolts from the transmission and remove the torque arm.

Track Rod (Tie Rod)
REMOVAL AND INSTALLATION
All Except 1971–75 Vega, 1975 Astre

1. Raise the car and support the rear axle.

2. Remove the mounting bolt at the body, and then remove the bolt at the axle bracket and remove the track rod.

Control Arms
REMOVAL AND INSTALLATION
Upper—1971–75 Vega, 1975 Astre

1. Raise the rear of the car and support the rear axle. An alternate procedure is to place the car on a drive-on hoist or over a grease pit.

2. Unbolt and remove the arm.

NOTE: *Remove and install one control arm at a time to prevent the axle from shifting out of alignment.*

3. Press out the bushings if they are to be

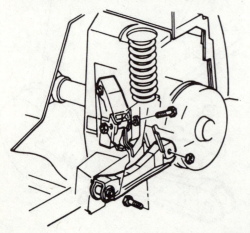

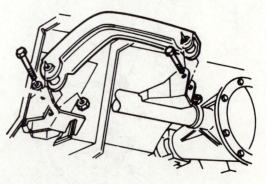

Rear upper and lower control arms—1971–75

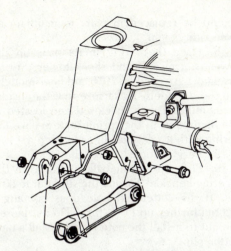

Lower control arm—Monza, Starfire, Skyhawk and 1976 and later Vegas

replaced. The new bushings will fit in only one direction. Press in the new bushings.

4. Replace the control arm. Check that the rear suspension is at or near its normal height, then torque the bolts to 60 ft lbs.

NOTE: *The special bolts must be used, and they must be tightened to the correct torque with the weight of the car on the axle.*

5. Repeat the procedure on the other side, if necessary.

Lower

This procedure is the same as that for Upper Control Arm Removal and Installation, with the exceptions that the stabilizer bar will have to be removed and mounting bolt torque is 80 ft lbs.

FRONT SUSPENSION

The independent front suspension, like the rear, is very similar to that used on some larger GM vehicles. Each wheel is suspended by unequal length control arms. The steering knuckle, which supports the wheel, is attached to the upper and lower control arms by ball joints. The coil spring is located between the lower control arm and the frame. The tubular shock absorber is mounted inside the spring. Vehicles equipped with the optional ride and handling package (standard on GT) have a stabilizer bar mounted in rubber bushings to the body and connecting the lower control arms.

Springs
REMOVAL AND INSTALLATION

NOTE: *Be extremely cautious when removing or installing coil springs.*

1. Raise the front of the car and place

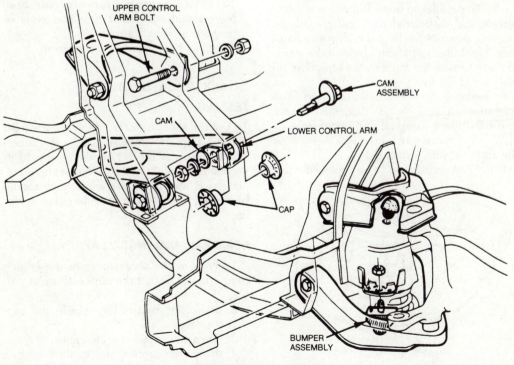

UPPER CONTROL ARM BOLT

CAM ASSEMBLY

CAM

LOWER CONTROL ARM

CAP

BUMPER ASSEMBLY

Front suspension—typical

SAFETY CHAIN   FLOOR JACK

WOOD

Removing coil spring

jackstands under the front crossmember braces. These braces run forward at a 45° angle from the crossmember supporting the front of the engine.

2. Remove the wheel, shock absorber, and stabilizer bar.

3. Support the lower control arm outer end with a hydraulic floor jack and a block of wood.

4. Securely fasten the spring to the lower control arm with a stout chain or cable.

5. To detach the tie rod, remove the cotter pin and castellated nut, and tap on the steering arm (not the tie rod end) with a hammer. Hold a heavy hammer behind the steering arm to take the force of the taps. The tie rod should fall free.

6. Remove the lower ball joint stud from the steering knuckle as described under lower Ball Joint Removal and Installation.

7. Very cautiously let the jack down until the spring is fully expanded.

If the coil springs are to be replaced, they

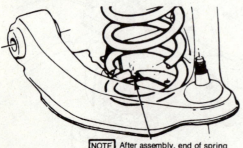

NOTE After assembly, end of spring must be visible through hole.

Positioning the front coil spring

should be replaced in pairs to maintain an even ride height.

8. Place the spring in its pads on the lower control arm and shock tower. Spring insulators are used on 1976 and later models. On these models, make sure that the insulator is indexed with its closed end located at the high point in the spring seat. Secure the spring with a safety chain as in Step 4.

9. Very cautiously raise the jack.

10. Place the lower ball joint stud in the steering knuckle. Torque the stud nut to 60 ft lbs. If the cotter pin hole does not align, tighten further up to $1/6$ turn. Do not loosen the nut to install the cotter pin. Install a new cotter pin.

11. Install the tie rod end to the steering arm. Torque the nut to 35 ft lbs. If the cotter pin hole does not align, tighten further up to a maximum of 50 ft lbs. Install a new cotter pin.

12. Replace the shock absorber as described under Front Shock Absorber Removal and Installation. Do not fasten the top mounting yet.

13. Replace the stabilizer bar, tightening the fasteners to the torque specified in Front Stabilizer Bar Installation.

14. Replace the wheel and lower the car to the floor. Install the upper end of the shock absorber.

NOTE: *All suspension fasteners must be of the original equipment type and must be torqued to specifications.*

15. Check the front end alignment.

Shock Absorbers
TESTING

To test the shock absorbers, bounce the front of the car up and down by hand a few times. When released, the car should return to its normal ride height and stop bouncing immediately. If the shocks are worn, they should be replaced in pairs to provide equal damping.

REMOVAL AND INSTALLATION

1. Pry out the access plug in the engine compartment so that the upper mount is visible.

2. Raise the front of the vehicle and support it safely.

3. Turn the wheels for clearance.

4. Hold the upper shock stud with a wrench. Loosen and remove the locknut.

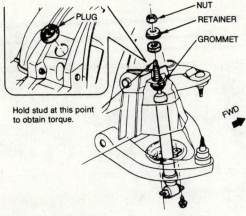

PLUG

NUT
RETAINER
GROMMET

Hold stud at this point to obtain torque.

FWD

Front shock absorber

5. Unbolt the lower end and pull the shock down and out.

6. Place the lower retainer and rubber grommet on the shock stud.

7. Put the shock in place and tighten the lower bolts. Torque to 20 ft lbs.

8. Place the upper grommet, retainer, and nut on the shock stud.

9. Hold the stud with a wrench and tighten the nut. Torque to 120 in. lbs.

Ball Joints

The ball joints connect the steering knuckle to the control arms. Excessive ball joint wear results in inaccurate steering, shimmy, and a generally unsafe condition.

CHECKING

1971–74—All; 1971–80—Upper

To check the ball joints for excessive wear:

1. Place jackstands under the lower control arms.

2. Turn the wheels straight ahead.

3. Lift and shake the wheel up and down vertically. If there is noticeable looseness, the ball joints are worn.

4. Grasp the top and bottom of the tire and rock it by pushing in on the top and pulling out on the bottom, then pulling out on the top and pushing in on the bottom. A ¼ in. play indicates worn ball joints. Make sure that loose wheel bearings do not result in a false reading.

1975–80 Lower Ball Joint

The lower ball joints incorporate wear indicators. They can be inspected visually; when the ½ in. diameter grease fitting is flush with, or inside the cover surface, replace the ball joint. Inspect the grease fitting with the car supported on its wheels so that the lower ball joint is in a loaded condition. Normal protrusion of the grease fitting is 0.050 in. beyond the cover surface.

Ball joint tightness can also be checked using the preceding procedure.

REMOVAL AND INSTALLATION
Upper

1. Raise the front of the car and place jackstands under the front crossmember braces. These braces run forward at a 45° angle from the crossmember supporting the front of the engine.

2. Remove the wheel.

3. Support the lower control arm with a hydraulic floor jack. Make sure that this jack is secure; it is restraining the coil spring.

4. Remove the cotter pin from the ball joint stud. Loosen but do not remove the nut.

5. The stud may now be pressed out upward. A special tool is available for this purpose.

6. To inspect the ball joint, replace the nut and screw it on all the way. Turn the nut and stud with a torque wrench. The torque required to turn the ball in the socket should be 1 to 4 ft lbs for a new joint. If the reading is too low or too high and the joint has been lubricated properly, replace the ball joint.

7. To remove the original joint from the control arm, grind off the rivets. Bolts and nuts are supplied with replacement ball joints.

NOTE: *The bolts and nuts supplied with the replacement joint must be used. Do not use substitutes.*

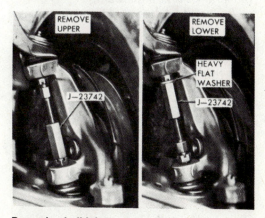

Removing ball joints

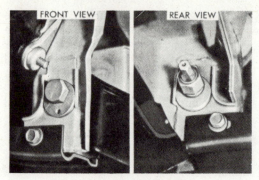

Caster and camber adjusting points

8. Bolt the new ball joint onto the control arm. Install a lubrication fitting.

9. Install the stud to the steering knuckle and torque the nut to 30 ft lbs. If the cotter pin hole does not align, tighten further up to ½ turn. Do not loosen the nut to install the cotter pin. Use a new cotter pin.

10. Replace the wheel and lower the car.

11. Check the front end alignment.

Lower

Steps 1 to 4 are the same as those for Upper Ball Joint Removal and Installation.

5. The stud may now be pressed out downward. A special tool is available for this purpose.

6. To inspect the ball joint, replace the stud nut and screw it on all the way. Turn the nut and stud with a torque wrench. If the torque required to turn the ball in the socket is zero, replace the ball joint. If there is measurable torque, the joint is usable.

7. The old joint must be pressed out of the control arm. A special tool is available for this operation.

8. When pressing in the new joint, position it so that the grease bleed vent in the rubber boot is facing inward.

9. Install a lubrication fitting in the new joint.

10. Install the stud to the steering knuckle and torque the nut to 60 ft lbs. If the cotter pin hole does not align, tighten further up to ½ turn. Do not loosen the nut to install the cotter pin. Use a new cotter pin.

11. Replace the wheel and lower the car.

12. Check the front end alignment.

Control Arms

REMOVAL AND INSTALLATION

Upper

Steps 1 to 8 are the same as those for Upper Ball Joint Removal and Installation.

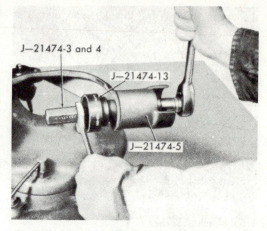

Removing upper control arm bushing

9. Remove the control arm pivot bolts and the control arm.

10. The bushings may be pressed out and replaced. Press in the new bushings.

11. Replace the control arm. The pivot should have the nuts on the inside of the arm. Hold the arm horizontal and torque the nuts to 60 ft lbs.

NOTE: *These bolts must be torqued. Do not use substitute bolts or nuts.*

12. Proceed with Steps 9 to 11 for Upper Ball Joint Removal and Installation.

Lower

Steps 1 to 7 are the same as for Front Spring Removal and Installation.

8. Mark the position of the lower control arm cam bolts and nuts, then remove them.

9. Proceed with Steps 6 to 9 for Lower Ball Joint Removal and Installation.

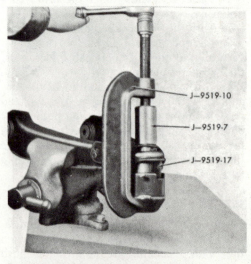

Removing lower control arm bushing

10. The bushings may be pressed out and replaced. Press in the new bushings.

11. Install the control arm. Make sure that the metal caps are installed in the bushings.

12. Install the cam bolts with the heads out. Replace the washers and nuts. Set the bolts to the marks made before removal. Torque the nuts to 125 ft lbs.

NOTE: *These bolts must be torqued. Do not use substitute bolts or nuts.*

13. Proceed with Steps 8 to 15 under Front Spring Removal and Installation.

Stabilizer Bar

The stabilizer bar can readily be installed on models on which this is an original equipment option if these models have the proper mounting holes in the lower control arms. The front stabilizer bar should be used in conjunction with the rear stabilizer bar; this is the arrangement used in the factory ride and handling package.

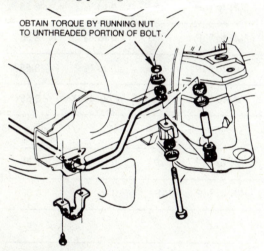

OBTAIN TORQUE BY RUNNING NUT TO UNTHREADED PORTION OF BOLT.

Front stabilizer bar

INSTALLATION

1. Hold the bar in place and install the body bushings and brackets, torquing the fasteners to 30 ft lbs.

2. Install the retainers, grommets, spacers, and nuts to the lower control arms. Torque the nuts to 10 ft lbs.

NOTE: *The nuts must be tightened to this torque in order to allow the stabilizer bar to function properly.*

Front End Alignment

The alignment adjustments must be made in this order: camber, caster, and toe-in. The toe-in adjustment can be made alone, but if caster or camber is changed, all three adjustments must be made in the order given. Refer to the Wheel Alignment Chart for specifications.

CAMBER

Camber is the inward or outward tilt, measured in degrees, of the wheel at the top. A wheel tilted outward at the top has positive (+) camber. A wheel tilted inward has negative (−) camber. Camber is adjusted by loosening the front lower control arm pivot nut and rotating the cam bolt to achieve the proper setting. Hold the cam bolt head while tightening the nut to 125 ft lbs.

NOTE: *This adjustment cannot be made accurately without special alignment equipment.*

CASTER

Caster is the backward or forward tilt from the vertical of the steering knuckle centerline at the top, measured in degrees. A steering knuckle centerline tilted backward at the top has positive (+) caster, while one tilted forward has negative (−) caster. Caster is adjusted by loosening the rear lower control arm pivot nut and rotating the cam bolt to achieve the proper setting. Hold the cam bolt head while tightening the nut to 125 ft lbs. Camber must be rechecked after setting caster.

NOTE: *This adjustment cannot be made accurately without special alignment equipment.*

TOE-IN

Toe-in is the amount, measured in inches, that the wheels are closer together at the front than at the rear. Toe-in must be checked after setting caster and/or camber. The wheels must be straight ahead and when adjusting toe-in.

1. Loosen the clamp bolt nut at each end of both tie rods and rotate the sleeves equally to obtain the proper adjustment. If the sleeves are not adjusted equally, the steering wheel will be crooked. Toe-in can be determined by measuring the distance between the center of the tire tread, front and rear, or by measuring the distance between the inside edges of the wheel rims, front and rear. If the wheel rims are used as the basis of measurement, the car should be rolled forward slightly and a second set of measurements taken. This avoids any error induced by bent wheel rims.

2. Make sure that the tie rod ends are in their normal position. Check that the clamps

Wheel Alignment Specifications

Year	Model	Caster Range (deg)	Caster Preferred Setting (deg)	Camber Range (deg)	Camber Preferred Setting (deg)	Toe-in (in.)	Steering Axis Inclination (deg)
VEGA, MONZA							
1972–73	Vega	1¼N to ¼N	¾N	¼N to ¾P	¼P	3/16 to 5/16	8.55
1974	Vega	1¾N to ¼P	¾N	¾N to 1¼P	¼P	3/16 to 5/16	8.55
1975–77	Vega/Monza	1¼N to ¼N	¾N	¼N to ¾P	¼P	0 to ⅛	8.55
1978	Monza	⅓N to 1⅓N	⅘N	⅓N to 7/10N	⅕P	0 to ⅛	8.55
1979–80	Monza	⅓N to 1⅓N	⅘N	7/10N to 3/10N	⅕P	⅛ to ¼	8.55
ASTRE, SUNBIRD							
1975–76	Astre	1¼N to ¼N	¾N	¼N to ¾P	¼P	0 to ⅛	8.55
1977	Astre/Sunbird	1¼N to ¼N	¾N	¼N to ¾P	¼P	0 to ⅛	8.55
1978	Sunbird	1¼N to ¼N	¾N	¼N to ¾P	¼P	0 to ⅛	8.55
1979–80	Sunbird	1¼N to ¼N	¾N	¾N to ¼P	¼N	⅛ out to 0	8.55
SKYHAWK							
1975–77	Skyhawk	1¼N to ¼N	¾N	½N to ¾P	¼P	0 to ⅛	8.55
1978–80	Skyhawk	¼N to 1¼N	¾N	¼N to ¾P	¼P	0 to ⅛	8.55
STARFIRE							
1975–76	Starfire	1¾N to ¼P	¾N	½N to 1 P	¼P	0–⅛	9
1977	Starfire	1¼N to ¼N	¾N	¼N to ¾P	¼P	0–⅛	9
1978–80	Starfire	⅓N to 1⅓N	⅘N	⅓N to 7/10P	⅕P	0–⅛	—

are positioned correctly on the sleeves and that they clear all parts when the steering wheel is turned. Torque the clamp bolts to 11 ft lbs.

STEERING

The steering gear is of the worm and sector, recirculating ball type. A collapsible, energy-absorbing column is used. Ball bearings imbedded in plastic are pressed between the upper and lower telescoping column sections. On impact, plastic pins in the steering shaft shear off, allowing the column and shaft to collapse. No service operations involving removal or disassembly of the steering column are given here. It is recommended that such critical and delicate operations be entrusted to qualified GM service personnel.

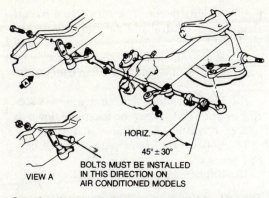

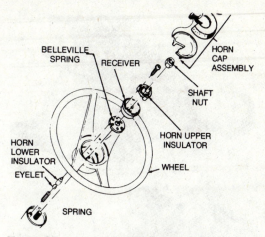

Steering linkage. Adjust toe in at the two outer tie rods

Monza GT or sport wheel-typical

Steering Wheel

REMOVAL AND INSTALLATION

Standard Wheel

1. Disconnect the battery ground cable.

2. Remove the two screws from the back of the wheel, allowing the shroud (horn actuator bar) to be removed.

3. Set the wheel in the straight ahead position. Mark the relationship of the wheel to the shaft, and remove the snap-ring and nut (1975 and later models). Remove the wheel nut.

4. Remove the steering wheel with a puller, using the two threaded holes in the wheel.

5. Replace the wheel in the straight ahead position, with the turn signal switch in the neutral position. Torque the wheel nut to 30 ft lbs. If the nut is overtightened, the wheel will rub.

6. Make sure that the lower horn insulator, eyelet, and spring are in place.

7. Position the shroud, seating the pin on the right side of the wheel in the hole in the shroud.

8. Replace the two screws in the rear of the wheel.

9. Connect the battery ground cable.

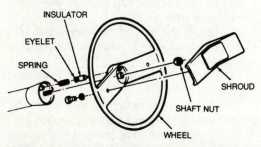

Monza standard steering wheel (typical). 1975 and later models have a snap ring in front of the nut

GT or Sport Wheel

1. Disconnect the battery ground cable.

2. Pry off the horn button.

3. Set the wheel in the straight ahead position. Mark the relationship of the wheel to the shaft.

4. Remove the wheel nut.

5. Remove the three screws and the upper horn insulator, receiver, and round belleville spring.

6. Remove the steering wheel with a puller, utilizing the two threaded holes in the wheel.

7. Replace the wheel in the straight ahead position, with the turn signal switch in the neutral position. Torque the wheel nut to 30 ft lbs. If the nut is overtightened, the wheel will rub.

8. Make sure that the lower horn insulator, eyelet, and spring are in place.

9. Install the belleville spring, receiver, upper horn insulator, and three screws.

10. Replace the horn button. Connect the battery ground cable.

TURN SIGNAL SWITCH REPLACEMENT

Standard Column

1. Remove the steering wheel as described under Steering Wheel Removal and Installation.

2. On 1971–75 models loosen the three captive cover screws and lift the cover off the shaft. On 1976 and later models the cover can be pryed off with a screwdriver.

3. The round lockplate must be pushed down to remove the wire snap-ring from the shaft. A special tool is available to press down the lockplate. This tool is an inverted U-

Removing the directional signal switch assembly

J-23653

Removing the lock plate retaining ring

shape with a hole for the shaft. The shaft nut is used to force this device down. Discard the snap-ring.

4. Remove the turn signal canceling cam, upper bearing preload spring, and thrust washer from the shaft.

5. Remove the signal lever screw and the lever.

6. Push the four-way flasher knob in and unscrew it.

7. Unplug the switch connector from the column and wrap the upper part of the connector with tape.

8. Remove the three switch mounting screws and pull the switch straight up. Guide the wiring connector through the column.

9. Tape the new switch connector. Feed the connector down through the column housing and under the mounting bracket.

10. Install the three switch mounting screws.

11. Replace the four-way flasher knob and

the turn signal lever. The turn signal switch should be in neutral and the four-way flasher knob out.

12. Place the thrust washer, upper bearing preload spring, and canceling cam on the shaft.

13. Place the lockplate and a new snap-ring on the shaft. Press the lockplate down as in Step 3 and install the new snap-ring.

14. Replace the cover with its three captive screws.

15. Replace the steering wheel.

Tilt Column

1. Remove the steering wheel.

2. With a screwdriver, pry off the cover from the steering shaft.

3. Remove the turn signal lever screw and lever.

4. Push the hazard warning knob in and remove the knob.

5. Depress the shaft lockplate and remove the retaining snap-ring. Remove the lockplate.

6. Slide the turn signal cancelling cam and upper bearing preload spring off the end of the shaft.

7. Remove the column mounting bracket and gently lower the column. Support the column.

8. Remove the signal switch wire protective cover and strip the wires from the protector. Do not damage the wires. Disconnect the switch connector from the bracket. Tape the wires close to the connectors to facilitate removal.

9. Remove the switch mounting screws and pull the switch straight up, guiding the wiring harness through the column.

10. Tape a new turn signal switch wiring harness and connector and feed the harness through the housing. Push the hazard warning switch in to aid in installation.

11. Reinstall the protective signal switch wire cover.

12. Install the column bracket and raise the column into position.

13. Install the mounting screws and clip the connector to the bracket on the steering column jacket.

14. Install the hazard warning knob and turn signal level.

15. Be sure the switch is in the neutral position and the hazard warning knob is out. Slide the upper bearing preload spring and cancelling cam onto the shaft.

16. Install the lockplate on the end of the

shaft. Compress the lockplate and install a new snap-ring.

17. Reinstall the cover on the end of the shaft.

18. Install the steering wheel.

Ignition Switch

REMOVAL AND INSTALLATION

1971–80 Vega, Monza
1975–76 Astre

The energy-absorbing column is fragile when disconnected and should not be subjected to any shock or excess pressure. Since the column will distort under its own weight, make sure that it is fully supported along its entire length while it is disconnected from the dashboard.

1. Disconnect the battery ground cable.

2. Remove the steering wheel.

3. On manual steering columns, remove the pot joint coupling clamp bolt.

4. On power steering columns, remove the flexible coupling pinch bolt.

5. Move the front seat back out of the way.

6. Remove the three floor pan bracket screws.

7. Remove the two column-to-instrument panel nuts and carefully lower the column far enough to allow the harness plugs to be disconnected.

8. Disconnect the turn signal and ignition switch harnesses.

9. Place the ignition switch in LOCK position.

10. Remove the two switch screws and the switch assembly.

11. When installing, make sure that the switch is in LOCK position.

12. Install the rod to the switch and the switch to the column. Do not use mounting screws longer than the original ones because they could interfere with the ability of the column to collapse.

NOTE: *The following is a mandatory column installation procedure, and must be followed exactly to prevent severe column damage.*

13. On power steering models, place the pot joint clamp over the lower end of the pot joint and assemble the intermediate shaft assembly (pot joint, intermediate shaft and flex coupling) to the steering gear stub shaft, aligning the flat on the stub shaft with the flat in the pot joint.

14. Position the column in the vehicle.

15. On manual steering models, place the pot joint clamp over the lower end of the pot joint and assemble the pot joint to the steering gear wormshaft with the flat in the pot joint. On power steering models, align the steering shaft flat with the flat in the flex coupling. When the shaft is bottomed against the coupling reinforcement, install and tighten bolt to 30 ft lbs.

16. Connect the turn signal and ignition switch wiring harnesses.

17. Loosely install the steering column bracket to instrument panel stud nuts.

18. Align the pot joint clamp with the groove across the end of the pot joint. Install bolt and nut, tightening nut to 55 ft lbs.

NOTE: *The bolt must pass through the shaft undercut.*

19. With the vehicle on the ground, tighten instrument panel nuts to 19 ft lbs.

20. Slide the toe plate down the column to the floorboard and install the three screws.

NOTE: *On power steering models, alignment flange on the toe plate must be engaged with the front of the toe pan before driving screws. On manual steering models, no side load is allowed during installation of the attaching screws. A side load could cause misalignment.*

21. On manual steering models: remove the alignment spacers. The minimum allowable clearance between the O.D. of the steering shaft and the I.D. of the column jacket lower plastic bushing after installation is 0.18 in.

22. Install the steering wheel.

23. Connect the battery ground cable.

1977–80 Astre, Sunbird
1975–80 Starfire, Skyhawk

1. Disconnect negative battery cable.

2. Place ignition switch in Off-Unlocked, or Acc (tilt wheel).

3. Remove toe pan cover (if applicable) and loosen toe clamp bolts.

4. Remove lower instrument panel trim and toe pan trim panel.

5. Remove automatic transmission shift indicator needle.

6. Remove steering column instrument panel bracket and let steering wheel rest on the driver's seat.

7. Remove the two dimmer switch retaining screws and remove the switch.

8. Remove two ignition switch attaching screws and lift switch off actuator rod.

9. Disconnect wiring.

10. To install, check that lock cylinder is still in Off-Unlocked or Acc (tilt wheel), and move sliding portion of switch until switch hole is positioned correctly. Hold the switch in this position with a 0.090 in. pin. Connect the wiring to the switch. Position switch over actuator rod, install attaching screws and remove the 0.090 in. pin. Reverse Steps 1 through 6 to complete installation.

Tie Rod Ends
REMOVAL AND INSTALLATION
All Models
Tie Rod Removal and Installation

1. Place the vehicle on a hoist.
2. Remove the cotter pins from the ball studs and remove the special nuts.
3. To remove the outer ball stud, tap on the steering arm at the tie rod end with a hammer while using a heavy hammer or similar tool as a backing.
4. Remove the inner ball stud from the relay rod using the same procedure as described in Step 3.
5. To remove the tie rod ends from the tie rod, loosen the clamp bolts and unscrew the end assemblies.
6. If the tie rod ends were removed, lu-

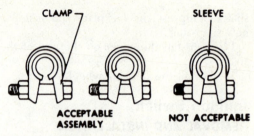

Correct positioning for the tie rod clamps

bricate the tie rod threads with chassis lube and install the ends on the tie rod making sure that both ends are threaded an equal distance from the tie rod.

7. Make sure that the threads on the ball studs and in the ball stud nuts are perfectly clean and smooth. Check the condition of the ball stud seals; replace if necessary.

NOTE: *If threads are not clean and smooth, the ball studs may turn in the tie rod ends when attempting to tighten nut.*

8. Install the ball studs in the steering arms and the relay rod.
9. Install the ball stud nut, tighten and install new cotter pins. Lubricate the tie rod ends.
10. Remove the vehicle from the hoist.
11. Adjust toe-in.

Brakes

Front disc brakes are standard equipment on all models, with power brakes available beginning 1975. The disc is 10 in. in diameter and 0.5 in. thick. Hub and disc are one-piece and the assembly is mounted to a one-piece steering knuckle and steering arm. The disc caliper design is similar to the single-piston Delco-Moraine disc brake used on other GM vehicles.

Rear brakes are drum-type. Unlike most other brake designs, the rear brakes on 1973–75 models are not automatically adjusted when the brakes are applied, but are adjusted when the parking brake is applied. For this reason, consistent parking in gear without using the parking brake is not recommended. Through 1975 the brakes are 9 in. in diameter. Beginning in 1976 the size was increased to 9.5 in. Beginning in 1976 self-adjusting rear drum brakes are used on all models. Adjustment occurs automatically when the brakes are applied during a reverse stop.

The tandem master cylinder pushrod is not adjustable, thus eliminating a pedal free travel adjustment.

Both front and rear hydraulic systems are routed to and from a distribution valve. Any significant change in the pressure difference between the front and rear systems moves a piston which activates a warning light switch, indicating pressure failure in one of the systems.

HYDRAULIC SYSTEM

Master Cylinder

No pedal play or travel adjustment is required. The warning switch assembly is mounted below the master cylinder and connected to it by two hydraulic lines. The switch is nonadjustable and nonserviceable.

REMOVAL AND INSTALLATION

1. On non power brakes disconnect the master cylinder pushrod from the brake pedal by detaching the clip and pin.
2. Disconnect the two brake lines and cap them to exclude dirt.
3. Unbolt the cylinder from the firewall.
4. On installation, torque the mounting nuts to 24 ft lbs.
NOTE: *The original equipment type nuts must be used, and they must be torqued for safety.*
5. Connect the brake lines.
6. Fill and bleed the system. Make sure that the reservoirs are full to within ¼ in. of the top.
7. Test the brake pedal before driving the car.

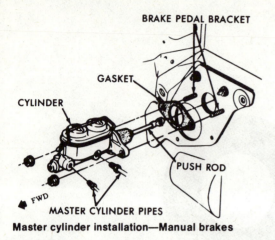

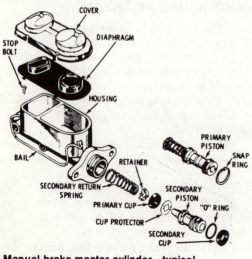

Master cylinder installation—Manual brakes

OVERHAUL

If the master cylinder leaks externally, or if the pedal sinks while being held down, the master cylinder is worn. There are three ways to correct the situation:

a. Buy a new master cylinder.

b. Trade in the worn unit on a rebuilt unit.

c. Rebuild the worn unit with a rebuilding kit.

The choice made will depend on the time and finances available.

1. Remove the unit from the car.

2. Remove the cover and drain the fluid. Depress the pushrod to pump the fluid out.

3. Pull back the boot. Hold the unit in a soft-jawed vise.

4. Remove the snap-ring and take the pushrod and retainer out.

5. Remove the primary piston. It need not be taken apart, since a new one is supplied in the rebuilding kit.

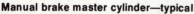

Manual brake master cylinder—typical

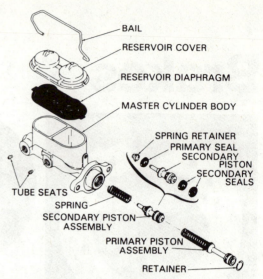

Power brake master cylinder—typical

6. Remove the secondary piston and spring by applying air pressure through the front outlet.

7. If the brass tube seats are damaged, drill them with a $^{13}/_{64}$ in. drill and tap the hole with a ¼ in. × 20 tap. Place a ½ to ¾ in. long by ¼ in. bolt through a thick washer and screw the bolt into the insert. Tighten the bolt to pull out the insert. Place the new seat in place and force it down by screwing in a spare brake line nut. Check for burrs.

NOTE: *No check valves are used in this unit.*

8. Clean all metal parts in denatured alcohol or clean, new brake fluid. Air dry the parts. Check that the cylinder bore is not pitted or corroded.

9. Check the identification marks on the secondary piston to make sure that an exact replacement piston is being installed.

10. Install the new seals on the secondary piston. The seal with the smallest inside diameter is the front seal and will have its lip facing the front. Install the seal retainer and the spring seat. The second seal lip will face front and the third seal lip will face the rear.

11. Coat the main cylinder bore and the secondary piston seals with clean brake fluid.

12. Place the spring on the secondary piston and insert the assembly in the bore.

13. Install the primary piston and the pushrod and retainer. Hold the pushrod in while installing the snap-ring.

14. Install the rubber boot.

15. Fill the reservoirs, plug the outlets, and work the pushrod several times to bleed the cylinder. Install the cover.

Bleeding brakes with special tool

16. Replace the unit in the car and bleed the system.

Power Brake Booster

REMOVAL AND INSTALLATION

1. Remove the vacuum hose from the check valve.

2. Remove the master cylinder-to-power booster nuts.

3. Remove the brake line distribution and switch mounting bolt from the fender skirt.

4. Pull forward on the master cylinder until the cylinder clears the power booster.

5. Carefully remove the master cylinder with the brake lines attached and set the master cylinder aside. Support the cylinder so that there is no stress on the brake lines. The master cylinder should be moved the minimum distance necessary.

6. Unbolt the power booster from the fire-wall.

7. Remove the brake pedal pushrod from the pedal pin.

8. Remove the power brake booster.

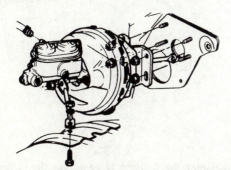

Power cylinder installation—except station wagon

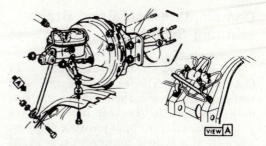

Power cylinder installation—station wagon

9. Installation is the reverse of removal. Be sure the brake lines are properly routed to provide sufficient clearance.

SYSTEM BLEEDING

The hydraulic system must be bled whenever the pedal feels spongy, indicating that compressible air has entered the system. The system must be bled whenever any component has been disconnected or there has been a leak. The manufacturer states that a soft pedal when the car is at rest is normal for the Vega brake system. The pedal should, however, have a solid feel during braking action.

1. Clean off the top of the master cylinder and remove the cover. Check that the fluid level in each reservoir is within ¼ in. of the top.

2. Attach a $7/32$ in. inside diameter hose to the bleeder valve at the first wheel to be bled. Mechanics customarily start at the wheel farthest from the master cylinder and work closer. Pour a few inches of brake fluid into a clear container and stick the end of the tube below the surface.

NOTE: *The tube and container of brake fluid are not absolutely necessary, but this is a very sloppy job without them.*

3. Open the bleed valve counterclockwise ⅓ turn with a ⅜ in. wrench. Have a helper slowly depress the pedal. Close the valve just before the pedal reaches the end of its travel. Have the helper let the pedal back up.

4. Check the fluid level. If the reservoir runs dry, the procedure will have to be re-started from the beginning.

5. Repeat Step 3 until no more bubbles come out the hose.

6. Repeat the bleeding operation, steps 3 to 5, at the other three wheels.

7. Check the master cylinder level again.

8. If repeated bleeding has no effect, there is an air leak, probably internally in the master cylinder or in one of the wheel cylinders.

Combination Valve and Brake Warning Switch

The combination valve is mounted on the frame and is connected to the hydraulic lines from the master cylinder. The proportioning section of the combination valveproportions outlet pressure to the rear brakes after a predetermined rear imput pressure has been reached. This is done to prevent rear wheel lock-up. The valve is designed to have a by-pass feature which assures full system pressure to the rear brakes if the front brake system fails and full system pressure to the front brakes if the rear brake system fails.

The warning switch is designed to constantly compare front and rear brake pressure from the master cylinder and turn on the light on the dash in case of front or rear system failure. The warning light switch portion of the combination valve is not serviceable. If the switch is found defective the combination valve must be replaced.

REMOVAL AND INSTALLATION

1. Disconnect the hydraulic lines at the combination valve. Plug the lines to prevent loss of fluid and to protect the system from dirt.
2. Disconnect the valve switch wire terminal and remove the combination valve.
3. To install reverse the above and bleed the brake system.

TESTING

1. Raise the vehicle on a hoist.
2. Attach a bleeder hose to a rear brake bleed screw and immerse the other end of the hose in a container partially filled with clean brake fluid. Make sure the master cylinder reservoirs are filled.
3. Turn the ignition switch to "On" and open the bleeder screw while a helper applies moderate pressure to the brake pedal. The warning lamp should light. Before the helper releases the brake pedal close the bleeder screw. Press down on the brake pedal and the light should go out.
4. Attach a bleeder hose to the front brake bleeder and repeat Step 5. Turn the ignition switch off.
5. If the warning lamp does not light during Steps 3 and 4 but does light when a jumper is connected to ground, the warning light switch portion of the combination valve is defective and the combination valve must be replaced.

FRONT BRAKES

The front disc brakes are of the single piston, sliding caliper type.

Disc Brake Calipers
REMOVAL AND INSTALLATION

1. Raise and support the front end safely.
2. Remove the front wheels.
3. Position a 7 inch "C" clamp on the caliper so that the solid side rests against the inside of the caliper and the screw end rests on the back side of the outer shoe.

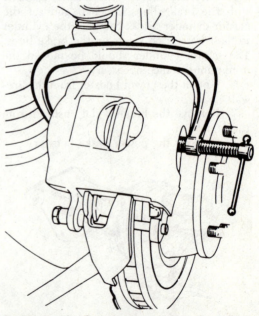

Positioning the C-clamp to compress the caliper piston

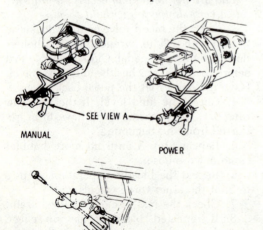

MANUAL

POWER

SEE VIEW A

VIEW A

Combination valve-typical mounting

4. Tighten the "C" clamp until the caliper moves enough to push the piston to the bottom of the piston bore. Remove the "C" clamp.

5. Pry off the two mounting pin stamped nuts and discard them. Remove the mounting pins.

6. Lift off the caliper. Lay it on the suspension members or hang it from a piece of wire. Do not let it hang on the brake line. Place a ½ in. thick block of wood between the brake pads to keep them in place, if you must leave the vehicle.

7. Remove the lining pads by sliding their ears to the mounting sleeve openings.

8. Remove the mounting pin sleeves and bushing assemblies.

9. Clean the caliper with denatured alcohol or brake fluid. Check the inside for leakage. Check the piston dust boot for damage or deterioration.

10. Install the new sleeves with bushings in the caliper grooves. The shouldered end of the sleeve must be to the outside.

11. Install the inner pad and slide the pad ears over the sleeve. Install the outer shoe.

12. Replace the caliper assembly.

13. Install the mounting pins from the outside to the inside. Press on the new stamped nuts with a socket that seats on the outer edge of the nut.

14. Replace the wheels and lower the car. Check the fluid level and press the brake pedal to adjust the front brakes.

OVERHAUL

1. Remove the caliper as described in Disc Brake Caliper Removal and Installation.

2. Disconnect the caliper hose from the steel brake line. Cap or tape the fittings to exclude dirt. Remove the hose fitting re-

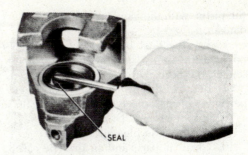

Removing the dust boot seal

tainer and remove the hose from the frame bracket.

3. Remove the caliper to the bench.

4. Clean the unit with brake fluid or denatured alcohol.

NOTE: *Any other solvents will destroy the rubber parts.*

5. Disconnect the hose and discard the copper gasket. Drain the fluid from the unit.

6. Place clean shop towels inside the caliper for padding and apply light air pressure to the fluid inlet. Use just enough pressure to ease out the piston. Do not attempt to catch

Mounting sleeve

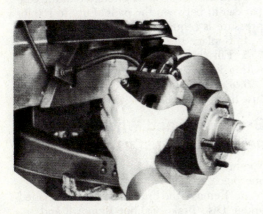

Removing the caliper

PRESS ON OUTER CIRCLE OF NUT

Installing new retaining nut

the piston with the hand, as this may be very dangerous.

7. Pry the dust boot out of the caliper bore with a screwdriver. Be careful not to scratch the bore. Discard it.

8. Remove the piston seal from the caliper bore, using a piece of wood or plastic so as to avoid scratches. Discard it.

9. Remove the bleeder valve.

10. Clean all parts and air dry. Be careful about using lubricated compressed air, which will deteriorate rubber parts.

11. Check the piston for scoring, nicks, corrosion, and worn or damaged plating. Replace it if it has any of these defects. Polishing with emery cloth or steel wool is not acceptable.

12. Check the caliper bore in the same way as the piston. Stains or slight corrosion may be polished out with crocus cloth. Clean the bore thoroughly after polishing.

13. Lubricate the caliper bore and the new piston seal with clean brake fluid. Position the seal in the caliper bore groove.

14. Lubricate the piston with clean brake fluid and install a new dust boot into the piston groove.

15. Insert the piston into its bore. Be careful not to unseat the seal. Force the piston to the bottom of the bore with 50 to 100 lbs pressure.

16. Position the dust boot in the caliper counterbore and seat it. Use either a seal installer, a suitable size socket, or a short piece of pipe. There is a retaining ring molded into the boot.

17. Replace the hose with a new copper gasket.

18. Connect the brake hose to the brake line at the frame bracket and replace the caliper on the car.

19. Bleed the brake system.

Disc Brake Pads
INSPECTION

1. Raise and support the front end safely.

2. Remove the front wheels.

3. Check both ends of the outer shoe by looking in at each end of the caliper. Check the lining thickness on the inner shoe by looking down through the inspection hole in the top of the caliper housing. Whenever the lining is worn to the approximate thickness of the metal shoe the lining should be removed. After removing the lining measure the lining thickness. The shoe and lining should be re-

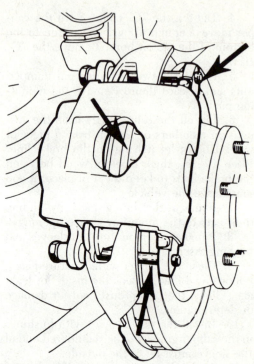

Lining inspection

placed at any time when the lining is worn to within 1/32 in. of a rivet or 1/32 in. of the shoe at any point. All four pads must be replaced as a matched set.

REMOVAL AND INSTALLATION

1. Remove the caliper and the lining pads, as described in Disc Brake Caliper Removal and Installation.

2. Before installing new pads, remove about half of the fluid from the master cylinder, using a perfectly clean dipper or suction device. If this is not done, the fluid will overflow and probably damage the paint.

3. Install the new pads, pushing the inner pad and the piston in far enough that the caliper can fit between the pads. Fifty to 100 lbs pressure is required to do this.

4. Replace the caliper.

5. Fill the master cylinder reservoirs to within ¼ in. of the top.

6. Press the brake pedal a few times to adjust the front brakes.

Brake Disc and Wheel Bearings
REMOVAL AND INSTALLATION

The brake disc (rotor) and the wheel hub are one piece.

1. Remove the brake caliper as described under Disc Brake Caliper Removal and Installation.

2. Remove the dust cap with a pair of water pump pliers or a screwdriver.

3. Remove the cotter pin and discard it. Remove the nut.

4. Pull on the disc and rattle it back and forth to loosen the outer bearing. Be careful not to get grease on the disc. Remove the washer and outer bearing.

5. Remove the disc-hub unit.

6. Insert a hammer handle through the hub and rap out the dust seal and inner bearing.

7. Wash all parts in solvent and air dry.

8. Check the bearings for pitting, scoring, or other signs of fatigue.

9. If either bearing is to be replaced, its outer race must also be replaced. Drive the old race out from behind with a brass drift. Start the new race into the hub squarely; tap it until it seats in the hub.

10. Pack both wheel bearings using wheel bearing grease made for disc brake cars. Ordinary grease will melt. Place a healthy glob of grease in the palm of one hand and force the edge of the bearing into it so that the grease fills the bearing. Do this until the whole bearing is packed. Grease packing tools are available which make this task much less messy.

11. Place the inner bearing into the hub and tap the seal flush with the hub. It is best to use a new seal.

12. Replace the disc-hub on the spindle.

13. Adjust the bearings as described under Wheel Bearing Adjustment. Replace the dust cap after installing a new cotter pin.

14. Replace the caliper.

DISC REFINISHING

If the disc is scored it may be machined to correct the damage. The minimum thickness for wear is cast into the disc. The original thickness is 0.500 in. The minimum thickness after refinishing is 0.470 in. The thickness at which a disc must be discarded is 0.440 in. No more than 0.002 in. run-out is allowable and total circumferential thickness variations must not exceed 0.0005 in. in 360°. The disc should have a nondirectional finish of 20 to 60 microinches. As these figures show, disc refinishing is a precision machine operation.

WHEEL BEARING ADJUSTMENT

1. Raise and support the front end safely.
2. Remove the hub cap. Remove the dust

cap with a pair of water pump pliers or a screwdriver.

3. Remove and discard the cotter pin. Loosen the spindle nut. Tighten it snugly to fully seat the bearings. Then loosen the nut again.

4. Rotate the wheel and tighten the spindle nut to 12 ft lbs. This is very roughly equivalent to finger tightness.

5. Back the nut off one flat and insert the new cotter pin. If the pin hole does not align, further back the nut off ½ flat or less.

6. Check that the wheel turns freely. Lock the cotter pin by spreading the ends.

7. If a dial indicator is available, the bearing end play may be checked. It should be 0.001 to 0.0008 in.

8. Tap the dust cap into place. Re-place the hub cap and lower the car.

REAR BRAKES

The rear drum brakes are of the two-shoe, leading and trailing shoe type. The brakes are self adjusting.

Brake Drums and Linings
REMOVAL AND INSTALLATION
1971–75

NOTE: *The brake linings are riveted or bonded to the brake shoes.*

1. Raise and support the vehicle safely.
2. Remove the wheel.
3. Pull off the drum by hand, tapping with a soft hammer if necessary. If the drum will not come off, it is probably being held by the linings. In this case, knock out the adjuster plug in the drum and release the adjuster rod from the trailing (rear) shoe by pushing in on the rod until it is clear of the

Rear brakes—1971–75

Drum knockout provision

shoe. The adjuster rod is at the 2 o'clock position on the left wheel and at the 10 o'clock position on the right. A new plug must be installed when the drum is replaced.

4. Release all tension from the parking brake equalizer. The equalizer is the device connecting the two rear wheel cables.

5. Detach the parking brake cable from the brake shoe lever. Do not allow the lever to swing forward, operating the brake adjuster.

6. Remove the shoe pullback spring with pliers.

7. Remove the brake retainer spring from the lower end of the shoes. Pull the shoes from the hold-down clips and remove the brakes with the strut and adjuster assembly attached.

8. Mark the front and rear shoes if they are to be reused. If any shoes are to be replaced all four must be replaced.

NOTE: *Replace the linings if they are less than 1/16 in. thick at any point.*

9. Separate the shoes and remove the strut and adjuster assembly from the trailing shoe.

10. Remove the parking brake lever. Remove the hold-down clips if they are broken or worn.

11. Press down on the adjuster locks and work free the rod assembly. A special tool is available for this operation. Slide the rod off the lever when both adjuster tangs are clear of the rod assembly.

12. Assemble the adjuster rod asembly to the strut, making sure that the index hole is lined up and seated. Slide the rod assembly over the adjuster locks until the lock index hole is about half covered by the rod assembly.

13. Apply a very light coat of grease to the

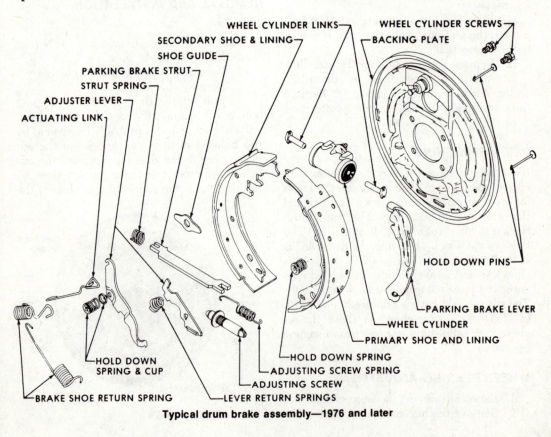

Typical drum brake assembly—1976 and later

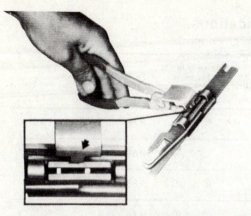

Adjuster assembly and tool—1971–75

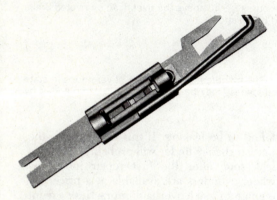

Adjuster position for new shoes—1971–75

backing plate surfaces rubbed by the shoes. Be extremely careful not to get grease on the linings.

NOTE: *At this point it is advisable to back off the parking brake adjuster nut several turns to aid in installing the brake shoes.*

14. Install the parking brake lever, park-

ing brake strut, and adjuster assembly to the trailing shoe.

15. Connect the shoes with the lower retaining spring.

16. Install the shoes in the hold-down clips with the lower retaining spring under the shoe anchor. Guide the adjuster assembly into position. Engage the shoes with the wheel cylinder.

17. Engage the parking brake lever to the leading shoe. Replace the shoe pullback spring.

18. Connect the parking brake cable to the lever, being careful not to move the brake shoe adjuster.

19. Replace the drums. Install the wheels. Adjust the parking brake equalizer. Operate the parking brake two or three times to adjust the brakes.

20. Adjust the parking brake as described under Handbrake Adjustment.

1976 and Later

1. Raise the car and support it on jackstands.

2. Slacken the parking brake cable.

3. Remove the rear wheel and brake drum.

4. Free the brake shoe return springs, actuator pull-back spring, hold-down pins and springs, and actuator assembly.

NOTE: *Special tools available from auto supply stores will ease spring and anchor pin removal, but the job may still be done with common hand tools.*

5. Disconnect the adjusting mechanism and spring, and remove the primary shoe.

6. Disconnect the parking brake lever from the secondary shoe and remove the shoe.

7. Clean and inspect all brake parts.

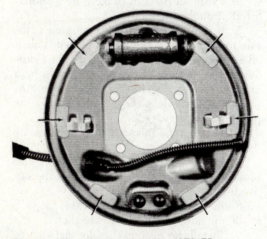

Flange plate contact surfaces—1971–75

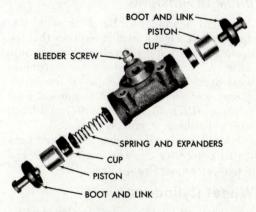

Wheel cylinder—exploded view

BOOT AND LINK
PISTON
CUP
BLEEDER SCREW
SPRING AND EXPANDERS
CUP
PISTON
BOOT AND LINK

Brake Specifications

(All measurements are given in in.)

Year	Model	Caliper Bore	Master Cylinder Bore	Wheel Cylinder Bore	Minimum Lining Thickness		Brake Diameter		Lug Nut Torque (ft lb)
					Front	Rear	Disc	Drum	
1971–75	All	1.875	0.875	0.75	①	①	9.88	9.0	70②
1976	All	2.50	0.875	0.6875	①	①	9.89⑤	9.5	80③
1977	All	1.875	0.75	0.6875	①	①	9.88④	9.5	80③
1978–80	All	2.50	0.875	0.6875	①	①	9.74	9.5	80③

① It is suggested that the lining be replaced when it measures $1/32$ in. above the rivet head on riveted brake shoes or $2/32$ in. above the metal shoe on the bonded brake shoes.
② 1975 Monza with aluminum wheels—80 ft lbs
③ 1976 and later Monza with aluminum wheels—90 ft lbs
④ Monza, Sunbird—9.74 in.
⑤ Monza—9.74 in.
NOTE: Minimum lining thickness is as recommended by the manufacturer. Because of variations in state inspection regulations, the minimum allowable thickness may be different than recommended by the manufacturer.

8. Check the wheel cylinders for seal condition and leaking.

9. Inspect the replacement shoes for nicks or burrs, lubricate the backing plate contact points, brake cable and levers, and adjusting screws, and then assemble.

10. Make sure that the right- and left-hand adjusting screws are not mixed. You can prevent this by working on one side at a time. This will also provide you with a reference for reassembly. The star-wheel should be nearest the secondary shoe when correctly installed.

11. Reverse the removal procedure for assembly. When completed, make an initial adjustment as previously described.

DRUM REFINISHING

Any light scoring can be done with fine emery cloth. Heavy scoring requires that the drum be trued and refinished (turned) on a lathe. All brake drums have the maximum wear diameter cast into them. If the inside diameter of a drum does not measure at least 9.030 in. (1971–75) or 9.590 (1977 and later) after refinishing, it must be replaced.

NOTE: *New brake drums are coated with rust preventive oil. This must be removed with a nonpetroleum solvent.*

Wheel Cylinders

It is the best practice to overhaul or replace both rear wheel cylinders if either one is found to be leaking. If this is not done, the undisturbed cylinder will probably develop a leak soon after the first repair job. New wheel cylinders are available at a price low enough to make overhaul impractical, except in emergency situations.

OVERHAUL

1. Disassemble the brake system as described under Brake Drum and Lining Removal and Installation.

2. Unbolt the wheel cylinder from the backing plate.

3. Remove and discard the rubber boots, the pistons, and the cups.

4. Clean all parts in brake fluid or denatured alcohol.

5. If there are any pits or roughness inside the cylinder, it must be replaced. Polish off any discolored area by revolving the cylinder around a piece of crocus cloth held by a finger. Do not polish the cylinder in a lengthwise direction. Clean the cylinder again after polishing. Air dry.

6. Replace the piston if it is scratched or damaged in any way.

7. Lubricate the cylinder bore with clean brake fluid and insert the spring and the expanders.

8. Install the new cups with the flat side to the outside. Do not lubricate them.

9. Install the pistons with the flat side to the inside. Do not lubricate them.

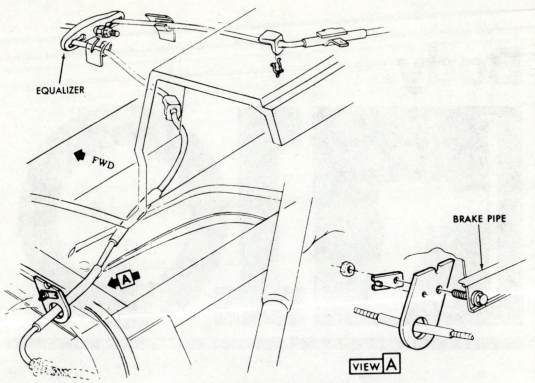

EQUALIZER

FWD

BRAKE PIPE

VIEW A

Parking brake cable routing

10. Press the new boots into the cylinder counterbores by hand. Do not lubricate them.

11. Replace the cylinder and tighten the bolts evenly.

12. Reassemble the brake system and bleed the brake hydraulic system.

HANDBRAKE

The handbrake (parking brake) must be adjusted periodically to compensate for lining wear and cable stretching. The adjuster is at the cable equalizer, above the driveshaft.

1. Raise and support the rear of the car.

2. Apply the parking brake one notch from the fully released position.

NOTE: *On 1977 and later models, it may be necessary to remove the driveshaft to gain access to the parking brake equalizer.*

3. Loosen the adjusting locknut and tighten the adjusting nut until a slight drag is felt when the rear wheels are rotated.

4. Tighten the locknut securely.

5. The rear wheels should rotate freely when the parking brake is fully released.

6. Lower the vehicle.

Body

10

You can repair most minor auto body damage yourself. Minor damage usually falls into one of several categories: (1) small scratches and dings in the paint that can be repaired without the use of body filler, (2) deep scratches and dents that require body filler, but do not require pulling, or hammering metal back into shape and (3) rust-out repairs. The repair sequences illustrated in this chapter are typical of these types of repairs. If you want to get involved in more complicated repairs including pulling or hammering sheet metal back into shape, you will probably need more detailed instructions. Chilton's *Minor Auto Body Repair, 2nd Edition* is a comprehensive guide to repairing auto body damage yourself.

TOOLS AND SUPPLIES

The list of tools and equipment you may need to fix minor body damage ranges from very basic hand tools to a wide assortment of specialized body tools. Most minor scratches, dings and rust holes can be fixed using an electric drill, wire wheel or grinder attachment, half-round plastic file, sanding block, various grades of sandpaper (#36, which is coarse through #600, which is fine) in both wet and dry types, auto body plastic,

primer, touch-up paint, spreaders, newspaper and masking tape.

Most manufacturers of auto body repair products began supplying materials to professionals. Their knowledge of the best, most-used products has been translated into body repair kits for the do-it-yourselfer. Kits are available from a number of manufacturers and contain the necessary materials in the required amounts for the repair identified on the package.

Kits are available for a wide variety of uses, including:

- Rusted out metal
- All purpose kit for dents and holes
- Dents and deep scratches
- Fiberglass repair kit
- Epoxy kit for restyling.

Kits offer the advantage of buying what you need for the job. There is little waste and little chance of materials going bad from not being used. The same manufacturers also merchandise all of the individual products used—spreaders, dent pullers, fiberglass cloth, polyester resin, cream hardener, body filler, body files, sandpaper, sanding discs and holders, primer, spray paint, etc.

CAUTION: *Most of the products you will be using contain harmful chemicals, so be extremely careful. Always read the complete label before opening the containers. When* *you put them away for future use, be sure they are out of children's reach!*

Most auto body repair kits contain all the materials you need to do the job right in the kit. So, if you have a small rust spot or dent you want to fix, check the contents of the kit before you run out and buy any additional tools.

ALIGNING BODY PANELS

Doors

There are several methods of adjusting doors. Your vehicle will probably use one of those illustrated.

Whenever a door is removed and is to be reinstalled, you should matchmark the position of the hinges on the door pillars. The holes of the hinges and/or the hinge attaching points are usually oversize to permit alignment of doors. The striker plate is also moveable, through oversize holes, permitting up-and-down, in-and-out and fore-and-aft movement. Fore-and-aft movement is made by adding or subtracting shims from behind the striker and pillar post. The striker should be adjusted so that the door closes fully and remains closed, yet enters the lock freely.

DOOR HINGES

Don't try to cover up poor door adjustment with a striker plate adjustment. The gap on each side of the door should be equal and uniform and there should be no metal-to-metal contact as the door is opened or closed.

1. Determine which hinge bolts must be loosened to move the door in the desired direction.

2. Loosen the hinge bolt(s) just enough to allow the door to be moved with a padded pry bar.

3. Move the door a small amount and check the fit, after tightening the bolts. Be sure that there is no bind or interference with adjacent panels.

4. Repeat this until the door is properly positioned, and tighten all the bolts securely.

Hood, Trunk or Tailgate

As with doors, the outline of hinges should be scribed before removal. The hood and trunk can be aligned by loosening the hinge bolts in their slotted mounting holes and moving the hood or trunk lid as necessary.

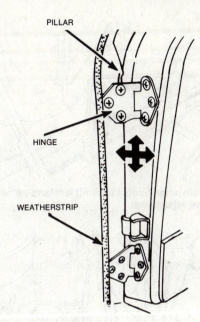

Door hinge adjustment

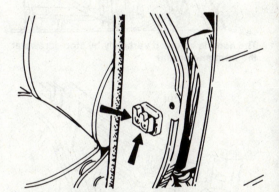

Move the door striker as indicated by arrows

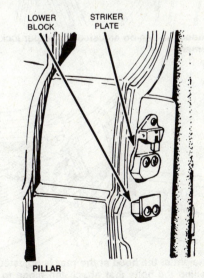

Striker plate and lower block

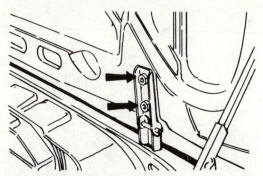

Loosen the hinge boots to permit fore-and-aft and horizontal adjustment

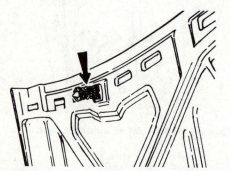

The hood is adjusted vertically by stop-screws at the front and/or rear

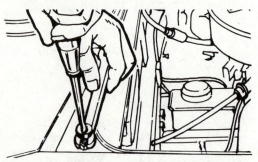

The hood pin can be adjusted for proper lock engagement

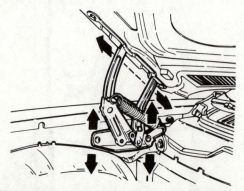

The height of the hood at the rear is adjusted by loosening the bolts that attach the hinge to the body and moving the hood up or down

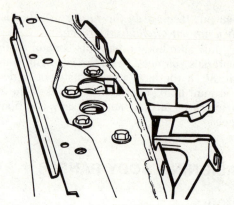

The base of the hood lock can also be repositioned slightly to give more positive lock engagement

The hood and trunk have adjustable catch locations to regulate lock engagement. Bumpers at the front and/or rear of the hood provide a vertical adjustment and the hood lockpin can be adjusted for proper engagement.

The tailgate on the station wagon can be adjusted by loosening the hinge bolts in their slotted mounting holes and moving the tailgate on its hinges. The latchplate and latch striker at the bottom of the tailgate opening can be adjusted to stop rattle. An adjustable bumper is located on each side.

RUST, UNDERCOATING, AND RUSTPROOFING

Rust

Rust is an electrochemical process. It works on ferrous metals (iron and steel) from the inside out due to exposure of unprotected surfaces to air and moisture. The possibility of rust exists practically nationwide—anywhere humidity, industrial pollution or chemical salts are present, rust can form. In coastal areas, the problem is high humidity and salt air; in snowy areas, the problem is chemical salt (de-icer) used to keep the roads clear, and in industrial areas, sulphur dioxide is present in the air from industrial pollution and is changed to sulphuric acid when it rains. The rusting process is accelerated by high temperatures, especially in snowy areas, when vehicles are driven over slushy roads and then left overnight in a heated garage.

Automotive styling also can be a contributor to rust formation. Spot welding of panels creates small pockets that trap moisture and form an environment for rust formation. Fortunately, auto manufacturers have been working hard to increase the corrosion protection of their products. Galvanized sheet metal enjoys much wider use, along with the increased use of plastic and various rust retardant coatings. Manufacturers are also designing out areas in the body where rust-forming moisture can collect.

To prevent rust, you must stop it before it gets started. On new vehicles, there are two ways to accomplish this.

First, the car or truck should be treated with a commercial rustproofing compound. There are many different brands of franchised rustproofers, but most processes involve spraying a waxy "self-healing" compound under the chassis, inside rocker panels, inside doors and fender liners and similar places where rust is likely to form. Prices for a quality rustproofing job range from $100–$250, depending on the area, the brand name and the size of the vehicle.

Ideally, the vehicle should be rustproofed as soon as possible following the purchase. The surfaces of the car or truck have begun to oxidize and deteriorate during shipping. In addition, the car may have sat on a dealer's lot or on a lot at the factory, and once the rust has progressed past the stage of light, powdery surface oxidation rustproofing is not likely to be worthwhile. Professional rustproofers feel that once rust has formed, rustproofing will simply seal in moisture already present. Most franchised rustproofing operations offer a 3–5 year warranty against rust-through, but will not support that warranty if the rustproofing is not applied within three months of the date of manufacture.

Undercoating should not be mistaken for rustproofing. Undercoating is a black, tar-like substance that is applied to the underside of a vehicle. Its basic function is to deaden noises that are transmitted from under the car. It simply cannot get into the crevices and seams where moisture tends to collect. In fact, it may clog up drainage holes and ventilation passages. Some undercoatings also tend to crack or peel with age and only create more moisture and corrosion attracting pockets.

The second thing you should do immediately after purchasing the car is apply a paint sealant. A sealant is a petroleum based product marketed under a wide variety of brand names. It has the same protective properties as a good wax, but bonds to the paint with a chemically inert layer that seals it from the air. If air can't get at the surface, oxidation cannot start.

The paint sealant kit consists of a base coat and a conditioning coat that should be applied every 6–8 months, depending on the manufacturer. The base coat must be applied before waxing, or the wax must first be removed.

Third, keep a garden hose handy for your car in winter. Use it a few times on nice days during the winter for underneath areas, and it will pay big dividends when spring arrives. Spraying under the fenders and other areas which even car washes don't reach will help remove road salt, dirt and other build-ups which help breed rust. Adjust the nozzle to a high-force spray. An old brush will help break up residue, permitting it to be washed away more easily.

It's a somewhat messy job, but worth it in the long run because rust often starts in those hidden areas.

At the same time, wash grime off the door sills and, more importantly, the under portions of the doors, plus the tailgate if you have a station wagon or truck. Applying a coat of wax to those areas at least once before and once during winter will help fend off rust.

When applying the wax to the under parts of the doors, you will note small drain holes. These holes often are plugged with undercoating or dirt. Make sure they are cleaned out to prevent water build-up inside the doors. A small punch or penknife will do the job.

Water from the high-pressure sprays in car washes sometimes can get into the housings for parking and taillights, so take a close look. If they contain water merely loosen the retaining screws and the water should run out.

Repairing Scratches and Small Dents

Step 1. This dent (arrow) is typical of a deep scratch or minor dent. If deep enough, the dent or scratch can be pulled out or hammered out from behind. In this case no straightening is necessary

Step 2. Using an 80-grit grinding disc on an electric drill grind the paint from the surrounding area down to bare metal. This will provide a rough surface for the body filler to grab

Step 3. The area should look like this when you're finished grinding

Step 4. Mix the body filler and cream hardener according to the directions

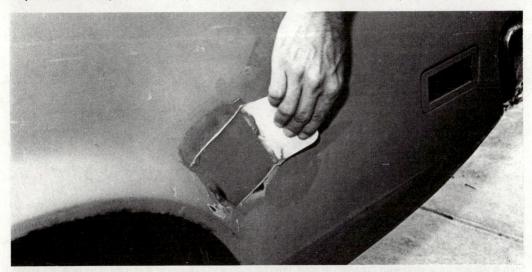

Step 5. Spread the body filler evenly over the entire area. Be sure to cover the area completely

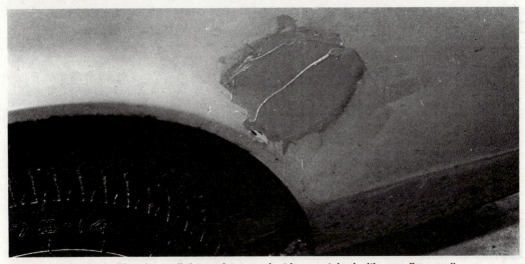

Step 6. Let the body filler dry until the surface can just be scratched with your fingernail

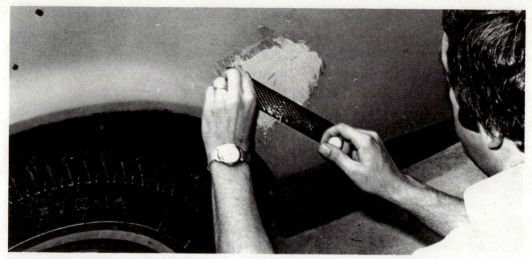

Step 7. Knock the high spots from the body filler with a body file

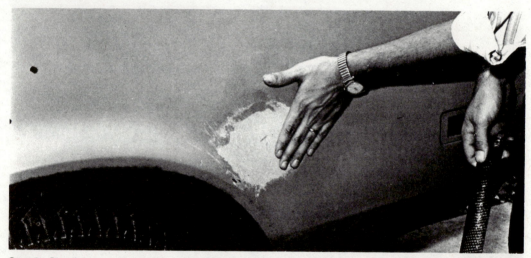

Step 8. Check frequently with the palm of your hand for high and low spots. If you wind up with low spots, you may have to apply another layer of filler

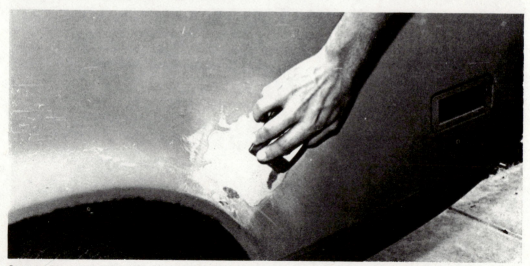

Step 9. Block sand the entire area with 320 grit paper

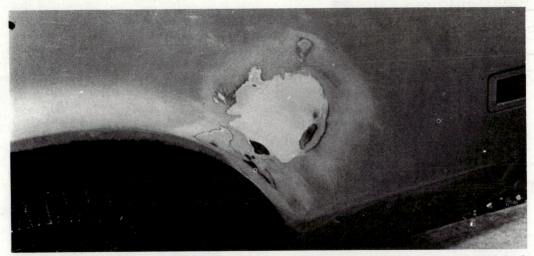

Step 10. When you're finished, the repair should look like this. Note the sand marks extending 2—3 inches out from the repaired area

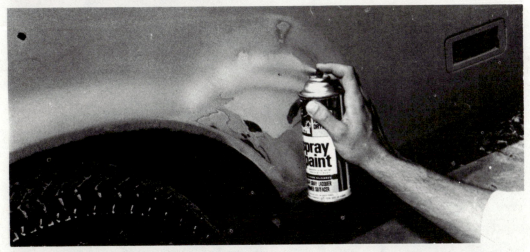

Step 11. Prime the entire area with automotive primer

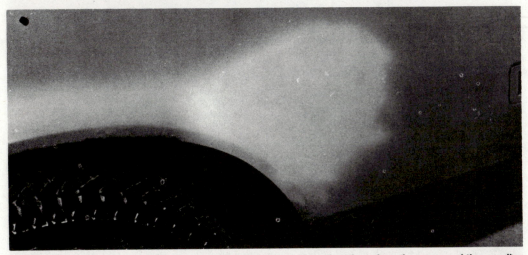

Step 12. The finished repair ready for the final paint coat. Note that the primer has covered the sanding marks (see Step 10). A repair of this size should be able to be spotpainted with good results

REPAIRING RUST HOLES

One thing you have to remember about rust: even if you grind away all the rusted metal in a panel, and repair the area with any of the kits available, *eventually* the rust will return. There are two reasons for this. One, rust is a chemical reaction that causes pressure under the repair from the inside out. That's how the blisters form. Two, the back side of the panel (and the repair) is wide open to moisture, and unpainted body filler acts like a sponge. That's why the best solution to rust problems is to remove the rusted panel and install a new one or have the rusted area cut out and a new piece of sheet metal welded in its place. The trouble with welding is the expense; sometimes it will cost more than the car or truck is worth.

One of the better solutions to do-it-yourself rust repair is the process using a fiberglass cloth repair kit (shown here). This will give a strong repair that resists cracking and moisture and is relatively easy to use. It can be used on large or small holes and also can be applied over contoured surfaces.

Step 1. Rust areas such as this are common and are easily fixed

Step 2. Grind away all traces of rust with a 24-grit grinding disc. Be sure to grind back 3—4 inches from the edge of the hole down to bare metal and be sure all traces of rust are removed

Step 3. Be sure all rust is removed from the edges of the metal. The edges must be ground back to un-rusted metal

Step 4. If you are going to use release film, cut a piece about 2″ larger than the area you have sanded. Place the film over the repair and mark the sanded area on the film. Avoid any unnecessary wrinkling of the film

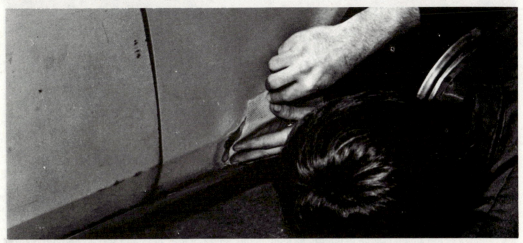

Step 5. Cut 2 pieces of fiberglass matte. One piece should be about 1″ smaller than the sanded area and the second piece should be 1″ smaller than the first. Use sharp scissors to avoid loose ends

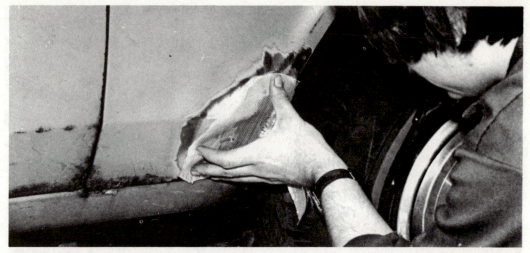

Step 6. Check the dimensions of the release film and cloth by holding them up to the repair area

Step 7. Mix enough repair jelly and cream hardener in the mixing tray to saturate the fiberglass material or fill the repair area. Follow the directions on the container

Step 8. Lay the release sheet on a flat surface and spread an even layer of filler, large enough to cover the repair. Lay the smaller piece of fiberglass cloth in the center of the sheet and spread another layer of repair jelly over the fiberglass cloth. Repeat the operation for the larger piece of cloth. If the fiberglass cloth is not used, spread the repair jelly on the release film, concentrated in the middle of the repair

Step 9. Place the repair material over the repair area, with the release film facing outward

Step 10. Use a spreader and work from the center outward to smooth the material, following the body contours. Be sure to remove all air bubbles

Step 11. Wait until the repair has dried tack-free and peel off the release sheet. The ideal working temperature is 65—90° F. Cooler or warmer temperatures or high humidity may require additional curing time

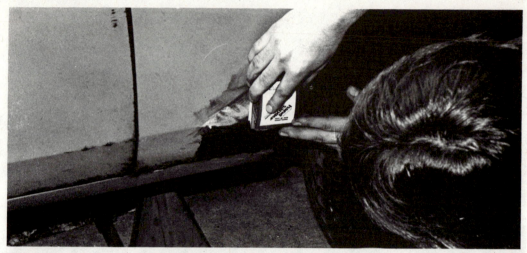

Step 12. Sand and feather-edge the entire area. The initial sanding can be done with a sanding disc on an electric drill if care is used. Finish the sanding with a block sander

Step 13. When the area is sanded smooth, mix some topcoat and hardener and apply it directly with a spreader. This will give a smooth finish and prevent the glass matte from showing through the paint

Step 14. Block sand the topcoat with finishing sandpaper

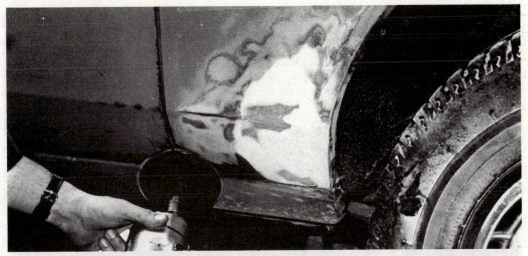

Step 15. To finish this repair, grind out the surface rust along the top edge of the rocker panel

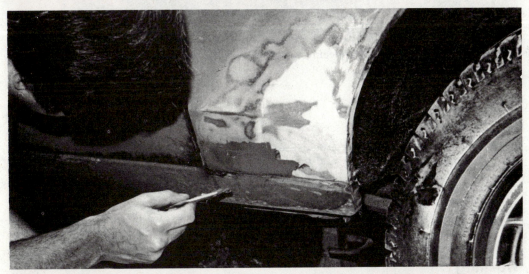

Step 16. Mix some more repair jelly and cream hardener and apply it directly over the surface

Step 17. When it dries tack-free, block sand the surface smooth

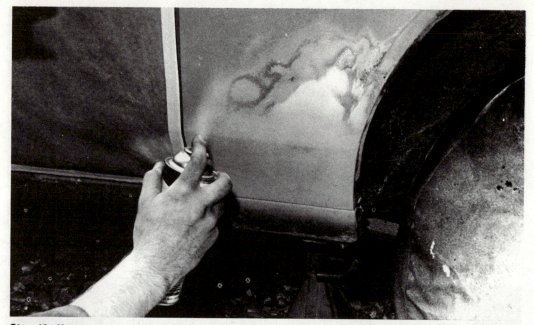

Step 18. If necessary, mask off adjacent panels and spray the entire repair with primer. You are now ready for a color coat

AUTO BODY CARE

There are hundreds—maybe thousands—of products on the market, all designed to protect or aid your car's finish in some manner. There are as many different products as there are ways to use them, but they all have one thing in common—the surface must be clean.

Washing

The primary ingredient for washing your car is water, preferably "soft" water. In many areas of the country, the local water supply is "hard" containing many minerals. The little rings or film that is left on your car's surface after it has dried is the result of "hard" water.

Since you usually can't change the local water supply, the next best thing is to dry the surface before it has a chance to dry itself.

Into the water you usually add soap. Don't use detergents or common, coarse soaps. Your car's paint never truly dries out, but is always evaporating residual oils into the air. Harsh detergents will remove these oils, causing the paint to dry faster than normal. Instead use warm water and a non-detergent soap made especially for waxed surfaces or a liquid soap made for waxed surfaces or a liquid soap made for washing dishes by hand.

Other products that can be used on painted surfaces include baking soda or plain soda water for stubborn dirt.

Wash the car completely, starting at the top, and rinse it completely clean. Abrasive grit should be loaded off under water pressure; scrubbing grit off will scratch the finish. The best washing tool is a sponge, cleaning mitt or soft towel. Whichever you choose, replace it often as each tends to absorb grease and dirt.

Other ways to get a better wash include:

• Don't wash your car in the sun or when the finish is hot.

• Use water pressure to remove caked-on dirt.

• Remove tree-sap and bird effluence immediately. Such substances will eat through wax, polish and paint.

One of the best implements to dry your car is a turkish towel or an old, soft bath towel. Anything with a deep nap will hold any dirt in suspension and not grind it into the paint.

Harder cloths will only grind the grit into the paint making more scratches. Always start drying at the top, followed by the hood and trunk and sides. You'll find there's always more dirt near the rocker panels and wheelwells which will wind up on the rest of the car if you dry these areas first.

Cleaners, Waxes and Polishes

Before going any farther you should know the function of various products.

Cleaners—remove the top layer of dead pigment or paint.

Rubbing or polishing compounds—used to remove stubborn dirt, get rid of minor scratches, smooth away imperfections and partially restore badly weathered paint.

Polishes—contain no abrasives or waxes; they shine the paint by adding oils to the paint.

Waxes—are a protective coating for the polish.

CLEANERS AND COMPOUNDS

Before you apply any wax, you'll have to remove oxidation, road film and other types of pollutants that washing alone will not remove.

The paint on your car never dries completely. There are always residual oils evaporating from the paint into the air. When enough oils are present in the paint, it has a healthy shine (gloss). When too many oils evaporate the paint takes on a whitish cast known as oxidation. The idea of polishing and waxing is to keep enough oil present in the painted surface to prevent oxidation; but when it occurs, the only recourse is to remove the top layer of "dead" paint, exposing the healthy paint underneath.

Products to remove oxidation and road film are sold under a variety of generic names—polishes, cleaner, rubbing compound, cleaner/polish, polish/cleaner, self-polishing wax, pre-wax cleaner, finish restorer and many more. Regardless of name there are two types of cleaners—abrasive cleaners (sometimes called polishing or rubbing compounds) that remove oxidation by grinding away the top layer of "dead" paint, or chemical cleaners that dissolve the "dead" pigment, allowing it to be wiped away.

Abrasive cleaners, by their nature, leave thousands of minute scratches in the finish, which must be polished out later. These should only be used in extreme cases, but are usually the only thing to use on badly oxidized paint finishes. Chemical cleaners are much milder but are not strong enough for severe cases of oxidation or weathered paint.

The most popular cleaners are liquid or paste abrasive polishing and rubbing compounds. Polishing compounds have a finer abrasive grit for medium duty work. Rubbing compounds are a coarser abrasive and for heavy duty work. Unless you are familiar with how to use compounds, be very careful. Excessive rubbing with any type of compound or cleaner can grind right through the paint to primer or bare metal. Follow the directions on the container—depending on type, the cleaner may or may not be OK for your paint. For example, some cleaners are not formulated for acrylic lacquer finishes.

When a small area needs compounding or heavy polishing, it's best to do the job by hand. Some people prefer a powered buffer for large areas. Avoid cutting through the paint along styling edges on the body. Small, hand operations where the compound is applied and rubbed using cloth folded into a thick ball allow you to work in straight lines along such edges.

To avoid cutting through on the edges when using a power buffer, try masking tape. Just cover the edge with tape while using power. Then finish the job by hand with the tape removed. Even then work carefully. The paint tends to be a lot thinner along the sharp ridges stamped into the panels.

Whether compounding by machine or by hand, only work on a small area and apply the compound sparingly. If the materials are spread too thin, or allowed to sit too long, they dry out. Once dry they lose the ability to deliver a smooth, clean finish. Also, dried out polish tends to cause the buffer to stick in one spot. This in turn can burn or cut through the finish.

WAXES AND POLISHES

Your car's finish can be protected in a number of ways. A cleaner/wax or polish/cleaner followed by wax or variations of each all provide good results. The two-step approach (polish followed by wax) is probably slightly better but consumes more time and effort. Properly fed with oils, your paint should never need cleaning, but despite the best polishing job, it won't last unless it's protected with wax. Without wax, polish must be renewed at least once a month to prevent oxidation. Years ago (some still swear by it today), the best wax was made from the Brazilian palm, the Carnuba, favored for its vegetable base and high melting point. However, modern synthetic waxes are harder, which means they protect against moisture better, and chemically inert silicone is used for a long lasting protection. The only problem with silicone wax is that it penetrates all layers of paint. To repaint or touch up a panel or car protected by silicone wax, you have to completely strip the finish to avoid "fish-eyes."

Under normal conditions, silicone waxes will last 4–6 months, but you have to be careful of wax build-up from too much waxing. Too thick a coat of wax is just as bad as no wax at all; it stops the paint from breathing.

Combination cleaners/waxes have become popular lately because they remove the old layer of wax plus light oxidation, while putting on a fresh coat of wax at the same time. Some cleaners/waxes contain abrasive cleaners which require caution, although many cleaner/waxes use a chemical cleaner.

Applying Wax or Polish

You may view polishing and waxing your car as a pleasant way to spend an afternoon, or as a boring chore, but it has to be done to keep the paint on your car. Caring for the paint doesn't require special tools, but you should follow a few rules.

1. Use a good quality wax.

2. Before applying any wax or polish, be sure the surface is completely clean. Just because the car looks clean, doesn't mean it's ready for polish or wax.

3. If the finish on your car is weathered, dull, or oxidized, it will probably have to be compounded to remove the old or oxidized paint. If the paint is simply dulled from lack of care, one of the non-abrasive cleaners known as polishing compounds will do the trick. If the paint is severely scratched or really dull, you'll probably have to use a rubbing compound to prepare the finish for waxing. If you're not sure which one to use, use the polishing compound, since you can easily ruin the finish by using too strong a compound.

4. Don't apply wax, polish or compound in direct sunlight, even if the directions on the can say you can. Most waxes will not cure properly in bright sunlight and you'll probably end up with a blotchy looking finish.

5. Don't rub the wax off too soon. The result will be a wet, dull looking finish. Let the wax dry thoroughly before buffing it off.

6. A constant debate among car enthusiasts is how wax should be applied. Some maintain pastes or liquids should be applied in a circular motion, but body shop experts have long thought that this approach results in barely detectable circular abrasions, especially on cars that are waxed frequently. They

advise rubbing in straight lines, especially if any kind of cleaner is involved.

7. If an applicator is not supplied with the wax, use a piece of soft cheesecloth or very soft lint-free material. The same applies to buffing the surface.

SPECIAL SURFACES

One-step combination cleaner and wax formulas shouldn't be used on many of the special surfaces which abound on cars. The one-step materials contain abrasives to achieve a clean surface under the wax top coat. The abrasives are so mild that you could clean a car every week for a couple of years without fear of rubbing through the paint. But this same level of abrasiveness might, through repeated use, damage decals used for special trim effects. This includes wide stripes, wood-grain trim and other appliques.

Painted plastics must be cleaned with care. If a cleaner is too aggressive it will cut through the paint and expose the primer. If bright trim such as polished aluminum or chrome is painted, cleaning must be performed with even greater care. If rubbing compound is being used, it will cut faster than polish.

Abrasive cleaners will dull an acrylic finish. The best way to clean these newer finishes is with a non-abrasive liquid polish. Only dirt and oxidation, not paint, will be removed.

Taking a few minutes to read the instructions on the can of polish or wax will help prevent making serious mistakes. Not all preparations will work on all surfaces. And some are intended for power application while others will only work when applied by hand.

Don't get the idea that just pouring on some polish and then hitting it with a buffer will suffice. Power equipment speeds the operation. But it also adds a measure of risk. It's very easy to damage the finish if you use the wrong methods or materials.

Caring for Chrome

Read the label on the container. Many products are formulated specifically for chrome, but others contain abrasives that will scratch the chrome finish. If it isn't recommended for chrome, don't use it.

Never use steel wool or kitchen soap pads to clean chrome. Be careful not to get chrome cleaner on paint or interior vinyl surfaces. If you do, get it off immediately.

Troubleshooting

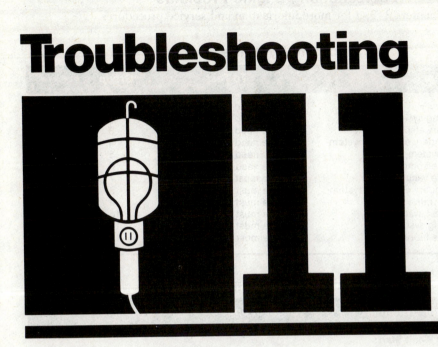

This section is designed to aid in the quick, accurate diagnosis of automotive problems. While automotive repairs can be made by many people, accurate troubleshooting is a rare skill for the amateur and professional alike.

In its simplest state, troubleshooting is an exercise in logic. It is essential to realize that an automobile is really composed of a series of systems. Some of these systems are interrelated; others are not. Automobiles operate within a framework of logical rules and physical laws, and the key to troubleshooting is a good understanding of all the automotive systems.

This section breaks the car or truck down into its component systems, allowing the problem to be isolated. The charts and diagnostic road maps list the most common problems and the most probable causes of trouble. Obviously it would be impossible to list every possible problem that could happen along with every possible cause, but it will locate MOST problems and eliminate a lot of unnecessary guesswork. The systematic format will locate problems within a given system, but, because many automotive systems are interrelated, the solution to your particular problem may be found in a number of systems on the car or truck.

USING THE TROUBLESHOOTING CHARTS

This book contains all of the specific information that the average do-it-yourself mechanic needs to repair and maintain his or her car or truck. The troubleshooting charts are designed to be used in conjunction with the specific procedures and information in the text. For instance, troubleshooting a point-type ignition system is fairly standard for all models, but you may be directed to the text to find procedures for troubleshooting an individual type of electronic ignition. You will also have to refer to the specification charts throughout the book for specifications applicable to your car or truck.

TOOLS AND EQUIPMENT

The tools illustrated in Chapter 1 (plus two more diagnostic pieces) will be adequate to troubleshoot most problems. The two other tools needed are a voltmeter and an ohmmeter. These can be purchased separately or in combination, known as a VOM meter.

In the event that other tools are required, they will be noted in the procedures.

Troubleshooting Engine Problems

See Chapters 2, 3, 4 for more information and service procedures.

Index to Systems

System	To Test	Group
Battery	Engine need not be running	1
Starting system	Engine need not be running	2
Primary electrical system	Engine need not be running	3
Secondary electrical system	Engine need not be running	4
Fuel system	Engine need not be running	5
Engine compression	Engine need not be running	6
Engine vacuum	Engine must be running	7
Secondary electrical system	Engine must be running	8
Valve train	Engine must be running	9
Exhaust system	Engine must be running	10
Cooling system	Engine must be running	11
Engine lubrication	Engine must be running	12

Index to Problems

Problem: Symptom	Begin at Specific Diagnosis, Number ____
Engine Won't Start:	
Starter doesn't turn	1.1, 2.1
Starter turns, engine doesn't	2.1
Starter turns engine very slowly	1.1, 2.4
Starter turns engine normally	3.1, 4.1
Starter turns engine very quickly	6.1
Engine fires intermittently	4.1
Engine fires consistently	5.1, 6.1
Engine Runs Poorly:	
Hard starting	3.1, 4.1, 5.1, 8.1
Rough idle	4.1, 5.1, 8.1
Stalling	3.1, 4.1, 5.1, 8.1
Engine dies at high speeds	4.1, 5.1
Hesitation (on acceleration from standing stop)	5.1, 8.1
Poor pickup	4.1, 5.1, 8.1
Lack of power	3.1, 4.1, 5.1, 8.1
Backfire through the carburetor	4.1, 8.1, 9.1
Backfire through the exhaust	4.1, 8.1, 9.1
Blue exhaust gases	6.1, 7.1
Black exhaust gases	5.1
Running on (after the ignition is shut off)	3.1, 8.1
Susceptible to moisture	4.1
Engine misfires under load	4.1, 7.1, 8.4, 9.1
Engine misfires at speed	4.1, 8.4
Engine misfires at idle	3.1, 4.1, 5.1, 7.1, 8.4

Sample Section

Test and Procedure	Results and Indications	Proceed to
4.1—Check for spark: Hold each spark plug wire approximately ¼″ from ground with gloves or a heavy, dry rag. Crank the engine and observe the spark.	→ If no spark is evident:	→ 4.2
	→ If spark is good in some cases:	→ 4.3
	→ If spark is good in all cases:	→ 4.6

Specific Diagnosis

This section is arranged so that following each test, instructions are given to proceed to another, until a problem is diagnosed.

Section 1—Battery

Test and Procedure	Results and Indications	Proceed to
1.1—Inspect the battery visually for case condition (corrosion, cracks) and water level.	If case is cracked, replace battery:	**1.4**
	If the case is intact, remove corrosion with a solution of baking soda and water (**CAUTION:** *do not get the solution into the battery*), and fill with water:	**1.2**

DIRT ON TOP OF BATTERY
PLUGGED VENT
CORROSION
LOOSE CABLE OR POSTS
CRACKS
LOW WATER LEVEL

Inspect the battery case

Test and Procedure	Results and Indications	Proceed to
1.2—Check the battery cable connections: Insert a screwdriver between the battery post and the cable clamp. Turn the headlights on high beam, and observe them as the screwdriver is gently twisted to ensure good metal to metal contact.	If the lights brighten, remove and clean the clamp and post; coat the post with petroleum jelly, install and tighten the clamp:	**1.4**
	If no improvement is noted:	**1.3**

TESTING BATTERY CABLE CONNECTIONS USING A SCREWDRIVER

Test and Procedure	Results and Indications	Proceed to
1.3—Test the state of charge of the battery using an individual cell tester or hydrometer.	If indicated, charge the battery. **NOTE:** *If no obvious reason exists for the low state of charge (i.e., battery age, prolonged storage), proceed to:*	**1.4**

°F

ADD THIS NUMBER TO THE HYDROMETER READING TO OBTAIN THE CORRECTED SPECIFIC GRAVITY

SUBTRACT THIS NUMBER FROM THE HYDROMETER READING TO OBTAIN THE CORRECTED SPECIFIC GRAVITY

Specific Gravity (@ 80° F.)

Minimum	Battery Charge
1.260	100% Charged
1.230	75% Charged
1.200	50% Charged
1.170	25% Charged
1.140	Very Little Power Left
1.110	Completely Discharged

The effects of temperature on battery specific gravity (left) and amount of battery charge in relation to specific gravity (right)

Test and Procedure	Results and Indications	Proceed to
1.4—Visually inspect battery cables for cracking, bad connection to ground, or bad connection to starter.	If necessary, tighten connections or replace the cables:	**2.1**

Section 2—Starting System
See Chapter 3 for service procedures

Test and Procedure	Results and Indications	Proceed to

Note: Tests in Group 2 are performed with coil high tension lead disconnected to prevent accidental starting.

2.1—Test the starter motor and solenoid: Connect a jumper from the battery post of the solenoid (or relay) to the starter post of the solenoid (or relay).

If starter turns the engine normally:	**2.2**
If the starter buzzes, or turns the engine very slowly:	**2.4**
If no response, replace the solenoid (or relay).	**3.1**
If the starter turns, but the engine doesn't, ensure that the flywheel ring gear is intact. If the gear is undamaged, replace the starter drive.	**3.1**

2.2—Determine whether ignition override switches are functioning properly (clutch start switch, neutral safety switch), by connecting a jumper across the switch(es), and turning the ignition switch to "start".

If starter operates, adjust or replace switch:	**3.1**
If the starter doesn't operate:	**2.3**

2.3—Check the ignition switch "start" position: Connect a 12V test lamp or voltmeter between the starter post of the solenoid (or relay) and ground. Turn the ignition switch to the "start" position, and jiggle the key.

If the lamp doesn't light or the meter needle doesn't move when the switch is turned, check the ignition switch for loose connections, cracked insulation, or broken wires. Repair or replace as necessary:	**3.1**
If the lamp flickers or needle moves when the key is jiggled, replace the ignition switch.	**3.3**

Checking the ignition switch "start" position

STARTER RELAY
(IF EQUIPPED)

2.4—Remove and bench test the starter, according to specifications in the engine electrical section.

If the starter does not meet specifications, repair or replace as needed:	**3.1**
If the starter is operating properly:	**2.5**

2.5—Determine whether the engine can turn freely: Remove the spark plugs, and check for water in the cylinders. Check for water on the dipstick, or oil in the radiator. Attempt to turn the engine using an 18″ flex drive and socket on the crankshaft pulley nut or bolt.

If the engine will turn freely only with the spark plugs out, and hydrostatic lock (water in the cylinders) is ruled out, check valve timing:	**9.2**
If engine will not turn freely, and it is known that the clutch and transmission are free, the engine must be disassembled for further evaluation:	**Chapter 3**

Section 3—Primary Electrical System

Test and Procedure	Results and Indications	Proceed to
3.1—Check the ignition switch "on" position: Connect a jumper wire between the distributor side of the coil and ground, and a 12V test lamp between the switch side of the coil and ground. Remove the high tension lead from the coil. Turn the ignition switch on and jiggle the key.	If the lamp lights:	**3.2**
	If the lamp flickers when the key is jiggled, replace the ignition switch:	**3.3**
	If the lamp doesn't light, check for loose or open connections. If none are found, remove the ignition switch and check for continuity. If the switch is faulty, replace it:	**3.3**

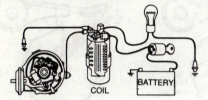

Checking the ignition switch "on" position

3.2—Check the ballast resistor or resistance wire for an open circuit, using an ohmmeter. See Chapter 3 for specific tests.	Replace the resistor or resistance wire if the resistance is zero. **NOTE:** *Some ignition systems have no ballast resistor.*	**3.3**

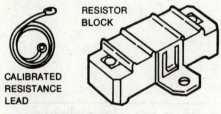

Two types of resistors

3.3—On point-type ignition systems, visually inspect the breaker points for burning, pitting or excessive wear. Gray coloring of the point contact surfaces is normal. Rotate the crankshaft until the contact heel rests on a high point of the distributor cam and adjust the point gap to specifications. On electronic ignition models, remove the distributor cap and visually inspect the armature. Ensure that the armature pin is in place, and that the armature is on tight and rotates when the engine is cranked. Make sure there are no cracks, chips or rounded edges on the armature.	If the breaker points are intact, clean the contact surfaces with fine emery cloth, and adjust the point gap to specifications. If the points are worn, replace them. On electronic systems, replace any parts which appear defective. If condition persists:	**3.4**

Test and Procedure	Results and Indications	Proceed to
3.4—On point-type ignition systems, connect a dwell-meter between the distributor primary lead and ground. Crank the engine and observe the point dwell angle. On electronic ignition systems, conduct a stator (magnetic pickup assembly) test. See Chapter 3.	On point-type systems, adjust the dwell angle if necessary. **NOTE:** *Increasing the point gap decreases the dwell angle and vice-versa.*	3.6
	If the dwell meter shows little or no reading;	3.5
	On electronic ignition systems, if the stator is bad, replace the stator. If the stator is good, proceed to the other tests in Chapter 3.	

Dwell is a function of point gap

3.5—On the point-type ignition systems, check the condenser for short: connect an ohmeter across the condenser body and the pigtail lead.	If any reading other than infinite is noted, replace the condenser	3.6

Checking the condenser for short

3.6—Test the coil primary resistance: On point-type ignition systems, connect an ohmmeter across the coil primary terminals, and read the resistance on the low scale. Note whether an external ballast resistor or resistance wire is used. On electronic ignition systems, test the coil primary resistance as in Chapter 3.	Point-type ignition coils utilizing ballast resistors or resistance wires should have approximately 1.0 ohms resistance. Coils with internal resistors should have approximately 4.0 ohms resistance. If values far from the above are noted, replace the coil.	4.1

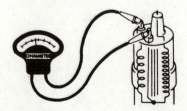

Check the coil primary resistance

Section 4—Secondary Electrical System
See Chapters 2–3 for service procedures

Test and Procedure	Results and Indications	Proceed to
4.1—Check for spark: Hold each spark plug wire approximately ¼″ from ground with gloves or a heavy, dry rag. Crank the engine, and observe the spark.	If no spark is evident:	**4.2**
	If spark is good in some cylinders:	**4.3**
	If spark is good in all cylinders:	**4.6**

Check for spark at the plugs

Test and Procedure	Results and Indications	Proceed to
4.2—Check for spark at the coil high tension lead: Remove the coil high tension lead from the distributor and position it approximately ¼″ from ground. Crank the engine and observe spark. **CAUTION: *This test should not be performed on engines equipped with electronic ignition.***	If the spark is good and consistent:	**4.3**
	If the spark is good but intermittent, test the primary electrical system starting at 3.3:	**3.3**
	If the spark is weak or non-existent, replace the coil high tension lead, clean and tighten all connections and retest. If no improvement is noted:	**4.4**
4.3—Visually inspect the distributor cap and rotor for burned or corroded contacts, cracks, carbon tracks, or moisture. Also check the fit of the rotor on the distributor shaft (where applicable).	If moisture is present, dry thoroughly, and retest per 4.1:	**4.1**
	If burned or excessively corroded contacts, cracks, or carbon tracks are noted, replace the defective part(s) and retest per 4.1:	**4.1**
	If the rotor and cap appear intact, or are only slightly corroded, clean the contacts thoroughly (including the cap towers and spark plug wire ends) and retest per 4.1: If the spark is good in all cases:	**4.6**
	If the spark is poor in all cases:	**4.5**

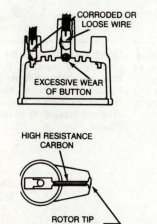

Inspect the distributor cap and rotor

Test and Procedure	Results and Indications	Proceed to
4.4—Check the coil secondary resistance: On point-type systems connect an ohmmeter across the distributor side of the coil and the coil tower. Read the resistance on the high scale of the ohmmeter. On electronic ignition systems, see Chapter 3 for specific tests.	The resistance of a satisfactory coil should be between 4,000 and 10,000 ohms. If resistance is considerably higher (i.e., 40,000 ohms) replace the coil and retest per 4.1. **NOTE:** *This does not apply to high performance coils.*	

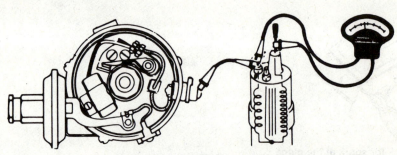

Testing the coil secondary resistance

4.5—Visually inspect the spark plug wires for cracking or brittleness. Ensure that no two wires are positioned so as to cause induction firing (adjacent and parallel). Remove each wire, one by one, and check resistance with an ohmmeter.	Replace any cracked or brittle wires. If any of the wires are defective, replace the entire set. Replace any wires with excessive resistance (over 8000 Ω per foot for suppression wire), and separate any wires that might cause induction firing.	4.6

Misfiring can be the result of spark plug leads to adjacent, consecutively firing cylinders running parallel and too close together

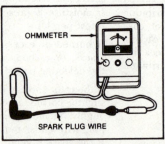

On point-type ignition systems, check the spark plug wires as shown. On electronic ignitions, do not remove the wire from the distributor cap terminal; instead, test through the cap

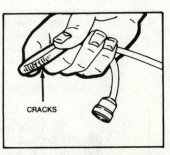

Spark plug wires can be checked visually by bending them in a loop over your finger. This will reveal any cracks, burned or broken insulation. Any wire with cracked insulation should be replaced

4.6—Remove the spark plugs, noting the cylinders from which they were removed, and evaluate according to the color photos in the middle of this book.	See following.	**See following.**

Test and Procedure	Results and Indications	Proceed to
4.7—Examine the location of all the plugs.	The following diagrams illustrate some of the conditions that the location of plugs will reveal.	4.8

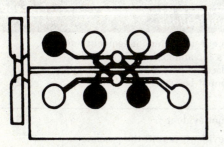

Two adjacent plugs are fouled in a 6-cylinder engine, 4-cylinder engine or either bank of a V-8. This is probably due to a blown head gasket between the two cylinders

The two center plugs in a 6-cylinder engine are fouled. Raw fuel may be "boiled" out of the carburetor into the intake manifold after the engine is shut-off. Stop-start driving can also foul the center plugs, due to overly rich mixture. Proper float level, a new float needle and seat or use of an insulating spacer may help this problem

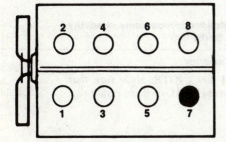

An unbalanced carburetor is indicated. Following the fuel flow on this particular design shows that the cylinders fed by the right-hand barrel are fouled from overly rich mixture, while the cylinders fed by the left-hand barrel are normal

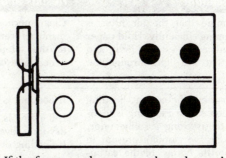

If the four rear plugs are overheated, a cooling system problem is suggested. A thorough cleaning of the cooling system may restore coolant circulation and cure the problem

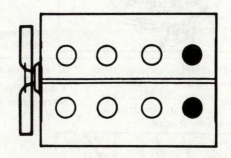

Finding one plug overheated may indicate an intake manifold leak near the affected cylinder. If the overheated plug is the second of two adjacent, consecutively firing plugs, it could be the result of ignition cross-firing. Separating the leads to these two plugs will eliminate cross-fire

Occasionally, the two rear plugs in large, lightly used V-8's will become oil fouled. High oil consumption and smoky exhaust may also be noticed. It is probably due to plugged oil drain holes in the rear of the cylinder head, causing oil to be sucked in around the valve stems. This usually occurs in the rear cylinders first, because the engine slants that way

Test and Procedure	Results and Indications	Proceed to
4.8—Determine the static ignition timing. Using the crankshaft pulley timing marks as a guide, locate top dead center on the compression stroke of the number one cylinder.	The rotor should be pointing toward the No. 1 tower in the distributor cap, and, on electronic ignitions, the armature spoke for that cylinder should be lined up with the stator.	4.8
4.9—Check coil polarity: Connect a voltmeter negative lead to the coil high tension lead, and the positive lead to ground (**NOTE:** *Reverse the hook-up for positive ground systems*). Crank the engine momentarily.  **Checking coil polarity**	If the voltmeter reads up-scale, the polarity is correct:	5.1
	If the voltmeter reads down-scale, reverse the coil polarity (switch the primary leads):	5.1

Section 5—Fuel System
See Chapter 4 for service procedures

Test and Procedure	Results and Indications	Proceed to
5.1—Determine that the air filter is functioning efficiently: Hold paper elements up to a strong light, and attempt to see light through the filter.	Clean permanent air filters in solvent (or manufacturer's recommendation), and allow to dry. Replace paper elements through which light cannot be seen:	5.2
5.2—Determine whether a flooding condition exists: Flooding is identified by a strong gasoline odor, and excessive gasoline present in the throttle bore(s) of the carburetor. 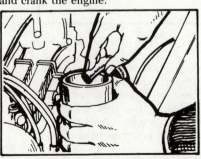 **If the engine floods repeatedly, check the choke butterfly flap**	If flooding is not evident:	5.3
	If flooding is evident, permit the gasoline to dry for a few moments and restart.	
	If flooding doesn't recur:	5.7
	If flooding is persistent:	5.5
5.3—Check that fuel is reaching the carburetor: Detach the fuel line at the carburetor inlet. Hold the end of the line in a cup (not styrofoam), and crank the engine.	If fuel flows smoothly:	5.7
	If fuel doesn't flow (**NOTE:** *Make sure that there is fuel in the tank*), or flows erratically:	5.4

Check the fuel pump by disconnecting the output line (fuel pump-to-carburetor) at the carburetor and operating the starter briefly

Test and Procedure	Results and Indications	Proceed to
5.4—Test the fuel pump: Disconnect all fuel lines from the fuel pump. Hold a finger over the input fitting, crank the engine (with electric pump, turn the ignition or pump on); and feel for suction.	If suction is evident, blow out the fuel line to the tank with low pressure compressed air until bubbling is heard from the fuel filler neck. Also blow out the carburetor fuel line (both ends disconnected):	5.7
	If no suction is evident, replace or repair the fuel pump:	5.7
	NOTE: *Repeated oil fouling of the spark plugs, or a no-start condition, could be the result of a ruptured vacuum booster pump diaphragm, through which oil or gasoline is being drawn into the intake manifold (where applicable).*	
5.5—Occasionally, small specks of dirt will clog the small jets and orifices in the carburetor. With the engine cold, hold a flat piece of wood or similar material over the carburetor, where possible, and crank the engine.	If the engine starts, but runs roughly the engine is probably not run enough.	
	If the engine won't start:	5.9
5.6—Check the needle and seat: Tap the carburetor in the area of the needle and seat.	If flooding stops, a gasoline additive (e.g., Gumout) will often cure the problem:	5.7
	If flooding continues, check the fuel pump for excessive pressure at the carburetor (according to specifications). If the pressure is normal, the needle and seat must be removed and checked, and/or the float level adjusted:	5.7
5.7—Test the accelerator pump by looking into the throttle bores while operating the throttle.	If the accelerator pump appears to be operating normally:	5.8
	If the accelerator pump is not operating, the pump must be reconditioned. Where possible, service the pump with the carburetor(s) installed on the engine. If necessary, remove the carburetor. Prior to removal:	5.8
5.8—Determine whether the carburetor main fuel system is functioning: Spray a commercial starting fluid into the carburetor while attempting to start the engine.	If the engine starts, runs for a few seconds, and dies:	5.9
	If the engine doesn't start:	6.1

Check for gas at the carburetor by looking down the carburetor throat while someone moves the accelerator

Test and Procedure	Results and Indications	Proceed to
5.9—Uncommon fuel system malfunctions: See below:	If the problem is solved:	**6.1**
	If the problem remains, remove and recondition the carburetor.	

Condition	Indication	Test	Prevailing Weather Conditions	Remedy
Vapor lock	Engine will not restart shortly after running.	Cool the components of the fuel system until the engine starts. Vapor lock can be cured faster by draping a wet cloth over a mechanical fuel pump.	Hot to very hot	Ensure that the exhaust manifold heat control valve is operating. Check with the vehicle manufacturer for the recommended solution to vapor lock on the model in question.
Carburetor icing	Engine will not idle, stalls at low speeds.	Visually inspect the throttle plate area of the throttle bores for frost.	High humidity, 32–40° F.	Ensure that the exhaust manifold heat control valve is operating, and that the intake manifold heat riser is not blocked.
Water in the fuel	Engine sputters and stalls; may not start.	Pump a small amount of fuel into a glass jar. Allow to stand, and inspect for droplets or a layer of water.	High humidity, extreme temperature changes.	For droplets, use one or two cans of commercial gas line anti-freeze. For a layer of water, the tank must be drained, and the fuel lines blown out with compressed air.

Section 6—Engine Compression
See Chapter 3 for service procedures

6.1—Test engine compression: Remove all spark plugs. Block the throttle wide open. Insert a compression gauge into a spark plug port, crank the engine to obtain the maximum reading, and record.	If compression is within limits on all cylinders:	**7.1**
	If gauge reading is extremely low on all cylinders:	**6.2**
	If gauge reading is low on one or two cylinders: (If gauge readings are identical and low on two or more adjacent cylinders, the head gasket must be replaced.)	**6.2**

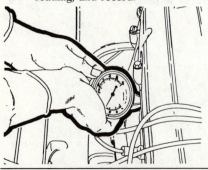

Checking compression

6.2—Test engine compression (wet): Squirt approximately 30 cc. of engine oil into each cylinder, and retest per 6.1.	If the readings improve, worn or cracked rings or broken pistons are indicated:	**See Chapter 3**
	If the readings do not improve, burned or excessively carboned valves or a jumped timing chain are indicated:	**7.1**
	NOTE: *A jumped timing chain is often indicated by difficult cranking.*	

Section 7—Engine Vacuum
See Chapter 3 for service procedures

Test and Procedure	Results and Indications	Proceed to
7.1—Attach a vacuum gauge to the intake manifold beyond the throttle plate. Start the engine, and observe the action of the needle over the range of engine speeds.	See below.	**See below**

INDICATION: normal engine in good condition

Proceed to: 8.1

Normal engine
Gauge reading: steady, from 17–22 in./Hg.

INDICATION: sticking valves or ignition miss

Proceed to: 9.1, 8.3

Sticking valves
Gauge reading: intermittent fluctuation at idle

INDICATION: late ignition or valve timing, low compression, stuck throttle valve, leaking carburetor or manifold gasket

Proceed to: 6.1

Incorrect valve timing
Gauge reading: low (10–15 in./Hg) but steady

INDICATION: improper carburetor adjustment or minor intake leak.

Proceed to: 7.2

Carburetor requires adjustment
Gauge reading: drifting needle

INDICATION: ignition miss, blown cylinder head gasket, leaking valve or weak valve spring

Proceed to: 8.3, 6.1

Blown head gasket
Gauge reading: needle fluctuates as engine speed increases

INDICATION: burnt valve or faulty valve clearance. Needle will fall when defective valve operates

Proceed to: 9.1

Burnt or leaking valves
Gauge reading: steady needle, but drops regularly

INDICATION: choked muffler, excessive back pressure in system

Proceed to: 10.1

Clogged exhaust system
Gauge reading: gradual drop in reading at idle

INDICATION: worn valve guides

Proceed to: 9.1

Worn valve guides
Gauge reading: needle vibrates excessively at idle, but steadies as engine speed increases

White pointer = steady gauge hand   Black pointer = fluctuating gauge hand

Test and Procedure	Results and Indications	Proceed to
7.2—Attach a vacuum gauge per 7.1, and test for an intake manifold leak. Squirt a small amount of oil around the intake manifold gaskets, carburetor gaskets, plugs and fittings. Observe the action of the vacuum gauge.	If the reading improves, replace the indicated gasket, or seal the indicated fitting or plug: If the reading remains low:	**8.1** **7.3**
7.3—Test all vacuum hoses and accessories for leaks as described in 7.2. Also check the carburetor body (dashpots, automatic choke mechanism, throttle shafts) for leaks in the same manner.	If the reading improves, service or replace the offending part(s): If the reading remains low:	**8.1** **6.1**

Section 8—Secondary Electrical System
See Chapter 2 for service procedures

Test and Procedure	Results and Indications	Proceed to
8.1—Remove the distributor cap and check to make sure that the rotor turns when the engine is cranked. Visually inspect the distributor components.	Clean, tighten or replace any components which appear defective.	**8.2**
8.2—Connect a timing light (per manufacturer's recommendation) and check the dynamic ignition timing. Disconnect and plug the vacuum hose(s) to the distributor if specified, start the engine, and observe the timing marks at the specified engine speed.	If the timing is not correct, adjust to specifications by rotating the distributor in the engine: (Advance timing by rotating distributor opposite normal direction of rotor rotation, retard timing by rotating distributor in same direction as rotor rotation.)	**8.3**
8.3—Check the operation of the distributor advance mechanism(s): To test the mechanical advance, disconnect the vacuum lines from the distributor advance unit and observe the timing marks with a timing light as the engine speed is increased from idle. If the mark moves smoothly, without hesitation, it may be assumed that the mechanical advance is functioning properly. To test vacuum advance and/or retard systems, alternately crimp and release the vacuum line, and observe the timing mark for movement. If movement is noted, the system is operating.	If the systems are functioning: If the systems are not functioning, remove the distributor, and test on a distributor tester:	**8.4** **8.4**
8.4—Locate an ignition miss: With the engine running, remove each spark plug wire, one at a time, until one is found that doesn't cause the engine to roughen and slow down.	When the missing cylinder is identified:	**4.1**

Section 9—Valve Train
See Chapter 3 for service procedures

Test and Procedure	Results and Indications	Proceed to
9.1—Evaluate the valve train: Remove the valve cover, and ensure that the valves are adjusted to specifications. A mechanic's stethoscope may be used to aid in the diagnosis of the valve train. By pushing the probe on or near push rods or rockers, valve noise often can be isolated. A timing light also may be used to diagnose valve problems. Connect the light according to manufacturer's recommendations, and start the engine. Vary the firing moment of the light by increasing the engine speed (and therefore the ignition advance), and moving the trigger from cylinder to cylinder. Observe the movement of each valve.	Sticking valves or erratic valve train motion can be observed with the timing light. The cylinder head must be disassembled for repairs.	**See Chapter 3**
9.2—Check the valve timing: Locate top dead center of the No. 1 piston, and install a degree wheel or tape on the crankshaft pulley or damper with zero corresponding to an index mark on the engine. Rotate the crankshaft in its direction of rotation, and observe the opening of the No. 1 cylinder intake valve. The opening should correspond with the correct mark on the degree wheel according to specifications.	If the timing is not correct, the timing cover must be removed for further investigation.	**See Chapter 3**

Section 10—Exhaust System

Test and Procedure	Results and Indications	Proceed to
10.1—Determine whether the exhaust manifold heat control valve is operating: Operate the valve by hand to determine whether it is free to move. If the valve is free, run the engine to operating temperature and observe the action of the valve, to ensure that it is opening.	If the valve sticks, spray it with a suitable solvent, open and close the valve to free it, and retest. If the valve functions properly: If the valve does not free, or does not operate, replace the valve:	**10.2** **10.2**
10.2—Ensure that there are no exhaust restrictions: Visually inspect the exhaust system for kinks, dents, or crushing. Also note that gases are flowing freely from the tailpipe at all engine speeds, indicating no restriction in the muffler or resonator.	Replace any damaged portion of the system:	**11.1**

Section 11—Cooling System
See Chapter 3 for service procedures

Test and Procedure	Results and Indications	Proceed to
11.1—Visually inspect the fan belt for glazing, cracks, and fraying, and replace if necessary. Tighten the belt so that the longest span has approximately ½″ play at its mid-point under thumb pressure (see Chapter 1).	Replace or tighten the fan belt as necessary:	**11.2**

Checking belt tension

11.2—Check the fluid level of the cooling system.	If full or slightly low, fill as necessary:	**11.5**
	If extremely low:	**11.3**
11.3—Visually inspect the external portions of the cooling system (radiator, radiator hoses, thermostat elbow, water pump seals, heater hoses, etc.) for leaks. If none are found, pressurize the cooling system to 14–15 psi.	If cooling system holds the pressure:	**11.5**
	If cooling system loses pressure rapidly, reinspect external parts of the system for leaks under pressure. If none are found, check dipstick for coolant in crankcase. If no coolant is present, but pressure loss continues:	**11.4**
	If coolant is evident in crankcase, remove cylinder head(s), and check gasket(s). If gaskets are intact, block and cylinder head(s) should be checked for cracks or holes.	
	If the gasket(s) is blown, replace, and purge the crankcase of coolant: **NOTE:** *Occasionally, due to atmospheric and driving conditions, condensation of water can occur in the crankcase. This causes the oil to appear milky white. To remedy, run the engine until hot, and change the oil and oil filter.*	**12.6**
11.4—Check for combustion leaks into the cooling system: Pressurize the cooling system as above. Start the engine, and observe the pressure gauge. If the needle fluctuates, remove each spark plug wire, one at a time, noting which cylinder(s) reduce or eliminate the fluctuation.	Cylinders which reduce or eliminate the fluctuation, when the spark plug wire is removed, are leaking into the cooling system. Replace the head gasket on the affected cylinder bank(s).	

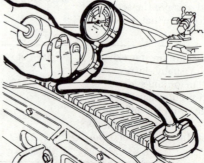

Pressurizing the cooling system

Test and Procedure	Results and Indications	Proceed to
11.5—Check the radiator pressure cap: Attach a radiator pressure tester to the radiator cap (wet the seal prior to installation). Quickly pump up the pressure, noting the point at which the cap releases.	If the cap releases within ± 1 psi of the specified rating, it is operating properly:	**11.6**
	If the cap releases at more than ± 1 psi of the specified rating, it should be replaced:	**11.6**

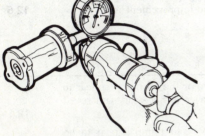

Checking radiator pressure cap

Test and Procedure	Results and Indications	Proceed to
11.6—Test the thermostat: Start the engine cold, remove the radiator cap, and insert a thermometer into the radiator. Allow the engine to idle. After a short while, there will be a sudden, rapid increase in coolant temperature. The temperature at which this sharp rise stops is the thermostat opening temperature.	If the thermostat opens at or about the specified temperature:	**11.7**
	If the temperature doesn't increase: (If the temperature increases slowly and gradually, replace the thermostat.)	**11.7**
11.7—Check the water pump: Remove the thermostat elbow and the thermostat, disconnect the coil high tension lead (to prevent starting), and crank the engine momentarily.	If coolant flows, replace the thermostat and retest per 11.6:	**11.6**
	If coolant doesn't flow, reverse flush the cooling system to alleviate any blockage that might exist. If system is not blocked, and coolant will not flow, replace the water pump.	

Section 12—Lubrication
See Chapter 3 for service procedures

Test and Procedure	Results and Indications	Proceed to
12.1—Check the oil pressure gauge or warning light: If the gauge shows low pressure, or the light is on for no obvious reason, remove the oil pressure sender. Install an accurate oil pressure gauge and run the engine momentarily.	If oil pressure builds normally, run engine for a few moments to determine that it is functioning normally, and replace the sender.	—
	If the pressure remains low:	**12.2**
	If the pressure surges:	**12.3**
	If the oil pressure is zero:	**12.3**
12.2—Visually inspect the oil: If the oil is watery or very thin, milky, or foamy, replace the oil and oil filter.	If the oil is normal:	**12.3**
	If after replacing oil the pressure remains low:	**12.3**
	If after replacing oil the pressure becomes normal:	—

Test and Procedure	Results and Indications	Proceed to
12.3—Inspect the oil pressure relief valve and spring, to ensure that it is not sticking or stuck. Remove and thoroughly clean the valve, spring, and the valve body.	If the oil pressure improves: If no improvement is noted:	— **12.4**
12.4—Check to ensure that the oil pump is not cavitating (sucking air instead of oil): See that the crankcase is neither over nor underfull, and that the pickup in the sump is in the proper position and free from sludge.	Fill or drain the crankcase to the proper capacity, and clean the pickup screen in solvent if necessary. If no improvement is noted:	**12.5**
12.5—Inspect the oil pump drive and the oil pump:	If the pump drive or the oil pump appear to be defective, service as necessary and retest per 12.1: If the pump drive and pump appear to be operating normally, the engine should be disassembled to determine where blockage exists:	**12.1** **See Chapter 3**
12.6—Purge the engine of ethylene glycol coolant: Completely drain the crankcase and the oil filter. Obtain a commercial butyl cellosolve base solvent, designated for this purpose, and follow the instructions precisely. Following this, install a new oil filter and refill the crankcase with the proper weight oil. The next oil and filter change should follow shortly thereafter (1000 miles).		

TROUBLESHOOTING EMISSION CONTROL SYSTEMS

See Chapter 4 for procedures applicable to individual emission control systems used on specific combinations of engine/transmission/model.

TROUBLESHOOTING THE CARBURETOR
See Chapter 4 for service procedures

Carburetor problems cannot be effectively isolated unless all other engine systems (particularly ignition and emission) are functioning properly and the engine is properly tuned.

Condition	Possible Cause
Engine cranks, but does not start	1. Improper starting procedure 2. No fuel in tank 3. Clogged fuel line or filter 4. Defective fuel pump 5. Choke valve not closing properly 6. Engine flooded 7. Choke valve not unloading 8. Throttle linkage not making full travel 9. Stuck needle or float 10. Leaking float needle or seat 11. Improper float adjustment
Engine stalls	1. Improperly adjusted idle speed or mixture **Engine hot** 2. Improperly adjusted dashpot 3. Defective or improperly adjusted solenoid 4. Incorrect fuel level in fuel bowl 5. Fuel pump pressure too high 6. Leaking float needle seat 7. Secondary throttle valve stuck open 8. Air or fuel leaks 9. Idle air bleeds plugged or missing 10. Idle passages plugged **Engine Cold** 11. Incorrectly adjusted choke 12. Improperly adjusted fast idle speed 13. Air leaks 14. Plugged idle or idle air passages 15. Stuck choke valve or binding linkage 16. Stuck secondary throttle valves 17. Engine flooding—high fuel level 18. Leaking or misaligned float
Engine hesitates on acceleration	1. Clogged fuel filter 2. Leaking fuel pump diaphragm 3. Low fuel pump pressure 4. Secondary throttle valves stuck, bent or misadjusted 5. Sticking or binding air valve 6. Defective accelerator pump 7. Vacuum leaks 8. Clogged air filter 9. Incorrect choke adjustment (engine cold)
Engine feels sluggish or flat on acceleration	1. Improperly adjusted idle speed or mixture 2. Clogged fuel filter 3. Defective accelerator pump 4. Dirty, plugged or incorrect main metering jets 5. Bent or sticking main metering rods 6. Sticking throttle valves 7. Stuck heat riser 8. Binding or stuck air valve 9. Dirty, plugged or incorrect secondary jets 10. Bent or sticking secondary metering rods. 11. Throttle body or manifold heat passages plugged 12. Improperly adjusted choke or choke vacuum break.
Carburetor floods	1. Defective fuel pump. Pressure too high. 2. Stuck choke valve 3. Dirty, worn or damaged float or needle valve/seat 4. Incorrect float/fuel level 5. Leaking float bowl

Condition	Possible Cause
Engine idles roughly and stalls	1. Incorrect idle speed 2. Clogged fuel filter 3. Dirt in fuel system or carburetor 4. Loose carburetor screws or attaching bolts 5. Broken carburetor gaskets 6. Air leaks 7. Dirty carburetor 8. Worn idle mixture needles 9. Throttle valves stuck open 10. Incorrectly adjusted float or fuel level 11. Clogged air filter
Engine runs unevenly or surges	1. Defective fuel pump 2. Dirty or clogged fuel filter 3. Plugged, loose or incorrect main metering jets or rods 4. Air leaks 5. Bent or sticking main metering rods 6. Stuck power piston 7. Incorrect float adjustment 8. Incorrect idle speed or mixture 9. Dirty or plugged idle system passages 10. Hard, brittle or broken gaskets 11. Loose attaching or mounting screws 12. Stuck or misaligned secondary throttle valves
Poor fuel economy	1. Poor driving habits 2. Stuck choke valve 3. Binding choke linkage 4. Stuck heat riser 5. Incorrect idle mixture 6. Defective accelerator pump 7. Air leaks 8. Plugged, loose or incorrect main metering jets 9. Improperly adjusted float or fuel level 10. Bent, misaligned or fuel-clogged float 11. Leaking float needle seat 12. Fuel leak 13. Accelerator pump discharge ball not seating properly 14. Incorrect main jets
Engine lacks high speed performance or power	1. Incorrect throttle linkage adjustment 2. Stuck or binding power piston 3. Defective accelerator pump 4. Air leaks 5. Incorrect float setting or fuel level 6. Dirty, plugged, worn or incorrect main metering jets or rods 7. Binding or sticking air valve 8. Brittle or cracked gaskets 9. Bent, incorrect or improperly adjusted secondary metering rods 10. Clogged fuel filter 11. Clogged air filter 12. Defective fuel pump

TROUBLESHOOTING FUEL INJECTION PROBLEMS

Each fuel injection system has its own unique components and test procedures, for which it is impossible to generalize. Refer to Chapter 4 of this Repair & Tune-Up Guide for specific test and repair procedures, if the vehicle is equipped with fuel injection.

TROUBLESHOOTING ELECTRICAL PROBLEMS

See Chapter 5 for service procedures

For any electrical system to operate, it must make a complete circuit. This simply means that the power flow from the battery must make a complete circle. When an electrical component is operating, power flows from the battery to the component, passes through the component causing it to perform its function (lighting a light bulb), and then returns to the battery through the ground of the circuit. This ground is usually (but not always) the metal part of the car or truck on which the electrical component is mounted.

Perhaps the easiest way to visualize this is to think of connecting a light bulb with two wires attached to it to the battery. If one of the two wires attached to the light bulb were attached to the negative post of the battery and the other were attached to the positive post of the battery, you would have a complete circuit. Current from the battery would flow to the light bulb, causing it to light, and return to the negative post of the battery.

The normal automotive circuit differs from this simple example in two ways. First, instead of having a return wire from the bulb to the battery, the light bulb returns the current to the battery through the chassis of the vehicle. Since the negative battery cable is attached to the chassis and the chassis is made of electrically conductive metal, the chassis of the vehicle can serve as a ground wire to complete the circuit. Secondly, most automotive circuits contain switches to turn components on and off as required.

Every complete circuit from a power source must include a component which is using the power from the power source. If you were to disconnect the light bulb from the wires and touch the two wires together (don't do this) the power supply wire to the component would be grounded before the normal ground connection for the circuit.

Because grounding a wire from a power source makes a complete circuit—less the required component to use the power—this phenomenon is called a short circuit. Common causes are: broken insulation (exposing the metal wire to a metal part of the car or truck), or a shorted switch.

Some electrical components which require a large amount of current to operate also have a relay in their circuit. Since these circuits carry a large amount of current, the thickness of the wire in the circuit (gauge size) is also greater. If this large wire were connected from the component to the control switch on the instrument panel, and then back to the component, a voltage drop would occur in the circuit. To prevent this potential drop in voltage, an electromagnetic switch (relay) is used. The large wires in the circuit are connected from the battery to one side of the relay, and from the opposite side of the relay to the component. The relay is normally open, preventing current from passing through the circuit. An additional, smaller, wire is connected from the relay to the control switch for the circuit. When the control switch is turned on, it grounds the smaller wire from the relay and completes the circuit. This closes the relay and allows current to flow from the battery to the component. The horn, headlight, and starter circuits are three which use relays.

It is possible for larger surges of current to pass through the electrical system of your car or truck. If this surge of current were to reach an electrical component, it could burn it out. To prevent this, fuses, circuit breakers or fusible links are connected into the current supply wires of most of the major electrical systems. When an electrical current of excessive power passes through the component's fuse, the fuse blows out and breaks the circuit, saving the component from destruction.

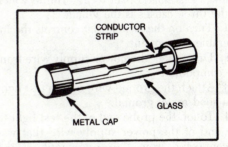

Typical automotive fuse

A circuit breaker is basically a self-repairing fuse. The circuit breaker opens the circuit the same way a fuse does. However, when either the short is removed from the circuit or the surge subsides, the circuit breaker resets itself and does not have to be replaced as a fuse does.

A fuse link is a wire that acts as a fuse. It is normally connected between the starter relay and the main wiring harness. This connection is usually under the hood. The fuse link (if installed) protects all the

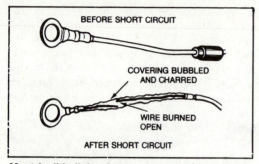

BEFORE SHORT CIRCUIT

COVERING BUBBLED AND CHARRED

WIRE BURNED OPEN

AFTER SHORT CIRCUIT

Most fusible links show a charred, melted insulation when they burn out

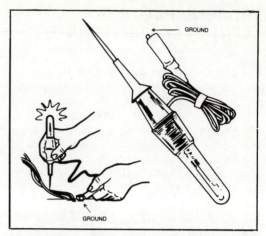

GROUND

GROUND

The test light will show the presence of current when touched to a hot wire and grounded at the other end

chassis electrical components, and is the probable cause of trouble when none of the electrical components function, unless the battery is disconnected or dead.

Electrical problems generally fall into one of three areas:

1. The component that is not functioning is not receiving current.

2. The component itself is not functioning.

3. The component is not properly grounded.

The electrical system can be checked with a test light and a jumper wire. A test light is a device that looks like a pointed screwdriver with a wire attached to it and has a light bulb in its handle. A jumper wire is a piece of insulated wire with an alligator clip attached to each end.

If a component is not working, you must follow a systematic plan to determine which of the three causes is the villain.

1. Turn on the switch that controls the inoperable component.

2. Disconnect the power supply wire from the component.

3. Attach the ground wire on the test light to a good metal ground.

4. Touch the probe end of the test light to the end of the power supply wire that was disconnected from the component. If the component is receiving current, the test light will go on.

NOTE: *Some components work only when the ignition switch is turned on.*

If the test light does not go on, then the problem is in the circuit between the battery and the component. This includes all the switches, fuses, and relays in the system. Follow the wire that runs back to the battery. The problem is an open circuit between the

battery and the component. If the fuse is blown and, when replaced, immediately blows again, there is a short circuit in the system which must be located and repaired. If there is a switch in the system, bypass it with a jumper wire. This is done by connecting one end of the jumper wire to the power supply wire into the switch and the other end of the jumper wire to the wire coming out of the switch. If the test light lights with the jumper wire installed, the switch or whatever was bypassed is defective.

NOTE: *Never substitute the jumper wire for the component, since it is required to use the power from the power source.*

5. If the bulb in the test light goes on, then the current is getting to the component that is not working. This eliminates the first of the three possible causes. Connect the power supply wire and connect a jumper wire from the component to a good metal ground. Do this with the switch which controls the component turned on, and also the ignition switch turned on if it is required for the component to work. If the component works with the jumper wire installed, then it has a bad ground. This is usually caused by the metal area on which the component mounts to the chassis being coated with some type of foreign matter.

6. If neither test located the source of the trouble, then the component itself is defective. Remember that for any electrical system to work, all connections must be clean and tight.

Troubleshooting Basic Turn Signal and Flasher Problems
See Chapter 5 for service procedures

Most problems in the turn signals or flasher system can be reduced to defective flashers or bulbs, which are easily replaced. Occasionally, the turn signal switch will prove defective.

F = Front   R = Rear   ● = Lights off   ○ = Lights on

Condition		Possible Cause
Turn signals light, but do not flash		Defective flasher
No turn signals light on either side		Blown fuse. Replace if defective. Defective flasher. Check by substitution. Open circuit, short circuit or poor ground.
Both turn signals on one side don't work		Bad bulbs. Bad ground in both (or either) housings.
One turn signal light on one side doesn't work		Defective bulb. Corrosion in socket. Clean contacts. Poor ground at socket.
Turn signal flashes too fast or too slowly		Check any bulb on the side flashing too fast. A heavy-duty bulb is probably installed in place of a regular bulb. Check the bulb flashing too slowly. A standard bulb was probably installed in place of a heavy-duty bulb. Loose connections or corrosion at the bulb socket.
Indicator lights don't work in either direction		Check if the turn signals are working. Check the dash indicator lights. Check the flasher by substitution.
One indicator light doesn't light		On systems with one dash indicator: See if the lights work on the same side. Often the filaments have been reversed in systems combining stoplights with taillights and turn signals. Check the flasher by substitution. On systems with two indicators: Check the bulbs on the same side. Check the indicator light bulb. Check the flasher by substitution.

Troubleshooting Lighting Problems
See Chapter 5 for service procedures

Condition	Possible Cause
One or more lights don't work, but others do	1. Defective bulb(s) 2. Blown fuse(s) 3. Dirty fuse clips or light sockets 4. Poor ground circuit
Lights burn out quickly	1. Incorrect voltage regulator setting or defective regulator 2. Poor battery/alternator connections
Lights go dim	1. Low/discharged battery 2. Alternator not charging 3. Corroded sockets or connections 4. Low voltage output
Lights flicker	1. Loose connection 2. Poor ground. (Run ground wire from light housing to frame) 3. Circuit breaker operating (short circuit)
Lights "flare"—Some flare is normal on acceleration—If excessive, see "Lights Burn Out Quickly"	High voltage setting
Lights glare—approaching drivers are blinded	1. Lights adjusted too high 2. Rear springs or shocks sagging 3. Rear tires soft

Troubleshooting Dash Gauge Problems

Most problems can be traced to a defective sending unit or faulty wiring. Occasionally, the gauge itself is at fault. See Chapter 5 for service procedures.

Condition	Possible Cause
COOLANT TEMPERATURE GAUGE	
Gauge reads erratically or not at all	1. Loose or dirty connections 2. Defective sending unit. 3. Defective gauge. To test a bi-metal gauge, remove the wire from the sending unit. Ground the wire for an instant. If the gauge registers, replace the sending unit. To test a magnetic gauge, disconnect the wire at the sending unit. With ignition ON gauge should register COLD. Ground the wire; gauge should register HOT.
AMMETER GAUGE—TURN HEADLIGHTS ON (DO NOT START ENGINE). NOTE REACTION	
Ammeter shows charge Ammeter shows discharge Ammeter does not move	1. Connections reversed on gauge 2. Ammeter is OK 3. Loose connections or faulty wiring 4. Defective gauge

Condition	Possible Cause

OIL PRESSURE GAUGE

Condition	Possible Cause
Gauge does not register or is inaccurate	1. On mechanical gauge, Bourdon tube may be bent or kinked. 2. Low oil pressure. Remove sending unit. Idle the engine briefly. If no oil flows from sending unit hole, problem is in engine. 3. Defective gauge. Remove the wire from the sending unit and ground it for an instant with the ignition ON. A good gauge will go to the top of the scale. 4. Defective wiring. Check the wiring to the gauge. If it's OK and the gauge doesn't register when grounded, replace the gauge. 5. Defective sending unit.

ALL GAUGES

Condition	Possible Cause
All gauges do not operate	1. Blown fuse 2. Defective instrument regulator
All gauges read low or erratically All gauges pegged	3. Defective or dirty instrument voltage regulator 4. Loss of ground between instrument voltage regulator and frame 5. Defective instrument regulator

WARNING LIGHTS

Condition	Possible Cause
Light(s) do not come on when ignition is ON, but engine is not started	1. Defective bulb 2. Defective wire 3. Defective sending unit. Disconnect the wire from the sending unit and ground it. Replace the sending unit if the light comes on with the ignition ON.
Light comes on with engine running	4. Problem in individual system 5. Defective sending unit

Troubleshooting Clutch Problems

It is false economy to replace individual clutch components. The pressure plate, clutch plate and throwout bearing should be replaced as a set, and the flywheel face inspected, whenever the clutch is overhauled. See Chapter 6 for service procedures.

Condition	Possible Cause
Clutch chatter	1. Grease on driven plate (disc) facing 2. Binding clutch linkage or cable 3. Loose, damaged facings on driven plate (disc) 4. Engine mounts loose 5. Incorrect height adjustment of pressure plate release levers 6. Clutch housing or housing to transmission adapter misalignment 7. Loose driven plate hub
Clutch grabbing	1. Oil, grease on driven plate (disc) facing 2. Broken pressure plate 3. Warped or binding driven plate. Driven plate binding on clutch shaft
Clutch slips	1. Lack of lubrication in clutch linkage or cable (linkage or cable binds, causes incomplete engagement) 2. Incorrect pedal, or linkage adjustment 3. Broken pressure plate springs 4. Weak pressure plate springs 5. Grease on driven plate facings (disc)

Troubleshooting Clutch Problems (cont.)

Condition	Possible Cause
Incomplete clutch release	1. Incorrect pedal or linkage adjustment or linkage or cable binding 2. Incorrect height adjustment on pressure plate release levers 3. Loose, broken facings on driven plate (disc) 4. Bent, dished, warped driven plate caused by overheating
Grinding, whirring grating noise when pedal is depressed	1. Worn or defective throwout bearing 2. Starter drive teeth contacting flywheel ring gear teeth. Look for milled or polished teeth on ring gear.
Squeal, howl, trumpeting noise when pedal is being released (occurs during first inch to inch and one-half of pedal travel)	Pilot bushing worn or lack of lubricant. If bushing appears OK, polish bushing with emery cloth, soak lube wick in oil, lube bushing with oil, apply film of chassis grease to clutch shaft pilot hub, reassemble. NOTE: Bushing wear may be due to misalignment of clutch housing or housing to transmission adapter
Vibration or clutch pedal pulsation with clutch disengaged (pedal fully depressed)	1. Worn or defective engine transmission mounts 2. Flywheel run out. (Flywheel run out at face not to exceed 0.005″) 3. Damaged or defective clutch components

Troubleshooting Manual Transmission Problems
See Chapter 6 for service procedures

Condition	Possible Cause
Transmission jumps out of gear	1. Misalignment of transmission case or clutch housing. 2. Worn pilot bearing in crankshaft. 3. Bent transmission shaft. 4. Worn high speed sliding gear. 5. Worn teeth or end-play in clutch shaft. 6. Insufficient spring tension on shifter rail plunger. 7. Bent or loose shifter fork. 8. Gears not engaging completely. 9. Loose or worn bearings on clutch shaft or mainshaft. 10. Worn gear teeth. 11. Worn or damaged detent balls.
Transmission sticks in gear	1. Clutch not releasing fully. 2. Burred or battered teeth on clutch shaft, or sliding sleeve. 3. Burred or battered transmission mainshaft. 4. Frozen synchronizing clutch. 5. Stuck shifter rail plunger. 6. Gearshift lever twisting and binding shifter rail. 7. Battered teeth on high speed sliding gear or on sleeve. 8. Improper lubrication, or lack of lubrication. 9. Corroded transmission parts. 10. Defective mainshaft pilot bearing. 11. Locked gear bearings will give same effect as stuck in gear.
Transmission gears will not synchronize	1. Binding pilot bearing on mainshaft, will synchronize in high gear only. 2. Clutch not releasing fully. 3. Detent spring weak or broken. 4. Weak or broken springs under balls in sliding gear sleeve. 5. Binding bearing on clutch shaft, or binding countershaft. 6. Binding pilot bearing in crankshaft. 7. Badly worn gear teeth. 8. Improper lubrication. 9. Constant mesh gear not turning freely on transmission mainshaft. Will synchronize in that gear only.

Condition	Possible Cause
Gears spinning when shifting into gear from neutral	1. Clutch not releasing fully. 2. In some cases an extremely light lubricant in transmission will cause gears to continue to spin for a short time after clutch is released. 3. Binding pilot bearing in crankshaft.
Transmission noisy in all gears	1. Insufficient lubricant, or improper lubricant. 2. Worn countergear bearings. 3. Worn or damaged main drive gear or countergear. 4. Damaged main drive gear or mainshaft bearings. 5. Worn or damaged countergear anti-lash plate.
Transmission noisy in neutral only	1. Damaged main drive gear bearing. 2. Damaged or loose mainshaft pilot bearing. 3. Worn or damaged countergear anti-lash plate. 4. Worn countergear bearings.
Transmission noisy in one gear only	1. Damaged or worn constant mesh gears. 2. Worn or damaged countergear bearings. 3. Damaged or worn synchronizer.
Transmission noisy in reverse only	1. Worn or damaged reverse idler gear or idler bushing. 2. Worn or damaged mainshaft reverse gear. 3. Worn or damaged reverse countergear. 4. Damaged shift mechanism.

TROUBLESHOOTING AUTOMATIC TRANSMISSION PROBLEMS

Keeping alert to changes in the operating characteristics of the transmission (changing shift points, noises, etc.) can prevent small problems from becoming large ones. If the problem cannot be traced to loose bolts, fluid level, misadjusted linkage, clogged filters or similar problems, you should probably seek professional service.

Transmission Fluid Indications

The appearance and odor of the transmission fluid can give valuable clues to the overall condition of the transmission. Always note the appearance of the fluid when you check the fluid level or change the fluid. Rub a small amount of fluid between your fingers to feel for grit and smell the fluid on the dipstick.

If the fluid appears:	It indicates:
Clear and red colored	Normal operation
Discolored (extremely dark red or brownish) or smells burned	Band or clutch pack failure, usually caused by an overheated transmission. Hauling very heavy loads with insufficient power or failure to change the fluid often result in overheating. Do not confuse this appearance with newer fluids that have a darker red color and a strong odor (though not a burned odor).
Foamy or aerated (light in color and full of bubbles)	1. The level is too high (gear train is churning oil) 2. An internal air leak (air is mixing with the fluid). Have the transmission checked professionally.
Solid residue in the fluid	Defective bands, clutch pack or bearings. Bits of band material or metal abrasives are clinging to the dipstick. Have the transmission checked professionally.
Varnish coating on the dipstick	The transmission fluid is overheating

TROUBLESHOOTING DRIVE AXLE PROBLEMS

First, determine when the noise is most noticeable.

Drive Noise: Produced under vehicle acceleration.

Coast Noise: Produced while coasting with a closed throttle.

Float Noise: Occurs while maintaining constant speed (just enough to keep speed constant) on a level road.

External Noise Elimination

It is advisable to make a thorough road test to determine whether the noise originates in the rear axle or whether it originates from the tires, engine, transmission, wheel bearings or road surface. Noise originating from other places cannot be corrected by servicing the rear axle.

ROAD NOISE

Brick or rough surfaced concrete roads produce noises that seem to come from the rear axle. Road noise is usually identical in Drive or Coast and driving on a different type of road will tell whether the road is the problem.

TIRE NOISE

Tire noise can be mistaken as rear axle noise, even though the tires on the front are at fault. Snow tread and mud tread tires or tires worn unevenly will frequently cause vibrations which seem to originate elsewhere; *temporarily, and for test purposes only,* inflate the tires to 40–50 lbs. This will significantly alter the noise produced by the tires,

but will not alter noise from the rear axle. Noises from the rear axle will normally cease at speeds below 30 mph on coast, while tire noise will continue at lower tone as speed is decreased. The rear axle noise will usually change from drive conditions to coast conditions, while tire noise will not. Do not forget to lower the tire pressure to normal after the test is complete.

ENGINE/TRANSMISSION NOISE

Determine at what speed the noise is most pronounced, then stop in a quiet place. With the transmission in Neutral, run the engine through speeds corresponding to road speeds where the noise was noticed. Noises produced with the vehicle standing still are coming from the engine or transmission.

FRONT WHEEL BEARINGS

Front wheel bearing noises, sometimes confused with rear axle noises, will not change when comparing drive and coast conditions. While holding the speed steady, lightly apply the footbrake. This will often cause wheel bearing noise to lessen, as some of the weight is taken off the bearing. Front wheel bearings are easily checked by jacking up the wheels and spinning the wheels. Shaking the wheels will also determine if the wheel bearings are excessively loose.

REAR AXLE NOISES

Eliminating other possible sources can narrow the cause to the rear axle, which normally produces noise from worn gears or bearings. Gear noises tend to peak in a narrow speed range, while bearing noises will usually vary in pitch with engine speeds.

Noise Diagnosis

The Noise Is:	Most Probably Produced By:
1. Identical under Drive or Coast	Road surface, tires or front wheel bearings
2. Different depending on road surface	Road surface or tires
3. Lower as speed is lowered	Tires
4. Similar when standing or moving	Engine or transmission
5. A vibration	Unbalanced tires, rear wheel bearing, unbalanced driveshaft or worn U-joint
6. A knock or click about every two tire revolutions	Rear wheel bearing
7. Most pronounced on turns	Damaged differential gears
8. A steady low-pitched whirring or scraping, starting at low speeds	Damaged or worn pinion bearing
9. A chattering vibration on turns	Wrong differential lubricant or worn clutch plates (limited slip rear axle)
10. Noticed only in Drive, Coast or Float conditions	Worn ring gear and/or pinion gear

Troubleshooting Steering & Suspension Problems

Condition	Possible Cause
Hard steering (wheel is hard to turn)	1. Improper tire pressure 2. Loose or glazed pump drive belt 3. Low or incorrect fluid 4. Loose, bent or poorly lubricated front end parts 5. Improper front end alignment (excessive caster) 6. Bind in steering column or linkage 7. Kinked hydraulic hose 8. Air in hydraulic system 9. Low pump output or leaks in system 10. Obstruction in lines 11. Pump valves sticking or out of adjustment 12. Incorrect wheel alignment
Loose steering (too much play in steering wheel)	1. Loose wheel bearings 2. Faulty shocks 3. Worn linkage or suspension components 4. Loose steering gear mounting or linkage points 5. Steering mechanism worn or improperly adjusted 6. Valve spool improperly adjusted 7. Worn ball joints, tie-rod ends, etc.
Veers or wanders (pulls to one side with hands off steering wheel)	1. Improper tire pressure 2. Improper front end alignment 3. Dragging or improperly adjusted brakes 4. Bent frame 5. Improper rear end alignment 6. Faulty shocks or springs 7. Loose or bent front end components 8. Play in Pitman arm 9. Steering gear mountings loose 10. Loose wheel bearings 11. Binding Pitman arm 12. Spool valve sticking or improperly adjusted 13. Worn ball joints
Wheel oscillation or vibration transmitted through steering wheel	1. Low or uneven tire pressure 2. Loose wheel bearings 3. Improper front end alignment 4. Bent spindle 5. Worn, bent or broken front end components 6. Tires out of round or out of balance 7. Excessive lateral runout in disc brake rotor 8. Loose or bent shock absorber or strut
Noises (see also "Troubleshooting Drive Axle Problems")	1. Loose belts 2. Low fluid, air in system 3. Foreign matter in system 4. Improper lubrication 5. Interference or chafing in linkage 6. Steering gear mountings loose 7. Incorrect adjustment or wear in gear box 8. Faulty valves or wear in pump 9. Kinked hydraulic lines 10. Worn wheel bearings
Poor return of steering	1. Over-inflated tires 2. Improperly aligned front end (excessive caster) 3. Binding in steering column 4. No lubrication in front end 5. Steering gear adjusted too tight
Uneven tire wear (see "How To Read Tire Wear")	1. Incorrect tire pressure 2. Improperly aligned front end 3. Tires out-of-balance 4. Bent or worn suspension parts

HOW TO READ TIRE WEAR

The way your tires wear is a good indicator of other parts of the suspension. Abnormal wear patterns are often caused by the need for simple tire maintenance, or for front end alignment.

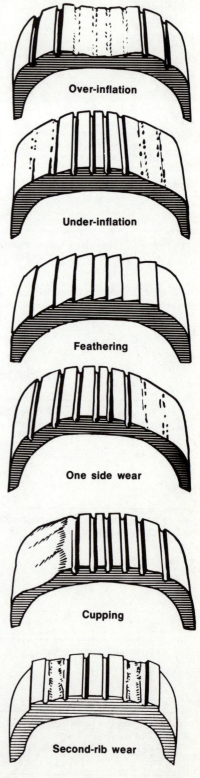

Excessive wear at the center of the tread indicates that the air pressure in the tire is consistently too high. The tire is riding on the center of the tread and wearing it prematurely. Occasionally, this wear pattern can result from outrageously wide tires on narrow rims. The cure for this is to replace either the tires or the wheels.

Over-inflation

This type of wear usually results from consistent under-inflation. When a tire is under-inflated, there is too much contact with the road by the outer treads, which wear prematurely. When this type of wear occurs, and the tire pressure is known to be consistently correct, a bent or worn steering component or the need for wheel alignment could be indicated.

Under-inflation

Feathering is a condition when the edge of each tread rib develops a slightly rounded edge on one side and a sharp edge on the other. By running your hand over the tire, you can usually feel the sharper edges before you'll be able to see them. The most common causes of feathering are incorrect toe-in setting or deteriorated bushings in the front suspension.

Feathering

When an inner or outer rib wears faster than the rest of the tire, the need for wheel alignment is indicated. There is excessive camber in the front suspension, causing the wheel to lean too much putting excessive load on one side of the tire. Misalignment could also be due to sagging springs, worn ball joints, or worn control arm bushings. Be sure the vehicle is loaded the way it's normally driven when you have the wheels aligned.

One side wear

Cups or scalloped dips appearing around the edge of the tread almost always indicate worn (sometimes bent) suspension parts. Adjustment of wheel alignment alone will seldom cure the problem. Any worn component that connects the wheel to the suspension can cause this type of wear. Occasionally, wheels that are out of balance will wear like this, but wheel imbalance usually shows up as bald spots between the outside edges and center of the tread.

Cupping

Second-rib wear is usually found only in radial tires, and appears where the steel belts end in relation to the tread. It can be kept to a minimum by paying careful attention to tire pressure and frequently rotating the tires. This is often considered normal wear but excessive amounts indicate that the tires are too wide for the wheels.

Second-rib wear

Troubleshooting Disc Brake Problems

Condition	Possible Cause
Noise—groan—brake noise emanating when slowly releasing brakes (creep-groan)	Not detrimental to function of disc brakes—no corrective action required. (This noise may be eliminated by slightly increasing or decreasing brake pedal efforts.)
Rattle—brake noise or rattle emanating at low speeds on rough roads, (front wheels only).	1. Shoe anti-rattle spring missing or not properly positioned. 2. Excessive clearance between shoe and caliper. 3. Soft or broken caliper seals. 4. Deformed or misaligned disc. 5. Loose caliper.
Scraping	1. Mounting bolts too long. 2. Loose wheel bearings. 3. Bent, loose, or misaligned splash shield.
Front brakes heat up during driving and fail to release	1. Operator riding brake pedal. 2. Stop light switch improperly adjusted. 3. Sticking pedal linkage. 4. Frozen or seized piston. 5. Residual pressure valve in master cylinder. 6. Power brake malfunction. 7. Proportioning valve malfunction.
Leaky brake caliper	1. Damaged or worn caliper piston seal. 2. Scores or corrosion on surface of cylinder bore.
Grabbing or uneven brake action—Brakes pull to one side	1. Causes listed under "Brakes Pull". 2. Power brake malfunction. 3. Low fluid level in master cylinder. 4. Air in hydraulic system. 5. Brake fluid, oil or grease on linings. 6. Unmatched linings. 7. Distorted brake pads. 8. Frozen or seized pistons. 9. Incorrect tire pressure. 10. Front end out of alignment. 11. Broken rear spring. 12. Brake caliper pistons sticking. 13. Restricted hose or line. 14. Caliper not in proper alignment to braking disc. 15. Stuck or malfunctioning metering valve. 16. Soft or broken caliper seals. 17. Loose caliper.
Brake pedal can be depressed without braking effect	1. Air in hydraulic system or improper bleeding procedure. 2. Leak past primary cup in master cylinder. 3. Leak in system. 4. Rear brakes out of adjustment. 5. Bleeder screw open.
Excessive pedal travel	1. Air, leak, or insufficient fluid in system or caliper. 2. Warped or excessively tapered shoe and lining assembly. 3. Excessive disc runout. 4. Rear brake adjustment required. 5. Loose wheel bearing adjustment. 6. Damaged caliper piston seal. 7. Improper brake fluid (boil). 8. Power brake malfunction. 9. Weak or soft hoses.

Troubleshooting Disc Brake Problems (cont.)

Condition	Possible Cause
Brake roughness or chatter (pedal pumping)	1. Excessive thickness variation of braking disc. 2. Excessive lateral runout of braking disc. 3. Rear brake drums out-of-round. 4. Excessive front bearing clearance.
Excessive pedal effort	1. Brake fluid, oil or grease on linings. 2. Incorrect lining. 3. Frozen or seized pistons. 4. Power brake malfunction. 5. Kinked or collapsed hose or line. 6. Stuck metering valve. 7. Scored caliper or master cylinder bore. 8. Seized caliper pistons.
Brake pedal fades (pedal travel increases with foot on brake)	1. Rough master cylinder or caliper bore. 2. Loose or broken hydraulic lines/connections. 3. Air in hydraulic system. 4. Fluid level low. 5. Weak or soft hoses. 6. Inferior quality brake shoes or fluid. 7. Worn master cylinder piston cups or seals.

Troubleshooting Drum Brakes

Condition	Possible Cause
Pedal goes to floor	1. Fluid low in reservoir. 2. Air in hydraulic system. 3. Improperly adjusted brake. 4. Leaking wheel cylinders. 5. Loose or broken brake lines. 6. Leaking or worn master cylinder. 7. Excessively worn brake lining.
Spongy brake pedal	1. Air in hydraulic system. 2. Improper brake fluid (low boiling point). 3. Excessively worn or cracked brake drums. 4. Broken pedal pivot bushing.
Brakes pulling	1. Contaminated lining. 2. Front end out of alignment. 3. Incorrect brake adjustment. 4. Unmatched brake lining. 5. Brake drums out of round. 6. Brake shoes distorted. 7. Restricted brake hose or line. 8. Broken rear spring. 9. Worn brake linings. 10. Uneven lining wear. 11. Glazed brake lining. 12. Excessive brake lining dust. 13. Heat spotted brake drums. 14. Weak brake return springs. 15. Faulty automatic adjusters. 16. Low or incorrect tire pressure.

Condition	Possible Cause
Squealing brakes	1. Glazed brake lining. 2. Saturated brake lining. 3. Weak or broken brake shoe retaining spring. 4. Broken or weak brake shoe return spring. 5. Incorrect brake lining. 6. Distorted brake shoes. 7. Bent support plate. 8. Dust in brakes or scored brake drums. 9. Linings worn below limit. 10. Uneven brake lining wear. 11. Heat spotted brake drums.
Chirping brakes	1. Out of round drum or eccentric axle flange pilot.
Dragging brakes	1. Incorrect wheel or parking brake adjustment. 2. Parking brakes engaged or improperly adjusted. 3. Weak or broken brake shoe return spring. 4. Brake pedal binding. 5. Master cylinder cup sticking. 6. Obstructed master cylinder relief port. 7. Saturated brake lining. 8. Bent or out of round brake drum. 9. Contaminated or improper brake fluid. 10. Sticking wheel cylinder pistons. 11. Driver riding brake pedal. 12. Defective proportioning valve. 13. Insufficient brake shoe lubricant.
Hard pedal	1. Brake booster inoperative. 2. Incorrect brake lining. 3. Restricted brake line or hose. 4. Frozen brake pedal linkage. 5. Stuck wheel cylinder. 6. Binding pedal linkage. 7. Faulty proportioning valve.
Wheel locks	1. Contaminated brake lining. 2. Loose or torn brake lining. 3. Wheel cylinder cups sticking. 4. Incorrect wheel bearing adjustment. 5. Faulty proportioning valve.
Brakes fade (high speed)	1. Incorrect lining. 2. Overheated brake drums. 3. Incorrect brake fluid (low boiling temperature). 4. Saturated brake lining. 5. Leak in hydraulic system. 6. Faulty automatic adjusters.
Pedal pulsates	1. Bent or out of round brake drum.
Brake chatter and shoe knock	1. Out of round brake drum. 2. Loose support plate. 3. Bent support plate. 4. Distorted brake shoes. 5. Machine grooves in contact face of brake drum (Shoe Knock). 6. Contaminated brake lining. 7. Missing or loose components. 8. Incorrect lining material. 9. Out-of-round brake drums. 10. Heat spotted or scored brake drums. 11. Out-of-balance wheels.

Troubleshooting Drum Brakes (cont.)

Condition	Possible Cause
Brakes do not self adjust	1. Adjuster screw frozen in thread. 2. Adjuster screw corroded at thrust washer. 3. Adjuster lever does not engage star wheel. 4. Adjuster installed on wrong wheel.
Brake light glows	1. Leak in the hydraulic system. 2. Air in the system. 3. Improperly adjusted master cylinder pushrod. 4. Uneven lining wear. 5. Failure to center combination valve or proportioning valve.

Appendix

General Conversion Table

Multiply by	To convert	To	
2.54	Inches	Centimeters	.3937
30.48	Feet	Centimeters	.0328
.914	Yards	Meters	1.094
1.609	Miles	Kilometers	.621
6.45	Square inches	Square cm.	.155
.836	Square yards	Square meters	1.196
16.39	Cubic inches	Cubic cm.	.061
28.3	Cubic feet	Liters	.0353
.4536	Pounds	Kilograms	2.2045
3.785	Gallons	Liters	.264
.068	Lbs./sq. in. (psi)	Atmospheres	14.7
.138	Foot pounds	Kg. m.	7.23
1.014	H.P. (DIN)	H.P. (SAE)	.9861
—	To obtain	From	Multiply by

Note: 1 cm. equals 10 mm.; 1 mm. equals .0394″.

Conversion—Common Fractions to Decimals and Millimeters

Common Fractions	Decimal Fractions	Millimeters (approx.)	Common Fractions	Decimal Fractions	Millimeters (approx.)	Common Fractions	Decimal Fractions	Millimeters (approx.)
1/128	.008	0.20	11/32	.344	8.73	43/64	.672	17.07
1/64	.016	0.40	23/64	.359	9.13	11/16	.688	17.46
1/32	.031	0.79	3/8	.375	9.53	45/64	.703	17.86
3/64	.047	1.19	25/64	.391	9.92	23/32	.719	18.26
1/16	.063	1.59	13/32	.406	10.32	47/64	.734	18.65
5/64	.078	1.98	27/64	.422	10.72	3/4	.750	19.05
3/32	.094	2.38	7/16	.438	11.11	49/64	.766	19.45
7/64	.109	2.78	29/64	.453	11.51	25/32	.781	19.84
1/8	.125	3.18	15/32	.469	11.91	51/64	.797	20.24
9/64	.141	3.57	31/64	.484	12.30	13/16	.813	20.64
5/32	.156	3.97	1/2	.500	12.70	53/64	.828	21.03
11/64	.172	4.37	33/64	.516	13.10	27/32	.844	21.43
3/16	.188	4.76	17/32	.531	13.49	55/64	.859	21.83
13/64	.203	5.16	35/64	.547	13.89	7/8	.875	22.23
7/32	.219	5.56	9/16	.563	14.29	57/64	.891	22.62
15/64	.234	5.95	37/64	.578	14.68	29/32	.906	23.02
1/4	.250	6.35	19/32	.594	15.08	59/64	.922	23.42
17/64	.266	6.75	39/64	.609	15.48	15/16	.938	23.81
9/32	.281	7.14	5/8	.625	15.88	61/64	.953	24.21
19/64	.297	7.54	41/64	.641	16.27	31/32	.969	24.61
5/16	.313	7.94	21/32	.656	16.67	63/64	.984	25.00
21/64	.328	8.33						

Conversion—Millimeters to Decimal Inches

mm	inches	mm	inches	mm	inches	mm	inches	mm	inches
1	.039 370	31	1.220 470	61	2.401 570	91	3.582 670	210	8.267 700
2	.078 740	32	1.259 840	62	2.440 940	92	3.622 040	220	8.661 400
3	.118 110	33	1.299 210	63	2.480 310	93	3.661 410	230	9.055 100
4	.157 480	34	1.338 580	64	2.519 680	94	3.700 780	240	9.448 800
5	.196 850	35	1.377 949	65	2.559 050	95	3.740 150	250	9.842 500
6	.236 220	36	1.417 319	66	2.598 420	96	3.779 520	260	10.236 200
7	.275 590	37	1.456 689	67	2.637 790	97	3.818 890	270	10.629 900
8	.314 960	38	1.496 050	68	2.677 160	98	3.858 260	280	11.032 600
9	.354 330	39	1.535 430	69	2.716 530	99	3.897 630	290	11.417 300
10	.393 700	40	1.574 800	70	2.755 900	100	3.937 000	300	11.811 000
11	.433 070	41	1.614 170	71	2.795 270	105	4.133 848	310	12.204 700
12	.472 440	42	1.653 540	72	2.834 640	110	4.330 700	320	12.598 400
13	.511 810	43	1.692 910	73	2.874 010	115	4.527 550	330	12.992 100
14	.551 180	44	1.732 280	74	2.913 380	120	4.724 400	340	13.385 800
15	.590 550	45	1.771 650	75	2.952 750	125	4.921 250	350	13.779 500
16	.629 920	46	1.811 020	76	2.992 120	130	5.118 100	360	14.173 200
17	.669 290	47	1.850 390	77	3.031 490	135	5.314 950	370	14.566 900
18	.708 660	48	1.889 760	78	3.070 860	140	5.511 800	380	14.960 600
19	.748 030	49	1.929 130	79	3.110 230	145	5.708 650	390	15.354 300
20	.787 400	50	1.968 500	80	3.149 600	150	5.905 500	400	15.748 000
21	.826 770	51	2.007 870	81	3.188 970	155	6.102 350	500	19.685 000
22	.866 140	52	2.047 240	82	3.228 340	160	6.299 200	600	23.622 000
23	.905 510	53	2.086 610	83	3.267 710	165	6.496 050	700	27.559 000
24	.944 880	54	2.125 980	84	3.307 080	170	6.692 900	800	31.496 000
25	.984 250	55	2.165 350	85	3.346 450	175	6.889 750	900	35.433 000
26	1.023 620	56	2.204 720	86	3.385 820	180	7.086 600	1000	39.370 000
27	1.062 990	57	2.244 090	87	3.425 190	185	7.283 450	2000	78.740 000
28	1.102 360	58	2.283 460	88	3.464 560	190	7.480 300	3000	118.110 000
29	1.141 730	59	2.322 830	89	3.503 903	195	7.677 150	4000	157.480 000
30	1.181 100	60	2.362 200	90	3.543 300	200	7.874 000	5000	196.850 000

To change decimal millimeters to decimal inches, position the decimal point where desired on either side of the millimeter measurement shown and reset the inches decimal by the same number of digits in the same direction. For example, to convert 0.001 mm to decimal inches, reset the decimal behind the 1 mm (shown on the chart) to 0.001; change the decimal inch equivalent (0.039″ shown) to 0.000039″.

Tap Drill Sizes

National Fine or S.A.E.		
Screw & Tap Size	Threads Per Inch	Use Drill Number
No. 5	44	37
No. 6	40	33
No. 8	36	29
No. 10	32	21
No. 12	28	15
1/4	28	3
5/16	24	1
3/8	24	Q
7/16	20	W
1/2	20	29/64
9/16	18	33/64
5/8	18	37/64
3/4	16	11/16
7/8	14	13/16
1 1/8	12	13/64
1 1/4	12	1 11/64
1 1/2	12	1 27/64

Tap Drill Sizes

National Coarse or U.S.S.		
Screw & Tap Size	Threads Per Inch	Use Drill Number
No. 5	40	39
No. 6	32	36
No. 8	32	29
No. 10	24	25
No. 12	24	17
1/4	20	8
5/16	18	F
3/8	16	5/16
7/16	14	U
1/2	13	27/64
9/16	12	31/64
5/8	11	17/32
3/4	10	21/32
7/8	9	49/64
1	8	7/8
1 1/8	7	63/64
1 1/4	7	1 7/64
1 1/2	6	1 11/32

Anti-Freeze Chart

Temperatures Shown in Degrees Fahrenheit +32 is Freezing

Cooling System Capacity Quarts	Quarts of ETHYLENE GLYCOL Needed for Protection to Temperatures Shown Below													
	1	2	3	4	5	6	7	8	9	10	11	12	13	14
10	+24°	+16°	+ 4°	−12°	−34°	−62°								
11	+25	+18	+ 8	− 6	−23	−47								
12	+26	+19	+10	0	−15	−34	−57°							
13	+27	+21	+13	+ 3	− 9	−25	−45							
14			+15	+ 6	− 5	−18	−34							
15			+16	+ 8	0	−12	−26							
16			+17	+10	+ 2	− 8	−19	−34	−52°					
17			+18	+12	+ 5	− 4	−14	−27	−42					
18			+19	+14	+ 7	0	−10	−21	−34	−50°				
19			+20	+15	+ 9	+ 2	− 7	−16	−28	−42				
20				+16	+10	+ 4	− 3	−12	−22	−34	−48°			
21				+17	+12	+ 6	0	− 9	−17	−28	−41			
22				+18	+13	+ 8	+ 2	− 6	−14	−23	−34	−47°		
23				+19	+14	+ 9	+ 4	− 3	−10	−19	−29	−40		
24				+19	+15	+10	+ 5	0	− 8	−15	−23	−34	−46°	
25				+20	+16	+12	+ 7	+ 1	− 5	−12	−20	−29	−40	−50°
26				+17	+13	+ 8	+ 3	− 3	− 9	−16	−25	−34	−44	
27				+18	+14	+ 9	+ 5	− 1	− 7	−13	−21	−29	−39	
28				+18	+15	+10	+ 6	+ 1	− 5	−11	−18	−25	−34	
29				+19	+16	+12	+ 7	+ 2	− 3	− 8	−15	−22	−29	
30				+20	+17	+13	+ 8	+ 4	− 1	− 6	−12	−18	−25	

For capacities over 30 quarts divide true capacity by 3. Find quarts Anti-Freeze for the ⅓ and multiply by 3 for quarts to add.

For capacities under 10 quarts multiply true capacity by 3. Find quarts Anti-Freeze for the tripled volume and divide by 3 for quarts to add.

To Increase the Freezing Protection of Anti-Freeze Solutions Already Installed

Cooling System Capacity Quarts	Number of Quarts of ETHYLENE GLYCOL Anti-Freeze Required to Increase Protection													
	From +20° F. to					From +10° F. to					From 0° F. to			
	0°	−10°	−20°	−30°	−40°	0°	−10°	−20°	−30°	−40°	−10°	−20°	−30°	−40°
10	1¾	2¼	3	3½	3¾	¾	1½	2¼	2¾	3¼	¾	1½	2	2½
12	2	2¾	3½	4	4½	1	1¾	2½	3¼	3¾	1	1¾	2½	3¼
14	2¼	3¼	4	4¾	5½	1¼	2	3	3¾	4½	1	2	3	3½
16	2½	3½	4½	5¼	6	1¼	2½	3½	4¼	5¼	1¼	2¼	3¼	4
18	3	4	5	6	7	1½	2¾	4	5	5¾	1½	2½	3¾	4¾
20	3¼	4½	5¾	6¾	7½	1¾	3	4¼	5½	6½	1½	2¾	4¼	5¼
22	3½	5	6¼	7¼	8¼	1¾	3¼	4¾	6	7¼	1¾	3¼	4½	5½
24	4	5½	7	8	9	2	3½	5	6½	7½	1¾	3½	5	6
26	4¼	6	7½	8¾	10	2	4	5½	7	8¼	2	3¾	5½	6¾
28	4½	6¼	8	9½	10½	2¼	4¼	6	7½	9	2	4	5¾	7¼
30	5	6¾	8½	10	11½	2½	4½	6½	8	9½	2¼	4¼	6¼	7¾

Test radiator solution with proper hydrometer. Determine from the table the number of quarts of solution to be drawn off from a full cooling system and replace with undiluted anti-freeze, to give the desired increased protection. For example, to increase protection of a 22-quart cooling system containing Ethylene Glycol (permanent type) anti-freeze, from +20° F. to −20° F. will require the replacement of 6¼ quarts of solution with undiluted anti-freeze.

Decimal Equivalent Size of the Number Drills

Drill No.	Decimal Equivalent	Drill No.	Decimal Equivalent	Drill No.	Decimal Equivalent
80	.0135	53	.0595	26	.1470
79	.0145	52	.0635	25	.1495
78	.0160	51	.0670	24	.1520
77	.0180	50	.0700	23	.1540
76	.0200	49	.0730	22	.1570
75	.0210	48	.0760	21	.1590
74	.0225	47	.0785	20	.1610
73	.0240	46	.0810	19	.1660
72	.0250	45	.0820	18	.1695
71	.0260	44	.0860	17	.1730
70	.0280	43	.0890	16	.1770
69	.0292	42	.0935	15	.1800
68	.0310	41	.0960	14	.1820
67	.0320	40	.0980	13	.1850
66	.0330	39	.0995	12	.1890
65	.0350	38	.1015	11	.1910
64	.0360	37	.1040	10	.1935
63	.0370	36	.1065	9	.1960
62	.0380	35	.1100	8	.1990
61	.0390	34	.1110	7	.2010
60	.0400	33	.1130	6	.2040
59	.0410	32	.1160	5	.2055
58	.0420	31	.1200	4	.2090
57	.0430	30	.1285	3	.2130
56	.0465	29	.1360	2	.2210
55	.0520	28	.1405	1	.2280
54	.0550	27	.1440		

Decimal Equivalent Size of the Letter Drills

Letter Drill	Decimal Equivalent	Letter Drill	Decimal Equivalent	Letter Drill	Decimal Equivalent
A	.234	J	.277	S	.348
B	.238	K	.281	T	.358
C	.242	L	.290	U	.368
D	.246	M	.295	V	.377
E	.250	N	.302	W	.386
F	.257	O	.316	X	.397
G	.261	P	.323	Y	.404
H	.266	Q	.332	Z	.413
I	.272	R	.339		

Index